MW01620459

Praise

Scenario-Based Training with X-Plane and Microsoft® Flight Simulator

"Author Williams draws from a rich background in aviation and computing to lead the industry in a direction that will change the way flight training is conducted in the future.

Incorporating routine use of simulation into flight training will transition us from focusing solely on "fundamental skills" to delivering a pilot who is truly ready to be a pilot-in-command—one who has developed the habit of identifying and managing the risks of flight.

While the FAA's first suggested way of implementing scenario-based training may have been a bit contrived and impractical, Willlams shows us how we harness the power of computing to make use of it to develop a higher level of pilot learning and much more capable pilots."

—John and Martha King
Co-chairmen and co-owners of King Schools, Inc.

"Let's be clear about one thing. I love teaching people how to fly and I am an unrepentant PC-based flight simulation fan. So when I see a new book that helps pilots—rated, aspiring, or virtual—learn how to better use their PC-based simulation software, I get excited. And when that book is written by Bruce Williams, I know it's going to be a first class training manual.

Scenario-Based Training with X-Plane and Microsoft Flight Simulator is Bruce's latest contribution to aviation education. What gives this book its educational heft is that Bruce shows you how to use your flight simulator to develop and reinforce your motor, perceptual, and cognitive flying skills. And he does this by creating real-world flying scenarios, then placing you and your joystick right in the middle of the mix to help you master your piloting performance.

Let's face it, most pilots can't spend as much time in the cockpit as they'd prefer. They can, however, do the next best thing by allowing Bruce Williams to become their book-based simulator instructor. So start your scenario-based training now by reading and applying the lessons found in Bruce's new book, *Scenario-Based Training with X-Plane and Microsoft Flight Simulator*."

—Rod Machado
Flight Instructor, AOPA National CFI spokesman,
and writer for AOPA Pilot *and* Flight Training Magazine

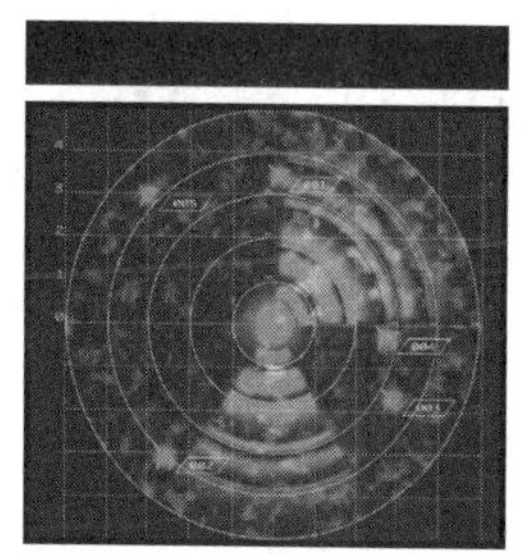

Scenario-Based Training with X-Plane and Microsoft® Flight Simulator

Using PC-Based Flight Simulations Based on FAA-Industry Training Standards

Bruce Williams

John Wiley & Sons, Inc.

Scenario-Based Training with X-Plane and Microsoft® Flight Simulator: Using PC-Based Flight Simulations Based on FAA-Industry Training Standards

Published by
John Wiley & Sons, Inc.
10475 Crosspoint Boulevard
Indianapolis, IN 46256
www.wiley.com

Copyright © 2012 by John Wiley & Sons, Inc., Indianapolis, Indiana
Published by John Wiley & Sons, Inc., Indianapolis, Indiana
Published simultaneously in Canada

ISBN: 978-1-118-10502-3
ISBN: 978-1-118-22400-7 (ebk)
ISBN: 978-1-118-23329-0 (ebk)
ISBN: 978-1-118-26222-1 (ebk)

Manufactured in the United States of America

10 9 8 7 6 5 4 3 2 1

No part of this publication may be reproduced, stored in a retrieval system or transmitted in any form or by any means, electronic, mechanical, photocopying, recording, scanning or otherwise, except as permitted under Sections 107 or 108 of the 1976 United States Copyright Act, without either the prior written permission of the Publisher, or authorization through payment of the appropriate per-copy fee to the Copyright Clearance Center, 222 Rosewood Drive, Danvers, MA 01923, (978) 750-8400, fax (978) 646-8600. Requests to the Publisher for permission should be addressed to the Permissions Department, John Wiley & Sons, Inc., 111 River Street, Hoboken, NJ 07030, (201) 748-6011, fax (201) 748-6008, or online at http://www.wiley.com/go/permissions.

Limit of Liability/Disclaimer of Warranty: The publisher and the author make no representations or warranties with respect to the accuracy or completeness of the contents of this work and specifically disclaim all warranties, including without limitation warranties of fitness for a particular purpose. No warranty may be created or extended by sales or promotional materials. The advice and strategies contained herein may not be suitable for every situation. This work is sold with the understanding that the publisher is not engaged in rendering legal, accounting, or other professional services. If professional assistance is required, the services of a competent professional person should be sought. Neither the publisher nor the author shall be liable for damages arising herefrom. The fact that an organization or Web site is referred to in this work as a citation and/or a potential source of further information does not mean that the author or the publisher endorses the information the organization or website may provide or recommendations it may make. Further, readers should be aware that Internet websites listed in this work may have changed or disappeared between when this work was written and when it is read.

For general information on our other products and services please contact our Customer Care Department within the United States at (877) 762-2974, outside the United States at (317) 572-3993 or fax (317) 572-4002.

Wiley publishes in a variety of print and electronic formats and by print-on-demand. Some material included with standard print versions of this book may not be included in e-books or in print-on-demand. If this book refers to media such as a CD or DVD that is not included in the version you purchased, you may download this material at http://booksupport.wiley.com. For more information about Wiley products, visit www.wiley.com.

Library of Congress Control Number: 2011942770

Trademarks: Wiley and the Wiley logo are trademarks or registered trademarks of John Wiley & Sons, Inc. and/or its affiliates, in the United States and other countries, and may not be used without written permission. Microsoft is a registered trademark of Microsoft Corporation. All other trademarks are the property of their respective owners. John Wiley & Sons, Inc. is not associated with any product or vendor mentioned in this book.

About the Author

Bruce Williams is the owner of BruceAir, LLC, an aviation consulting, training, and pilot-services company based in Seattle, WA (www.BruceAir.com).

He has been a pilot since the early 1970s, and he is a certified flight instructor and FAASTeam representative in the Seattle area. Today, he focuses on training for technically advanced aircraft (TAA) and stall/spin/upset courses in an Extra 300L aerobatic aircraft.

During a 15-year career at Microsoft, he worked on six versions of Microsoft Flight Simulator. While at Microsoft, he was also a technical editor, multimedia producer and editor, and business development manager.

In the 1980s, he edited the *Western Flyer* (now the *General Aviation News*), a biweekly newspaper dedicated to the world of general aviation. He is also the author of *Microsoft Flight Simulator as a Training Aid: A Guide for Pilots, Instructors, and Virtual Aviators*, published in 2007 by ASA, and many features on a variety of topics for magazines and other periodicals.

About the Technical Editor

Doug Holland, an Architect Evangelist at Microsoft Corporation, took to the sky on his first solo flight in a Cessna 172 at KEDU (University Airport in Davis, CA) on March 1, 2008. Doug is also a member of the Civil Air Patrol, US Air Force Auxiliary, participating in search and rescue flights. He lives with his wife and four children in Northern California.

Credits

Acquisitions Editor
Paul Reese

Senior Project Editor
Adaobi Obi Tulton

Technical Editor
Doug Holland

Senior Production Editor
Debra Banninger

Copy Editor
Luann Rouff

Editorial Manager
Mary Beth Wakefield

Freelancer Editorial Manager
Rosemarie Graham

Associate Director of Marketing
David Mayhew

Marketing Manager
Ashley Zurcher

Business Manager
Amy Knies

Production Manager
Tim Tate

Vice President and Executive Group Publisher
Richard Swadley

Vice President and Executive Publisher
Neil Edde

Associate Publisher
Jim Minatel

Project Coordinator, Cover
Katie Crocker

Compositor
Happenstance Type-O-Rama

Proofreader
Nancy Carrasco

Indexer
Robert Swanson

Cover Image
© iStock / Ryan Tacay
© iStock / Nicolas Holzapfel
© iStock / George Cairns

Cover Designer
LeAndra Young

Acknowledgments

Only the true pioneers of aviation — Otto Lilienthal, the Wright brothers, the original fighter pilots of World War I — discovered how to fly. Those of us who have taken to the skies after them benefit immeasurably by learning from others.

More than most pilots, I've enjoyed and benefited from the patience, advice, experience, skill, and generosity of a remarkable group of aviators who represent the best of the flying community. I owe whatever skills I've acquired as a pilot and instructor to mentors such as Yoda, Dula, Patty, Cubes, Curly, Rod, John and Martha, Sean, and many others who have taken me under their wings. Thank you, all.

I also owe a special debt to the colleagues with whom I worked at Microsoft for so many years. They did the hard work of making Microsoft Flight Simulator fly.

Books are collaborations, and the team at Wiley made this book possible. Paul Reese, the acquisition editor, persuaded me to undertake the project, laid the cornerstone, and organized the editorial team. Project editor Adaobi Obi Tulton, copy editor Luann Rouff, and technical editor Doug Holland caught and corrected my errors and polished the text and graphics. The finished project is the result of their professionalism, expertise, and attention to detail.

Contents at a Glance

Contents

Introduction

Scenario-Based Training is the first book designed to work with both of the most popular PC-based flight simulations, X-Plane and Microsoft Flight Simulator X (FSX), and to emphasize the latest scenario-based approach to flight training developed by the FAA/Industry Training Standards (FITS) consortium.

It's directed at three primary audiences:

- People serious about learning to fly who want to make the most practical and effective use of PC-based flight simulations during their training and proficiency flying
- Flight instructors and flight schools that want a guide to including PC-based simulations in logical, efficient training programs
- Virtual aviators — enthusiasts who may not be "real" pilots but who are serious about having fun with PC-based simulations and want to enhance their knowledge and skills

Scenario-Based Training emphasizes a practical approach to the two fundamental training programs that most pilots complete, regardless of their ultimate goals in flying:

- The private pilot certificate in single-engine airplanes
- The instrument rating in single-engine airplanes

The two syllabi presented here follow the requirements for those certificates and ratings as issued in the United States by the FAA, but the basic knowledge and skills in the lessons apply regardless of where you fly.

Scenario-Based Training also includes additional challenges for aviators who aspire to fly more advanced aircraft on missions such as charter, cargo, and medical assistance flights.

NOTE **Of course, *Scenario-Based Training* is not a substitute for training with a qualified flight instructor. If you're a pilot, talk to your flight instructor about how you can best include PC-based simulations and flight training devices in your training program.**

The FITS Approach to Flight Training

FITS is a partnership between the FAA, industry, and academia designed to improve flight training and enhance the safety of general aviation (GA, as it's often called, includes all types of flying except military and airline operations). FITS focuses on programs that are more convenient, more accessible, less expensive, and more relevant to today's pilots than traditional approaches to flight training.

FITS also emphasizes the use of flight simulation, scenarios, self-evaluation, and pilot decision-making, not a series of separate flying skills learned only in the cockpit. This approach, to use a bad pun only once, best fits the challenges of learning to fly and operating in today's complex aviation environment.

The FITS approach also works well if you're a virtual aviator. The scenarios at the heart of the program are challenges of increasing complexity that provide structure to the free-form world of virtual flying; and the completion criteria — learner-centered grading standards and grids — serve as a scoring system that you can use to gauge your progress through a series of adventures that will help you develop and hone fundamental flying skills.

CROSS-REFERENCE **For detailed information about FITS, see Chapter 9.**

A Guided Tour

Scenario-Based Training isn't a comprehensive handbook for either X-Plane or FSX. You'll find guides to the essential features of each simulation in Chapters 6 and 7, but the best sources for the latest details about setting up and using X-Plane and FSX are the websites for each product and the documentation included when you install X-Plane or FSX on your computer.

Likewise, *Scenario-Based Training* doesn't attempt to teach all the details of aerodynamics, aircraft systems and instruments, navigation, flying techniques, and other subjects that pilots must master. Those topics are described authoritatively in the official FAA training handbooks and other resources cited in the lessons. Those references, described in Chapter 2 are available for download or via links at this book's website at `www.wiley.com/go/flightsimulatortraining`.

In short, it's best to think of *Scenario-Based Training* as an interactive guided tour through the process of learning how to think like a pilot. To use this book to best effect and for maximum enjoyment, you'll want to explore the references to develop (or refresh) your knowledge of the fundamentals of both PC-based simulations and real-world flying.

Part

I

Before You Take Off

In This Part

Chapter 1: What You Need to Use This Book
Chapter 2: Essential Resources on the Website
Chapter 3: Using PC-Based Simulations Effectively
Chapter 4: Scenario-Based Training for Virtual Aviators
Chapter 5: Choosing a PC-Based Simulation: X-Plane or FSX?
Chapter 6: A Quick Guide to X-Plane
Chapter 7: A Quick Guide to Microsoft Flight Simulator X

CHAPTER 1

What You Need to Use This Book

If you're like most pilots, you enjoy gadgets — they're one of aviation's main attractions — and when you get serious about using a PC-based simulation to complement flight training or the hobby of virtual flying, it's tempting to set up an elaborate home cockpit.

But aside from the desire to learn and a commitment to work through the lessons in this book in a logical sequence, here's all you need to use this book effectively:

- X-Plane version 9 or Microsoft Flight Simulator X (FSX)
- A suitable computer with a single display, a basic joystick, and a mouse (a keyboard usually isn't required after you start the simulation); even a laptop can suffice (see Figure 1-1)
- Web access to download the scenarios and background reading for the lessons
- A PDF reader, such as the free Adobe Reader, to read the FAA training handbooks, view charts, and use other resources that complement this book

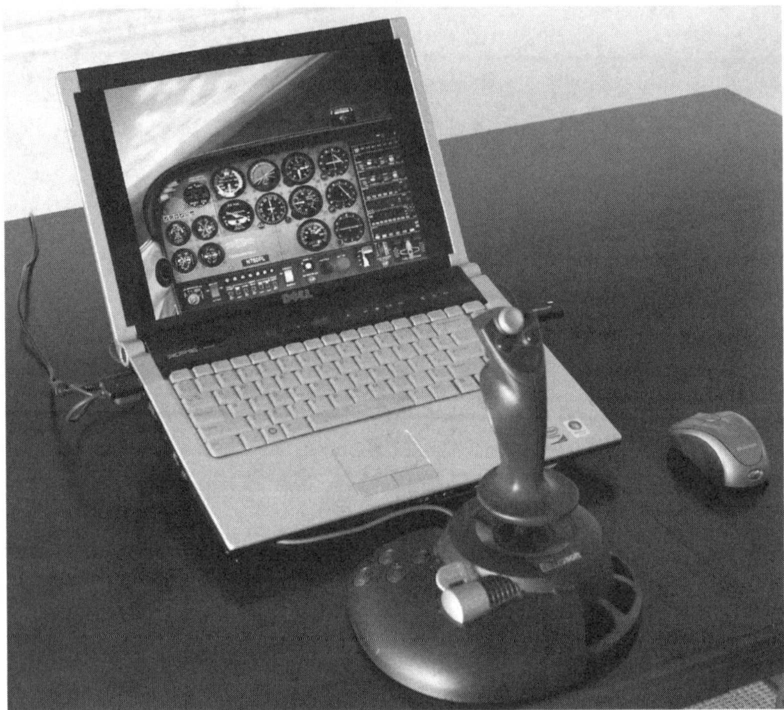

Figure 1-1: The minimum required setup for X-Plane or FSX: a laptop, mouse, and joystick

CROSS-REFERENCE For more information about using PC-based simulations in training, see Chapter 8.

Supported Flight Simulations

Pilots and flight simulation enthusiasts engage in passionate debates about the relative merits of X-Plane (see Figure 1-2) versus FSX (see Figure 1-3) — you'll find a chapter devoted to the subject later in this book — but either product can be equally effective when used properly as a training tool.

The scenarios in this book are based on preset initial conditions — location, time of day, weather, and so forth — stored in files that you can open in either X-Plane or FSX. You can find separate sets of these scenarios for each simulation at this book's website at `www.wiley.com/go/flightsimulatortraining`.

These scenarios assume a standard installation of either X-Plane or FSX, and they are based in the Pacific Northwest, a region presented well in both simulations. Enhanced scenery and features such as advanced navigation displays are not required.

Figure 1-2: X-Plane 9 package

Figure 1-3: FSX package

Both X-Plane and FSX include sets of supplied aircraft, and except for some advanced lessons, the scenarios in this book use the Cessna 172 Skyhawk (see Figure 1-4), which has long been the most popular training and personal aircraft in the world.

Photo courtesy of Cessna Aircraft Company

Figure 1-4: Cessna 172 Skyhawk

CROSS-REFERENCE **For more information about selecting the best simulation for your circumstances, see Chapter 5.**

X-Plane

If you use X-Plane, the lessons in this book require X-Plane Situations (`.sit` files) created in X-Plane 9, the latest version available when this book was in production.

The Situations have not been tested in earlier versions of X-Plane or in X-Plane 10, which is scheduled for release in late 2011.

You can learn about and order X-Plane at the product's website, at `www.x-plane.com`. Links are also available at this book's website.

Microsoft Flight Simulator X (FSX)

If you use Microsoft Flight Simulator, the lessons in this book are based on Flights (`.flt`, `.wx`, and `.fssave` files) created in FSX.

Microsoft changed the format of the `.flt` and `.wx` files after Flight Simulator 2004, so the Flights provided on this book's website will not work with versions earlier than FSX.

You can learn about and order FSX at the product's website at `www.microsoft.com/games/flightsimulatorx/`. Links are also available at this book's website.

Microsoft Flight

Microsoft announced the successor to FSX, "Microsoft Flight" ("simulator" is not part of the new title) on August 31, 2010. According to the company's announcement, Microsoft Flight is "inspired by the best-selling Flight Simulator," but few details about the scope and features of Microsoft Flight were available as this book was being finalized in the summer of 2011.

It may be possible to use the FSX Flights (the `.flt`, `.wx`, and `.fssave` files available at this book's website) with Microsoft Flight, but you may find that the scenery, database of navigation aids, cockpit instrumentation, and other details in the new game do not support all of the goals of the scenarios.

For the latest official information about Microsoft Flight, visit the product's website. A link is available at this book's website at `www.wiley.com/go/flightsimulatortraining`.

Computer and Accessories

One of the most common questions about using PC-based simulations is "What kind of computer do I need?"

The short answers are as follows:

- For X-Plane, a suitable computer running Windows, or a Mac (OS X version 10.4 or later); X-Plane also runs under Linux
- For FSX, a suitable computer running Windows (XP SP1 through Windows 7)

You can find the latest minimum system specifications at the websites for each product.

Of course, the minimum processor and system memory requirements listed by the manufacturers are just that — minimums. More speed and memory are always preferable. For example, in 2006, Microsoft recommended the following specifications for a good experience with FSX, shown in Table 1-1.

Table 1-1: FSX Recommended System

COMPONENT	SPECIFICATION
CPU	3.6 GHz+
Memory (RAM)	2 GB+
Video card	512 MB+

FSInsider.com: Optimizing Visuals and Performance

Those specifications also exceed the minimum requirements for X-Plane and should deliver good performance with that simulation.

Because the scenarios in this book don't require add-ons or depend on high-definition scenery, you can probably get by with a recent mid-range system. Most computers made in the last three years or so are sufficiently powerful, provided, most crucially, that they include a separate graphics processor (video card) that supports DirectX 9 or later (if you run Windows). Many new high-performance laptops intended for playing games and enjoying multimedia are also suitable for running PC-based flight simulations.

If you're shopping for a new computer, look for a model that is designed for games, entertainment, or graphics-intensive applications such as video editing. Bargain-priced computers often don't include dedicated video cards, and they may skimp on system memory (RAM).

Because development of new computers and components such as video cards continues apace, it's impossible for a book to offer definitive, up-to-the-moment advice about the latest hardware. To get help equipping and tweaking your computer for optimum performance, visit the enthusiast websites, forums, and other online resources for each simulation noted at this book's website.

Joysticks and Flight Yokes

The focus of the scenarios in this book isn't developing "stick and rudder" skills that prepare you adequately to take the controls of a real airplane. As explained in Chapter 3, developing and honing the muscle memories required to fly an airplane precisely and smoothly requires practice in a real airplane under the guidance of a qualified instructor. Simply put, PC-based simulations can't provide all of the visual and motion (kinesthetic) cues and control responses necessary to develop a pilot's feel for flying, especially as you begin flight training.

Nevertheless, all that's required for the purposes of this book is a joystick (see Figure 1-5) or a yoke (see Figure 1-6) that provides an intuitive, fundamentally correct way to control the virtual airplane — its pitch and roll (and optionally, yaw). It's also helpful to have a lever for the throttle, and switches and knobs to operate elevator trim, flaps, and other secondary aircraft controls and systems.

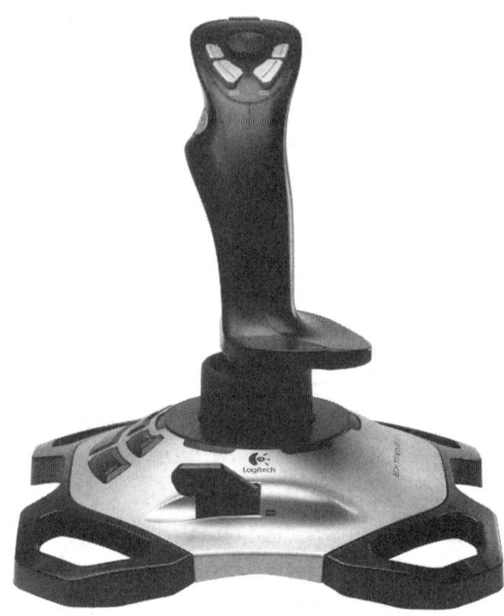

Figure 1-5: Logitech Extreme 3D Pro Joystick

Fortunately, most joysticks and flight yokes available today offer those features, and current models connect to your computer via a standard USB port. The choice of which joystick or yoke to use is entirely up to you. Many models are available from such manufacturers as CH Products, Saitek, Logitech, and Thrustmaster. You can find links to the manufacturers at this book's website.

Some virtual pilots insist on using a flight yoke, not a joystick, because most civilian training and personal aircraft made since the 1950s feature primary controls that resemble the steering wheels in cars. But many new airplanes, such as the Cirrus SR models and the Cessna Corvalis and Skycatcher series, are equipped with side-stick or hybrid controls that are neither pure yokes nor joysticks (see Figure 1-7).

Figure 1-6: CH Products Eclipse Yoke

Figure 1-7: Side-stick control in a Cirrus SR22.

Pilots, even those with many years of experience with conventional flight yokes, quickly adapt to the new controls, and soon the mechanism used to bank the wings and raise or lower the nose becomes irrelevant. That experience also applies to joysticks and yokes used with PC-based simulations.

I suggest you try various joysticks and yokes and then choose the model that you find the most comfortable and the easiest to use — and the best fit for your budget. It's also important to consider how you use your computer. A joystick, small and easy to put aside, may be the best option if you have limited space and often switch from flying to email and other tasks. If you dedicate a computer to virtual flying, attaching a yoke to your computer desk may be the better setup.

Rudder Pedals and Radio Stacks

Virtual pilots often want to equip their home cockpits with rudder pedals and separate consoles to simulate radios and other systems. Those components are important if you want to earn FAA approval for a flight training device (FTD), but they aren't necessary for using the scenarios effectively.

However, if you can't suspend your disbelief and enjoy virtual flying without those accessories, you can find links to manufacturers at this book's website.

Mouse with Scroll Wheel

A mouse is essential, regardless of whether you use a joystick or a yoke bristling with buttons and levers. You can use a mouse like your hand to operate naturally and realistically many on-screen cockpit controls — including heading and course selectors; radio-tuning knobs; and the throttle, flap, and trim controls. Any standard mouse equipped with two buttons and a wheel will suffice.

CROSS-REFERENCE **For more information about using a mouse, see Chapters 6 and 7.**

Multiple Displays

The view from your virtual cockpit may sometimes seem crowded or limited. Computer displays have become less cumbersome (and cheaper) and many recent video cards support multiple monitors. If you find it helpful to expand your virtual field of view by adding a second (or even three or four displays) to your system, you can configure X-Plane or FSX to display inside and outside views and other features, such as radios and accessories, on different monitors.

However, multiple displays aren't necessary to use the scenarios effectively; and like rudder pedals and separate consoles for radios and other controls, multiple monitors add to the complexity, cost, and everyday utility of your virtual cockpit.

CROSS-REFERENCE **For more information about using multiple displays, see Chapters 6 and 7.**

Additional Software and Web Access

X-Plane and Microsoft Flight Simulator have inspired developers all over the world to enhance the basic simulations. You can download thousands of aircraft; enhanced scenery; interactive air traffic control; and specialized avionics that emulate specific models of GPS navigators, autopilots, and the like. Other products support virtual flying with others online or enhance the use of PC-based simulations as training tools. Some add-ons are free; others are sold as supplemental products.

As noted earlier, no add-ons are required to fly the scenarios in the private pilot and instrument rating courses in this book. You're free, of course, to enhance your virtual flying with as many options as you like. You can find links to information about add-ons at the website for this book.

CROSS-REFERENCE **For more information about the resources that complement this book, see Chapter 2.**

Glass Cockpits and Flying RNAV (GPS) Procedures

New and recently updated aircraft are typically equipped with electronic flight displays — so-called *glass cockpits* (see Figure 1-8). Older aircraft are often updated with a GPS receiver and moving map, because GPS has become increasingly important in real-world instrument flying for all phases of flight.

You can find glass cockpit and GPS add-ons for both X-Plane and FSX that can help you learn about this new technology, but those supplements aren't necessary for the scenarios in this book, which focuses on fundamental knowledge and skills that apply regardless of whether you fly an aircraft with conventional instruments or the latest touch-screen, flat-panel displays.

Photo courtesy of Cessna Aircraft Company

Figure 1-8: Garmin G1000 system in a late-model Cessna 172 Skyhawk

In addition, the cockpits in the basic versions of X-Plane and FSX rely on conventional instruments — "steam gauges," as they're known to pilots (see Figures 1-9 and 1-10). Accurately rendering the latest flat-panel cockpit displays and emulating all of their functions usually requires multiple computers and several large displays, a setup that defeats one of the primary purposes of this book.

Figure 1-9: Default Cessna 172 Skyhawk instrument panel in X-Plane 9

Figure 1-10: Default Cessna 172 Skyhawk instrument panel in FSX

For similar reasons, details about using specific IFR-approved, GPS-based navigation systems, especially when flying the latest RNAV (GPS) approaches, are beyond the scope of this book.

The GPS in the consumer version of X-Plane 9 supports only basic GPS functions. The emulation of the Garmin GNS500 series navigation system in FSX is more detailed, but it does not include a current database of procedures, and you can't use it to practice the latest instrument approaches, which are based on the Wide Area Augmentation System (WAAS).

To fly the latest GPS (RNAV) procedures, you need one or more add-ons for X-Plane or FSX. Options include the RealityXP GNS430W/GNS530W accessories (for either X-Plane or FSX) and the G1000 and Avidyne add-ons from Flight1Aviation Technologies that work with FSX.

For more information about add-ons for X-Plane and FSX, see the links on the book's website.

Virtual Flying with Others

Finally, you may want to share your virtual cockpit with fellow aviators or mentors. Both X-Plane and FSX enable you to connect with others over the Internet or a local network, but this capability isn't required to fly the scenarios described in this book.

You can find links to information about sharing your cockpit at each simulation's website. To learn more about interactive ATC services such as VATSIM and PilotEdge, see the links at the website for this book at `www.wiley.com/go/flightsimulatortraing`.

CHAPTER 2

Essential Resources on the Website

The website for this book, `www.wiley.com/go/flightsimulatortraining`, is an essential complement to the text. It's home to:

- Additional resources that help you set up, learn about, enjoy, and customize X-Plane and FSX
- Situation and Flight files that help you use X-Plane and FSX effectively and efficiently with the scenarios in this book
- Resources, including official FAA pilot-training handbooks, that provide the background knowledge required to prepare for and complete each lesson
- Charts that help you plan and complete each virtual flight

Additional Resources for X-Plane and FSX

As noted earlier, this book isn't a detailed user guide for X-Plane or FSX, and neither the author nor the publisher can provide technical support for the simulations; add-on aircraft and features; or flight yokes, joysticks, and other accessories.

That said, this book's website is a good place to start if you have questions about either simulation. It includes links to the websites for X-Plane and FSX, and developers of add-on products for X-Plane and FSX.

The official websites for the products include documentation, tips, links to technical support, and other information that can help you set up and use X-Plane and FSX (see Figures 2-1 and 2-2). They're the best and most current sources of reliable information about each simulation.

Figure 2-1: X-Plane support page

If you have specific questions about, or problems with, joysticks and other devices or with add-on aircraft, scenery, or features, visit the websites of the manufacturers and developers of those accessories. These websites provide software updates, current documentation, support forums, and other useful information.

You can also often get help and advice from the worldwide communities of X-Plane and FSX users. Links to popular forums are available at this book's website.

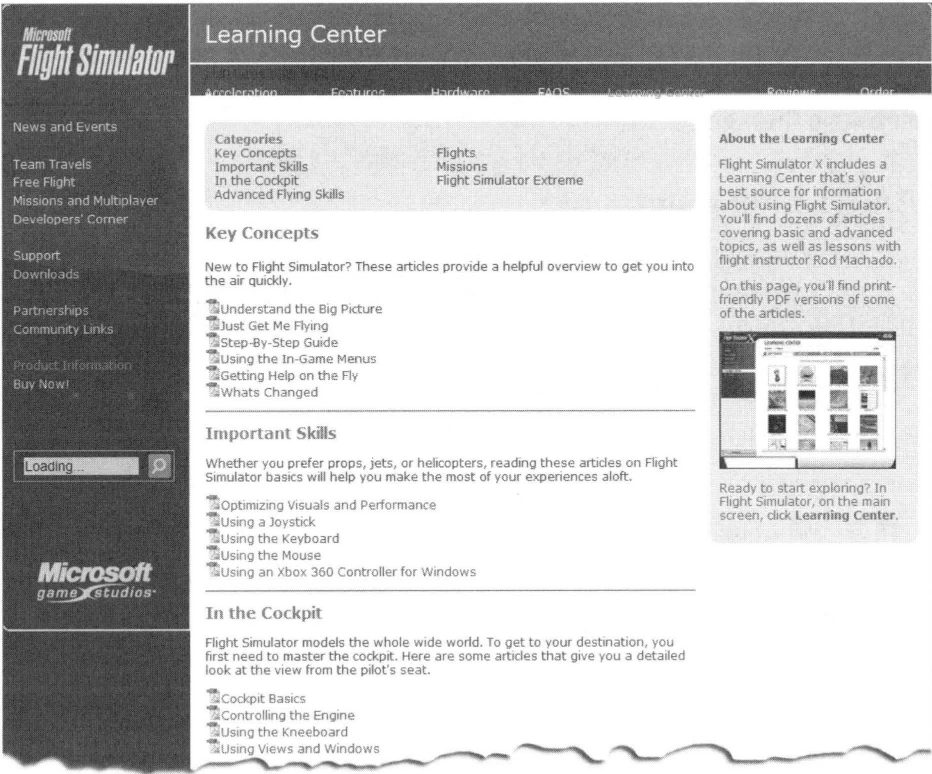

Figure 2-2: FSX Learning Center page

Scenarios

The scenarios for the lessons described later in this book depend on *Situations* (`.sit` files for X-Plane) and *Flights* (`.flt`, `.wx`, and `.fssave` files for FSX). The files for each simulation are collected in `.zip` files on the website.

The Situations and Flights establish the starting conditions for each lesson (aircraft type, location, weather, and so forth). For more information about copying the appropriate files to your computer, see Chapter 10.

Resources for Further Learning

You can find many comprehensive guides to the knowledge and flying skills required to earn a private pilot certificate or instrument rating. Those books and interactive training programs suit a variety of learning styles and vary in price from around $40 to several hundred dollars.

Instead of rewriting or recapitulating that large body of work, however, this book relies on a range of texts and other resources that are both authoritative and a terrific value — they're free downloads available from the FAA and other sources on the web.

FAA Training Handbooks

The FAA training handbooks and references listed below provide the essential background for each lesson. They are the same guides that flight instructors and students use during training, and they're the definitive texts that pilot examiners and FAA inspectors rely on when conducting flight tests (see Figure 2-3).

The following handbooks and manuals, available in PDF format on this book's website, were current as of summer 2011:

- *Pilot's Handbook of Aeronautical Knowledge* (FAA-H-8083-25A)
- *Airplane Flying Handbook* (FAA-H-8083-3A)
- *Instrument Flying Handbook* (FAA-H-8083-15A)
- *Instrument Procedures Handbook* (FAA-H-8261-1A)
- *Advanced Avionics Handbook* (FAA-H-8083-6)
- *NACO Aeronautical Chart User's Guide*
- *Aviation Weather* (AC 00-6A)
- *Aviation Weather Services* (AC 00-45G CHG1)
- *Risk Management Handbook* (FAA-H-8083-2)
- *Aeronautical Information Manual* (AIM)
- *Pilot/Controller Glossary* (P/CG)
- *FAA Practical Test Standards — Private Pilot SEL* (FAA-S-14A with Change 1)
- *FAA Practical Test Standards — Instrument Rating Airplane SEL* (FAA-S-8081-4E with Changes 1 and 2)

You can search for the latest editions of these books and other publications, such as the bi-monthly magazine *FAA Safety Briefing*, on the FAA website, `www.faa.gov`.

Note that most of the handbooks contain glossaries of aviation terms. The glossary at the end of this book defines key phrases; for comprehensive lists and definitions, you should check the glossaries in the individual handbooks.

Figure 2-3: Essential FAA handbooks

FITS

This book's website hosts the complete versions of the generic FAA-Industry Training Standards syllabi (see Figure 2-4) on which the lessons are based:

- FITS Generic Private Airplane Single Engine Land Syllabus
- FITS Generic Instrument-Airplane Single Engine Rating Syllabus

You can find the latest versions of these syllabi and supporting FITS documents at the FAA-Industry Training Standards website, which you can link to from this book's website at `www.wiley.com/go/flightsimulatortraining`.

Figure 2-4: FITS logo

For more information about FITS, see Chapter 9.

Additional Free Resources

Several organizations devoted to promoting and supporting aviation offer free training and safety aids that you can download or use on the web. Most of the lessons that follow in this book include references to these resources.

Some of the best offerings are available from the AOPA Air Safety Institute (see Figure 2-5). Materials at the ASI include:

Figure 2-5: AOPA Air Safety Institute logo

- Safety Advisors and related publications on a wide range of topics (see Figure 2-6)
- Interactive courses

- Current and back issues of *Flight Training* magazine, published by AOPA
- Videos from AOPA Live

Figure 2-6: AOPA ASI Safety Advisors

You'll also find links at this book's website to user guides and other documentation available from avionics manufacturers and developers of add-on features for X-Plane and FSX.

Charts

The sample charts printed in this book and available via links on the website are based on the editions published by FAA AeroNav Products. They were current as of the summer of 2011. The charts, in PDF format, include:

- Seattle Sectional South
- Seattle Sectional North (see Figure 2-7)
- Seattle Terminal Area Chart
- Low-altitude en route chart 1
- Low-altitude en route chart 2
- Low-altitude en route chart 11
- Low-altitude en route chart 12
- Low-altitude en route chart 13
- Low-altitude en route chart 14

Figure 2-7: Excerpt from the Seattle sectional chart

The sectional charts and terminal area chart are basic navigation tools for pilots operating under visual flight rules (VFR). The low-altitude en route charts are used when flying under instrument flight rules (IFR).

NOTE **Obviously, these charts should not be used for real-world navigation. When operating a real aircraft, you should obtain and use only current, approved charts.**

The website also includes PDF versions of airport diagrams, excerpts from the official Airport/Facility Directory (A/FD), and instrument procedure charts.

You can download or view the latest editions of these charts and airport information from several sources on the web. The *NACO Aeronautical Chart User's Guide,* included among the FAA handbooks available on this book's website, explains the symbols and terms used on aviation charts.

Online Charts and Flight Planning

Sometimes it's convenient to use online charts that you can view in a web browser. Several websites offer charts that also support basic interactive flight-planning. For example, you can draw courses and estimate distances and flight times (see Figure 2-8). Good sources for online charts and detailed information about airports and navigation aids include:

- `http://SkyVector.com`
- `http://RunwayFinder.com`
- `http://Airnav.com`
- `http://AvCharts.com`

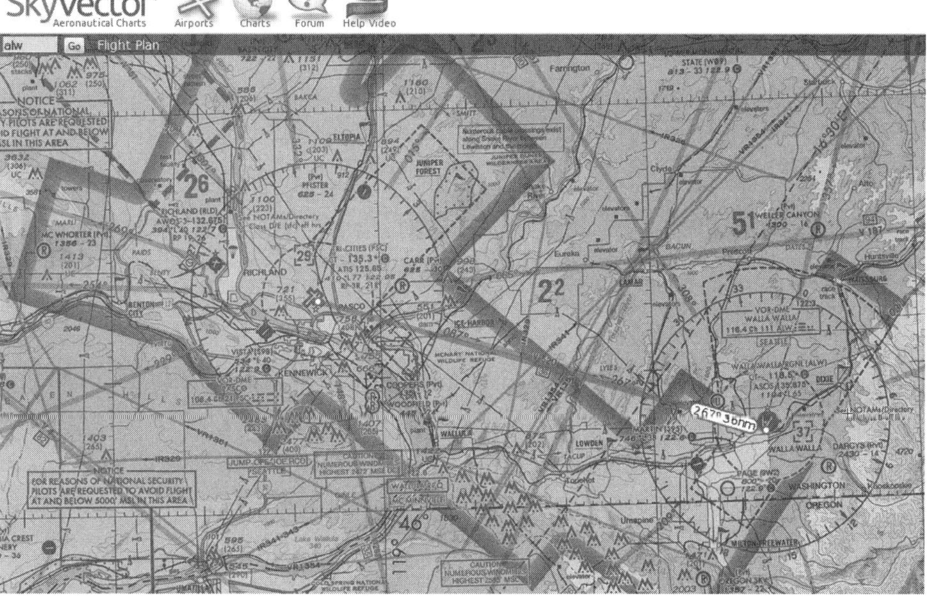

Figure 2-8: Course plotted on a chart at SkyVector

Many of the lessons that follow recommend that you gather information and practice flight planning at one of the preceding sites.

NOTE **As this book went to press, FAA AeroNav Services announced that as of April 2012 individuals will no longer have access to charts and related information on the FAA website. For updated information about where to download current charts and airport information, see this book's website,** **`www.wiley.com/go/flightsimulatortraining`.**

CHAPTER 3

Using PC-Based Simulations Effectively

PC-based flight simulations have been popular since the introduction of Microsoft Flight Simulator in the early 1980s, and as soon as such "games" appeared, pilots and instructors started arguing about if and how they should be used in formal flight training.

The first issue — *if* PC-based simulations have a place in training — is settled. A growing literature documents the beneficial role that simulations — especially PC-based simulations — can play in modern flight training. (You can find links to articles from periodicals, case studies, and research papers published by academics at this book's website.) Both the FAA and the general aviation community, through approval of PC-based flight simulation devices and the FAA-Industry Training Standards (FITS) program described later in this book, endorse the use of simulation in all phases of flight training. Indeed, FITS syllabi — including those designed for new students training to fly in visual flight conditions — *depend* on simulation.

The Great Debate

Today, arguments about the merits of PC-based simulation center on the second question — *how* PC-based simulations should be used — and that discussion typically focuses on three key issues:

- The minimum level of "realism" required to use PC-based simulations effectively
- When to introduce simulation
- How best to integrate simulation with in-flight lessons

Uncertainty surrounding those concerns frequently arises because many instructors and pilots aren't familiar with PC-based simulations, and they may have experience with purpose-built, expensive simulators used in the military and commercial aviation. By comparison, PC-based simulations, usually promoted as games, don't look like "real simulators." And so, as in most debates, it's helpful to begin by defining key terms.

Simulators, FTDs, and Simulations

Technological leaps have blurred the lines that just a few years ago distinguished the capabilities of full-motion simulators from the features of the home cockpits that hobbyists set up in their basements and garages. Recent changes to the definitions of, and the regulations governing the use of, FAA-approved simulators have added to the aviation community's confusion about these tools.

Key Categories

The FAA recognizes four general categories of flight simulation systems:

- Full Flight Simulator (FFS)
- Flight Training Device (FTD)
- Basic Aviation Training Device (BATD)
- Advanced Aviation Training Device (AATD)

The first two categories are described in 14 CFR Part 60 of the FAA regulations. BATD and AATD are covered in Advisory Circular AC 61-126, *Qualification and Approval of Personal Computer-Based Aviation Training Devices.*

NOTE ***CFR*** **means "Code of Federal Regulations." Most pilots call the sections of the CFR that govern the FAA the "FARs," meaning the FAA regulations. The FAA publishes Advisory Circulars to offer detailed guidance and background on many topics, including pilot training. "ACs," as they're known in the aviation community, are not regulations, but they are statements of official FAA policy and recommendations.**

Each category of simulator and training device includes levels that describe the increasing sophistication, capability, and fidelity of the systems.

Full Flight Simulators

The term *Full Flight Simulator* (FFS) replaces *airplane simulator,* previously defined in AC 120-45A. According to current FAA regulations, an FFS (see Figure 3-1) is a

> ... replica of a specific type, make, model, or series aircraft. It includes the equipment and computer programs necessary to represent aircraft operations in ground and flight conditions, a visual system providing an out-of-the-flight deck view, a system that provides cues at least equivalent to those of a three-degree-of-freedom motion system, and has the full range of capabilities of the systems installed in the device....
>
> 14 CFR 60, Appendix F

Figure 3-1: A Full Flight Simulator (courtesy of CAE)

The core of that definition remains "replica of a specific type, make, model, or series aircraft." In other words, a flight simulator duplicates the performance and feel of a particular airplane, and it must recreate an airplane's cockpit with great fidelity, including exact reproductions of the real aircraft's physical controls, instrumentation, and switches.

Flight Training Devices (FTDs)

The same regulations update the definition of a Flight Training Device (FTD) to

> ... a replica of aircraft instruments, equipment, panels, and controls in an open flight deck area or an enclosed aircraft flight deck replica. It includes the equipment and computer programs necessary to represent aircraft (or set of aircraft) operations in ground and flight conditions having the full range of capabilities of the systems installed in the device ... for a specific FTD qualification level.
>
> 14 CFR 60, Appendix F

That description drops the requirement that an FTD (see Figure 3-2) must mimic a specific make or model of an aircraft. The degree to which a particular FTD must emulate an aircraft's controls, instruments, and switches depends on the device's certification level; but in general, an FTD doesn't have to duplicate every switch.

Figure 3-2: A typical FTD, produced by Precision Flight Controls

For example, a Level 4 FTD, the least sophisticated type

> ... may have an open airplane-specific flight deck area, or an enclosed airplane-specific flight deck and at least one operating system. Air/ground logic is required (no aerodynamic programming required). All displays may be flat/LCD panel representations or actual representations of displays in the aircraft. All controls, switches, and knobs may be touch sensitive activation (not capable of manual manipulation of the flight controls) or may physically replicate the aircraft in control operation.
>
> 14 CFR 60, Appendix F

Level 5 and 6 FTDs must replicate the cockpits and flight characteristics of aircraft with increasing precision.

Basic and Advanced Aviation Training Devices

In 1997, the FAA published AC 61-126, *Qualification and Approval of Personal Computer-Based Aviation Training Devices*, which, as the title implies, discussed the use of PC-based simulations. PCATDs, as the devices were known, included software like Microsoft Flight Simulator, hardware (usually one or more consoles that incorporated a flight yoke and other controls and switches), and a display (typically an off-the-shelf computer monitor). Because the technology was new, the FAA restricted the use of PCATDs to a few basic tasks required during primary and instrument flight training.

Technological advances and the aviation community's experience with PCATDs led the FAA to update the definition and expand the use of PC-based simulations. AC 61-136, *FAA Approval of Basic Aviation Training Devices* (BATD) and *Advanced Aviation Training Devices* (AATD), issued in 2008, retired the PCATD category. It describes the PC-based training devices that the FAA now approves for use in aviation training.

The core requirements for BATDs and AATDs are more general than those specified for flight simulators and FTDs. For example, according to AC 61-136, a BATD (see Figure 3-3) "provides a training platform for at least the procedural aspects of flight relating to an integrated ground and flight instrument training curriculum."

The more sophisticated AATD "provides a training platform for both procedural and operational performance tasks related to ground and flight training towards private pilot, commercial pilot, and airline transport pilot certificates, a flight instructor certificate, and instrument rating."

Figure 3-3: Hardware for a CR12 Basic Aviation Training Device from Precision Flight Controls.

The hardware specifications for BATDs and ATTDs are similar. For example, a BATD "must provide certain physical controls and may provide some virtual controls," described as follows:

> (1) Physical flight and aircraft system controls should be recognizable as to their function and how they are to be manipulated solely from their appearance. Physical flight and aircraft system controls eliminate the use of interfaces such as a keyboard, mouse, or gaming joystick to control the represented aircraft model in simulated flight.
>
> (2) For the purposes of this AC, virtual control is any input device to control aspects of the simulation (such as setting aircraft configuration, location, and weather) and to program, pause, or freeze the device. Virtual controls should be primarily for the instructor's use...
>
> (4) The physical arrangement, appearance, and operation of controls, instruments, and switches ... should model at least one aircraft in the family of aircraft represented as closely as practicable. Manufacturers are expected to use their best efforts to recreate the appearance, arrangement, operation, and function of realistically placed physical switches and other required controls representative of a generic aircraft instrument panel.
>
> FAA Advisory Circular AC 61-136

The Deeper Distinction

It's as easy to distinguish superficially between an FFS and a BATD as it is to see the differences between a single-engine trainer and an airliner. But there's more than technology behind the differences between types of simulation devices. They're intended for fundamentally different uses.

Simply put, an FFS is a substitute for a specific aircraft; and in many circumstances, pilots using an FFS can receive all the training required to operate the simulated airplane and earn a type rating for that aircraft without ever leaving the ground. In fact, airline pilots who have completed training for a new type in an FFS, and who may never have been in the cockpit of the real aircraft that the simulator emulates, often make their first flights in regular revenue service with passengers on board.

To achieve the level of fidelity necessary to meet that goal, the specifications for an FFS are extensive, detailed, and stringent. As noted earlier, they require that a simulator duplicate a specific cockpit. The FFS must also have a wide-view, high-resolution display; "flying" characteristics that closely mimic those of the real airplane throughout its normal flight envelope; a sophisticated sound system; and, usually, motion that accurately recreates the feel of flying.

Level 4, 5, and 6 FTDs are by definition less comprehensive representations of specific aircraft or broad types of airplanes, and as such, the requirements they must meet are less stringent. They also can't be used to complete all of the training pilots must receive. To earn type ratings or similar approvals to act as the pilot in command of an aircraft simulated by an FTD, pilots eventually must fly the real airplane — or train in an appropriate FFS.

A BATD or AATD, however, is not intended to be a replacement for a specific aircraft, or even a series of related aircraft — it's not a *simulator*. In fact, as their full names imply, BATDs and AATDs are not even *flight* training devices.

Instead, BATDs and AATDs are *Aviation Training Devices* (ATDs) intended to complement aircraft — and ground-school classrooms — throughout a training program. The FAA explains the distinction this way:

> Instructors have typically taught flight task procedural skills almost exclusively during in-flight training and aeronautical knowledge during ground training. However, based on the available data, the FAA has determined that instructors can successfully teach procedural understanding of certain flight tasks during ground and flight training using [BATDs and AATDs]... .
>
> FAA Advisory Circular AC 61-136

The key to using PC-based simulations effectively, then, is understanding that like BATDs and AATDs, they are tools to help pilots grasp general principles and practice basic procedures through hands-on experience.

Where X-Plane and FSX Fit In

You may have noticed that the discussion of BATDs and AATDs hasn't mentioned X-Plane or FSX. The reason is straightforward — neither product by itself meets the FAA standards for a "training device," which by definition must include software and hardware, such as flight controls and cockpit switches:

> Physical flight and aircraft system controls [of an ATD] should be recognizable as to their function and how they are to be manipulated solely from their appearance. Physical flight and aircraft system controls eliminate the use of interfaces such as a keyboard, mouse, or gaming joystick to control the represented aircraft model in simulated flight.
>
> FAA Advisory Circular AC 61-136

The only significant physical difference between X-Plane or FSX, configured as described in Chapter 1, and a BATD is the use of a "gaming" joystick for primary flight control and a mouse to operate the virtual switches and other controls depicted on the cockpit display. The FAA requirements for a BATD restrict the use of a mouse and keyboard as follows:

> Except for setup and/or fault mode entry, neither the keyboard nor the mouse may be used to set or position any feature of the BATD in the represented aircraft for the maneuvers or flight training to be accomplished ... The pilot must operate the additional equipment needed in order to accomplish a training procedure ... in the same manner in which it would be operated in the represented aircraft. For example, [by using] landing gear, wing flaps, cowl flaps, carburetor heat control, and mixture, propeller, and throttle controls.
>
> FAA Advisory Circular AC 61-136

The latest flight yokes, throttle quadrants, and other accessories developed for hobbyists, however, meet the FAA requirement that they be "recognizable as to their function and how they are to be manipulated solely from their appearance" (see Figure 3-4). Many BATDs use such off-the-shelf cockpit controls.

Ultimately, it's just the presence of a keyboard and mouse that disqualifies a typical home setup running X-Plane or FSX as a BATD. To borrow a famous line from the 1980 movie *Airplane!*, however, "That's not important right now" — because, as you'll see in the sections that follow, either X-Plane or FSX can fulfill the training goals established for BATDs and AATDs.

Figure 3-4: A control console designed for use with X-Plane or FSX from Precision Flight Controls

ATD Instructional Features

In addition to the physical characteristics described earlier, an ATD must help an instructor use the devices effectively with students. AC 61-136 lists the key features that an ATD must provide for an instructor, including:

> (1) The instructor must be able to pause/freeze the system at any point for the purpose of administering instruction regarding the task.
>
> (2) If a training session begins with the "aircraft in the air" and ready for the performance of a particular procedural task, the instructor must be able to manipulate the following system parameters independently of the simulation:
>
> Aircraft geographic location,
> Aircraft heading,
> Aircraft airspeed,
> Aircraft altitude, and
> Wind direction, speed, and turbulence.
>
> (3) The system must be capable of recording both a horizontal and vertical track of aircraft movement for later playback and review.
>
> (4) The instructor must be able to disable any of the instruments prior to or during a training session, and be able to simulate failure of any of the instruments without stopping or freezing the simulation to affect the failure.
>
> (5) The ATD must have at least a navigational area database that is local to the training facility to allow reinforcement of procedures learned during actual flight in that area.
>
> FAA Advisory Circular AC 61-136, Appendix 2

As described in Chapters 6 and 7, both simulations meet those requirements.

For example, the Instructor's Operating Station (IOS) in X-Plane mimics features of the control panels that instructors use to change the weather and fail instruments and systems. FSX includes a feature called *Shared Aircraft* that an instructor can use to fly along with a student, plus an IFR training panel for the Cessna 172 Skyhawk. You can also set up system failures in FSX. In addition, X-Plane and FSX include flight analysis and replay features to review a flight and evaluate a student's performance.

Flight Dynamics

No issue generates more heated debated among users of PC-based simulations — including pilots and flight instructors — than the perceived realism of the "flight" characteristics (also known as the *flight models*, or, more formally, the *flight dynamics*) of different programs.

Because BATDs and AATDs are aviation training devices, not flight simulators, the FAA lays out only general standards for the flight models that drive them. Note that throughout the following descriptions, there is no requirement that a flight model replicate the characteristics of a specific airplane:

> (1) Flight dynamics of the ATD should be comparable to the way the represented training aircraft performs and handles. However, there is no requirement for an ATD to have control loading to exactly replicate any particular aircraft...
>
> (2) Aircraft performance parameters (such as maximum speed, cruise speed, stall speed, maximum climb rate, hovering/sideward/forward/rearward flight) should be comparable to the aircraft or family of aircraft being represented.
>
> (3) Aircraft vertical lift component must change as a function of bank, comparable to the way the aircraft or family of aircraft being represented performs and handles.
>
> (4) Changes in flap setting, slat setting, gear position, collective control or cyclic control must be accompanied by changes in flight dynamics, comparable to the way the aircraft or family of aircraft represented performs and handles.
>
> (5) The presence and intensity of wind and turbulence must be reflected in the handling and performance qualities of the simulated aircraft and should be comparable to the way the aircraft or family of aircraft represented performs and handles.
>
> FAA Advisory Circular AC 61-136, Appendix 2

Stated in more familiar terms, the virtual airplane inside an ATD must bank left when you move the yoke to the left. The nose must pitch up when you pull back on the flight controls. Changing power should make the aircraft speed up or slow down (or affect its rate of climb or descent). The rates at which the airplane rolls, pitches, and yaws should be "comparable" to the way a given airplane or family of similar aircraft responds to a pilot's actions (see Figure 3-5).

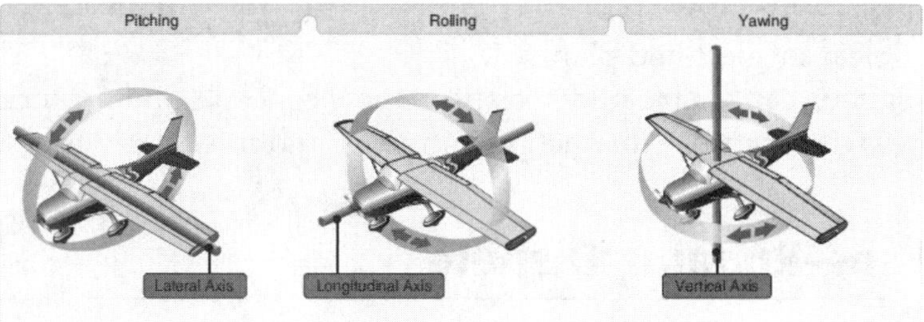

Figure 3-5: The pitch, roll, and yaw axes of an airplane

For the purposes of this book, then, there's no meaningful distinction between the "blade element theory" at the core of X-Plane and the classic "six-degree-of-freedom" model employed in FSX. (If you're interested in the technical details of each approach, see the links to more information at this book's website.) Both simulations, in fact, exceed the general requirements for the flight model at the heart of an ATD. The choice of which PC-based simulation to use depends largely on personal perception of how the virtual aircraft respond and on other considerations, as described in Chapter 5.

The Consensus

Even conservative instructors who question the role of PC-based simulation in flight training agree that ATDs, and by extension, X-Plane and FSX, have some value, especially in learning the skills required for flight by reference to instruments. The FAA summarizes that consensus this way:

> Flight simulation devices meeting acceptable FAA standards are very beneficial when used under the supervision of an authorized instructor. Pilots can use the devices to learn procedural tasks such as holding pattern entries, instrument approach procedures, missed approach procedures, and some operational performance tasks.
>
> FAA Advisory Circular AC 61-136

Many instructors have also long recognized that PC-based simulations can help new students, even those learning to fly under visual flight rules.

Airplane cockpits are noisy, stressful settings in which tasks such as scanning for other aircraft and monitoring chatter on the radio can interfere with the goals of a training flight; and no matter how well an instructor and student prepare for a lesson, bad weather, mechanical problems, and similar circumstances beyond their control — for example, a crowded airport traffic pattern — can interfere with or defeat the best-laid plans.

PC-based simulations can enable pilots to absorb new concepts and practice specific procedures without those distractions, stresses, and interruptions.

Echoes of Long-Running Disputes

The general agreement about the role of PC-based simulation often breaks down, however, when aviators discuss broader application of the tools. The ensuing debates frequently echo other enduring disputes among flight instructors and pilots.

For example, some experienced instructors assert that all pilots should learn to fly in simple airplanes (preferably equipped with a tailwheel); others argue gliders (sailplanes) would be even better primary trainers. Learning in such aircraft, those aviators reason, promotes and reinforces basic airmanship — "stick-and-rudder" flying — much as learning to handle a car with a manual transmission helps student drivers develop a better feel for the road.

There's little doubt that such basic training would benefit most pilots. However, that approach isn't practical today, because few tailwheel aircraft are available for primary training (instructors qualified to teach in tailwheel aircraft are also scarce, and insurance rates are high). For similar reasons, primary training in gliders is feasible only at institutions such as the United States Air Force Academy. The introduction of Light Sport Aircraft (LSA) may provide more opportunities for back-to-basics primary instruction, but most LSA are based on the modern nosewheel design, and many arrive from the manufacturer equipped with electronic flight and engine instruments as sophisticated as those found in modern high-performance airplanes.

Another disagreement focuses on the concept of "integrated flight instruction," the phrase the FAA uses to describe how instructors should correlate the view of the natural horizon beyond the cockpit windows to the gauges on the airplane's instrument panel:

> When introducing basic flight maneuvers to a beginning pilot, it is recommended that the "Integrated" or "Composite" method of flight instruction be used. This means the use of outside references and flight instruments to establish and maintain desired flight attitudes and airplane performance. When beginning pilots use this technique, they achieve a more precise and competent overall piloting ability. Although this method of airplane control may become second nature with experience, the beginning pilot must make a determined effort to master the technique...
>
> AIRPLANE FLYING HANDBOOK (3-3)

Many instructors assert that this concept leads to heads-down flying and dependence on instruments — and when applied improperly, it can — but the sentences that follow the description of integrated flight instruction include this admonition:

> The airplane's attitude is established and maintained by positioning the airplane in relation to the natural horizon. At least 90 percent of the pilot's attention should be devoted to this end, along with scanning for other airplanes.
>
> AIRPLANE FLYING HANDBOOK (3-3)

Indeed, the *Airplane Flying Handbook* recognizes the tendency to rely on instruments, and its guidance emphasizes that beginning pilots should use the view outside as the primary reference for controlling the aircraft:

> The most common error made by the beginning student is to make pitch or bank corrections while still looking inside the cockpit. Control pressure is applied, but the beginning pilot, not being familiar with the intricacies of flight by references to instruments ... will invariably make excessive attitude corrections and end up "chasing the instruments." Airplane attitude by reference to the natural horizon, however, is immediate in its indications, accurate, and presented many times larger than any instrument could be.
>
> AIRPLANE FLYING HANDBOOK (3-4)

The problem of instrument-panel fixation resonates with the instructors of students who begin flight training after logging many hours of virtual flying time in X-Plane or FSX. Those new pilots tend to focus on instruments because even astonishingly realistic scenery rendered on a typical PC display can't replace the "seat of the pants" feel and panoramic view provided by an airplane in flight. Breaking that habit can prove especially challenging.

Disagreements about using PC-based simulations in flight training also recapitulate points in more recent controversies about the proper role of Technically Advanced Aircraft (TAA) in basic flight training. (TAA, generally speaking, are aircraft equipped with flat-panel, computer-driven displays that replace most conventional mechanical instruments, so-called *steam gauges*.) Many flight training experts legitimately worry that the proliferation of dazzling cockpit displays distracts new pilots from the fundamentals of flying and contributes to the decline of such vital skills as *pilotage* — navigating by reference to visible landmarks and a chart.

Nevertheless, the debate about TAA is fast becoming irrelevant. Almost all new aircraft, even basic training and personal aircraft, leave the factory with "glass cockpits," and the owners of older aircraft are rapidly replacing the original needles and dials with retrofitted flat-panel displays. If you start training today at a flight school equipped with airplanes built or updated in the last 10–15 years, you will probably learn in an airplane equipped with at least some electronic instruments.

Likewise, the FAA and the aviation industry encourage the use of ATDs, even in the earliest stages of flight training. For example, Lesson 2 of the generic FAA/ Industry Training Standards (FITS) Private Pilot Syllabus introduces the student to the "Airplane Cockpit and Fundamental Flight Maneuvers" not in the airplane, but in a "visual training device" — in other words, a BATD or AATD.

Limitations of Training Devices

Even as enthusiasm for the use of ATDs grows, experts also concur on key limitations of training conducted with ATDs, namely:

- You shouldn't use a typical PC-based simulation to develop and hone stick-and-rudder flying skills.
- Self-instruction can negate the benefits of using simulation. A self-tutored pilot can develop bad habits, miss critical information, and have to unlearn or make up for those deficiencies at later stages of flight training.

The first point recognizes the fundamental purpose of ATDs and the limitations of the flight models and physical controls of those devices. (In fact, even pilots who regularly train in "real" simulators complain that the devices are more sensitive to control inputs and therefore harder to "fly" than the real airplanes those FFSs represent.)

The second issue applies more generally. Self-study can take you only so far, and without guidance from an experienced mentor, you're likely to go astray without realizing that you haven't mastered key concepts and skills. You shouldn't learn surgery from a book.

Logging Simulation Time

One other issue often muddies discussions about the use of PC-based simulations in flight training: How much credit can you earn when "flying" a simulation?

As noted earlier, X-Plane and FSX alone aren't approved ATDs. You can't receive credit for hours you spend "flying" X-Plane or FSX toward the requirements for a pilot certificate or rating. In fact, the advisory circular on BATDs and AATDs notes:

> An authorized instructor must administer and properly endorse the training [using an approved ATD] to satisfy the regulatory requirements.
>
> FAA Advisory Circular AC 61-136

Nevertheless, if you use either X-Plane or FSX during ground training sessions, your instructor can endorse that time as ground instruction.

To learn more about logging time while operating an ATD under the supervision of an authorized instructor, see AC 61-136, which, for example, lists the following credits for time spent using a BATD, including:

> Not more than 10 hours toward instrument rating flight instruction time ... ;
>
> Not more than 2.5 hours of training permitted ... in the introduction to the operation of flight instruments.

AC 61-136 also notes that:

> The flight experience allowance for the use of a BATD and the flight experience allowance for an AATD, an FTD or a flight simulator towards obtaining an instrument rating may be combined. However, that combination may not exceed ... [20 hours] ... .

Other Uses for PC-Based Simulations

With all of the preceding information in mind, how can aspiring pilots and their instructors use X-Plane and FSX most effectively? As the scenario-based lessons that follow demonstrate, PC-based simulations help students understand concepts, develop procedural skills, and prepare for flight lessons in the aircraft. Simulations are also helpful when a flight lesson doesn't go well and a student needs review and more practice. PC-based simulations have other uses, however, including some for which they're better suited than an approved ATD.

Animating Demonstrations

Sometimes a simulation is best used as a demonstration tool. For example, instead of drawing on a whiteboard or showing static PowerPoint slides to a ground school class, an instructor can connect a computer running X-Plane or FSX to a projector or large display to show how the flight instruments react in real time. Such interactive demonstrations can also help drill students on checklists, understand navigation, and so forth.

In fact, an instructor can use X-Plane or FSX to animate the discussion of most topics covered in a typical ground school curriculum.

Exploiting Portability

PC-based simulations like X-Plane and FSX needn't be used only at a flight school. Instructors and students who "fly" the same simulation can connect over the web or a local area network and conduct lessons much as people use Skype and similar tools to hold video conferences.

At present, remote use of PC-based simulations isn't envisioned in the FAA guidance on ATDs, but it has great potential. Like the distance learning already embraced by airlines and providers of advanced training for business jets, connecting PC-based simulations can help time-pressed students prepare for flight lessons (especially in urban areas where commuting to and from the airport adds unnecessary stress and expense), keep students motivated, and make training more enjoyable.

Summary

To resist including PC-based simulations in flight training is as counterproductive and ultimately futile as banning tablet computers and the web from classrooms (and, more pertinently to this discussion, from tasks such as flight planning). The challenge for instructors and pilots contemplating the effective application of PC-based simulation is the same as that posed by all of the developments noted earlier — namely, how to use rapidly evolving technology appropriately and wisely.

CHAPTER

4

Scenario-Based Training for Virtual Aviators

Perhaps you're a dedicated flight-simulation hobbyist who has logged thousands of hours flying X-Plane or FSX. You may be a pilot for a virtual airline or a dedicated user of VATSIM or another simulated air traffic control service. Or you may be new to virtual flying, taking it up as a pastime or as a prelude to starting real flight training. What can this book and scenario-based training offer you?

Learning Like a Real Pilot

For all but the most casual virtual pilots, realism is the main attraction of simulated flying — and the more you learn about real-world aviation, the more you'll enjoy virtual flying at whatever level appeals to you.

Flight simulation hobbyists who have never been pilots typically learn about virtual flying by trial and error and by tapping the many sources of information now available online. Worldwide, active communities have formed around X-Plane and FSX, and you can find a lot of advice about flying — even lessons — in online forums and magazines such as *Computer Pilot* and *PC Pilot*.

Some of the instruction available to virtual aviators is thorough and of high quality. For example, FSX includes a series of interactive lessons with Rod Machado, a widely respected flight instructor, writer, and speaker. Flying virtually with Machado can help you acquire basic knowledge and skills, and practice selected instrument-flying procedures.

Unfortunately, you also run across misinformation, and too often lessons don't follow a logical sequence or cover topics completely. Of course, those limitations aren't a big deal in the world of virtual flying — no one is at risk and there are no FAA regulations to break. (And, sadly, flight training in the real world isn't always as systematic and complete as it should be.) Still, haphazard learning can detract from the enjoyment of virtual flying, just as it does in real-world flight training.

Even if your goal is to fly simulated jets for a virtual airline, reviewing the basics and honing core skills such as the instrument scan will help you get more enjoyment out of the hobby of virtual flying. As online air traffic and other forms of interactive flying proliferate, you'll be more welcome in those communities and more comfortable joining in if you've acquired fundamental knowledge and polished your flying procedures.

As future versions of X-Plane and other PC-based simulations such as Microsoft Flight are released with increasingly detailed and realistic weather, airport environments, avionics, interactive ATC, and other features, building a solid foundation of real-world flying knowledge and skills will become ever more important.

A Systematic Approach

Scenario-based training (SBT) — described in detail in Chapter 9 — was developed to improve the quality of real-world flight training and to address safety issues; it's also an excellent way to help flight simulation enthusiasts get more out of virtual flying. In particular:

- SBT and the grading standards create structure for the free-form world of flight simulation, much like virtual airlines and similar community activities.
- The learner-centered grading method described in Chapter 9 is a way to "score" both your knowledge of aviation and the flights you make without resorting to complicated "missions" with sensitive scoring systems.
- SBT organizes the background information required to understand the procedures and techniques that real pilots use to fly safely and efficiently.

Starting Over?

Even if you've enjoyed virtual flying for years and think you've moved beyond the basics, you can still acquire important knowledge and skills by working through the scenarios, including some of the introductory lessons, and that experience will make virtual flying more fun. Many pilots who show up for training at their first real flying jobs, usually at an air freight company or regional airline, are surprised by how hard they must work to hone basic flying skills — or to master knowledge and procedures they didn't acquire during their initial training and flying experience.

You aren't required, of course, to follow a specific sequence of scenarios, but you'll benefit from reviewing the resources available via this book's website and proceeding through the lessons generally in order.

Learning to Fly

If your interest in flight simulation is part of a larger aspiration to become a pilot, you'll also benefit from taking the lessons and scenarios seriously and in a logical sequence. The authoritative resources described in Chapter 2 are tools that instructors and aviators in training use every day; and by completing the lessons, you'll start to understand how real-world aviation works. Of course, if you're already in flight training or plan to start soon, you should talk to your instructor about how to integrate PC-based simulation in your lessons and ground school sessions.

The learn-to-fly information from *AOPA Flight Training* (see Figure 4-1) is especially helpful if you have questions about choosing a flight school and finding an instructor — and what you'll have to learn.

Figure 4-1: AOPA Flight Training website

Experienced pilots often remind newly licensed flyers that a pilot certificate or new rating is a "license to learn," and that "a good pilot is always learning." The same could be said about periodically reviewing the fundamentals of any activity — including virtual flying.

CHAPTER 5

Choosing a PC-Based Simulation: X-Plane or FSX?

Like airplane owners who argue passionately about the advantages of flying low-wing Pipers versus high-wing Cessnas, virtual aviators have long engaged in a simmering debate about the merits of the leading PC-based flight simulations: X-Plane and FSX.

As explained in Chapter 3, both X-Plane and FSX support the learning environment that you need in order to use simulation as a complement to flight training — especially when following the approach advocated in this book.

Determining which simulation to use depends mostly on such factors as the type of computer you prefer (essentially, Windows or Mac), how much you enjoy tweaking and customizing software, and your own perception of how well each simulation immerses you in the illusion of flight — and perhaps whether you prefer factory-built airplanes (FSX) or homebuilt ("experimental") aircraft (X-Plane).

CROSS-REFERENCE **For more information that may help you decide which simulation is best for you, see Chapters 6 and 7. You can quickly compare the key features of each simulation, and assess how each simulation looks on a typical computer display.**

Essential Features

Both X-Plane and FSX offer the key features — essentially the software components — of a basic aviation training device (BATD) that support their effective use in flight training, including the following:

- Detailed display of cockpit instruments and essential controls (see Figures 5-1 and 5-2)
- Flight characteristics representative of the aircraft depicted in the simulation
- Enough airports, navigation aids, and related details to support accurate navigation and airport operations
- Scenery in sufficient detail to support basic visual navigation and operations around airports (see Figures 5-3 and 5-4)
- Realistic simulation of weather (wind, clouds, visibility, and so forth)
- Features for instructors to change ambient conditions, simulate failures, and review the details of a simulated flight

Figure 5-1: The Cessna 172 cockpit in X-Plane

Figure 5-2: The Cessna 172 cockpit in FSX

Figure 5-3: A typical airport environment in X-Plane

Figure 5-4: A typical airport environment in FSX

CROSS-REFERENCE **For more information about BATDs, see Chapter 3.**

Basic Decision Tree

The best choice of simulation for you largely depends on the following factors:

- The type of computer you prefer. If you run Windows, either simulation works well. Although FSX can function on newer Macs that can run Windows, that's not an ideal configuration. If you're a Mac fan, X-Plane is the simulation of choice. If you're dedicated to Linux, X-Plane is also the default choice.
- Your ability to set up and tweak your computer (especially if you want to run X-Plane on Linux). Basic installation of either product works well under Windows or Mac OS. Configuring and customizing X-Plane, however,

may require more knowledge of how your system works than is necessary for setting up FSX.

- Your "user-interface aesthetic." The menus and dialog boxes in X-Plane are utilitarian and not as polished as their counterparts in FSX (see Figures 5-5 and 5-6). The X-Plane interface isn't difficult to use, but if you prefer software with a friendly face, FSX may be the better choice.
- How much you like to customize and tinker with a simulation, especially with aircraft characteristics. For example, X-Plane includes Airfoil-Maker, a supplemental application that you can use to change the modeling of a wide range of aerodynamic factors. FSX offers a more limited range of "realism" settings in the core simulation. (If you're an experienced programmer, you can use the free FSX Software Development Kit to adjust many details of FSX and to create add-on features.)

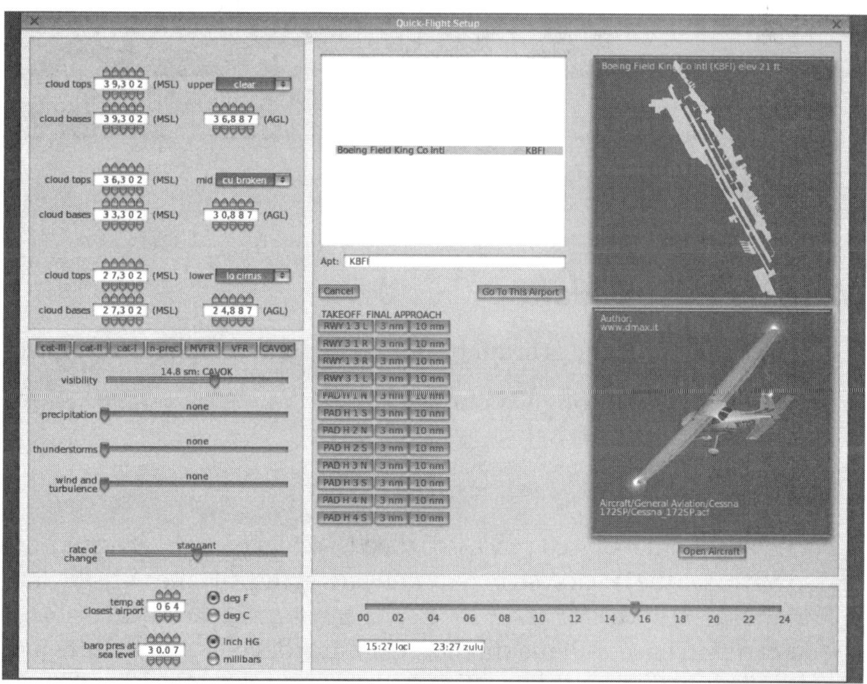

Figure 5-5: The X-Plane Quick-Flight Setup dialog box

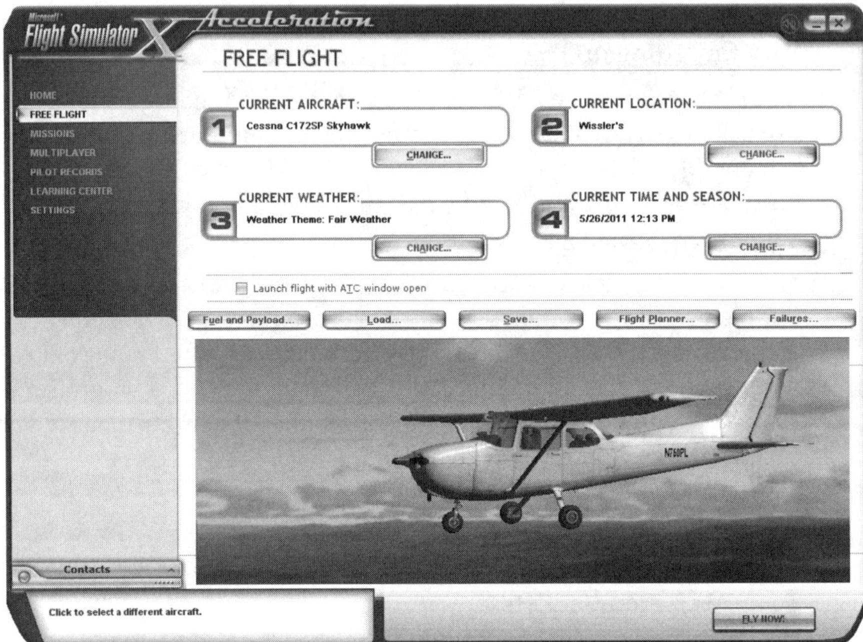

Figure 5-6: The FSX Free Flight dialog box

More Details: X-Plane

As noted earlier, X-Plane is available for all popular PC-platforms, including:

- Windows (XP through Windows 7)
- Mac OS
- Linux

For details about required processor speed, system memory, graphics adapters, and so forth, see the latest system requirements at the X-Plane website (link available at this book's website at `www.wiley.com/go/flightsimulatortraining`).

You can purchase X-Plane directly from the developer's website and from some online retailers and stores. For the latest information about where to buy X-Plane, visit X-Plane.com and community websites (links available at this book's website). X-Plane is updated frequently, and you can download revisions from the X-Plane website.

More Details: FSX

FSX runs only on Windows (XP SP2 through Windows 7). For details about required processor speed, system memory, graphics, and so forth, see the product website and the latest system requirements described in Microsoft Knowledge Base Article 925724 (links available at this book's website).

The scenarios in this book require only FSX Standard Edition, but Deluxe Edition and FSX Acceleration (which includes the FSX SP1) are also supported. The best deal available as this book went to press is the Gold Edition of FSX, which includes both FSX Deluxe and FSX Expansion and the service pack. Because FSX was released in 2008, it's often easiest to purchase the software from the online Microsoft store or an online retailer.

Add-Ons

If you plan to use X-Plane or FSX for entertainment as well as a training aid, other considerations may inform your decision.

For example, both simulations have spawned large communities of users around the world, and many add-ons (free and for purchase) are available for each product. FSX, because it is the last version in one of the longest-running titles in the history of PC software, has held the advantage in this arena, and developers continue to create a variety of add-ons for FSX. However, Microsoft's decision to stop producing Flight Simulator in favor of Microsoft Flight has ceded momentum to X-Plane, at least temporarily.

If you want to use a specific aircraft or cockpit layout while flying the scenarios in this book, investigate what's available for each simulation. Models of most common training and personal aircraft are available for both X-Plane and FSX, and you can find a wide range of aircraft instruments (including glass-cockpit displays) for each simulation. Some are available as free downloads or shareware. Others are offered as packaged products.

Note that the quality and sophistication of add-ons varies. To learn more about specific add-ons, see the links available at this book's website and popular community forums for X-Plane and FSX, where you can often find reviews and comments from customers.

Cockpit Controls

As noted in Chapter 1, both X-Plane and FSX work with popular flight yokes, joysticks, rudder pedals, throttle quadrants, and similar accessories. In fact, manufacturers of those accessories often provide configuration files for X-Plane and FSX that you can download from their websites.

The main factors that affect the compatibility of devices like flight yokes are the operating system on your computer and the number of USB connectors your system offers; but most of the popular controls work with Windows versions ranging from Windows XP to Windows 7 and newer releases of Mac OS.

If your computer can run X-Plane or FSX, it will probably work with popular cockpit controls. As always, however, it's a good idea to visit the manufacturer's website to confirm the system requirements for each device you want to add to your home cockpit.

Realism

Partisans of X-Plane and FSX often base their preference on the realism of the flight models (the way the airplanes behave in the air). As noted in "Flight Dynamics" in Chapter 3, those debates are largely moot, at least as they pertain to the use of BATDs as complements to real-world flight training.

Disputes about how well the simulated aircraft fly are sometimes confused because vocal fans may have little (or no) experience at the controls of real aircraft. The characteristics of the flight yoke or joystick used as the primary control also strongly influence impressions about flying qualities. Reasonably priced devices made for the consumer market currently can't replicate the precision and range of motion of real aircraft controls, and even high-end devices made for approved flight training devices (FTDs) often don't provide the tactile feedback of their counterparts in an actual aircraft. Experienced pilots also develop a feel for flight based on *kinesthesia*, the (often unconscious) perception of motion and reaction to control inputs in a real airplane. Those cues are missing in a simulation planted firmly on the ground, and their absence can create subtle expectations that strongly influence the perception of how well a virtual airplane "flies."

Some virtual pilots think X-Plane flies more smoothly than FSX. Others prefer the way FSX handles. In the end, the choice is up to you: high-wing or low-wing?

Help and Support

Both X-Plane and FSX include resources to help you learn about, use, and customize the simulations.

X-Plane provides a user-guide in PDF format (and as a wiki at the X-Plane website), a Help feature, plus forums on a range of subjects, including add-on aircraft and features.

FSX includes the Learning Center (on the Help menu). In effect, it's a user guide on disk (see Figure 5-7). Additional help is available on the FSInsider website.

Figure 5-7: The FSX Learning Center

You can also find magazine articles (print and electronic editions), books, and myriad videos and blog items on the web that can help you get up to speed on and master specific features of X-Plane or FSX. You'll find links to some of these resources at this book's website.

NOTE **Neither the author nor Wiley can provide support for X-Plane and Microsoft Flight Simulator, add-on aircraft and features, or joysticks and other accessories. If you have questions about these products, contact the developer or manufacturer. The web-based communities for X-Plane and FSX are also good places to find answers and get advice from experienced users.**

CHAPTER 6

A Quick Guide to X-Plane

This chapter will get you started with the Desktop Edition of X-Plane (see Figure 6-1), whether you're new to PC-based simulations or trying X-Plane after years of virtual flying in Microsoft Flight Simulator. It highlights key features that will help both pilots and instructors use the simulation effectively with the scenarios that follow later in this book.

Figure 6-1: The X-Plane 9 box art

The guided tour that follows is like a first flying lesson. It gives you an overview of X-Plane, but it doesn't attempt to explain every feature in detail. Of course, if you're a pilot (even a pilot in training) or an instructor, you have an advantage. The simulated cockpit looks familiar, and you should need only a little practice to become comfortable at the controls.

Getting Help for X-Plane

For detailed information about X-Plane, see the *X-Plane Operation Manual* (provided as a PDF document on the X-Plane discs) and the support page at the X-Plane website, `http://x-plane.com` (see Figure 6-2). These references are the best sources of current information about the simulation.

Figure 6-2: Support page at the X-Plane website.

The support pages of the X-Plane website host several key documents and tutorials that help you install and configure X-Plane, including the following:

- Quick Start Guide for New Users
- Installation on a Windows PC
- Installation on a Macintosh

- Installation in Linux
- System Requirements
- Updating Graphics Drivers in Windows
- Setting Up X-Plane for Best Performance (Optimizing Frame Rate)
- X-Plane Desktop Frequently Asked Questions
- Cheat Sheet for Menus and Default Keys

You will also find a support wiki, forums, other sources of useful information, and plug-ins (add-on aircraft and features) for X-Plane.

The Cessna 172 Cockpit in X-Plane

The standard cockpit for the Cessna 172 Skyhawk displays all the instruments and controls in one window (see Figure 6-3).

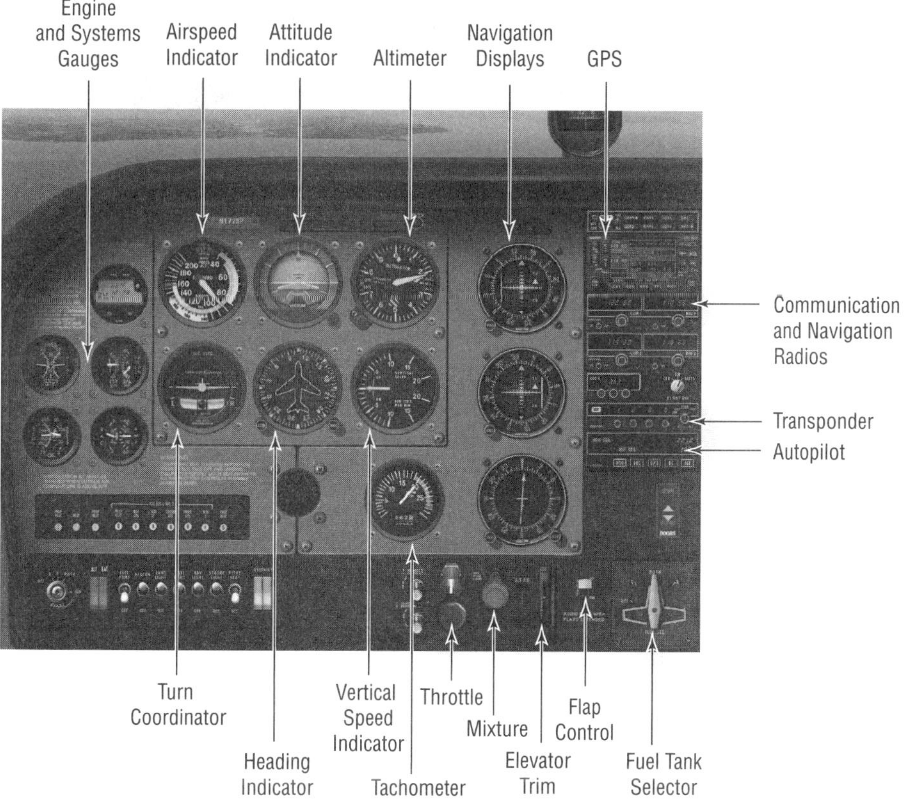

Figure 6-3: The standard Cessna 172 cockpit in X-Plane

You can slide the instrument panel down to provide a better view straight ahead (see Figure 6-4), look left and right, and even hide the instrument panel (for more information, see the discussion of the View menu later in this chapter and "Getting a Better View" in Chapter 11).

Figure 6-4: The instrument panel lowered for a better view of the runway

Using a Mouse in the Cockpit

You can use the mouse to operate most controls in the X-Plane cockpit (for example, tuning the radios, adjusting elevator trim, and extending and retracting the flaps) as if you were using your hand. Point to the control with the mouse, and when the pointer changes shape, click or drag the lever or knob (see Figures 6-5 and 6-6).

For more information about using the mouse in the X-Plane cockpit, see "Controlling Instruments and Avionics with the Mouse" in the *X-Plane Operation Manual.*

NOTE **You can also assign functions to buttons and other controls on a yoke or joystick (see the discussion of the X-Plane Settings menu below). Yoke and joystick levers and switches are usually the best mechanisms for adjusting primary controls such as the throttle and elevator trim.**

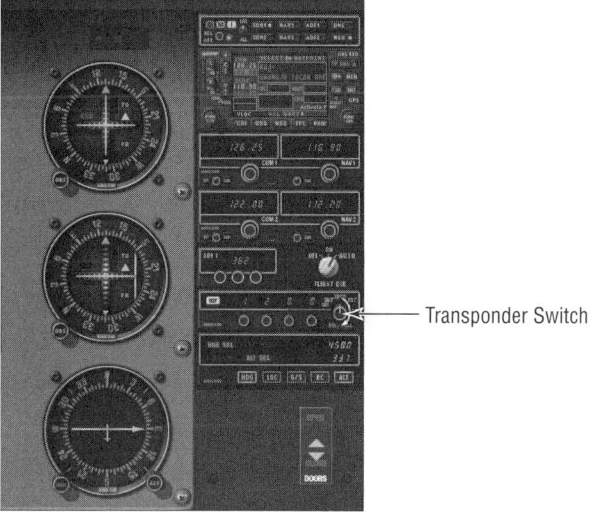

Figure 6-5: Using the mouse to operate the switch on the transponder in X-Plane

Figure 6-6: Using the mouse to operate the flap lever in X-Plane

Important X-Plane Commands

The *X-Plane Operation Manual* provides detailed descriptions of the menus and commands available in X-Plane, but a few features deserve special attention here. Note that many menus include keyboard shortcuts enclosed in brackets. You can press the indicated keys instead of opening the menu and clicking the command.

The File Menu

The File menu (see Figure 6-7) includes the Load Situation command, which you use to open the X-Plane Situations associated with each of the lessons in this book (see Figure 6-8).

Figure 6-7: The Load Situation command on the File menu in X-Plane

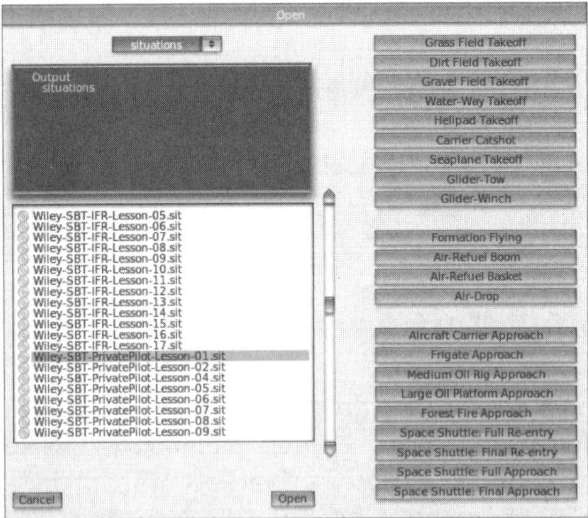

Figure 6-8: Situations for the lessons as listed in the Open dialog box

As explained later in this chapter, you also use commands on the File menu to capture screenshots of the X-Plane window, turn the movie recorder on and off, and load flight data recordings to replay your flights.

The Aircraft Menu

The Aircraft menu (see Figure 6-9) includes commands for changing aircraft, adjusting your aircraft's weight and fuel load, setting instrument and equipment failures, and so forth.

Figure 6-9: The Aircraft menu in X-Plane

You can also use the commands on the Aircraft menu to display or hide descriptions of the instruments when you point to them with the mouse (see Figure 6-10), and to display or hide the special mouse cursors that help you tune radios and operate cockpit controlsAa. You may want to hide these aids after you gain experience flying in X-Plane.

Figure 6-10: Description of the turn and slip indicator (turn coordinator) displayed in the X-Plane cockpit

The Location Menu

The Location menu (see Figure 6-11) includes commands for displaying interactive maps.

You can use these maps to check your position, drag your airplane to a new position, and adjust the airplane's altitude, heading, and speed. (You can also use the Location menu to move your airplane to Mars.)

You'll probably use the Local Map command often during your virtual flights. The Local Region map includes tabs for several types of maps, including one that mimics an aviation sectional chart (see Figure 6-12).

Press the Plus and Minus keys to zoom in and out on the map.

Figure 6-11: The Location menu in X-Plane

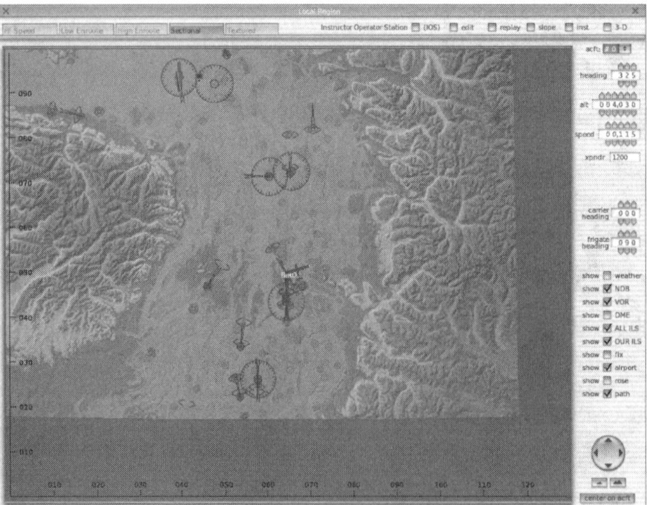

Figure 6-12: The Sectional chart display of the Local Region map

The Environment Menu

The Environment menu (see Figure 6-13) includes commands that you use to change the weather and date and time of day. You can use these commands after you load a Situation to customize the cloud layers, visibility, and other settings (see Figure 6-14).

Figure 6-13: The Environment menu in X-Plane

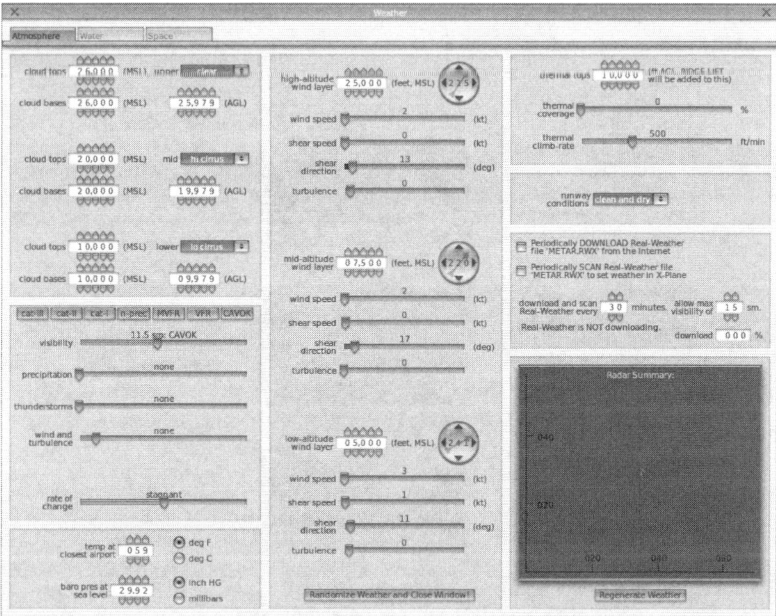

Figure 6-14: The Weather dialog box in X-Plane

The Settings Menu

The Settings menu (see 6-15) includes two important commands: Joystick & Equipment and Quick-Flight Setup. You use these commands to adjust (calibrate) your yoke or joystick and to assign functions to buttons, levers, and switches on those devices.

Figure 6-15: The Settings menu in X-Plane

Use the Quick-Flight Setup dialog box (see Figure 6-16) to move your airplane quickly to a different airport, change key weather conditions, and make other basic adjustments.

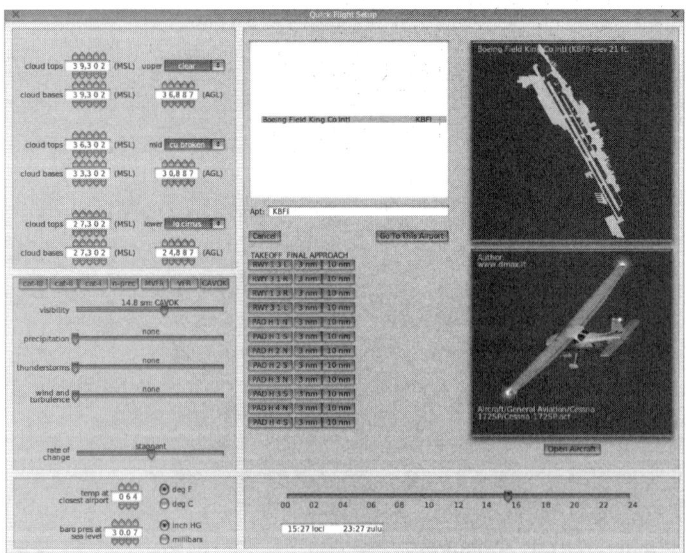

Figure 6-16: The Quick-Flight Setup dialog box in X-Plane

The View Menu

The View menu (see Figure 6-17) includes commands for changing views, switching between the normal and transparent instrument panel displays, and other commands that change your perspective. As the *X-Plane Operation Manual* notes, the best way to understand the many options for looking around in X-Plane is to experiment with the commands on this menu.

Figure 6-17: The View menu in X-Plane

CROSS-REFERENCE **You can find examples of useful views in "Getting a Better View" in Chapter 11.**

The Special Menu

The Special menu (see Figure 6-18) includes commands for adjusting the flight characteristics of your aircraft.

For the purposes of the lessons in this book, it's best to use the default settings for the Cessna 172 Skyhawk.

CROSS-REFERENCE **To learn more about the Plugins menu, which you use to work with add-on aircraft, scenery, and features, see the *X-Plane Operation Manual.***

Figure 6-18: The Special menu in X-Plane

Recording Flights in X-Plane

X-Plane includes features to help you record flights. You can:

- Capture individual screens as you fly.
- Record flight data and replay a flight in X-Plane.
- Record movies that you can edit and share with others.

Capturing Screens

To capture individual screens as you fly, press Ctrl+Period (if you use this feature often, you can assign this function to a button on your yoke or joystick). You can capture both internal pictures of the cockpit and external views of your airplane (see Figure 6-19).

X-Plane captures the images as .png files and saves them in the directory where you installed X-Plane on your hard drive.

NOTE **If you're an instructor, you can use screen captures to create realistic illustrations for PowerPoint presentations and lesson plans.**

Figure 6-19: External view of the Cessna 172 captured in X-Plane

Recording and Replaying Flights

X-Plane provides two ways to record your flights:

- A flight data recorder that saves a "situation movie file" (.smo file). An .smo file stores data about the airplane's position, velocity, and so forth, just like a flight data recorder (the so-called black box) on an airliner. You can replay "situation movies" only within X-Plane, but just as when you are flying in real-time, you can change the viewpoint during the replay.
- A QuickTime recorder that stores a flight as a movie, which you can edit and share with people who do not have X-Plane.

You use Save Replay and Toggle Movie commands on the File menu to record flights. The Save Replay command stores flight data. The Toggle Movie command records a QuickTime movie.

For more information about these features, see "The File Menu" in the *X-Plane Operation Manual.*

NOTE **Note that recording QuickTime movies rapidly consumes space on your hard drive. If you record a long flight, you may quickly gobble up available space on the disk.**

Instructor Operating Station

X-Plane includes an Instructor Operating Station (IOS) that provides many of the features of the instructor's control panel in a flight training device (FTD). You can run the IOS on the same computer as X-Plane (if you have a video card that supports two displays) or on a separate computer (provided you have a second copy of X-Plane) connected to the primary system via a network or the web.

With the IOS, shown in Figure 6-20, you can:

- Observe the student's airplane on an interactive map.
- Monitor key instruments in the student's airplane.
- Fail instruments and systems on the aircraft without interfering with the pilot flying X-Plane.
- Change the time of day and weather.
- Move the aircraft to a new location and adjust its altitude, speed, heading, and so forth.

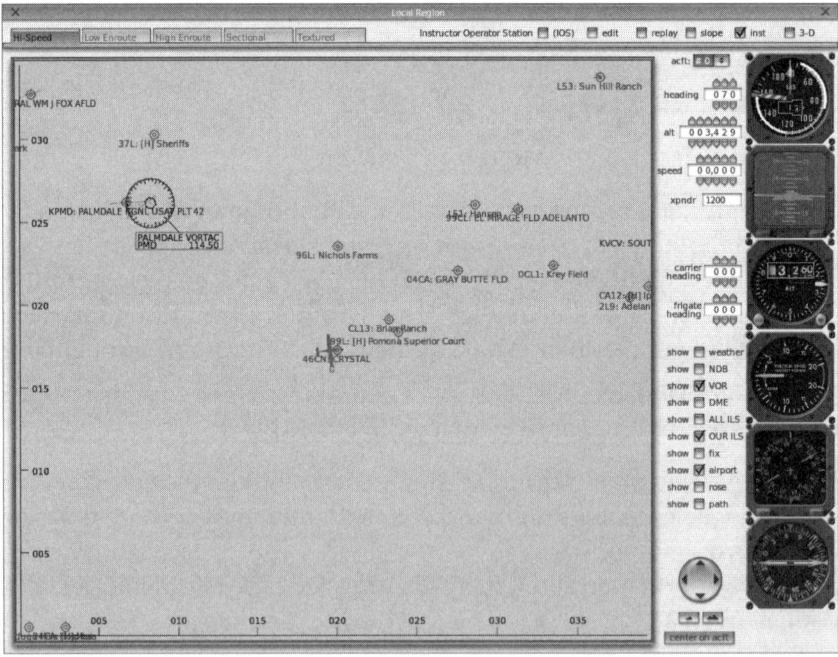

Figure 6-20: Instructor Operating Station in X-Plane

For more information about the IOS, see the *X-Plane Operation Manual*.

CHAPTER 7

A Quick Guide to Microsoft Flight Simulator X

This chapter helps you get started with FSX (see Figure 7-1), whether you're new to PC-based simulations or trying FSX after years of virtual flying in X-Plane. It highlights key features that will help both pilots and instructors use the simulation effectively with the scenarios that follow later in this book.

Figure 7-1: The FSX box art

The guided tour that follows is like a first flying lesson. It gives you an overview of FSX, but it doesn't attempt to explain every feature in detail. Of course, if you're a pilot (even a pilot in training) or instructor, you have an advantage. The simulated cockpit looks familiar, and you should need only a little practice to become comfortable at the controls.

Getting Help for FSX

FSX Learning Center, part of the Help system (see Figure 7-2) installed when you set up FSX on your computer, is a web-like guide to the simulation that features a visual table of contents to help you find specific information about a wide variety of topics (see Figure 7-3). It's the primary source of information about FSX.

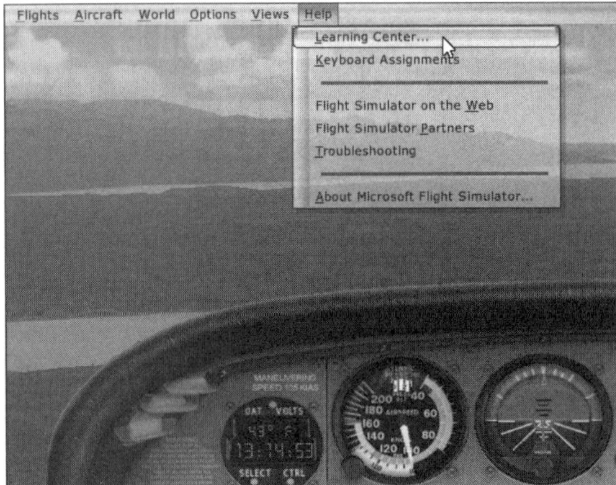

Figure 7-2: FSX Learning Center command on the Help menu

Guides to key features and other information about setting up, optimizing, and troubleshooting FSX are also available at the official FSInsider website (see Figure 7-4).

The Community Links page at the FSInsider website (`http://www.microsoft.com/games/fsinsider/`) includes information about forums and other resources offered by the worldwide community of FSX virtual aviators and developers of add-on aircraft, scenery, and features for FSX.

Figure 7-3: The Key Topics page of the FSX Learning Center

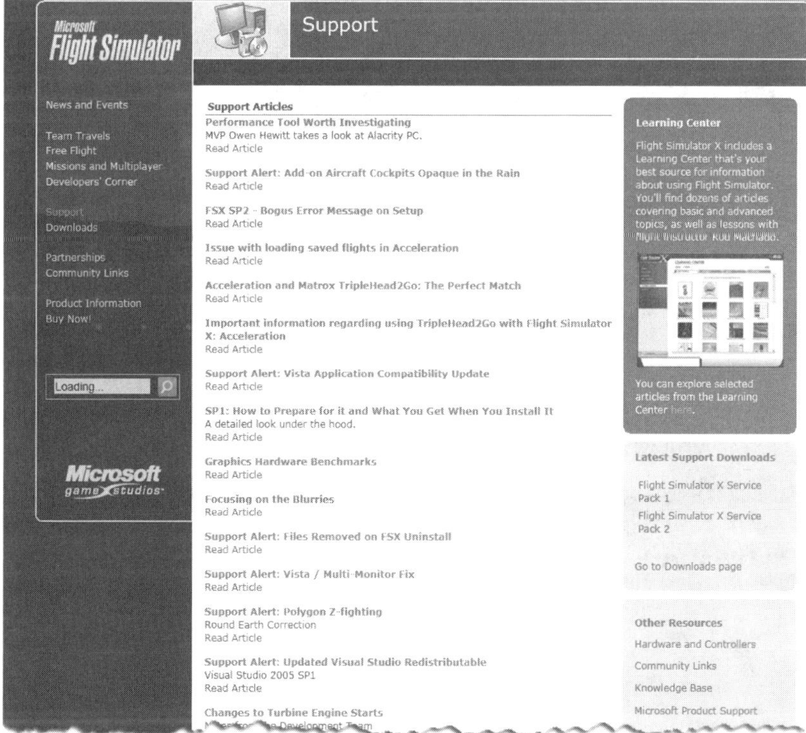

Figure 7-4: The Support page at the FSInsider website

The Cessna 172 Cockpit in FSX

The standard cockpit for the Cessna 172 Skyhawk displays the primary instruments and controls in one window (see Figure 7-5).

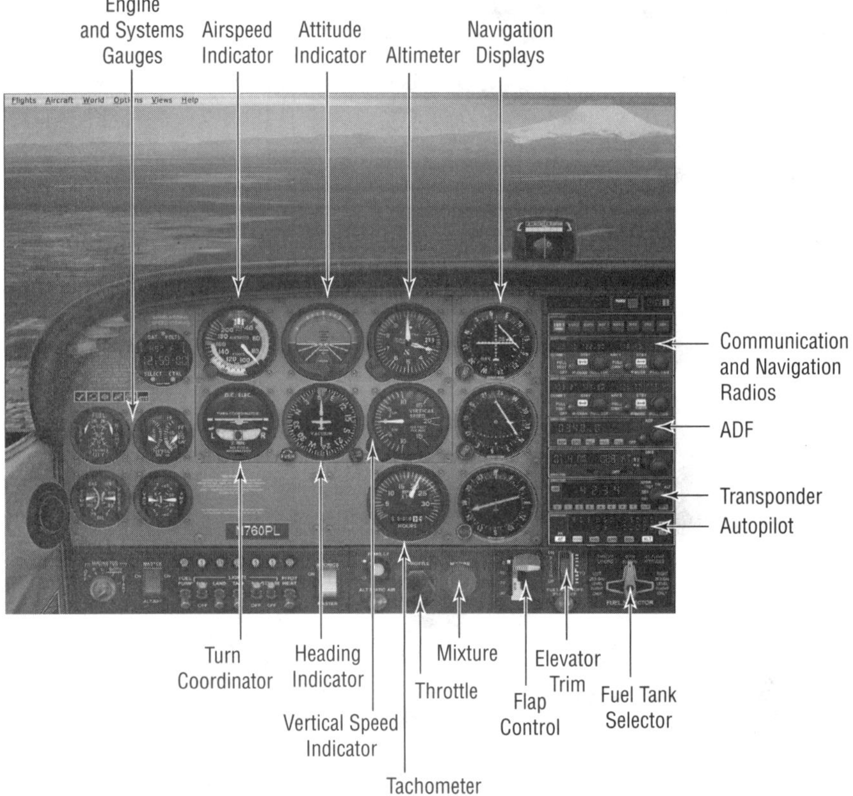

Figure 7-5: The standard 2D Cessna 172 cockpit in FSX

You can display and hide the GPS and other features, such as the Map and the Kneeboard, by clicking icons on the instrument panel (see Figure 7-6). These features appear in new windows (see Figure 7-7) that you can move around the screen with the mouse.

Figure 7-6: The instrument-panel icons to display and hide the GPS and other features

Figure 7-7: The GPS displayed in a window in FSX

Using a Mouse in the Cockpit

You can use the mouse to operate most controls in the FSX cockpit (for example, tuning the radios, adjusting elevator trim, and extending and retracting the flaps) as if you were using your hand. Point to the control with the mouse, and when the pointer changes shape, click or drag the lever or knob (see Figures 7-8 and 7-9). You can also roll the mouse wheel to operate many controls.

Figure 7-8: Using the mouse to press buttons on the autopilot in FSX

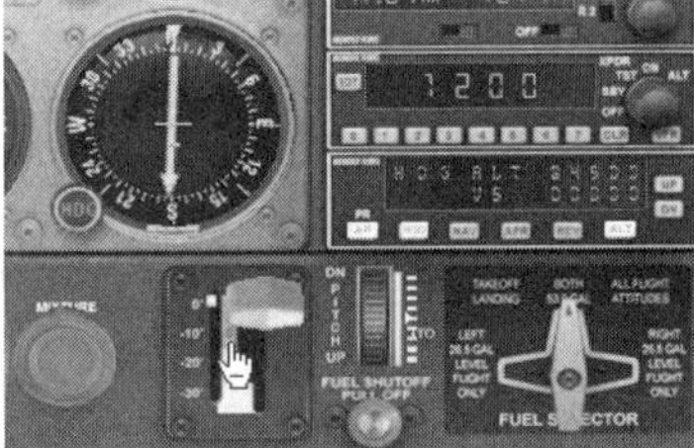

Figure 7-9: Using the mouse to operate the flap lever in FSX

For more information, see "The Mouse as a Cockpit Tool" in the FSX Learning Center.

NOTE **The Important Skills section of the FSX Learning Center also includes the topics "Using the Mouse," "Using Joysticks and Yokes," and "Using the Keyboard," which will help you operate cockpit controls easily and efficiently.**

Important FSX Menus

The FSX Learning Center includes detailed descriptions of the menus and commands available in FSX, but a few features deserve special attention here. Note that many menus include keyboard shortcuts next to the command names. You can press the indicated keys to choose the command instead of opening the menu and clicking the command.

NOTE **To learn more about choosing commands in FSX, see "Using the In-Game Menus" in the FSX Learning Center. You can also assign functions to buttons and other controls on a yoke or joystick. Yoke and joystick levers and switches are usually the best mechanisms for adjusting primary controls such as the throttle and elevator trim. For more information, see "Using a Joystick" and "Customizing Joystick Assignments" in the FSX Learning Center.**

The Flights Menu

The Flights menu (see Figure 7-10) includes the Load command, which you use to open the FSX Flights associated with each of the lessons in this book (see Figure 7-11). You can also use the Reset command to restart a Flight.

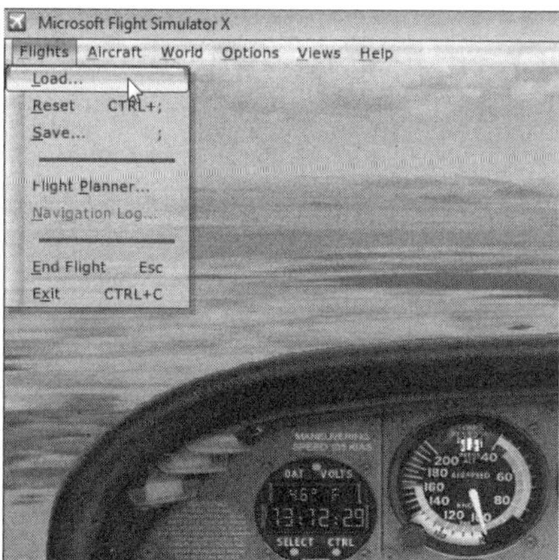

Figure 7-10: The Flights menu in FSX

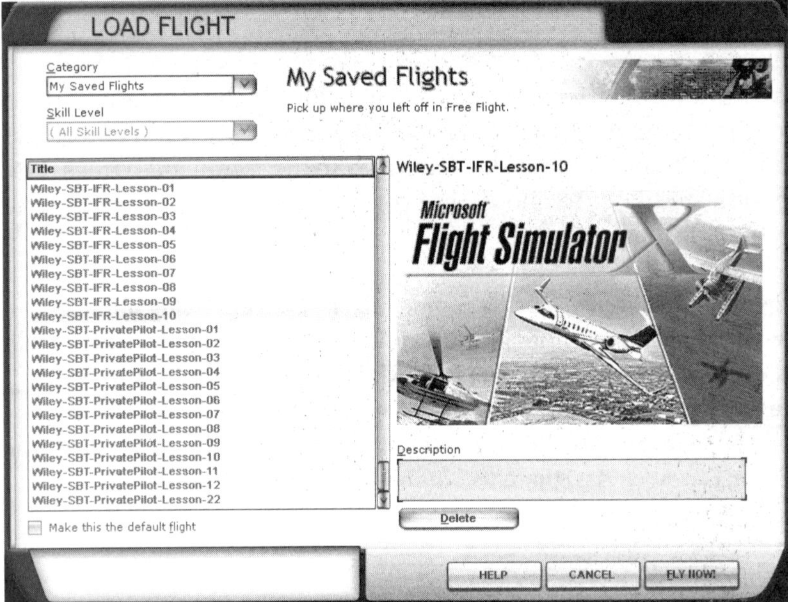

Figure 7-11: Flights for the lessons as listed in the Load Flight dialog box

The Aircraft Menu

The Aircraft menu (see Figure 7-12) includes the Select Aircraft command, which you use to switch to a different airplane (see Figure 7-13).

Figure 7-12: The Aircraft menu in FSX

Figure 7-13: The Select Aircraft dialog box in FSX

The Aircraft menu also includes the Kneeboard command to display helpful information as you fly (see Figure 7-14).

Figure 7-14: The Kneeboard in FSX

NOTE **The Kneeboard feature in FSX includes lists of key assignments, checklists, and other useful information. For more information, see "Using the Kneeboard" in the FSX Learning Center.**

You can use the Realism Settings command to adjust the flying qualities of the current aircraft (see Figure 7-15).

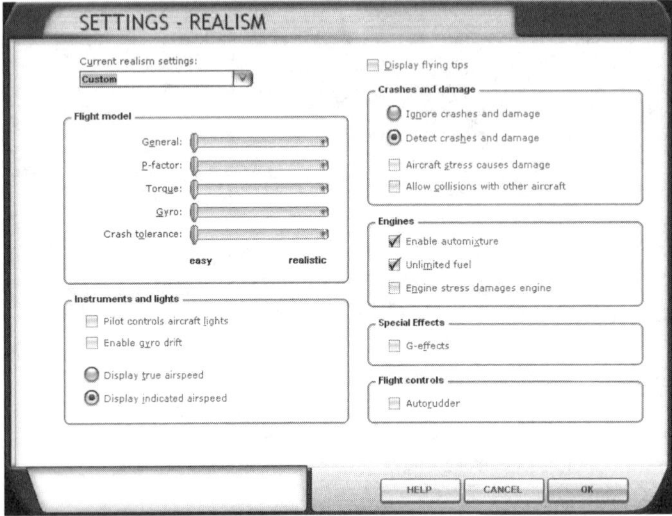

Figure 7-15: The Settings-Realism dialog box in FSX

To set up instrument and systems failures, choose the Failures command (see Figure 7-16).

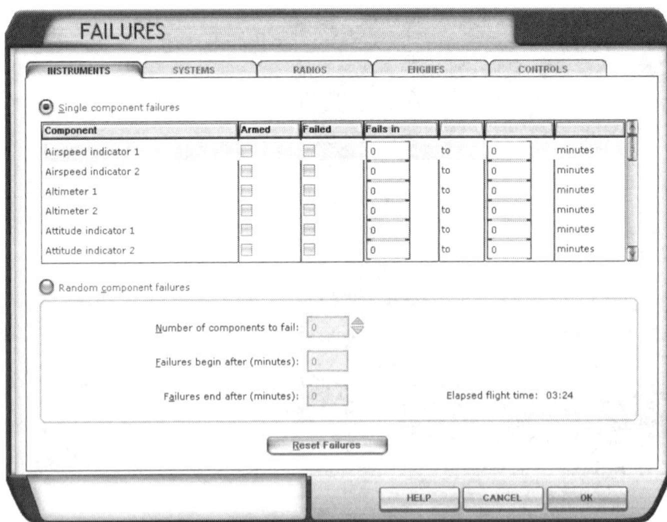

Figure 7-16: The Failures dialog box in FSX

Use the tabs on the Failures dialog box to fail the aircraft's instruments, systems, radios, or engine. You can choose to have a failure take effect immediately, randomly, or within specified time during a flight.

The World Menu

The World menu (see Figure 7-17) includes commands to change the time, season, and weather (see Figure 7-18).

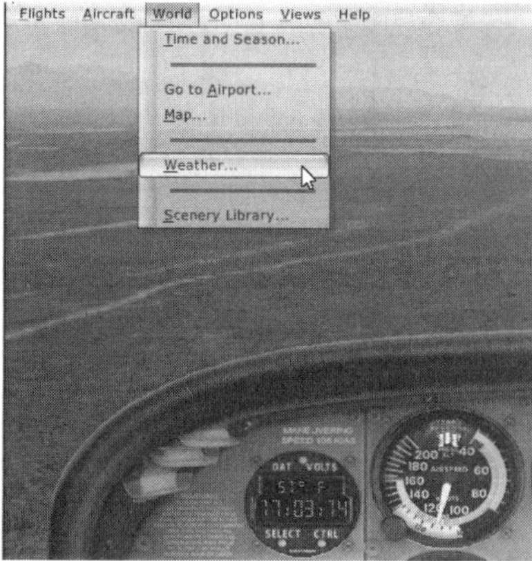

Figure 7-17: The World menu in FSX

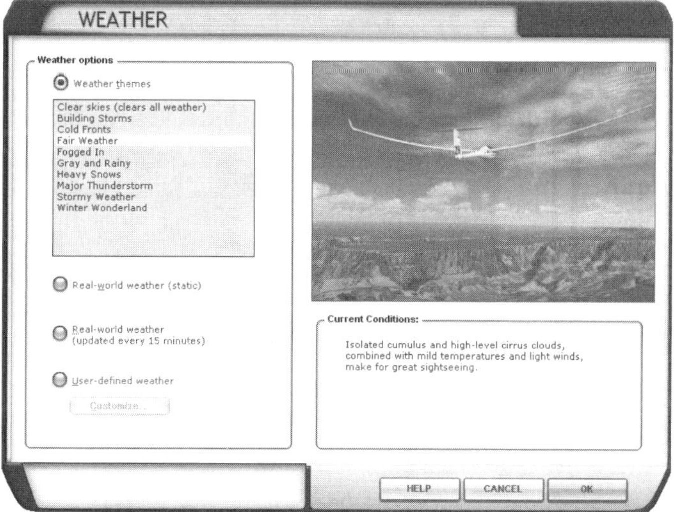

Figure 7-18: The Weather dialog box

You can use the Go to Airport command on the World menu to move your aircraft to a new airport (see Figure 7-19).

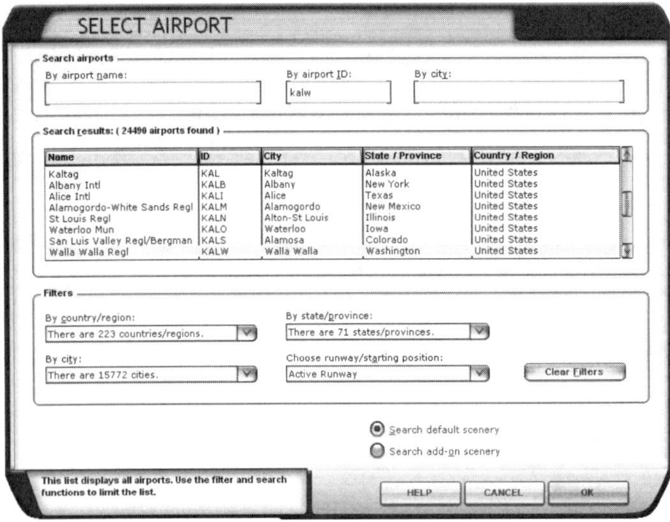

Figure 7-19: The Select Airport dialog box

The Map command displays an interactive map (see Figure 7-20) that you can use to reposition your aircraft and change its heading, altitude, and speed. You can also click airports and navigation aids on the map to display information about them.

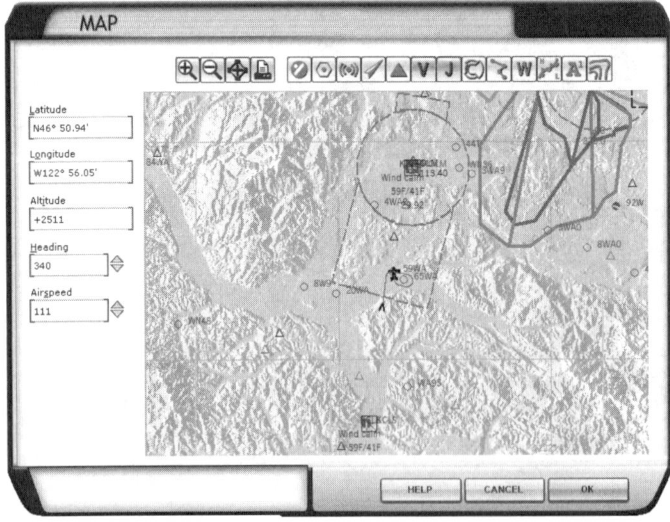

Figure 7-20: The Map in FSX

NOTE **For more information about using the interactive map in FSX, see "Using the Map" in the FSX Learning Center.**

The Options Menu

The Options menu (see Figure 7-21) includes the Flight Analysis command, which you can use to review your flight path and other information at any time during a flight (see Figure 7-22).

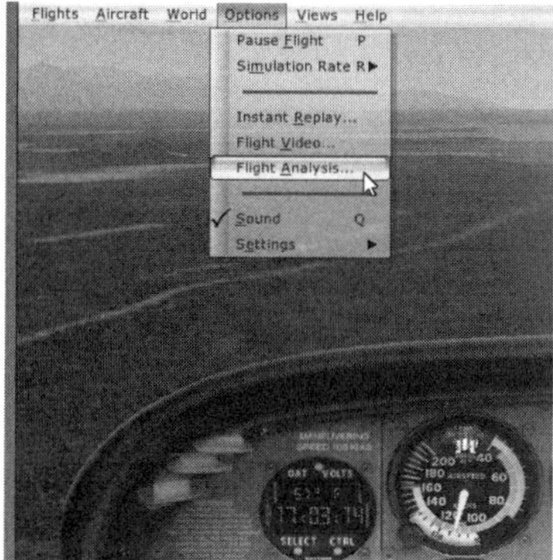

Figure 7-21: The Options menu in FSX

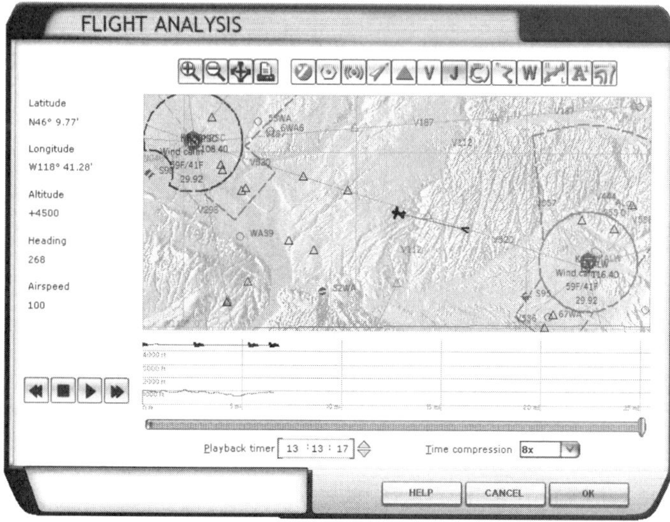

Figure 7-22: The Flight Analysis display in FSX

To record a flight, choose the Flight Video command (for more information, see "Recording Flights in FSX," later in this chapter).

The Views Menu

The Views menu (see Figures 7-23 and 7-24) includes commands for changing views, switching among different cockpit displays, opening new views, and other commands that change your perspective.

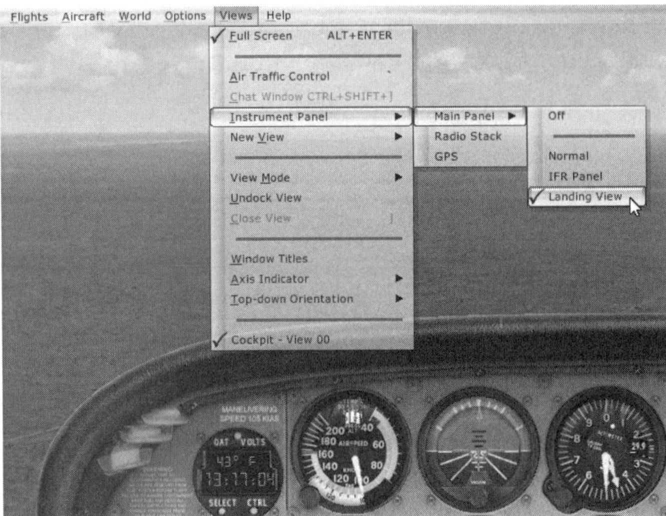

Figure 7-23: The Instrument Panel commands on the View menu in FSX

Figure 7-24: The View Mode commands on the View menu in FSX

NOTE **The best way to understand the different views and perspectives available in FSX is to experiment with the commands on the Views menu. For more information, see "Using Views and Windows" in the FSX Learning Center.**

The Cessna 172 Skyhawk in FSX includes an IFR training panel (see Figure 7-25) that minimizes the outside view (which isn't relevant when you're in the clouds) and devotes almost all of the window to the flight instruments, avionics, and controls. You can switch between the normal 2D panel and the IFR training panel by choosing it on the Views menu or by clicking an instrument panel icon on the IFR training panel (see Figure 7-26).

Figure 7-25: The Cessna 172 IFR training panel in FSX

Figure 7-26: The icons to switch between the IFR training panel and the standard instrument panel in FSX

Recording Flights in FSX

FSX includes features to help you record flights. You can:

- Capture individual screens as you fly.
- Replay a flight — until you reset that flight or start a new flight.
- Record flight data and replay a flight at any time in FSX.

Capturing Screens

To capture individual screens as you fly, press the V key (if you use this feature often, you can assign this function to a button on your yoke or joystick). You can capture both internal views of the cockpit and external views of your airplane (see Figure 7-27).

Figure 7-27: External view of the Cessna 172 captured in FSX

FSX captures screen images as .bmp files and saves them in the Flight Simulator X Files folder of the Pictures directory on your hard drive. Before sharing the images, you may want to use a graphics program to convert the .bmp files into a more compact format, such as .jpg or .png.

NOTE **If you're an instructor, you can use screen captures to create realistic illustrations for PowerPoint presentations and lesson plans.**

Recording and Replaying Flights

As its name implies, the Instant Replay command on the Options menu (see Figure 7-28) plays back all or part of the current flight. You can replay a flight until you end or reset that flight or begin a new flight.

The Flight Video command on the Options menu is a bit misleading. It doesn't record videos in a familiar movie format like .mpg or .avi. Instead, it acts like the flight data recorder (the so-called black box) on an airliner. It stores information about the airplane's position, velocity, and so forth in a data file with the extension .fsr. You can store these files for replay at any time and share them with other virtual aviators who have FSX installed on their systems.

You can replay these "videos" only within FSX (by choosing the Flight Video command on the Options menu); but just as when you are flying in real time, you can change the viewpoint during the replay.

Figure 7-28: The Options menu in FSX

NOTE **To learn more about recording and replaying flights, see "Flight Videos" in the FSX Learning Center.**

Using the Shared Aircraft Feature

The Shared Aircraft feature in FSX provides a way for two people to fly together in the same aircraft. This feature is especially useful for instructors who want to observe and help a student.

You can connect two computers running FSX via a local network or over the Internet. Just as in a real aircraft, the two pilots flying together can transfer the flight controls. One pilot can operate the primary flight controls while the other works with the radios and other systems.

NOTE **For detailed information about the Shared Aircraft feature, see "Sharing an Aircraft in Multiplayer" in the FSX Learning Center.**

Part

II

Getting the Most from X-Plane and FSX

In This Part

CHAPTER

8

Beyond the Basics: Additional Advice about Using Simulations Effectively

Whether you're an instructor, student pilot, certificated pilot, or virtual aviator, here are some additional tips about using this book and X-Plane or FSX to enhance your training and proficiency flying — and increase your enjoyment of virtual flying.

Developing Situational Awareness

First, make sure that you focus on what PC-based simulation does well. Most people develop the basic skills required to fly straight-and-level, turn, climb, and descend with just a few hours of practice. The most challenging part of flight training is learning how to think like a pilot. For all the reasons described in Chapter 3, PC-based simulations are excellent tools for exercising mental skills — specifically, for developing and honing "situational awareness" and aeronautical decision making (ADM). If you need to work on the finer points of aircraft control, fly a real airplane.

The lessons that follow are based on the goals of the scenario-based training (SBT) approach adopted by the FAA Industry Training Standards initiative, described in more detail in Chapter 9. As you explore the scenarios, keep in mind that the scenarios in this book are a starting point. The great advantage of a PC-based simulation is its flexibility. The lessons follow a logical sequence, but you may not find a given scenario useful if you already know about the knowledge and skills it is designed to teach. You may want to repeat some lessons. Whether you're an instructor or a pilot at any stage of training, you are free to adapt, skip, and replace the scenarios to suit your needs.

Using Other Airplane Types

The scenarios in this book are based on the Cessna 172 Skyhawk, which, for several reasons, is well suited for the purposes outlined in the preceding section:

- Most training aircraft in use today have performance and handling characteristics similar to those of the Skyhawk. For example, the Piper Archer, like the latest Skyhawk SP, has a 180-hp engine; it cruises at about 120 knots; and it has a range of 500–600 nm.
- The basic layout of the instrument panel (the so-called *six-pack*) and avionics follows standards established by the General Aviation Manufacturers Association (GAMA), formalized in 14 CFR Part 23 of the regulations that manufacturers must follow. For example, the essential flight instruments of the Cessna 172 Skyhawk (FSX) and the Piper Malibu (X-Plane) are arranged in the same basic pattern (see Figures 8-1 and 8-2).

Figure 8-1: Arrangement of basic flight instruments in the Cessna 172 Skyhawk (FSX)

Figure 8-2: Arrangement of basic flight instruments in the Piper Malibu (X-Plane)

- You can learn fundamental skills, such as interpreting the flight instruments, the actions for performing basic maneuvers, and even advanced instrument procedures, regardless of the aircraft you fly.
- Relying on the Skyhawk, which is included in the basic versions of both X-Plane and FSX, simplifies setup and use of those simulations.

However, if your real (or favorite) airplane is a Piper Cherokee, Beechcraft Bonanza, or other type, and if flying the Skyhawk distracts you from the general goals of the scenarios, you can substitute any aircraft available for X-Plane or FSX. Just choose a different airplane (see Figures 8-3 and 8-4) after you load a Situation (X-Plane) or Flight (FSX).

Figure 8-3: Choosing an aircraft in X-Plane

Figure 8-4: Choosing an aircraft in FSX

Keep in mind that many scenarios begin with the aircraft already in the air with the autopilot on. Switching aircraft, especially to a model with major differences in performance from the Skyhawk, may cause the scenario to begin with the aircraft flying at an unrealistic airspeed — probably too slowly. You may need to adjust power and other settings to stabilize the aircraft. If you plan to fly a scenario again, after you switch aircraft and stabilize it, save the Situation (X-Plane) or Flight (FSX) with a new name.

Choosing Conventional Gauges or Glass

Almost all new aircraft, even basic trainers and personal airplanes, are now delivered with high-tech "glass cockpits" such as the Garmin G1000 system (see Figure 8-5.)

For several reasons, however, the scenarios in this book are based on the conventional cockpits as depicted in X-Plane and FSX:

- Many aircraft still in use at flight schools are older models with conventional cockpit instruments.
- The simulation of the G1000 in FSX includes only the core features of that advanced avionics system, and G1000 cockpits are available only as add-ins for X-Plane.
- It's often difficult to see the instruments and data on the virtual displays unless you have a large monitor or several screens.
- Many variables and differences between glass systems complicate their use in a generic syllabus. For example, there are now several versions of the system software for the G1000 in the Cessna 172 that differ significantly in basic functions, such as the display of engine and system information.

- Most instructors and pilots agree that it's easier to transition to glass from conventional instruments rather than vice-versa. Core skills such as instrument interpretation are transferrable to glass cockpits with a little practice. Switching from feature-rich electronic displays to the "raw data" of conventional instruments is usually more challenging.

Photo courtesy of Cessna Aircraft Company

Figure 8-5: The G1000 system standard in new Cessna 172 Skyhawks

If you want to use a G1000 or similar system with the Skyhawk in X-Plane or FSX, you have several options. The better solutions involve buying an add-on module (such as the *Garmin G1000 Student Simulator* from Flight1Aviation Technologies) that simulates advanced avionics within X-Plane or FSX or that supports connections to glass cockpit hardware in a flight training device (FTD).

For more information about these options, visit the resources for each simulation at this book's website at `www.wiley.com/go/flightsimulatortraining`.

Adding Randomness

Instructors and pilots often overcomplicate the use of PC-based simulations. For example, to achieve the laudable goal of scenarios that present the pilot with realistic situations (equipment failures, challenging weather, and so forth), some users create elaborate scenarios that rely on programmed triggers, employing tools like *Scenario Builder* from Flight1Aviation Technologies or the mission-creation and failure features built into X-Plane and FSX. That approach can create excellent lessons, but simpler, low-tech solutions can also work.

A Dice-Based Failure Scheme

To add random challenges to any simulated flight, you can "roll the dice" (or, usually, one die) to choose which issue arises. (If you're a high-tech pilot or instructor, use a dice-rolling application on your smartphone.)

For example, at any point in a flight, you can roll a die (or spin a homemade "failure wheel") and then use a table like the example shown in Table 8-1 to determine which problem the pilot must solve.

Table 8-1: Rolling a Failure

NUMBER	RESULT
1	Engine failure
2	Vacuum pump failure
3	Electrical system failure
4	Minimum fuel
5	Unacceptable weather at planned destination
6	Navigation radio failure

Whether you're an instructor or flying solo for practice, you can use a similar table, like the example shown in 8-2, to decide when to trigger an event.

Table 8-2: Triggering an Event

NUMBER	RESULT
1	Immediately
2	Within the next 5 minutes
3	Within the next 5–10 minutes
4	Within the next 10–15 minutes
5	Within the next 15–20 minutes
6	Within the last 10 minutes of a flight

The challenges you can create with this simple system are limited only by your imagination. For example, you can mix equipment failures with other realistic events, such as a sick passenger, an amended clearance from air traffic control, or a blocked runway at your intended destination. Even a simple randomizer like dice can ensure that scenarios don't become repetitions of canned events at predictable times.

If you've connected two computers running X-Plane or FSX, you can use the Instructor Operating Station (IOS) to induce failures and change the weather without interrupting the student. The Shared Cockpit feature in FSX supports similar capabilities.

Many of the scenarios in the private pilot and instrument-rating lessons that follow include tables that give you a head start on creating realistic events that test your ability to make effective decisions and take the appropriate actions to resolve challenges.

Using the Charts and Data

Aviation charts are updated regularly, as are the databases in GPS units and flight management systems in aircraft cockpits. Most of the details that change aren't important for the purposes of learning the fundamentals of navigation and gathering information from charts. The general procedures for tracking a VOR radial or flying an ILS apply even if the frequency of the ground station changes or the decision altitude on the approach is adjusted.

However, if underlying data changes, you may find that the details of a particular scenario have fallen out of sync with the latest charts and diagrams. This issue is most common with GPS-based procedures. For that reason, and the limitations of the GPS devices simulated in X-Plane and FSX (see Figures 8-6 and 8-7), most of the scenarios that follow rely on conventional navigation aids.

Figure 8-6: The GPS simulation in X-Plane offers only basic functionality.

Figure 8-7: The GPS in FSX offers more features and a larger display than that in X-Plane.

If you want to emphasize GPS-based navigation in the supplied scenarios or create new scenarios that focus on GPS procedures, consider purchasing an add-on from RealityXP or another developer of similar enhancements.

Simulating Air Traffic Control

The virtual air traffic control built into X-Plane and FSX is essentially a special effect, added to enhance the ambiance of virtual flying. Like a computerized language course, it's a rough approximation of the real conversation between air traffic controllers and pilots, and it can have some value in acclimating pilots to radio communication.

For training purposes at this stage of PC-simulation, it's usually best for the instructor to play the role of ATC to help the student learn the lingo.

When you're flying solo, online services such as VATSIM and PilotEdge are attractive alternatives. They use the web to connect users of X-Plane and FSX to enthusiasts who enjoy playing the role of air traffic controller. These services have devoted followings around the world, and the virtual controllers pride themselves on recreating ATC as accurately as the PC-based simulations emulate flight.

To learn more about these options, see the links at the website for this book.

Complementing Formal Training

Scenario-Based Training highlights key concepts, makes suggestions, and passes along specific tips that both pilots and instructors may find useful in formal flight training. However, it isn't a textbook that covers all the knowledge an aspiring pilot must master. For example, it doesn't attempt to explain aircraft performance, weather, regulations, human factors, and the details of aircraft systems, among other important subjects. You can, however, learn about these topics in the free FAA training handbooks and other resources described in Chapter 2.

As you follow the lessons in this book, you can also use additional sources, such as the interactive training programs available at Cessna Pilot Centers — or complete courses published by Aviation Supplies and Academics (ASA), Jeppesen, and other providers. Many pilots enjoy the comprehensive and entertaining guides written and published by Rod Machado, especially the following:

- *Rod Machado's Private Pilot Handbook*
- *Rod Machado's Instrument Pilot's Handbook*

All the resources just noted cover the same subjects. Some emphasize videos and interactive quizzes. Others approach the topics more like traditional textbooks. In the end, if you're using this book in conjunction with formal flight instruction, the choice of which texts and supplementary training materials to use depends on your learning style, the syllabus approved by your flight school, and your instructor's recommendations. To explore some of the possibilities, visit the links at this book's website at `www/wiley.com/go/flightsimulatortraining`.

CHAPTER

9

Scenario-Based Training and FITS

FAA-Industry Training Standards (FITS), whose logo is shown in Figure 9-1, is a joint initiative between the aviation industry and the Federal Aviation Administration to:

- Make pilot training more relevant as technology rapidly transforms aircraft cockpits.
- Help flight instructors use new tools (especially simulation) and teaching methods to increase the effectiveness and efficiency of flight instruction.

Figure 9-1: FITS logo

The ultimate goal is to reduce the number of aviation accidents and incidents by emphasizing and addressing the perennial cause of most crashes — pilot error.

The FITS approach includes several key components:

- Scenario-based training (SBT)
- Extensive use of simulation
- Aeronautical decision making (ADM)
- Risk management
- Learner-centered grading

Often overlooked amid the jargon, however, is an important and beneficial side effect of scenario-based training — it makes learning to fly (and the hobby of virtual flying) more interesting, challenging, and fun. In other words, SBT creates "adventures for learning" that:

- Give you realistic reasons — missions — to fly.
- Present real-world challenges such as changing weather, equipment malfunctions, pressures from passengers, and other unexpected circumstances that pilots must handle even on routine flights.
- Help you measure your progress against specific goals.

In short, FITS focuses on teaching you to *think* like a pilot.

The FITS Approach

FITS is collaborative effort between the FAA and everyone involved in general aviation — including manufacturers of aircraft and avionics, universities, pilot groups, insurers, and flight schools. It was originally created to address the challenges posed by the introduction of technically advanced aircraft (TAA), which are equipped with sophisticated electronic cockpit displays and autopilots. More recently, the program has expanded its goals to update the process of training and evaluating pilots regardless of the type of aircraft they fly. A key objective all along has been adapting the process of flight instruction without having to overhaul the regulations that govern flight training and pilot certification (specifically, Part 61 of 14 CFR — the Code of Federal Regulations — known to pilots as "the FARs"):

> FITS itself was not intended for training on non-TAA aircraft. However, the concepts at the core of the FITS program (i.e., risk management, aeronautical decision-making, situational awareness, and single pilot resource management) are not unique to FITS or to [TAA], and many flight training professionals strongly believe that these concepts should be integrated more effectively into other areas of flight training.
>
> FAA/Industry Training Standards (FITS) Questions and Answers

Middle Tennessee State University reviewed data on a set of its students trained with a FITS syllabus in 2005. That study, available on the FITS website, notes that by the end of a combination private pilot/instrument rating program, students who used the FITS syllabus had fewer setbacks than those who followed a traditional training program.

In particular, the study noted, the FITS-trained pilots were:

- More comfortable with their IFR flying skills
- More comfortable using the automation in TAA
- More conservative when operating under IFR

The FITS concept isn't intended just for students in the early phases of their flight training, however. It's becoming a key component of the flight reviews that most pilots must complete every two years, instrument proficiency checks and aircraft checkouts, and the practical tests pilots must pass to earn new certificates and ratings.

Scenario-Based Training

Scenarios form the core of a FITS syllabus. In fact, in the aviation community FITS is almost synonymous with SBT. The FITS consortium defines *scenario-based training* as

> … [A] training system that uses a highly structured script of real-world experiences to address flight-evaluation in an operational environment. Consistent with the concept of training the way you fly and flying the way you train, FITS places more emphasis on whole task training and uses carefully planned scenarios … to address … flight-training objectives in a real world operational environment … Ideally, all flight training should include some degree of scenario-based training, which helps develop decision-making, risk management, and single pilot resource management skills (SRM).
>
> FAA/Industry Training Standards (FITS) Questions and Answers

That description will sound familiar to airline pilots, who for many years have practiced their skills in simulators using a method called *line-oriented flight training (LOFT).* Now applied during all phases of training for airline crews, LOFT "began in the mid-1970s as a means to provide pilot training that is more representative of actual flight operations than is maneuver-based training alone" (FAA Advisory Circular AC 120-35C).

The objectives described earlier are also fundamental goals of this book; and, as you'll see, PC-based simulations can help even the smallest flight schools and independent flight instructors incorporate the concepts and techniques that underlie FITS and SBT into their training programs.

JOHN KING ON SCENARIO-BASED TRAINING

John King, co-owner of King Schools in San Diego, California, and one of the most respected leaders in flight training today, is a passionate advocate of scenario-based training. The following excerpt from a letter to the editor published in the May 2011 issue of *Flight Training* magazine explains his support for SBT:

> **As an industry it is essential that we move from focusing on teaching fundamental skills to delivering a pilot who is truly ready to be a pilot-in-command — one who has developed the habit of identifying and managing the risks of flight. The FAA's first suggested way of implementing scenario-based training may have been a bit contrived and impractical; however, scenario-based training, when designed thoughtfully and executed well, excels at providing this higher level of pilot learning.**
>
> **King Schools developed the Cessna Sport/Private Pilot course used by Cessna Pilot Centers to put every lesson into a practical, realistic setting that includes a purpose and a set of risks to be managed. From the very first lesson, and for every lesson thereafter, the customer and the instructor identify the risks of each flight and discuss a strategy for managing them. This puts the learning into context, provides a better understanding of why they are learning things, requires application in a realistic situation, and develops correlation of knowledge and skill. It is a more fun way to learn. And it is efficient, too — Cessna Pilot Centers are graduating customers in the minimum required times.**
>
> **Scenario-based training may be a surprising case where the FAA actually got us all started in the right direction, and it is clear that the FAA intends for us all to head in that direction. The FAA's guidance to designated examiners strongly recommends they use scenarios to evaluate the applicant's single-pilot risk management skills. The applicant who has been trained using scenarios is likely to do much better on the flight test.**
>
> **LETTER TO THE EDITOR, FLIGHT TRAINING MAGAZINE, MAY 2011**

PC-Based Simulations and SBT

The FITS/SBT approach to flight training depends on simulation because, as explained in Chapter 3 and Chapter 8, virtual flying is usually the best way to learn about and practice new concepts and skills before developing and honing them in a real airplane cockpit.

The simulation component of FITS relies on flight training devices (FTDs) and aviation training devices (ATD), and when used under the supervision of an instructor, time spent "flying" those approved devices can be credited toward some of the requirements for pilot certificates and ratings and for maintaining instrument-flying currency. Figure 9-2 shows an example of such an approved device.

Figure 9-2: A typical ATD, manufactured by Precision Flight Controls

However, as the scenarios that follow demonstrate, X-Plane or FSX, running on a standard PC equipped with only basic accessories like a joystick, often can be as useful as ATDs in achieving the fundamental goals of scenario-based training. You just can't count the time you spend "flying" X-Plane or FSX on a PC toward the requirements for a pilot certificate or rating.

In other words, flight schools and individual instructors who may not be able to afford or have space for a dedicated ATD can still meet the core goals of FITS by making creative use of PC-based simulations.

Aeronautical Decision Making and Risk Management

Some flight instructors and pilots are wary of FITS-based training programs because they worry that the new approach doesn't devote enough time or emphasis to "stick-and-rudder flying" — the basic skills required to control and maneuver an airplane in all phases of flight. That perception arises from the importance FITS places on contemporary topics, especially aeronautical decision making (ADM) and risk management.

However, integrating ADM and risk management into all phases of flight training doesn't have to detract from learning and polishing the fundamental flying skills described in such classic texts as *Stick and Rudder: An Explanation of the Art of Flying* by Wolfgang Langeweische (McGraw-Hill, 1990). Adopting the new approach shouldn't be an "either FITS or mastering airplane control" proposition.

Of course, among a host of other skills, pilots still must know how to avoid inadvertent stalls and spins, land in a crosswind, and fly an instrument approach to minimums in fog. The current emphasis on ADM and risk management stems from the unpleasant reality that most accidents and incidents ultimately are the result of a pilot's mistakes or lapses in judgment — not mechanical failure, unexpected weather, or other factors beyond a pilot's control. According to the 2010 edition of the Nall Report, a summary and analysis of general-aviation accidents published annually by the AOPA Air Safety Institute:

> Pilot-related categories [that is, accidents attributed primarily to pilot error] made up 70% of non-commercial fixed-wing accidents in 2009 and 63% of fatal accidents. While the judgment leading to any pilot-related accident could be called into question, fuel-management and weather accidents can be seen primarily as failures of flight planning and in-flight decision-making. Accidents occurring during takeoff and climb, maneuvering, descent and approach, and landing tend to result more directly from deficient airmanship, though it may have been faulty decision-making that placed the pilots in situations beyond their skills.
>
> AOPA ASI Joseph T. Nall Report 2010

Even when an airplane crashes in bad weather, the weather itself is rarely the primary cause. One of the most common types of accident today is known as *controlled flight into terrain (CFIT)*. A CFIT accident typically occurs when a pilot attempts to continue flight as low clouds, rain, fog, or other phenomena reduce or eliminate forward visibility. Rarely is anything wrong with the airplane. But the pilots press on. They may not have an instrument rating or be current — that is, meet the legal requirements to operate under instrument flight rules. The airplane may not be equipped for IFR flight. Perhaps, fearing they'll get in trouble with the FAA, they don't want to ask for help from air traffic control. And they smack into a hillside or hit an antenna, tower, or other obstruction.

Most often, the probable cause of such accidents as determined by the NTSB reads simply "continued flight into [instrument meteorological conditions] under VFR."

> Examination of the components, not destroyed by the post-crash fire, did not reveal any anomalies that would have contributed to the accident... The National Transportation Safety Board determines the probable cause(s) of this [accident] as follows: The pilot's continued flight into IMC conditions. Factors were the low ceiling and dark night conditions.
>
> NTSB report on accident FTW93FA168

Teaching Judgment

The fundamental assumption underlying the ADM and risk management components of FITS is that the elusive ability "judgment" can be taught and practiced. As you'll discover in the lessons that follow, the FITS approach to these topics involves such concepts as:

- Single pilot resource management
- The 3P Model (perceive, process, perform)
- The 5P Check (plan, plane, pilot, passengers, programming)
- Setting personal minimums

Although the preceding frameworks may seem like gimmicks at first, they're actually systematic attempts to guide a continuous internal dialog that poses and answers the question "What should you do?" before and throughout a flight. Practiced in the context of well-crafted scenarios that mimic the challenges pilots face even during routine flights, these checklists and procedures can help aviators develop the mental habits that are as indispensible to a pilot as a fine touch on the controls.

Learner-Centered Grading

The last premise underlying FITS is *learner-centered grading*. In traditional training, the student often passively absorbs information from the instructor, and the instructor provides constructive criticism and advice. As the name implies, self-evaluation is the key to learner-centered grading. The instructor guides the student (in FITS parlance, the PT — "pilot in training") through discussions before and after each lesson. During a flight, the PT is often expected to identify and correct mistakes. This approach is intended to engage the PT and develop the habits of ADM and risk management from the first lesson.

The "grades" in learner-centered grading are related to the levels of learning described in the *Aviation Instructor's Handbook*:

- **Rote:** The ability to repeat something learned
- **Understanding:** Comprehending or grasping the meaning of something
- **Application:** Putting something to use
- **Correlation:** Associating what has been learned with previous or subsequent learning

In a FITS syllabus, these concepts translate into specific "desired outcomes" that you can think of as the "passing grades" for each lesson. If you're a flight simulation enthusiast, think of the grading system as one way to score each of the adventures (scenarios) that follow.

FITS Grading Standards

The specific definitions for the desired outcomes vary with the phase of instruction. In general, however, they follow the pattern described here:

- **Describe:** After completing the scenario, the PT will be able to describe the physical characteristics and cognitive elements of the scenario activities. Instructor assistance is required to successfully execute the maneuver.
- **Explain:** After completing the scenario, the PT will be able to describe the scenario activity and understand the underlying concepts, principles, and procedures that comprise the activity. Significant instructor effort will be required to successfully execute the maneuver.
- **Practice:** After completing the scenario, the pilot in training will be able to plan and execute the scenario. Coaching, instruction, and/or assistance from the CFI will correct deviations and errors identified by the CFI.
- **Perform:** After completing the scenario, the PT will be able to perform the activity without assistance from the CFI. Errors and deviations will be identified and corrected by the PT in an expeditious manner. At no time will successful completion of the activity be in doubt. ("Perform" will be used to signify that the PT is satisfactorily demonstrating proficiency in traditional piloting and systems operation skills.)
- **Not Observed:** Any event not accomplished or required.

Each lesson involves a combination of tasks, so the desired outcomes vary according to whether a specific skill is new or being reviewed or polished.

The letter- or number-based scores traditionally assigned at the end of a flying lesson focus on how well a student answers specific questions ("What's the stall speed for this airplane?") or performs a given task (for example, maintaining altitude within ±100 feet while flying a 360-degree steep turn). The grades in a FITS program focus on the PT's deeper understanding of the concepts behind facts and on the student's ability to identify and correct mistakes while flying the airplane.

As you'll see in the lessons that follow, each scenario includes a learner-centered grading grid that lists core and sub-activities and the desired outcome for each goal. Table 9-1 shows an example grid.

Table 9-1: Sample Learner-Centered Grading Table

SCENARIO ACTIVITIES	SCENARIO SUB-ACTIVITIES	DESIRED OUTCOME
Flight Planning	1. Scenario planning 2. Weight & balance calculations 3. Preflight SRM briefing 4. Decision-making and risk management	1. Perform 2. Perform 3. Perform 4. Explain/Practice
Normal preflight and cockpit procedures	1. Normal pre-takeoff checklist procedures 2. GPS programming 3. MFD setup 4. PFD setup	1. Perform 2. Explain/Practice 3. Practice 4. Explain/Practice
Engine start and taxi	1. Engine start 2. Taxi 3. SRM/SA	1. Perform 2. Explain/Perform 3. Perform 4. Manage/Decide
Before takeoff checks	1. Normal and abnormal indications 2. Aircraft automation management 3. ADM and risk management	1. Perform 2. Explain/Practice 3. Manage/Decide

From: FITS Generic Private Pilot Syllabus

Further Reading

FAA/Industry Training Standards (FITS): Questions and Answers

FITS Generic Private Airplane Single Engine Land Syllabus

Aviation Instructor's Handbook (FAA-H-8083-9A)

Risk Management Handbook (FAA-H-8083-2)

CHAPTER 10

Using the Scenarios in This Book

The scenarios in this book provide a logical path, based on the generic syllabi published on the FAA/Industry Training Standards (FITS) website, through the background knowledge and experience pilots must acquire to earn a private pilot certificate and the instrument rating in single-engine airplanes. The lessons are also designed to promote easy, efficient, and effective use of PC-based simulation as a complement to flight training (and to provide entertaining challenges for virtual aviators).

According to the *Aviation Instructor's Handbook* (pp. 2–26), a good scenario:

- Has a clear set of objectives
- Is tailored to the needs of the student
- Capitalizes on the nuances of the local environment

The scenarios in this book also strive to meet the specific goals of scenario-based training (SBT) described in Chapter 9, in the background information about FITS, and in the introductions to the specific private pilot and instrument rating syllabi.

Starting Points: Situations and Flights

To meet goals noted above, each lesson in the chapters that follow is supported by a *Situation* (X-Plane) or *Flight* (FSX) that serves as a starting point for the scenario.

It's important to understand that the scenarios aren't interactive lessons. Instead, they establish the initial conditions (see Figures 10-1 and 10-2) for a virtual flight, including the following:

- Type of aircraft
- Location
- Time of day
- Weather (wind, visibility, cloud cover, and so forth)
- Initial state of the aircraft (altitude, speed, heading, radio frequencies, lights, and so forth)

Figure 10-1: Load Situation command in X-Plane

Figure 10-2: Load Flight command in FSX

In other words, the Situations (.sit files for X-Plane) and Flights (.flt and associated .wx files in FSX) are templates that save time setting up a scenario; allow easy repetition of lessons; and promote consistency, especially for instructors who use PC-based simulation with several students.

The scenarios may begin in the air or on the ground, depending on the purpose of a particular lesson. Lessons that start in the air usually begin with the autopilot turned on to help ensure a stable start.

Flying in the Pacific Northwest

Most of the scenarios in this book are based in the Pacific Northwest, a region that offers a wide range of topography and weather, plus opportunities to explore a variety of situations that include busy urban airports and rural airstrips, complex airspace, wide-open spaces, and challenging instrument approaches, all without having to fly long distances during a particular lesson (see Figure 10-3). Basing the lessons in one area also makes it easier to use charts, airport directories, and other supplemental information.

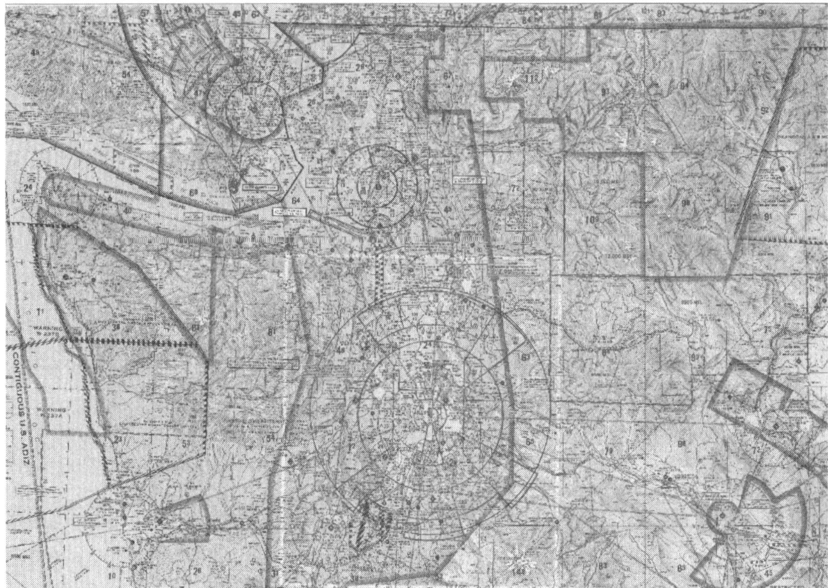

Figure 10-3: Part of Washington state, as shown on an aviation sectional chart

Of course, you can adapt the scenarios or add lessons to emphasize the areas where you fly. Keep in mind, however, that one of the advantages of using PC-based simulation is testing your knowledge and skill while flying in unfamiliar territory. If you can aviate and navigate confidently far from home, local flying is a snap.

Preparing for a Lesson

All good training requires preparation. To get the most from the scenarios in this book, you should complete a preflight checklist that includes:

- Reviewing the provided references to ensure that you understand the basic concepts
- Reviewing the objectives, especially the Student-Centered Grading sheet, that specify the knowledge and skills you should acquire during the lesson
- Exploring the appropriate charts, Airport/Facility Directory (A/FD) entries, and other information pertinent to the flight (see Figure 10-4)
- Checking aircraft performance data, especially for flights that include trips to other airports, to validate your flight planning

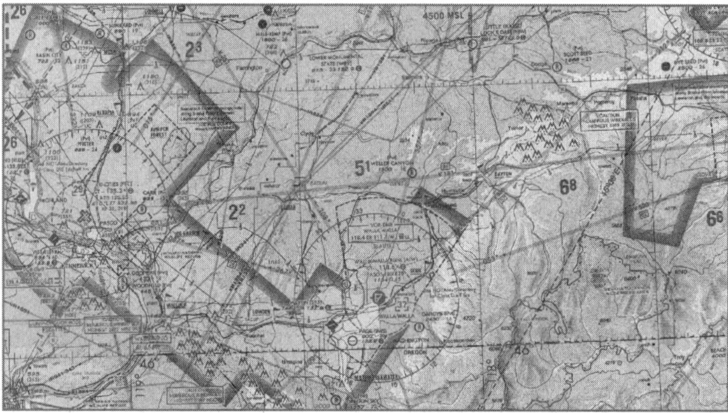

Wind Direction Indicators

Traffic Patterns

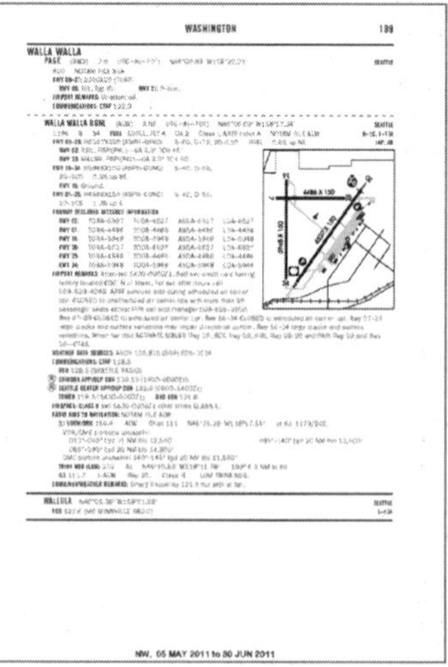

WASHINGTON 189

WALLA WALLA

NW, 05 MAY 2011 to 30 JUN 2011

Figure 10-4: Samples of pages from the A/FD, the *Pilot's Handbook of Aeronautical Knowledge*, and the Seattle sectional chart

Installing the Scenarios

The scenarios are consolidated in folders (.zip files) that you can download from the book's website. Two .zip files are available for each simulation, one for the private pilot lessons, the other for the instrument-rating scenarios:

- `Wiley-SBT-PrivatePilot-X-Plane.zip`
- `Wiley-SBT-IFR-X-Plane.zip`
- `Wiley-SBT-PrivatePilot-FSX.zip`
- `Wiley-SBT-IFR-FSX.zip`

Download the appropriate sets of .zip files from `www.wiley.com/go/flightsimulatortraining` to your computer and then use the instructions in the following sections to extract and copy the files to the appropriate directory for X-Plane or FSX.

NOTE **If you need help using folders and files in Windows, visit the topics "Working with Files and Folders" and "Compress and Uncompress Files (zip files)" in the Windows help system or online at `windows.microsoft.com`. You can find the appropriate instructions for the Mac OS in the sections about the Finder in the Mac help system and online at `support.apple.com`.**

Installing the Situations for X-Plane

To install the Situations for X-Plane:

1. Navigate to the folder that contains the .zip files for X-Plane that you downloaded from this book's website.
2. If you're using Windows, right-click the folder, click Extract All, and then follow the prompts to copy the files to the Situations folder on your hard drive.

   In Windows, the default path of the Situations folder for X-Plane 9 is `C:\Documents and Settings\`*`[User Name]`*`\Desktop\X-Plane 9\Output\Situations`.

If you're running X-Plane on a Mac, locate the X-Plane Situations folder in the Finder and extract all the files into that folder.

NOTE **For more information about Situations in X-Plane, see the *X-Plane Operation Manual* or the wiki at the X-Plane website.**

Installing the Flights for FSX

To install the Flights for FSX:

1. Navigate to the folder that contains the .zip files for FSX that you downloaded from this book's website. Note that each Flight includes three files: a .flt file that stores the initial state of the aircraft, a complementary .wx file that stores information about the weather, and an .fssave file.
2. Right-click the folder, click Extract All, and then follow the prompts to copy the files to the Flight Simulator X Files folder on your hard drive.

The default path of the Flight Simulator X Files folder is `C:\Users\[User Name]\Documents\Flight Simulator X Files`.

NOTE For more information about using Flights in FSX, see the topic "All About Flights" in the FSX Learning Center.

Naming Conventions

The filenames for the lessons are designed to make them easy to find in the lists that appear when you choose the Load Situation command (X-Plane) or Load Flight command (FSX), as shown in Figures 10-5 and 10-6, respectively.

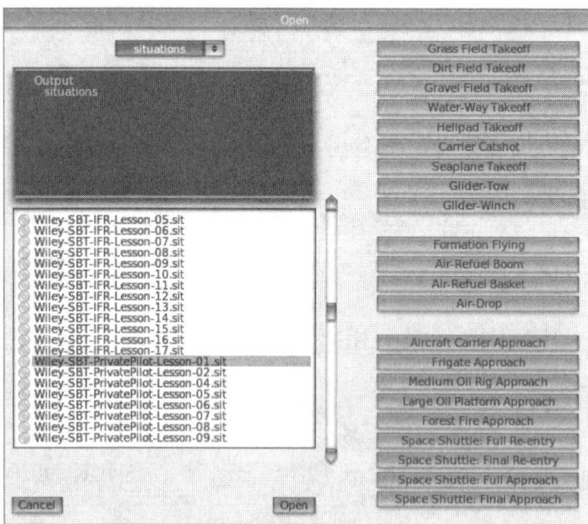

Figure 10-5: Load Situation dialog box in X-Plane showing Situations for the lessons

Figure 10-6: Load Flight dialog box in FSX showing Flights for the lessons

The files for the private pilot lessons follow this pattern:

- Wiley-SBT-PrivatePilot-Lesson-*xx*, where *xx* is the corresponding lesson number from this book

The files for the instrument rating lessons follow this pattern:

- Wiley-SBT-IFR-Lesson-*xx*, where *xx* is the corresponding lesson number from this book

CROSS-REFERENCE **For the more information about how to start the scenarios, see Chapter 6 or Chapter 7.**

Part

III

Flying Fundamentals

In This Part

CHAPTER

11

Flying Fundamentals

Because PC-based simulations can't reproduce the "feel" of flying, you have to work harder to fly a simulation as smoothly and precisely as a real airplane. (Many pilots assert that even full-flight simulators with sophisticated motion systems are also more difficult to fly than the real airplanes that the devices emulate; see Figure 11-1). In particular, you must rely on the instruments more than you should in a real airplane when flying in visual conditions.

Figure 11-1: Pilots training in a Gulfstream simulator (courtesy of CAE)

The lack of "feel" in a PC-based simulation may help when practicing instrument flight, because you don't sense conflicts between perceived motion and what instruments tell you. Spatial disorientation isn't an issue in a simulator attached firmly to the ground. However, even pilots flying on instruments, who must learn to disregard sensory cues and depend on the gauges for aircraft control, find that the environment still provides subtle hints — such as the sound of the engine and slipstream — that, with experience, help them maintain control of the airplane.

Fortunately, some of the same basic skills and techniques that pilots use to fly real airplanes smoothly and precisely also help you compensate for the lack of sensory inputs and master the art of virtual flying.

Integrated Flight Instruction

The instrument panel may be more important in PC-based simulation than it is in an airplane, but you shouldn't let it dominate your approach to flying. The FAA has long promoted the concept of "integrated" or "composite" flight instruction (see Figure 11-2) to help new pilots learn to correlate the view out the window with the information provided by the instruments; and that approach can help you divide your attention appropriately, especially as you develop a feel for a simulation.

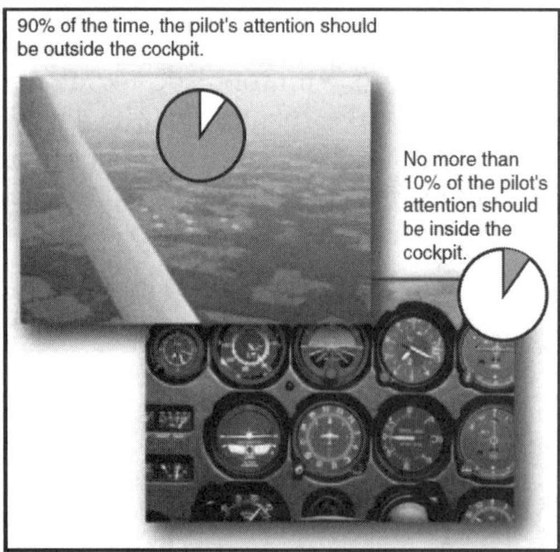

Figure 11-2: The concept of integrated flight instruction (Figure 3-2 of the *Airplane Flying Handbook*)

As noted in Chapter 3, the principles of integrated flight instruction are often overlooked or improperly emphasized in real flight training. Many instructors and pilots focus on the instruments, not the view outside; but the basic idea is an especially useful concept when learning to fly a simulation, and both X-Plane and FSX provide specific features to help you avoid the pitfalls of fixating on the instrument panel.

To review, the *Airplane Flying Handbook* (p. 3-3) defines integrated flight instruction as "... the use of outside references and flight instruments to establish and maintain desired flight attitudes and airplane performance." The order of the statements in that definition is important. Note what the *Airplane Flying Handbook* says in the expanded discussion of the technique:

> The airplane's attitude is established and maintained by positioning the airplane in relation to the natural horizon. At least 90 percent of the pilot's attention should be devoted to this end, along with scanning for other airplanes... The airplane's attitude is confirmed by referring to flight instruments, and its performance checked. If airplane performance, as indicated by flight instruments, indicates a need for correction, a specific amount of correction must be determined, then applied with reference to the natural horizon. The airplane's attitude and performance are then rechecked by referring to flight instruments. The pilot then maintains the corrected attitude by reference to the natural horizon.
>
> AIRPLANE FLYING HANDBOOK (P. 3-3)

In other words:

- Look outside to determine the aircraft's attitude by reference to the real horizon.
- Briefly check the instruments to confirm the airplane's attitude.
- Use the natural horizon outside as a reference while applying specific corrections to achieve the appropriate attitude.
- Check the instruments again to confirm that the airplane is doing what you want it to.

The *Airplane Flying Handbook* offers additional specific advice about how to divide your attention:

> The pilot should monitor the airplane's performance by making numerous quick glances at the flight instruments. No more than 10 percent of the pilot's attention should be inside the cockpit. The pilot must develop the skill to instantly focus on the appropriate flight instrument, and then immediately return to outside reference to control the airplane's attitude.
>
> AIRPLANE FLYING HANDBOOK (P. 3-4)

This sequence of using the natural horizon and gauges follows the same principle of *control and performance instruments* that is one key to accurate, smooth instrument flying. (You'll learn more about control and performance instruments in the instrument rating lessons.) When flying in visual conditions, the natural horizon is the primary "control instrument," used to determine the aircraft's attitude and initiate corrections; the gauges on the panel just confirm that the airplane is performing as expected.

NOTE For an introduction to the control and performance instruments, see p. 2-12 in the *Pilot's Handbook of Aeronautical Knowledge.* You can find a more detailed discussion of the topic in Chapter 4, "Airplane Attitude Instrument Flying," of the *Instrument Flying Handbook.*

Getting a Better View

Given the limited view of the outside world in a typical configuration of a PC-based simulation, how, then, can you emphasize the outside view and rely less on the instruments? Fortunately, both X-Plane and FSX include options that expand the outside view while still providing essential information that helps compensate for the lack of motion cues in a simulation.

These features are helpful both when you're learning the basics of controlling the simulated airplanes and during critical phases of flight, such as takeoff and landing.

X-Plane: Panel Views

In X-Plane, you can de-emphasize the instrument panel and expand the outside view with three main options.

The Toggle Transparent Cockpit command on the View menu (see Figure 11-3) dims the instrument panel (see Figure 11-4). You can also press the semicolon character (;) to turn the transparent cockpit view on and off.

Figure 11-3: Toggle Transparent Cockpit command on the View menu in X-Plane

Figure 11-4: Transparent Cockpit in X-Plane

To slide the instrument panel down and devote more space to the outside view (see Figures 11-5 and 11-6), press the down arrow key. To move the panel back up to see more cockpit controls, press the up arrow key. You can press these keys repeatedly to adjust the amount of the panel you see.

Figure 11-5: Full-panel view in X-Plane

Figure 11-6: Instrument panel lowered in X-Plane

NOTE **You can also assign the panel-adjustment keys to buttons on your flight yoke or joystick. For more information, see "Joystick Configuration and Calibration" in the X-Plane Operation Manual.**

Another option in X-Plane is Full-Screen with HUD view (see Figure 11-7), which removes the instrument panel and presents basic information about the aircraft's attitude, speed, altitude, and heading on a transparent display, like those used in modern fighter aircraft.

NOTE **To learn more about cockpit views available in X-Plane, see the discussion of the View menu in the *X-Plane Operation Manual*.**

Figure 11-7: HUD view in X-Plane

FSX: Panel Views

The Views menu in FSX, includes several options for changing and adjusting the appearance of the cockpit (see Figure 11-8).

Figure 11-8: The Views menu in FSX

You can use the Landing View option to quickly lower the instrument panel and expand the outside view, as shown in Figure 11-9.

Figure 11-9: Landing view in FSX

To switch quickly between the normal 2D cockpit and the Landing View panel, click the appropriate icon on the instrument panel (see Figure 11-10).

Figure 11-10: To switch panel views, click the control panel icon.

NOTE **To learn more about cockpit and panel views in FSX, see the topic "Using Views and Windows" in the FSX Learning Center.**

The Mini-panel view replaces the standard instrument panel in FSX with a row of basic instruments you can use to monitor the aircraft's performance (see Figure 11-11).

In FSX, press the W key to cycle through normal panel view, Mini-panel view, and full-screen view, which hides the entire instrument panel.

NOTE **To reduce the need for the keyboard, you can assign view commands to buttons on your flight yoke or joystick. For more information, see "Customizing Joystick Assignments" in the FSX Learning Center.**

You can adjust the transparency of the instrument panel in FSX by pressing Ctrl+Shift+T and then the + (plus) or – (minus) key to make the panel more or less opaque (see Figure 11-12).

Figure 11-11: Mini-panel view in FSX

Figure 11-12: Transparent instrument panel in FSX

The Cessna 172 in FSX also has a special IFR instrument panel (see Figure 11-13) that uses most of the screen to provide an enhanced view of the full instrument panel. This view (which you can choose from the Views menu) is most useful in the lessons for the instrument rating.

Figure 11-13: The IFR panel in FSX

The Golden Rule of Flying

The most important concept to help you fly accurately and smoothly is best described by a simple equation:

Pitch+Power+(Configuration)=Performance

In other words, if you establish and maintain a precise pitch attitude (the angle of the nose relative to the horizon) and set the power at a specific value with the throttle, the airplane will fly at a predictable airspeed, and it will maintain altitude or climb or descend at a particular rate (see Figures 11-14 and 11-15).

"Configuration," in the Cessna 172 Skyhawk, refers to the position of the flaps. In more complex airplanes, you can also extend or retract the landing gear or make other changes that affect the aircraft's configuration and performance.

Translated into a procedure, the golden-rule equation means that you should use the following sequence whenever you need to change the airplane's state — for example, to transition from straight-and-level flight to a climb or descent:

1. Establish the appropriate pitch attitude.
2. Set power by adjusting the throttle.
3. Confirm the aircraft's configuration.
4. Allow the airplane to stabilize at the expected airspeed and/or rate of climb or descent.
5. Adjust the elevator trim control to relieve the pressure on the yoke or joystick.

Figure 11-14: In X-Plane, a stable descent at 500 fpm at about 90 KIAS with 10° of flaps

Figure 11-15: In FSX, a stable configuration for level flight with 10° of flaps

Knowing "the numbers" for your airplane — pitch attitude, power setting, and configuration — for the basic phases of flight helps you quickly establish stable flight without having to fiddle repeatedly with the flight, power, and trim controls.

CROSS-REFERENCE **To review "the numbers" for the basic phases of flight in the Skyhawk, see Chapter 12.**

In effect, applying the golden rule is like dialing a set of values for airspeed and altitude (or rate of climb or descent) into a sophisticated autopilot that can control both aircraft attitude and power (via auto-throttles) to maintain the commanded performance.

The Four Fundamentals

The scenarios later in this book offer many opportunities to learn about the four fundamentals of flight (straight-and-level, turns, climbs, and descents). The *Airplane Flying Handbook* and *Instrument Flying Handbook* devote entire chapters to thorough discussions of the recommended techniques and procedures for performing these basic maneuvers. However, reviewing a few key points here, even if you're a pilot or an experienced virtual aviator, can help you avoid common frustrations associated with flying PC-based simulations.

Often the quickest way to grasp the essentials of a task is to review the typical errors that people make when trying to accomplish it. The following sections point out these mistakes to help you identify areas that you may want to review and focus on as you develop your simulation-flying skills.

NOTE **For detailed discussions of basic flying techniques, see Chapter 3, "Basic Flight Maneuvers," in the *Airplane Flying Handbook* and Chapter 5, "Airplane Basic Flight Maneuvers," in the *Instrument Flying Handbook*.**

Straight-and-Level Flight

As the name of this maneuver implies, an airplane in straight-and-level flight is flying in a specific direction (heading) while maintaining a particular altitude (see Figure 11-16).

The *Airplane Flying Handbook* (p. 3-6) notes the difficulties that pilots typically encounter as they try to achieve the goal of straight-and-level flight, including:

- Attempting to use improper reference points on the airplane to establish attitude
- Attempting to establish or correct airplane attitude using flight instruments rather than outside visual reference
- Habitually flying with one wing low
- "Chasing" the flight instruments rather than adhering to the principles of attitude flying
- Too tight a grip on the flight controls, resulting in overcontrol and lack of feel

Figure 11-16: Straight-and-level flight in the Cessna 172 in X-Plane

- Pushing or pulling on the flight controls rather than exerting pressure against the airstream
- Improper scanning and/or devoting insufficient time to outside visual reference. (Head in the cockpit.)
- Fixation on the nose (pitch attitude) reference point
- Unnecessary or inappropriate control inputs
- Failure to make timely and measured control inputs when deviations from straight-and-level flight are detected

To reduce the effects of these tendencies while flying X-Plane or FSX:

- Don't restrict yourself to the forward, over-the-nose view. Use keyboard shortcuts or switches on the yoke or joystick to look around as you fly. For example, looking left and right to check the alignment of the wings helps you avoid subtle banks that make you wander off heading (see Figure 11-17).
- Relax! Don't strangle the yoke or joystick. Use smooth, small, and precise control pressures to maintain the airplane's attitude.
- When flying visually, devote most of your attention to the big natural horizon outside the cockpit. Use the views and features described earlier in this chapter to help you de-emphasize the instrument panel, and check the gauges to confirm performance, not to control the airplane.
- Be patient. Don't react instantly to changes in the aircraft's attitude or twitching needles on the gauges. Allow the aircraft to ride the ripples in the air and "make timely and measured control inputs" to reestablish straight-and-level flight.

Figure 11-17: Looking at the left wing in FSX

Level Turns

According to the *Airplane Flying Handbook* (p. 3-12), common errors in the performance of level turns (see Figure 11-18) include many of the same problems described for straight-and-level flight, plus the following:

- Failure to adequately clear the area before beginning the turn
- Attempting to execute the turn solely by instrument reference
- Attempting to sit up straight, in relation to the ground, during a turn, rather than riding with the airplane

Figure 11-18: A level turn in the Cessna 172 in X-Plane

To avoid these tendencies while flying X-Plane or FSX:

- Get in the habit of scanning for other aircraft, even in the virtual skies. Use the keyboard shortcuts or switches on the yoke or joystick to look around, especially before you begin a turn.
- As noted earlier, use the views and features in the simulation to deemphasize the instrument panel; and check the gauges to confirm performance, not to control the airplane.
- Don't tilt your head "against the turn." Even while sitting at the controls of a simulation that's anchored to the ground, virtual aviators often lean.

Climbs and Climbing Turns

Many of the considerations just discussed also apply to climbs and descents. According to the *Airplane Flying Handbook* (p. 3-15), common errors in the performance of climbs and climbing turns (see Figure 11-19) include the following:

- Attempting to establish climb pitch attitude by referencing the airspeed indicator, resulting in "chasing" the airspeed
- Applying elevator pressure too aggressively, resulting in an excessive climb angle
- Applying elevator pressure too aggressively during level-off
- Fixation on the nose during straight climbs, resulting in climbing with one wing low
- Inability to keep pitch and bank attitude constant during climbing turns
- Attempting to exceed the airplane's climb capability

Figure 11-19: A climbing right turn in FSX

You can reduce these errors by applying the previously discussed principles; in particular:

- Look around as you establish and maintain a climb or climbing turn. Don't stare over the nose.
- Follow the pitch-power-trim sequence when you transition to a climb and use small, smooth, and precise inputs to establish the appropriate climb attitude.
- Don't rush through the maneuver. Give the airplane time to stabilize and then use the controls to adjust the aircraft's attitude to achieve the desired performance.
- Remember that a light, single-engine airplane like the Cessna 172 can't climb like a jet fighter.

Descents, Glides, and Descending Turns

You can make descents at different rates and airspeeds by using different power settings. In an airplane such as the Cessna 172, from level cruising flight, you can establish a normal descent at approximately 500 feet per minute by reducing power by 300–500 rpm and lowering the nose slightly (see Figure 11-20). A "normal glide" in an airplane with an engine means a descent with the power reduced to idle and with a pitch attitude that establishes and maintains the airplane's best glide speed.

Figure 11-20: A descent at 105 KIAS and 500 fpm in X-Plane

According to the *Airplane Flying Handbook* (p. 3-19), common errors in the performance of descents, glides, and descending turns include the following:

- Failure to adequately clear the area
- Failure to slow the airplane to approximate glide speed prior to lowering pitch attitude
- Attempting to establish/maintain a normal glide solely by reference to flight instruments
- Inability to stabilize the glide (chasing the airspeed indicator)
- Failure to lower pitch attitude during gliding turn entry, resulting in a decrease in airspeed
- Inadequate pitch control during recovery from straight glides
- Failure to maintain constant bank angle during gliding turns

While flying X-Plane or FSX, the following tips will help you reduce these problems:

- Look around as you establish and maintain a descent, glide, or descending turn. Don't stare over the nose.
- Follow the pitch-power-trim sequence when you transition to a descent or glide and use small, smooth, and precise inputs to establish the appropriate attitude and power setting.
- Fly methodically. Give the airplane time to stabilize and then use the controls to adjust the aircraft's attitude to achieve the desired result.

Using the Trim Control

The most abused control on the airplane is the elevator trim (see Figures 11-21 and 11-22). It's an essential tool in a real airplane, and understanding and using the trim properly can reduce many of the frustrations new virtual aviators encounter when they start flying PC-based simulations.

NOTE **You can find thorough discussions of trim systems in the *Pilot's Handbook of Aeronautical Knowledge* (p. 5-10) and the *Airplane Flying Handbook* (p. 3-6). For information about trim technique in instrument flying, see the *Instrument Flying Handbook* (p. 5-12).**

Figure 11-21: The trim control in the Cessna 172 cockpit in X-Plane

Figure 11-22: The trim control in the Cessna 172 cockpit in FSX

The *Airplane Flying Handbook* describes the importance of trim this way:

> Proper trim technique is a very important and often overlooked basic flying skill. An improperly trimmed airplane requires constant control pressures, produces pilot tension and fatigue, distracts the pilot from scanning, and contributes to abrupt and erratic airplane attitude control.
>
> AIRPLANE FLYING HANDBOOK (P. 3-6)

Unfortunately, many pilots use the trim as if it were a primary flight control:

> Attempting to "fly the airplane with the trim tabs" is a common fault in basic flying technique even among experienced pilots.
>
> AIRPLANE FLYING HANDBOOK (P. 3-7)

Virtual aviators often make the same mistake. Remember that adjusting the trim is the *last* step in the control sequence:

> The airplane attitude must be established and held first, then control pressures trimmed out so that the airplane will maintain the desired attitude in "hands off" flight.
>
> AIRPLANE FLYING HANDBOOK (P. 3-7)

You can adjust the elevator trim in the Cessna 172 Skyhawk in X-Plane or FSX by pointing to the control with the mouse and then clicking the left button or rolling the mouse wheel. It's usually more convenient, however, to use buttons or toggles on your flight yoke or joystick for this function. Experiment with the switches on the controller you use to determine default assignments for applying nose-down and nose-up trim. If you prefer to use other switches, reassign the trim functions using the Joystick & Equipment command on the Settings menu in X-Plane; in FSX, see "Customizing Joystick Assignments" in the Learning Center.

Using the Rudder

If trim is the most abused aircraft control, rudder is the most neglected. The rudder is also a special problem for pilots flying PC-based simulations.

NOTE You can find thorough discussions of the rudder in the *Pilot's Handbook of Aeronautical Knowledge* (p. 5-7) and Chapter 3, "Basic Flight Maneuvers," in the *Airplane Flying Handbook*.

The rudder pedals available for home cockpits (and even many aviation training devices) often don't provide realistic precision or "feel." They're useful reminders of the role the rudder plays in flying, and adding pedals to a PC-simulation setup can help you develop the habit of including your feet in the dance of the controls. If you fly with a joystick, you can also twist the stick to apply left and right rudder inputs.

The limitations of most consumer-grade rudder pedals, however, mean you must make a special effort to understand and use the rudder properly when you fly a real airplane. Keep in mind the advice about stick-and-rudder skills in Chapter 3.

If you prefer not to complicate virtual flying with rudder pedals or the twisting action on a joystick (and the lack of rudder pedals isn't a major limitation except when landing or taking off with a crosswind and practicing maneuvers such as slips), X-Plane and FSX provide automatic rudder features. If X-Plane doesn't see a rudder axis on the controller connected to your computer, it attempts to compensate for yaw automatically. FSX includes the Autorudder option in the Settings-Realism dialog box (see Figure 11-23), which, as the name implies, coordinates rudder inputs as you maneuver the airplane.

NOTE **For more information about the options for simulating rudder controls in X-Plane, see the *X-Plane Operation Manual*. For FSX, see "Changing Realism Settings" in the Learning Center.**

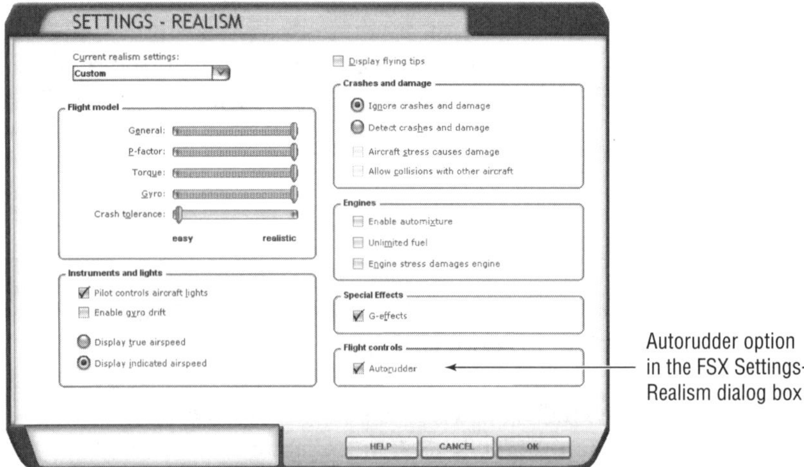

Figure 11-23: Autorudder option in FSX

CHAPTER 12

Flying the Cessna 172 Skyhawk

The Cessna 172 Skyhawk (see Figure 12-1) is the most popular airplane ever produced. It entered production in 1955; and even after a hiatus from 1986–1997, Cessna has built more than 43,000 of the type, and it remains in production today.

Figure 12-1: The Cessna 172 in flight in FSX

The Skyhawk is an excellent trainer and personal aircraft because its basic systems don't overwhelm new pilots, and it's reliable and easy to maintain. The Skyhawk is a good choice for this book, because if you're taking flying lessons or plan to start training soon, the odds are good you'll fly a Cessna 172. If you're a pilot, you've probably logged at least a few hours in a Skyhawk.

X-Plane and FSX simulate the Cessna 172 SP, a model with a 180-hp engine (20 hp more than previous versions, achieved by changing the propeller and increasing maximum engine rpm to 2,700). Most of the other basic specifications of the airplane match those of recent models, and the generic information in the following sections of this chapter applies to virtual flights. Obviously, if you're planning a flight in a real Cessna 172, you must refer to the Airplane Flight Manual (AFM) for that specific aircraft to determine its unique operating weights, performance, and limitations.

Skyhawk Tips from the AOPA ASI

The AOPA Air Safety Institute offers a free publication, *Cessna 172 Skyhawk Safety Highlights* (see Figure 12-2), that provides a general description of the airplane, explains common errors that have led to incidents and accidents, and includes quizzes about aircraft systems and operating limitations. It's a good reference to have at hand during your virtual flights.

Figure 12-2: *Cessna 172 Skyhawk Safety Highlights*, published by the AOPA Air Safety Institute

NOTE **To download a free PDF copy of the *Cessna 172 Skyhawk Safety Highlights*, visit the AOPA ASI website (`www.aopa.org/asf/`) and search for the document's title.**

Key Specifications

The Cessna 172 Skyhawk is typical of many light, fixed-gear aircraft powered by a single-piston engine. Fully loaded, it weighs in at less than 2,500 lbs, takes off and lands at about 60 knots, and can cruise some 600 miles at a true airspeed of approximately 120 knots. Tables 12-1 and 12-2 provide some basic information about the Skyhawk.

Table 12-1: Skyhawk Basic Specifications

ITEM	INFORMATION
Maximum ramp weight	2,457 lbs
Maximum takeoff/landing weight	2,450 lbs
Maximum usable fuel	57 gallons / 318 lbs
Typical empty weight	1,691 lbs
Typical useful load	766 lbs
Full-fuel payload	448 lbs

Table 12-2: Skyhawk Basic Airspeeds

PHASE OF FLIGHT	AIRSPEED (KIAS)
Normal climb	70–80
En route (cruise) climb (sea-level)	75–85
Short-field takeoff (flaps 10°)	57 at 50 ft
En route (cruise) climb (10,000 ft)	70–80
Best ROC (sea-level)	79
Best ROC (10,000 ft)	71
Best angle of climb (sea-level)	60
Best angle of climb (10,000 ft)	65
Landing approach (flaps UP)	65–75
Landing approach (flaps 30°)	60–70
Short-field approach (flaps 30°)	62
Maneuvering speed	99
Maximum flap extended speed (10°)	110
Maximum flap extended speed (10°–30°)	85

NOTE **To learn more about the terms and abbreviations used when describing aircraft specifications, see Chapter 8, "Flight Manuals and Other Documents," and Chapter 10, "Aircraft Performance," in the *Pilot's Handbook of Aeronautical Knowledge*.**

Cessna 172: Cockpit Tour

The following sections describe the layout of the standard, 2D Cessna 172 instrument panels in X-Plane and FSX. You can fly either simulation in a "virtual cockpit" that displays a 3D-like view; but for the purposes of this book, the standard 2D instrument panel usually works best. The instruments are more detailed, and it's easier to operate the basic cockpit controls.

You can find recommendations about using the standard cockpit views in X-Plane and FSX in the section "Getting a Better View" in Chapter 11.

NOTE **To learn more about the cockpit views in X-Plane, see the discussion of the View menu in the *X-Plane Operation Manual*. For more information about the cockpit views in FSX, see the topic "Using Views and Windows" in the FSX Learning Center.**

Until the introduction of advanced "glass cockpit" displays, Skyhawks were equipped with standard flight instruments and communications and navigation radios designed for personal aircraft. The primary flight instruments in such cockpits are arranged in a "six-pack" directly in front of the pilot. The avionics — radios, autopilot, and GPS — are aligned vertically to the right of flight instruments, and two navigation displays form a column between the flight instruments and the avionics stack (see Figure 12-3).

Figure 12-3: Photo of the instrument panel of a Cessna 172 SP manufactured in 2000

Both X-Plane and FSX reproduce the key features of that cockpit realistically, with a few concessions that make the display and operation of cockpit instruments and controls feasible on a typical computer display.

NOTE **To learn more about cockpit instruments and controls, see Chapter 7, "Flight Instruments," in the *Pilot's Handbook of Aeronautical Knowledge* and Chapter 3, "Flight Instruments," in the *Instrument Flying Handbook*. For more information about engine and system gauges, see Chapter 6, "Aircraft Systems," in the *Pilot's Handbook of Aeronautical Knowledge*.**

X-Plane Default Cockpit View

You will probably spend most of your flying time in X-Plane in the default 2D cockpit view (see Figure 12-4).

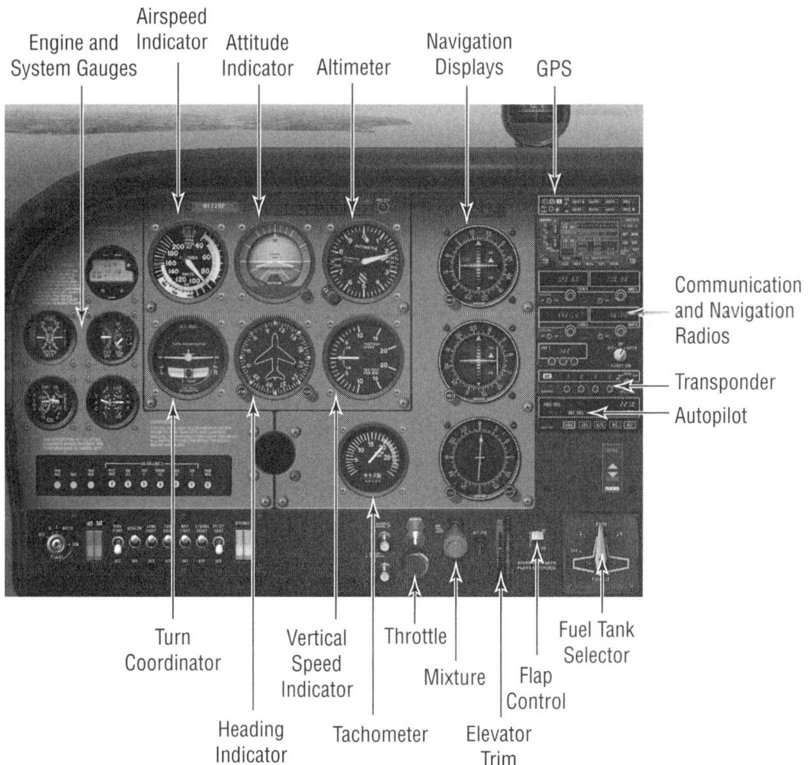

Figure 12-4: Primary features of the standard, 2D Cessna 172 panel in X-Plane

You can use the mouse to operate most controls in the X-Plane cockpit (for example, tuning the radios, adjusting elevator trim, and extending and retracting the flaps) as if you were using your hand. Point to the control with the mouse, and when the pointer changes shape, click or drag the lever or knob (see Figures 12-5 and 12-6).

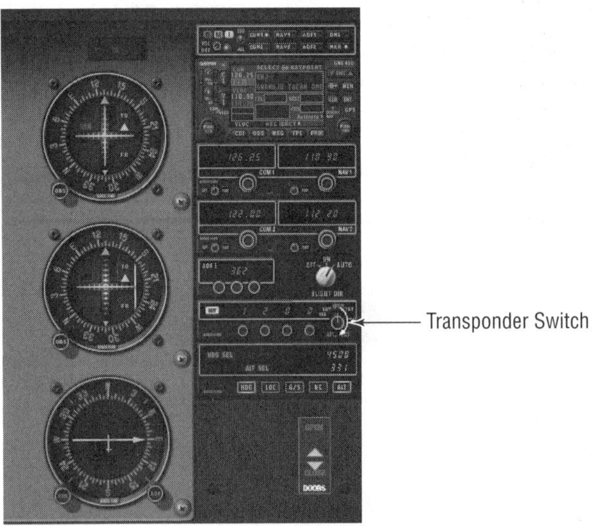

Figure 12-5: Using the mouse to operate the switch on the transponder in X-Plane

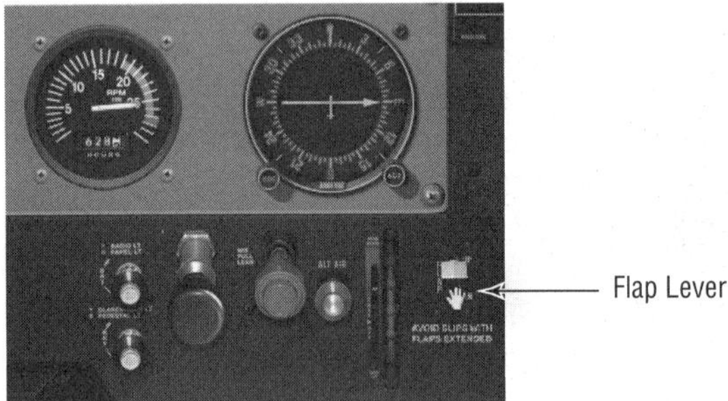

Figure 12-6: Using the mouse to operate the flap lever in X-Plane

NOTE **For more information about using the mouse in the X-Plane cockpit, see "Controlling Instruments and Avionics with the Mouse" in the *X-Plane Operation Manual*.**

You can also assign functions to buttons and other controls on a yoke or joystick (see the discussion of the X-Plane Settings menu later in this chapter). Yoke and joystick levers and switches are usually the best mechanisms for adjusting primary controls such as the throttle and elevator trim.

FSX: Default Cockpit View

You will probably spend most of your flying time in FSX in the default 2D cockpit view (see Figure 12-7).

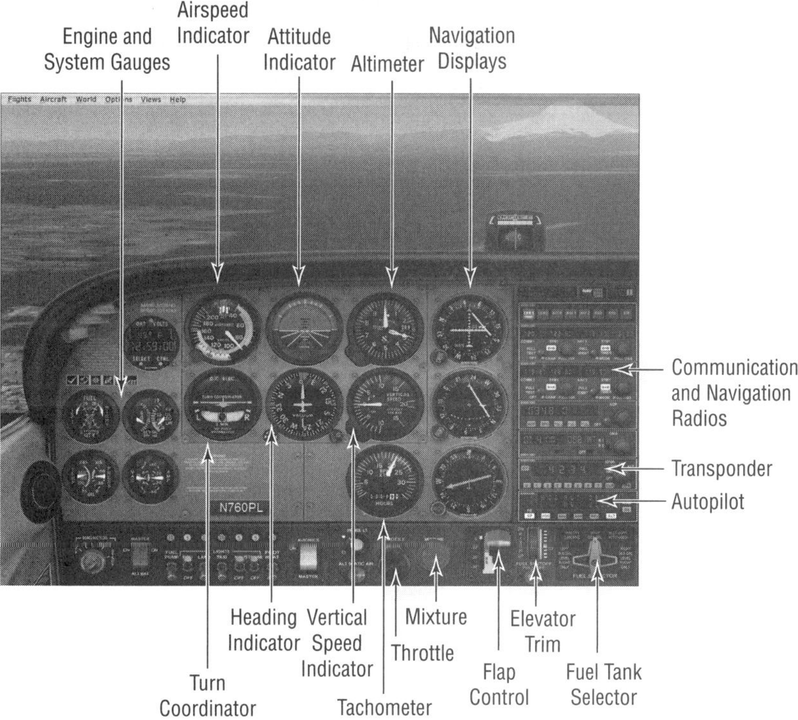

Figure 12-7: Primary features of the standard, 2D Cessna 172 panel in FSX

You can use the mouse to operate most controls in the FSX cockpit (for example, tuning the radios, adjusting elevator trim, and extending and retracting the flaps) as if you were using your hand. Point to the control with the mouse, and when the pointer changes shape, click or drag the lever or knob, or roll the mouse wheel (see Figures 12-8 and 12-9).

Figure 12-8: Using the mouse to operate autopilot controls in FSX

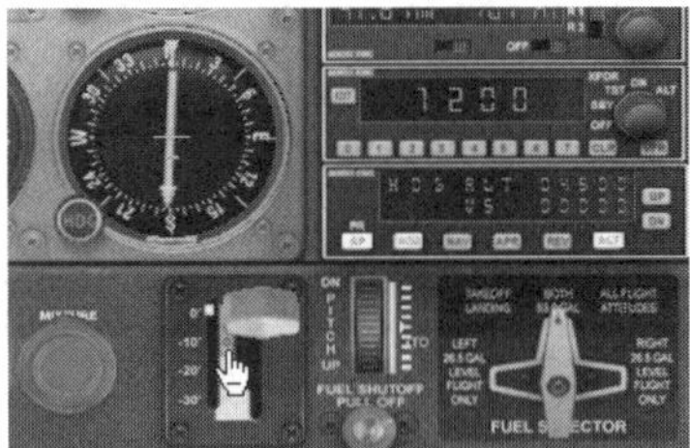

Figure 12-9: Using the mouse to operate the flap lever in FSX

Flying Tips

The tables and illustrations that follow show how to apply the Golden Rule of Flying (see Chapter 11) to set pitch, power, and configuration to achieve stable flight for common situations. If you learn and apply these settings, you can quickly establish the Skyhawk in stable flight for situations such as normal cruise, climbs and descents, the traffic pattern, and instrument approaches. As described next, you can make small adjustments to pitch, power, and flap settings to tweak the performance indicated in the configuration tables.

Configuration Tables

The following tables provide guidelines for use with X-Plane and FSX. Keep in mind that they are not a substitute for the information and procedures in the official AFM. Performance calculations for real-world flying must be based on the details of a specific aircraft and ambient conditions.

NOTE You can create your own configuration tables regardless of the type of airplane you fly. Use the autopilot to stabilize the airplane and observe how changes in pitch, power, and configuration affect indicated airspeed and rate of climb and descent.

When flying an aircraft like the Skyhawk, equipped with a fixed-pitch propeller, remember the following guidelines:

- Smoothly reducing power by about 100 rpm slows the airplane by 5–10 KIAS (level flight) or starts a descent of about 100 fpm at the original airspeed.
- Increasing power by 100 rpm results in an increase of 5–10 KIAS (level flight) or initiates a climb of about 100 fpm.
- To maintain indicated airspeed in a turn (up to about 30° of bank), increase power about 100 rpm as you roll into the turn, and reduce power to the original setting as you roll the wings level.
- Little change in trim should be required until you add or reduce power by more than about 200 rpm. Adding or reducing power more than that amount significantly changes the volume of air that the propeller blows over the horizontal stabilizer, affecting the force created by the tail.

Remember to be patient, and experiment with small, incremental changes in power to see how they affect aircraft performance as the airplane stabilizes, typically 30–60 seconds after you add or reduce power.

NOTE Knowing the basic configurations for your airplane becomes vitally important if you experience instrument malfunctions. If you know the pitch, power, configuration, and resulting performance for different situations, you can establish the airplane in stable flight, even if, for example, the airspeed indicator displays erroneous information.

X-Plane Configurations

The following sections describe configurations for typical phases of flight in the X-Plane Cessna 172.

Initial Climb after Takeoff

Table 12-3 and Figure 12-10 show typical pitch-power-configuration values for an initial climb in the X-Plane Cessna 172. The actual rate of climb achieved at 80 KIAS depends on the aircraft's weight and the density altitude.

Figure 12-10: Initial climb configuration in the X-Plane Cessna 172

Table 12-3: Initial Climb in the X-Plane Cessna 172

ITEM	VALUE
Pitch	+5
Power	Maximum available rpm (2,300–2,500)
Flaps	0°
Airspeed	80 KIAS
Rate of Climb (sea-level)	+800–900 fpm

En Route Climb

Table 12-4 and Figure 12-11 show typical pitch-power-configuration values for an en route climb in the X-Plane Cessna 172. Lowering the nose to fly at 90 KIAS makes it easier to watch for other aircraft, helps cool the engine, and is a good compromise between distance traveled and climb rate. The actual rate of climb achieved at 90 KIAS depends on the aircraft's weight and the density altitude. This configuration is also a good foundation for normal climbs when flying on instruments.

Figure 12-11: En route climb configuration in the X-Plane Cessna 172

Table 12-4: En Route Climb Configuration in the X-Plane Cessna 172

ITEM	VALUE
Pitch	+2
Power	Maximum available rpm (2,400–2,500)
Flaps	0°
Airspeed	90 KIAS
Rate of Climb (sea-level)	+600–700 fpm

Normal Cruise

Table 12-5 and Figure 12-12 show typical pitch-power-configuration values for normal cruise in the X-Plane Cessna 172. Indicated airspeed decreases at higher altitudes.

Figure 12-12: Normal cruise configuration in the X-Plane Cessna 172

Table 12-5: Normal Cruise in the X-Plane Cessna 172

ITEM	VALUE
Pitch	+0
Power	2,500 rpm
Flaps	0°
Airspeed	110–115 KIAS
Rate of Climb	0 fpm

Low-Speed Cruise/Initial Approach Speed

Table 12-6 and Figure 12-13 show typical pitch-power-configuration values for low-speed cruise in the X-Plane Cessna 172. This configuration is useful as you approach an airport and during the initial phases of instrument approaches. Note that this configuration also results in an indicated airspeed below the limit for extending the first 10° of flaps (110 KIAS).

Figure 12-13: Low-speed cruise configuration in the X-Plane Cessna 172

Tale 12-6: Low-Speed Cruise in X-Plane Cessna 172

ITEM	VALUE
Pitch	+0
Power	2,100 rpm
Flaps	0°
Airspeed	90 KIAS
Rate of Climb	0 fpm

En Route Descent

Table 12-7 and Figure 12-14 show typical pitch-power-configuration values for an en route descent in the X-Plane Cessna 172. Use this configuration to maintain normal speed and a comfortable rate of descent from cruise altitude, especially when flying on instruments. You can, of course, increase speed by adding power and/or lowering the pitch attitude.

Figure 12-14: En route descent configuration in the X-Plane Cessna 172

Table 12-7: En Route Descent in X-Plane Cessna 172

ITEM	VALUE
Pitch	–1
Power	2,300 rpm
Flaps	0°
Airspeed	105–110 KIAS
Rate of Descent	–500 fpm

Traffic Pattern

Table 12-8 and Figure 12-15 show typical pitch-power-configuration values for joining and flying the downwind leg of the traffic pattern in the X-Plane Cessna 172. This configuration also establishes the airplane at or near the maximum indicated airspeed allowed for extending more than 10° of flaps (85 KIAS). The configuration is also useful for establishing level flight at the minimum descent altitude on a nonprecision instrument approach.

Figure 12-15: Traffic pattern configuration in the X-Plane Cessna 172

Table 12-8: Traffic Pattern Configuration in X-Plane Cessna 172

ITEM	VALUE
Pitch	0
Power	2,000 rpm
Flaps	10°
Airspeed	85–90 KIAS
Rate of Descent	0 fpm

Final Approach

Table 12-9 and Figure 12-16 show typical pitch-power-configuration values for flying a normal final approach at about 65 KIAS in the X-Plane Cessna 172.

Figure 12-16: Final approach configuration in the X-Plane Cessna 172

Table 12-9: Final Approach Configuration in X-Plane Cessna 172

ITEM	VALUE
Pitch	–2
Power	1,600 rpm
Flaps	30° (full down)
Airspeed	65 KIAS
Rate of Descent	300–500 fpm

ILS Approach (Flaps 10°)

Table 12-10 and Figure 12-17 show typical pitch-power-configuration values for flying an ILS approach at about 90 KIAS with 10° flaps in the X-Plane Cessna 172. This configuration provides a stable descent at an airspeed that prepares the airplane for landing or a missed approach.

Figure 12-17: ILS approach with flaps configuration in the X-Plane Cessna 172

Table 12-10: ILS Approach at 90 KIAS Configuration in X-Plane Cessna 172

ITEM	VALUE
Pitch	–1
Power	1,900 rpm
Flaps	10°
Airspeed	90 KIAS
Rate of Descent	–500 fpm

ILS Approach (Flaps 0°)

Table 12-11 and Figure 12-18 show typical pitch-power-configuration values for flying an ILS approach at about 100 KIAS with 0° flaps in the X-Plane Cessna 172. This configuration provides a stable descent at a higher airspeed, which may be helpful when fitting into the flow at busy airports.

Figure 12-18: ILS approach with no flaps configuration in the X-Plane Cessna 172

Table 12-11: ILS Approach at 100 KIAS Configuration in X-Plane Cessna 172

ITEM	VALUE
Pitch	–1
Power	2,000–2,100 rpm
Flaps	0°
Airspeed	100–105 KIAS
Rate of Descent	–500 fpm

FSX Configurations

The following sections describe configurations for typical phases of flight in the FSX Cessna 172.

Initial Climb after Takeoff

Table 12-12 and Figure 12-19 show typical pitch-power-configuration values for an initial climb in the FSX Cessna 172. The actual rate of climb achieved at 80–85 KIAS depends on the aircraft's weight and the density altitude.

Figure 12-19: Initial climb configuration in the FSX Cessna 172

Table 12-12: Initial Climb in FSX Cessna 172

ITEM	VALUE
Pitch	+5
Power	Maximum available rpm (2,400–2,500)
Flaps	0°
Airspeed	80–85 KIAS
Rate of Climb (sea-level)	+800–900 fpm

En Route Climb

Table 12-13 and Figure 12-20 show typical pitch-power-configuration values for an en route climb in the FSX Cessna 172. Lowering the nose to fly at 90 KIAS makes it easier to watch for other aircraft, helps cool the engine, and is a good compromise between distance traveled and climb rate. The actual rate of climb achieved at 90 KIAS depends on the aircraft's weight and the density altitude. This configuration is also a good foundation for normal climbs when flying on instruments.

Figure 12-20: En route climb configuration in the FSX Cessna 172

Table 12-13: En Route Climb Configuration in the FSX Cessna 172

ITEM	VALUE
Pitch	+4
Power	Maximum available rpm (2,400–2,500)
Flaps	0°
Airspeed	90 KIAS
Rate of Climb (sea-level)	+600–700 fpm

Normal Cruise

Table 12-14 and Figure 12-21 show typical pitch-power-configuration values for normal cruise in the FSX Cessna 172. Indicated airspeed decreases at higher altitudes.

Figure 12-21: Normal cruise configuration in the FSX Cessna 172

Table 12-14: Normal Cruise in the FSX Cessna 172

ITEM	VALUE
Pitch	+0
Power	2,500 rpm
Flaps	0°
Airspeed	105–110 KIAS
Rate of Climb	0 fpm

Low-Speed Cruise/Initial Approach Speed

Table 12-15 and Figure 12-22 show typical pitch-power-configuration values for low-speed cruise in the FSX Cessna 172. This configuration is useful as you approach an airport and during the initial phases of instrument approaches. Note that this configuration also results in an indicated airspeed below the limit (110 KIAS) for extending the first 10° of flaps.

Figure 12-22: Low-speed cruise configuration in the FSX Cessna 172

Table 12-15: Low-Speed Cruise in FSX Cessna 172

ITEM	VALUE
Pitch	+1
Power	2,200 rpm
Flaps	0°
Airspeed	90 KIAS
Rate of Climb	0 fpm

En Route Descent

Table 12-16 and Figure 12-23 show typical pitch-power-configuration values for en route descent in the FSX Cessna 172. Use this configuration to maintain normal speed and a comfortable rate of descent from cruise altitude, especially when flying on instruments. You can, of course, increase speed by adding power and/or lowering the pitch attitude.

Figure 12-23: En route descent configuration in the FSX Cessna 172

Table 12-16: En Route Descent in FSX Cessna 172

ITEM	VALUE
Pitch	–1
Power	2,300 rpm
Flaps	0°
Airspeed	105–110 KIAS
Rate of Descent	–500 fpm

Traffic Pattern

Table 12-17 and Figure 12-24 show typical pitch-power-configuration values for joining and flying the downwind leg of the traffic pattern in the FSX Cessna 172. This configuration also establishes the airplane at or near the maximum indicated airspeed (85 KIAS) allowed for extending more than 10° of flaps. This configuration is also useful for establishing level flight at the minimum descent altitude on a nonprecision instrument approach.

Figure 12-24: Traffic pattern configuration in the FSX Cessna 172

Table 12-17: Traffic Pattern Configuration in FSX Cessna 172

ITEM	VALUE
Pitch	+1
Power	2,200 rpm
Flaps	10°
Airspeed	80–85 KIAS
Rate of Descent	0 fpm

Final Approach

Table 12-18 and Figure 12-25 show typical pitch-power-configuration values for flying a normal final approach at about 65 KIAS in the FSX Cessna 172.

Figure 12-25: Final approach configuration in the FSX Cessna 172

Table 12-18: Final Approach Configuration in FSX Cessna 172

ITEM	VALUE
Pitch	–1
Power	1,600–1,700 rpm
Flaps	30° (full down)
Airspeed	65 KIAS
Rate of Descent	500 fpm

ILS Approach (Flaps 10°)

Table 12-19 and Figure 12-26 show typical pitch-power-configuration values for flying an ILS approach at about 90 KIAS with 10° flaps in the FSX Cessna 172. This configuration provides a stable descent at an airspeed that prepares the airplane for landing or a missed approach.

Figure 12-26: ILS approach with flaps configuration in the FSX Cessna 172

Table 12-19: ILS Approach at 90 KIAS Configuration in FSX Cessna 172

ITEM	VALUE
Pitch	–1
Power	2,100 rpm
Flaps	10°
Airspeed	90 KIAS
Rate of Descent	–500 fpm

ILS Approach (Flaps 0°)

Table 12-20 and Figure 12-27 show typical pitch-power-configuration values for flying an ILS approach at about 100 KIAS with 0° flaps in the FSX Cessna 172. This configuration provides a stable descent at a higher airspeed, which may be helpful when fitting into the flow at busy airports.

Figure 12-27: ILS approach with no flaps configuration in the FSX Cessna 172

Table 12-20: ILS Approach at 100 KIAS Configuration in FSX Cessna 172

ITEM	VALUE
Pitch	–2
Power	2,000–2,100 rpm
Flaps	0°
Airspeed	100–105 KIAS
Rate of Descent	–500 fpm

Cessna 172 Performance Data

The appendix to the *Pilot's Handbook of Aeronautical Knowledge* includes several basic performance tables for the C172R that are useful for planning and checking performance for the scenarios later in this book. Figures 12-28 and 12-29 show two of these tables: one for a short-field (maximum performance) takeoff and one for cruise performance, respectively.

Appendix

Short Field Takeoff Distance at 2,450 Pounds for a Cessna Model 172R

CONDITIONS:

Flaps 10°
Full Throttle Prior to Brake Release
Paved, level, dry runway
Zero Wind
Lift Off: 51 KIAS
Speed at 50 Ft: 57 KIAS

Press Alt In Feet	0°C		10°C		20°C		30°C		40°C	
	Grnd Roll Ft	Total Ft To Clear 50 Ft Obst	Grnd Roll Ft	Total Ft To Clear 50 Ft Obst	Grnd Roll Ft	Total Ft To Clear 50 Ft Obst	Grnd Roll Ft	Total Ft To Clear 50 Ft Obst	Grnd Roll Ft	Total Ft To Clear 50 Ft Obst
S. L.	845	1510	910	1625	980	1745	1055	1875	1135	2015
1000	925	1660	1000	1790	1075	1925	1160	2070	1245	2220
2000	1015	1830	1095	1970	1185	2125	1275	2290	1365	2455
3000	1115	2020	1205	2185	1305	2360	1400	2540	1505	2730
4000	1230	2245	1330	2430	1435	2630	1545	2830	1655	3045
5000	1355	2500	1470	2715	1585	2945	1705	3175	1830	3430
6000	1500	2805	1625	3060	1750	3315	1880	3590	2020	3895
7000	1660	3170	1795	3470	1935	3770	2085	4105	2240	4485
8000	1840	3620	1995	3975	2150	4345	2315	4775	---	---

NOTES:

1. Short field technique as specified in Section 4.
2. Prior to takeoff from fields above 3000 feet elevation, the mixture should be leaned to give maximum RPM in a full throttle, static runup.
3. Decrease distances 10% for each 9 knots headwind. For operation with tail winds up to 10 knots, increase distances by 10% for each 2 knots.
4. For operation on dry, grass runway, increase distances by 15% of the "ground roll" figure.
5. Where distance value has been deleted, climb performance is minimal.

A-1

Figure 12-28: Short-field takeoff/landing performance table for a typical Cessna 172

Cruise Performance for a Cessna Model 172R

CONDITIONS:
2450 Pounds
Recommended Lean Mixture At All Altitudes (Refer to Section 4, Cruise)

PRESS ALT FT	RPM	20°C BELOW STANDARD TEMP			STANDARD TEMPERATURE			20°C ABOVE STANDARD TEMP		
		% BHP	KTAS	GPH	% BHP	KTAS	GPH	% BHP	KTAS	GPH
2000	2250	---	---	---	79	115	9.0	74	114	8.5
	2200	79	112	9.1	74	112	8.5	70	111	8.0
	2100	69	107	7.9	65	106	7.5	62	105	7.1
	2000	61	101	7.0	58	99	6.6	55	97	6.4
	1900	54	94	6.2	51	91	5.9	50	89	5.8
4000	2300	--	---	---	79	117	9.1	75	117	8.6
	2250	80	115	9.2	75	114	8.6	70	114	8.1
	2200	75	112	8.6	70	111	8.1	66	110	7.6
	2100	66	106	7.6	62	105	7.1	59	103	6.8
	2000	58	100	6.7	55	98	6.4	53	95	6.2
	1900	52	92	6.0	50	90	5.8	49	87	5.6
6000	2350	--	---	---	80	120	9.2	75	119	8.6
	2300	80	117	9.2	75	117	8.6	71	116	8.1
	2250	76	115	8.7	71	114	8.1	67	113	7.7
	2200	71	112	8.1	67	111	7.7	64	109	7.3
	2100	63	105	7.2	60	104	6.9	57	101	6.6
	2000	56	98	6.4	53	96	6.2	52	93	6.0

NOTE:

1. Cruise speeds are shown for an airplane equipped with speed fairings. Without speed fairings, decrease speeds shown by 2 knots.

A-3

Figure 12-29: Cruise performance table for a typical Cessna 172

NOTE **To learn more about performance tables, see Chapter 10, "Aircraft Performance," in the *Pilot's Handbook of Aeronautical Knowledge*.**

Part

IV

Private Pilot Scenarios

In This Part

CHAPTER

13

Introduction to the Private Pilot Syllabus

The lessons in this part of the book guide you through a realistic training program to earn an FAA private pilot certificate. The syllabus of 30 lessons covers ground and flight training, solo flights, and preparation for the FAA private pilot practical test.

The lessons and scenarios are based on the *FITS Generic Private Pilot ASEL Syllabus* published in October 2007. It is one of several documents available in the Generic Curriculums and Curriculum Guides section of the FAA/Industry Training Standards (FITS) website.

For the purposes of this book, the lessons are adapted for use with X-Plane and FSX, as described in Chapters 3 and 9. For example, in the FITS syllabus, some of the lessons are ground sessions. However, you can take to the virtual skies in X-Plane or FSX to see the concepts in action as you review the background information in FAA training handbooks and other sources. Even lessons that focus on learning about the instruments and cockpit controls begin in the air (with the autopilot on). Of course, if you're involved in real flight training, you should follow your instructor's guidance.

INFORMATION FROM *LET'S GO FLYING!* AND AOPA *FLIGHT TRAINING*

AOPA hosts two websites that answer common questions about learning to fly and help you during flight training. For more information, visit `www.aopa.org/letsgoflying/` (see Figure 13-1) and `http://flighttraining.aopa.org/`.

Figure 13-1: The *Let's Go Flying!* website

What Is a Private Pilot?

The private pilot certificate (see Figure 13-2) is the first goal of most people who pursue flight training. Even aspiring airline and military pilots usually begin their careers by training for and earning a private pilot certificate with a single-engine land rating. (Outside the U.S., this basic credential is often known as the "PPL," or private pilot license; but the FAA issues pilot *certificates*, not licenses.)

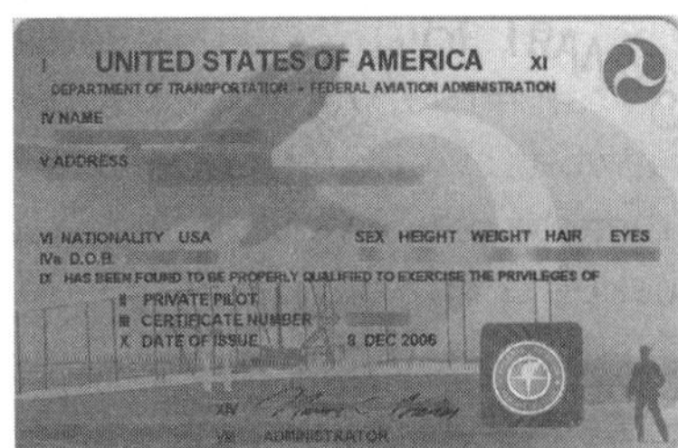

Figure 13-2: An FAA-issued private pilot certificate

NOTE **The FAA issues two other basic pilot certificates: the *recreational pilot certificate* and the *sport pilot certificate*. These certificates allow you to fly small, uncomplicated airplanes, with significant restrictions on where and when you can fly. However, they are alternatives for pilots who may not meet the medical standards for the private pilot certificate or those who just want to enjoy flying on sunny days. Few pilots have pursued the recreational pilot certificate (according to the FAA, there were only 252 such certificates active in 2008), but interest in the sport pilot certificate is growing with the introduction of new light sport aircraft (LSA). For more information about earning a sport pilot certificate, visit `http://sportpilot.org`, a website hosted by the Experimental Aircraft Association (EAA).**

As the name "private pilot" implies, the private pilot certificate is designed for personal flying, but unless you pursue a career in aviation, it's the only "license" you need. With a private pilot certificate, you can:

- Take family, friends, and colleagues on flights of any length.
- Fly at altitudes up to 18,000 feet (flight at and above that altitude requires an instrument rating).
- Fly aircraft with fixed landing gear and a single engine that produces 200 horsepower or less.
- Take off and land at any public-use, civilian airport (although as a practical matter, you won't have much reason to fly into airline hubs like JFK and LAX).
- Use an airplane for business travel, provided you're not being compensated as pilot or accepting payment from others.
- Fly under visual flight rules (VFR), day or night.
- Split direct costs (rental fees, fuel, and so forth) equally with your passengers. You can't, however, operate an "air taxi," offering to take people on trips like an airline or charter company.

You can add ratings to a private pilot certificate that allow you to fly:

- Under instrument flight rules (IFR)
- Floatplanes (seaplanes)
- Gliders (sailplanes)
- Multi-engine aircraft
- Helicopters (rotorcraft)
- Jets and large aircraft (those weighing more than 12,500 pounds)

NOTE **You can earn a private pilot certificate in a glider (sailplane), floatplane, or helicopter and then add a land airplane rating after you receive additional training and pass specific tests. You can even complete all of your initial flight training in a multi-engine airplane and add a single-engine rating later. Most pilots, however, learn to fly in single-engine airplanes equipped with wheels.**

To earn additional ratings, you must complete specific training with an instructor, and you must also pass a practical test given by a pilot examiner. Some ratings, like the instrument rating, require you to pass a computerized knowledge test.

You can also expand the variety of aircraft you fly by training with an instructor who endorses your logbook. No FAA tests are required for these approvals, which allow you to fly aircraft with more powerful engines, tailwheels, or retractable landing gear (see Figure 13-3).

Photo credit: Pat DuLaney

Figure 13-3: With the proper logbook endorsements, a private pilot can fly a high-performance aerobatic airplane such as the Extra 300L pictured here.

Basic Requirements

The legal minimums required to earn a private pilot certificate are spelled out in the FAA regulations, specifically 14 CFR Part 61. They include the following:

- 40 hours of total flight time, including at least 20 hours of dual instruction and 10 hours of solo practice
- The total flight time must include several "cross-country" flights — flights of varying distance to practice navigation to airports other than your home airfield

- 3 hours of training at night
- 3 hours of instruction in basic instrument flying skills
- Practice flying at airports with control towers

Flight schools that focus on students who want to pursue a career as a pilot may also provide training under Part 141 of the regulations. Part 141 flight schools follow a detailed training program and record-keeping standards specifically approved by the FAA. Graduates of Part 141 flight schools can earn a private pilot certificate with 35 hours of total flight time. Nevertheless, given the complexity of today's aircraft, operating procedures, and other factors, most students require 50–70 hours total flight time to earn a private pilot certificate.

Those are the basic FAA rules. Insurance requirements and the individual policies at businesses that rent aircraft usually require pilots to receive additional training, gain experience, or earn specific ratings before they're allowed to fly new models of aircraft.

NOTE **To review the detailed requirements for student pilots and earning a private pilot certificate, see 14 CFR Part 61, Subparts C (Student Pilots) and E (Private Pilots).**

Essential References

The private pilot lessons rely on a set of key references (see Figure 13-4).

Figure 13-4: Essential resources for private pilot training

All of the following key references (current as of the summer of 2011) are available in PDF versions at the website for this book, which also provides links to other resources:

- *Pilot's Handbook of Aeronautical Knowledge* (FAA-H-8083-25A)
- *Airplane Flying Handbook* (FAA-H-8083-3A)
- *Aeronautical Information Manual* (AIM). Updated semiannually.
- *Aviation Weather* (AC 00-6A)
- *Aviation Weather Services* (AC 00-45G)
- *Private Pilot Practical Test Standards for Airplane* (FAA-S-8081-14A, effective August 1, 2002, updated February 2, 2008); often referred to as the "PTS"
- *Instrument Flying Handbook* (FAA-H-8083-15A). This book focuses on the knowledge and skills required for earning an instrument rating, but it provides excellent background for the basic instrument flying abilities that private pilots must demonstrate.

Most lessons also refer to supplemental publications, such as Safety Advisors published by the AOPA Air Safety Institute.

You can find a complete list of references for all the tasks included in the Private Pilot PTS on page 3 of that booklet, including the following:

- 14 CFR Parts 61 and 91 (the FARs) and NTSB Part 831: Aircraft Accident/Incident Investigation Procedures
- Pilot Operating Handbook and FAA-approved manual for the airplane used for the practical test
- Current navigation charts
- Current Airport/Facility Directory
- FAA advisory circulars

CROSS-REFERENCE **For details about many free references and resources for pilots and virtual aviators, see Chapter 2.**

Three-Phase Private Pilot Syllabus

Like a typical training program for a private pilot certificate, the lessons in this part of the book are organized in three main phases:

- Pre-solo
- Cross-country
- Preparation for the practical test

Of course, unless you're using the instructional features of X-Plane or FSX, you'll fly each of the lessons solo.

As described in Chapter 9, each lesson includes specific objectives, recommended background reading and practice, and a grading grid that helps you evaluate your knowledge and skills.

The lessons follow the logical progression in the FITS syllabus, but you can, of course, skip or repeat scenarios and fly the scenarios in any sequence.

Keep in mind that the first lessons may be useful even if you're already a pilot, have experience with FSX or X-Plane, or are switching from one simulation to the other. They help you review key features of the simulations described in Chapters 6 and 7, and they give you a chance to practice fundamental flying skills so that you can become more comfortable with the controls and "flying" qualities of the simulation installed on your computer.

CHAPTER

14

Private Pilot Lesson 1: Introductory Flight

Think of this lesson as an introductory flight or first flight lesson.

Scenario

There's no need to conjure up an elaborate scenario with "what-ifs" and "roll of the dice" problems to solve during this initial experience. Still, it's useful to start thinking like a pilot even during early lessons. Every flight — even a local sightseeing hop — has a purpose and goals, and you should assess those objectives before you climb into the cockpit.

NOTE **If you're not yet involved in real flight training, visit the *Let's Go Flying!* website (`www.aopa.org/letsgoflying`) to learn more about becoming a pilot and about the aviation community.**

Objectives

Before a real first flying lesson, an instructor should answer your questions about the process of flight training and ensure that you understand the basic parts of an airplane (see Figure 14-1) and the key instruments and controls in the cockpit. During the lesson, you see what the world looks like from the pilot's seat and learn how to use key visual references during basic flight maneuvers.

Photo credit: Cessna Airplane Company

Figure 14-1: A student and instructor prepare for a flight lesson

Those basic goals also apply to this first virtual flight, which:

- Introduces you to the key references and resources that you'll use throughout the private pilot course
- Provides a low-stress environment so that you can become comfortable with the basic layout of the cockpit of your virtual airplane
- Gives you the opportunity to practice using key features described in Chapter 6 (for X-Plane) and Chapter 7 (for FSX), such as using the mouse to operate cockpit controls, changing the view, viewing your position on the map, and getting help
- Introduces the learner-centered grading system that is one of the keys to scenario-based training

In fact, the generic FITS syllabus suggests that the first lesson (not an introductory flight) use a flight training device so that the instructor and student can discuss the instruments and controls without the distractions and stresses associated with flying an airplane. The Situations (X-Plane) and Flights (FSX) for this lesson follow that advice; but to take advantage of PC simulation, they begin in the air (with the autopilot on) so that you can practice right away in an interactive, realistic environment.

Completion Standards

The detailed goals for this lesson are outlined in the table at the end of this chapter. In general, before you move on to the next lesson, you should be able to:

- Identify the key controls and instruments in the cockpit of your virtual airplane

- Use controls on the flight yoke or joystick to look around
- Hide or dim the instrument panel to enhance the view of the outside world
- Use the integrated help features of X-Plane or FSX
- Understand the functions of the key flight controls

The grading sheet uses standard FITS terminology to help you assess your progress. As noted in "FITS Grading Standards" in Chapter 9, you should be able, as appropriate, to describe, explain, practice, or perform the concept or task associated with each goal for a lesson. As you advance through the lessons, you may also encounter goals that require you to manage situations and decide on appropriate actions.

If you aren't working with an instructor, you can still grade yourself according to these standards. Just imagine that you must explain the concepts and demonstrate the tasks to a fellow virtual aviator or friend. As the old saying goes, you know you've learned a subject when you can teach it.

References and Resources

If you're starting real flight lessons, your instructor should give you a guided tour of an airplane and help you understand what's involved in learning to fly. You can accomplish the same goal yourself by reviewing the following references and resources before you climb into the cockpit:

TITLE	CHAPTER/SECTION	TOPIC/NOTES
Pilot's Handbook of Aeronautical Knowledge	Chapter 1, "Introduction to Flying"	FAA Reference Material (pp. 1-9–1-11) and The Student Pilot (pp. 1-16–1-20)
	Chapter 2, "Aircraft Structure"	Lift and Basic Aerodynamics (p. 2-2), Major Components (pp. 2-3–2-6), Performance Instruments (p. 2-12), Control Instruments (p. 2-12), Navigation Instruments (p. 2-12)
This book	Chapter 6 (X-Plane) or Chapter 7 (FSX)	–

CROSS-REFERENCE For more information about the references and resources that complement the lessons in this book, see Chapter 2.

Preflight Briefing

As noted earlier, this lesson begins in the air, as if your instructor has made the takeoff and guided you to the practice area. Now you can explore the cockpit of your virtual aircraft and experiment with the key features X-Plane or FSX. Take as much time as you like and stop the flight when you're confident that you've met the objectives. Don't worry about getting back to an airport and landing. Just as during a real introductory flight, the instructor would be responsible for those tasks.

Location and Weather

The lesson begins in the air between Walla Walla, WA (KALW) and Pullman, WA (KPUW). It's a beautiful day, and you're flying in a rural area well away from busy airports (see Figure 14-2).

Figure 14-2: Area around Walla Walla, WA, on the Seattle sectional chart, as shown on SkyVector

Situations and Flights

This lesson uses the following files for X-Plane and FSX:

- X-Plane: `Wiley-SBT-PrivatePilot-Lesson-01.sit`
- FSX: `Wiley-SBT-PrivatePilot-Lesson-01.flt`

CROSS-REFERENCE **For more information about using Situations (X-Plane) and Flights (FSX), see Chapter 10.**

Tips for This Lesson

The overall goals for this lesson are becoming familiar with basic features of the simulation that you use and the cockpit instrument controls in your virtual Cessna 172 Skyhawk. The following sections offer specific tips to help you meet those objectives.

Yoke and Joystick Controls

Experiment with the buttons and switches on the flight yoke or joystick that you use. Don't worry about memorizing all the functions at this point. With a little practice, you'll become comfortable with the most important controls, such the "hat" switch at the top of a joystick, which is typically used to change your view left, right, and forward. You can also reassign functions to buttons and switches.

To change the functions assigned to yoke and joystick buttons and switches:

- In X-Plane, on the Settings menu, choose the Joystick & Equipment command.
- In FSX, on the Options menu, point to Settings, and then click Controls.

Autopilot Controls

The autopilots in the X-Plane and FSX versions of the Cessna 172 offer the same basic functions, such as holding altitude and tracking a heading or course defined by the GPS or VOR navigation receivers.

The autopilot in the X-Plane Cessna 172 is a generic device (see Figure 14-3). The FSX version closely emulates the Bendix/King KAP 140 autopilot installed in many Skyhawks (see Figure 14-4). In addition to holding altitude, the FSX version can establish a climb or descent at a rate you specify (within the performance limits of the Cessna 172).

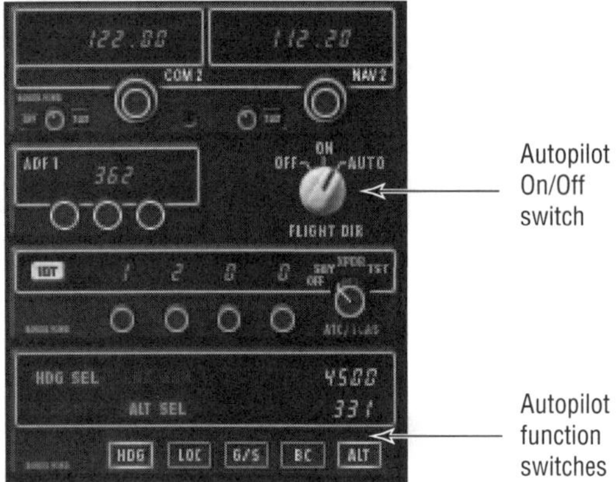

Figure 14-3: Autopilot controls in the X-Plane Cessna 172

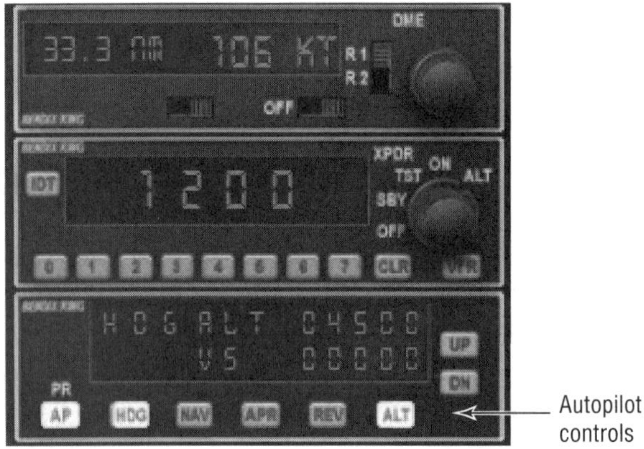

Figure 14-4: Autopilot controls in the FSX Cessna 172

This lesson begins with the autopilot on in heading and altitude hold modes. Experiment with the autopilot by using the mouse to:

- Move the "bug" on the heading indicator (see Figures 14-5 and 14-6). The airplane banks left or right to turn to the new heading.
- Switch the altitude hold function (ALT) on and off; and in FSX, to select a rate of climb or descent.

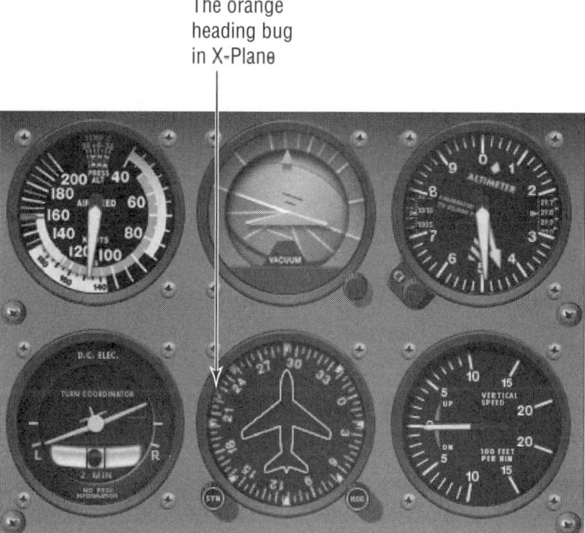

Figure 14-5: Heading bug on the heading indicator in X-Plane

Figure 14-6: Heading bug on the heading indicator in FSX

To learn more about the autopilot:

- In X-Plane, see "Using the Autopilot" in the *X-Plane Operation Manual.*
- In FSX, see the topic "Using an Autopilot" in the Learning Center.

Interactive Map

X-Plane and FSX include interactive maps that you can use to check your position and obtain information about airports and navigation aids. You can also drag the symbol for your airplane to change its position and fill in boxes to reset your altitude, speed, and heading.

To learn more about using the interactive maps:

- For X-Plane, see the discussion of the Location menu in Chapter 6.
- For FSX, see the discussion of the World menu in Chapter 7.

Objectives and Desired Outcome Grading Sheet

SCENARIO ACTIVITIES	SCENARIO SUB-ACTIVITIES	DESIRED OUTCOME
Learn the key components and cockpit features of a typical airplane.	–	Describe
Review common questions about flight training and pilot certification.	–	Describe/Discuss
Learn key features of X-Plane or FSX.	Change views.	Practice
	Use the mouse to operate cockpit controls.	Practice
	Adjust the height of, dim, and hide the instrument panel.	Practice
	Observe your location on the simulation's interactive map.	Practice
	Explore the simulation's integrated help system and web-based resources.	Practice

CHAPTER 15

Private Pilot Lesson 2: Fundamental Flight Maneuvers

This lesson introduces fundamental flight maneuvers and reviews the functions of instruments and cockpit controls.

Scenario

As in the first lesson, at this early stage of flight training there's no need to concoct an elaborate scenario with a detailed decision tree. To help you start thinking like a pilot, it's sufficient to assume that you're taking a friend on a short sightseeing flight near the mouth of the Columbia River in the area around Astoria, OR (KAST). You need to maneuver the airplane to enjoy the scenery, but you also must keep passengers in mind. Fly smoothly at a safe altitude and leave aggressive maneuvers such as steep turns for another day.

Objectives

The primary goal of this flight is practicing the four fundamental flight maneuvers:

- Straight-and-level
- Turns
- Climbs
- Descents

During the flight you should also:

- Review and practice the operation of cockpit controls and instruments.
- Practice looking around as you fly, especially looking left and right to clear the area before you begin turns.
- Use the features in X-Plane or FSX to minimize or hide the instrument panel.
- Practice using the natural horizon and other visual cues, not the gauges on the instrument panel, to control the airplane.

You can also practice identifying landmarks that you can use as checkpoints when you begin navigating on your own. Objects that look familiar at ground level may be hard to identify from the air, and it's important to learn which features make good checkpoints. Especially in a simulation, it's often best to use landmarks like major rivers, coastlines, and big lakes with distinctive shapes (see Figure 15-1). The *Pilot's Handbook of Aeronautical Knowledge* offers the following advice:

> Appropriate checkpoints ... should be easy-to-locate points such as large towns, large lakes and rivers, or combinations of recognizable points such as towns with an airport, towns with a network of highways, and railroads entering and departing.
>
> Pilot's Handbook of Aeronautical Knowledge (p. 15-19)

Finally, it's never too early to learn about collision avoidance and to practice techniques for seeing and avoiding other aircraft.

Figure 15-1: Scenery in X-Plane near Astoria, OR

Completion Standards

The detailed goals for this lesson are outlined in the table at the end of this chapter. In general, before you move on to the next lesson, you should:

- Understand the fundamentals of the basic flight maneuvers.
- Be able to use buttons and switches on the flight yoke or joystick to look around and to adjust the throttle and elevator trim.
- Be able to use the mouse to move the heading bug and other key cockpit controls.
- Know how to hide or dim the instrument panel to enhance the view of the outside world.

The practical test standards for private pilots set the following benchmarks for most flight maneuvers:

- **Altitude:** Maintain within ±100 feet
- **Airspeed:** Maintain within ±10 knots

- **Bank angle:** Establish and maintain within ±5°
- **Heading:** Maintain within ±10°, or when turning, roll out within ±10° of the intended heading

You don't have to meet those standards at this point in your training, but you should strive to achieve them as you practice.

References and Resources

To prepare for this lesson, review the following references and resources.

TITLE	CHAPTER/SECTION	TOPIC/NOTES
Pilot's Handbook of Aeronautical Knowledge	Chapter 4, "Aerodynamics of Flight"	Aerodynamic Forces in Flight Maneuvers (pp. 4–19)
	Chapter 13, "Airport Operations"	Collision Avoidance (pp. 13–17)
	Chapter 16, "Aeromedical Factors"	Motion Sickness (pp. 16–11) and Vision in Flight (pp. 16–17)
	Chapter 17, "Aeronautical Decision-Making"	Situational Awareness (pp. 17–23)
Airplane Flying Handbook	Chapter 3, "Basic Flight Maneuvers"	Review all topics (pp. 3-1–3-19)
Private Pilot Practical Test Standards	Introduction	General Information and Practical Test Standards Concept
AOPA ASI Safety Advisor *Collision Avoidance*	–	–
This book	Chapter 11, "Flying Fundamentals"	In particular, note the section "Integrated Flight Instruction"
	Chapter 12, "Flying the Cessna 172 Skyhawk"	Review the configuration tables for your simulation.

CROSS-REFERENCE **For more information about the references and resources that complement the lessons in this book, see Chapter 2.**

Preflight Briefing

In the generic FITS private pilot syllabus, this lesson utilizes a flight training device. As in Lesson 1 of this book, the Situation (X-Plane) or Flight (FSX) for this scenario begins in the air; assume your instructor has guided you to the practice area. You don't need to take off or land.

When the flight begins, the autopilot is on in heading and altitude hold modes. Use the heading bug to make the first few turns and observe both the natural horizon and primary flight instruments as the airplane turns. Try to correlate the outside and instrument panel views, and then use similar bank and pitch angles when you begin maneuvering the airplane on your own.

Take as much time as you like and stop the flight when you're confident that you've met the objectives. Don't worry about returning to an airport and landing.

Location and Weather

The lesson begins in the air near Astoria, OR (KAST), as shown in Figure 15-2. It's a beautiful day for sightseeing.

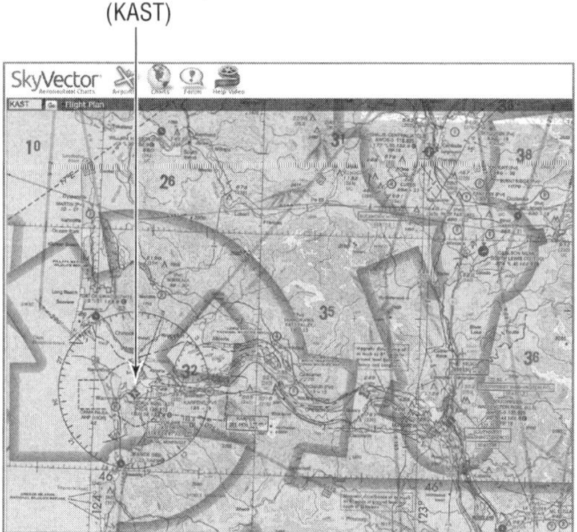

Figure 15-2: The area around Astoria, OR, on the Seattle sectional chart as shown on SkyVector.

Situations and Flights

This lesson uses the following files for X-Plane and FSX:

- X-Plane: `Wiley-SBT-PrivatePilot-Lesson-02.sit`
- FSX: `Wiley-SBT-PrivatePilot-Lesson-02.flt`

CROSS-REFERENCE **For more information about using Situations (X-Plane) and Flights (FSX), see Chapter 10.**

Tips for This Lesson

Here are a few suggestions to help you get the most from this lesson:

- Shrink or hide the instrument panel for most of this flight. Use the natural horizon to help you develop a feel for the controls.
- Frequently compare the view from the cockpit with the interactive map in your simulation. Cross-checking will help you learn how the simulated scenery compares to important features on the map.
- Review the area around Astoria on the Seattle sectional chart (available as a PDF file at this book's website or online at `http://SkyVector.com`) and compare key features on the chart with the scenery in your simulation.
- Use a light touch on the controls and practice applying the configuration tables in Chapter 12 of this book to help you fly precisely and smoothly.

What-Ifs

This is a typical local flight; but challenges can arise even on short trips. For example, your passengers might feel airsick. How can you assist them without losing control of the airplane or becoming so distracted that you wander off the intended flight path and get lost? Here are some suggestions:

- Tell your passengers where to find airsickness bags — did you make sure to bring some along?
- Given what you've learned about the autopilot, could you use it to help stabilize the aircraft?

- Shrink or hide the instrument panel to focus on the outside view. You'll fly more smoothly.
- Enlist the help of passengers in spotting and announcing other airplanes in the vicinity (see Figure 15-3). Encouraging passengers to enjoy the view, not the details of the instrument panel, reduces the likelihood of airsickness.

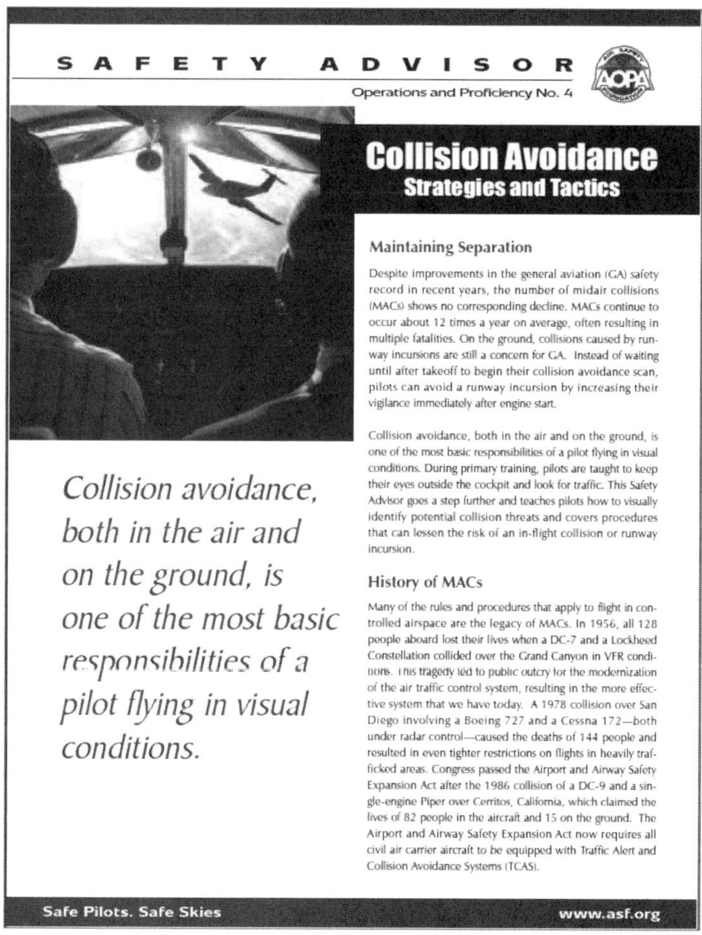

SAFETY ADVISOR

Operations and Proficiency No. 4

AOPA

Collision Avoidance
Strategies and Tactics

Collision avoidance, both in the air and on the ground, is one of the most basic responsibilities of a pilot flying in visual conditions.

Maintaining Separation

Despite improvements in the general aviation (GA) safety record in recent years, the number of midair collisions (MACs) shows no corresponding decline. MACs continue to occur about 12 times a year on average, often resulting in multiple fatalities. On the ground, collisions caused by runway incursions are still a concern for GA. Instead of waiting until after takeoff to begin their collision avoidance scan, pilots can avoid a runway incursion by increasing their vigilance immediately after engine start.

Collision avoidance, both in the air and on the ground, is one of the most basic responsibilities of a pilot flying in visual conditions. During primary training, pilots are taught to keep their eyes outside the cockpit and look for traffic. This Safety Advisor goes a step further and teaches pilots how to visually identify potential collision threats and covers procedures that can lessen the risk of an in-flight collision or runway incursion.

History of MACs

Many of the rules and procedures that apply to flight in controlled airspace are the legacy of MACs. In 1956, all 128 people aboard lost their lives when a DC-7 and a Lockheed Constellation collided over the Grand Canyon in VFR conditions. This tragedy led to public outcry for the modernization of the air traffic control system, resulting in the more effective system that we have today. A 1978 collision over San Diego involving a Boeing 727 and a Cessna 172—both under radar control—caused the deaths of 144 people and resulted in even tighter restrictions on flights in heavily trafficked areas. Congress passed the Airport and Airway Safety Expansion Act after the 1986 collision of a DC-9 and a single-engine Piper over Cerritos, California, which claimed the lives of 82 people in the aircraft and 15 on the ground. The Airport and Airway Safety Expansion Act now requires all civil air carrier aircraft to be equipped with Traffic Alert and Collision Avoidance Systems (TCAS).

Safe Pilots. Safe Skies www.asf.org

Figure 15-3: *Collision Avoidance*, a Safety Advisor from AOPA ASI

Objectives and Desired Outcome Grading Sheet

SCENARIO ACTIVITIES	SCENARIO SUB-ACTIVITIES	DESIRED OUTCOME
Practice using basic flight and cockpit controls.	Use the mouse to operate cockpit controls.	Practice/Perform
	Use the yoke or joystick controls to adjust the throttle and elevator trim.	Practice/Perform
Use the features of X-Plane or FSX to change your view.	Use the yoke or joystick buttons to look around.	Practice/Perform
	Use the view features to shrink and hide the instrument panel.	Practice/Perform
Practice the fundamental flight maneuvers.	Straight-and-level	Practice
	Turns	Practice
	Climbs	Practice
	Descent	Practice
Practice identifying landmarks.	–	Practice
Learn about the Practical Test Standards.	Review the introductory material of the PTS.	Describe

CHAPTER

16

Private Pilot Lesson 3: Ground Reference Maneuvers

This lesson focuses on several elements from the corresponding scenario in the generic FITS private pilot syllabus.

Scenario

Imagine that you sell crop insurance. A hailstorm recently passed over one of your customer's fields. You plan to take him along on a short flight to survey the damage from the air.

Like the previous lessons, this scenario doesn't involve emergencies or complicated decision trees. However, it helps you apply and combine some of the basic flying skills that you've practiced as isolated, abstract skills.

Objectives

The primary goal of this flight is learning about the rectangular course, an important ground reference maneuver. The rectangular course (sometimes called the "rectangular pattern") tests your ability to fly precisely while dividing your attention between flying a specific path over the ground and monitoring altitude and airspeed (see Figure 16-1).

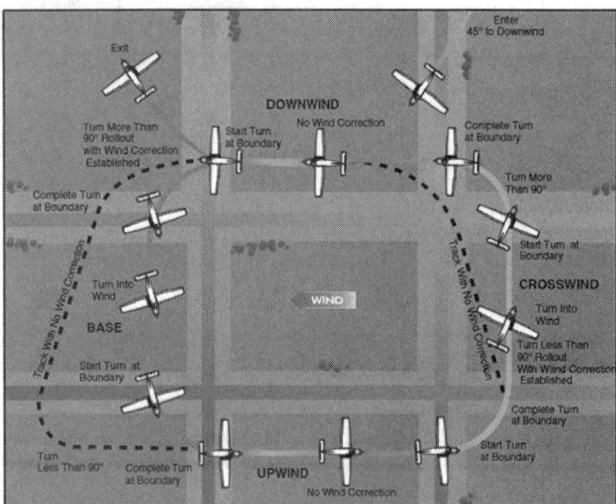

Figure 16-1: Flying a rectangular course, as shown in Figure 6-4 of the *Airplane Flying Handbook*

The *Airplane Flying Handbook* describes the rectangular course as follows:

> The rectangular course is a training maneuver in which the ground track of the airplane is equidistant from all sides of a selected rectangular area on the ground. The maneuver simulates the conditions encountered in an airport traffic pattern. While performing the maneuver, the altitude and airspeed should be held constant.
>
> Like those of other ground track maneuvers, one of the objectives is to develop division of attention between the flightpath and ground references, while controlling the airplane and watching for other aircraft in the vicinity. Another objective is to develop recognition of drift toward or away from a line parallel to the intended ground track. This will be helpful in recognizing drift toward or from an airport runway during the various legs of the airport traffic pattern. The airplane should be flown parallel to and at a uniform distance about one-fourth to one-half mile away from the field boundaries, not above the boundaries.
>
> AIRPLANE FLYING HANDBOOK (P. 6-4)

In addition, this scenario introduces you to:

- Basic navigation — pilotage
- Information about airports on a sectional chart
- The standard airport traffic pattern

The flight back toward the Pullman airport also gives you an opportunity to practice and apply the fundamental flight maneuvers that you practiced in previous lessons.

Completion Standards

The detailed goals for this lesson are outlined in the table at the end of this chapter.

At this point, you should be comfortable looking around and using the basic controls in the cockpit. When flying the fundamental maneuvers, you should be at the Perform level in the FITS grading standards — that is, able to fly consistently within the limits established by the practical test standards. Don't worry, however, if you need more practice flying rectangular patterns.

You should also be able to use the heading indicator, the sectional chart, and the interactive map in X-Plane or FSX to help you return to the vicinity of the Pullman airport.

Using the descriptions of airport symbols and information blocks in the *Aeronautical Chart Users Guide*, you should be able to describe the basic features of the Pullman airport (see Figure 16-2), including the following:

- Official three-letter identifier for the airport
- Runway type, orientation, and length
- Airport elevation above mean sea level
- Basic airport type — whether it is home to a control tower or it is an airport with common traffic advisory frequency (CTAF)

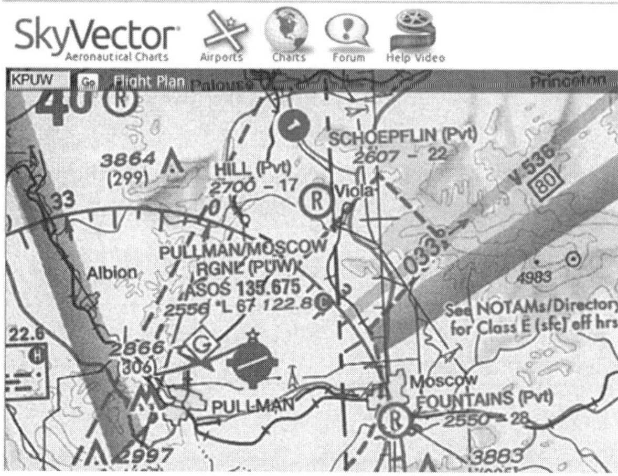

Figure 16-2: Detailed view of the Pullman airport on the Seattle sectional chart

NOTE **Note that on most U.S. aeronautical charts, the official identifiers for airports use three letters or a combination of letters and numbers. For example, on the sectional chart, the identifier for Pullman is PUW. In most GPS-based navigation units and in some official publications, however, many public-use airports in the U.S. use identifiers that begin with the letter "K," assigned to the U.S. long ago by international convention. In general, airport identifiers that begin with "K," like KPUW, report current weather to the National Weather Service and the FAA. Adding "K" to airports with three-letter identifiers (the practice in this book) also helps to distinguish an airport from a nearby navigation aid that might, like Pullman, share the same designation.**

References and Resources

To prepare for this lesson, review the following references and resources. The AOPA Air Safety Institute publications are valuable supplements to the official information in the FAA references.

TITLE	CHAPTER/SECTION	TOPIC/NOTES
Pilot's Handbook of Aeronautical Knowledge	Chapter 15, "Navigation"	Introduction (p. 15-1) and Sectional Charts (p. 15-2)
Airplane Flying Handbook	Chapter 6, "Ground Reference Maneuvers"	Purpose and Scope and Maneuvering by Reference to Ground Objects (p. 6-1), Drift and Ground Track Control (p. 6-2), and Rectangular Course (p. 6-4)
	Chapter 7, "Airport Traffic Pattern"	Review this chapter in preparation for later lessons.
Aeronautical Chart Users Guide	VFR Aeronautical Chart Symbols	Aeronautical Information: Airports (p. 11)
Private Pilot Practical Test Standards	Task VI: Ground Reference Maneuvers	Rectangular Course (p. 1-22)
AOPA ASI Safety Advisor *Operations at Nontowered Airports*	–	–
AOPA ASI Safety Advisor *Maneuvering Flight—Hazardous to Your Health?*	–	–

CROSS-REFERENCE **For more information about the references and resources that complement the lessons in this book, see Chapter 2.**

Preflight Briefing

This lesson begins in the air over the farm fields north of Pullman, WA (KPUW). You're in position to select a field and turn to start flying a rectangular course (see Figure 16-3). Fly the first couple of laps to the left before trying a right-hand pattern. The autopilot is on in heading and altitude hold modes to ensure a stable start to the flight. Turn it off when you're ready to start flying.

Figure 16-3: View of the area where you should fly the rectangular pattern as seen in FSX

The practical test standards specify that you should fly ground reference maneuvers at 600 to 1,000 ft. above ground level (AGL). The area north of Pullman is generally at an elevation of about 2,500 ft. above mean sea level (MSL). For this lesson, you should fly the rectangular course at 3,500 ft. as shown on the altimeter (generally speaking, your altimeter displays the airplane's altitude above MSL).

Practice as many laps as you like, left and right, around the pattern, before you climb to 5,500 ft. and turn to a heading of about 160 degrees to fly back toward the Pullman airport. The goals of this lesson don't include landing. It's sufficient for you to get to the vicinity of the airport and consider how you would fly a standard traffic pattern.

Location and Weather

The lesson begins in the air near Pullman, WA (KPUW), as shown in Figure 16-4. The skies are mostly clear with light winds from the west.

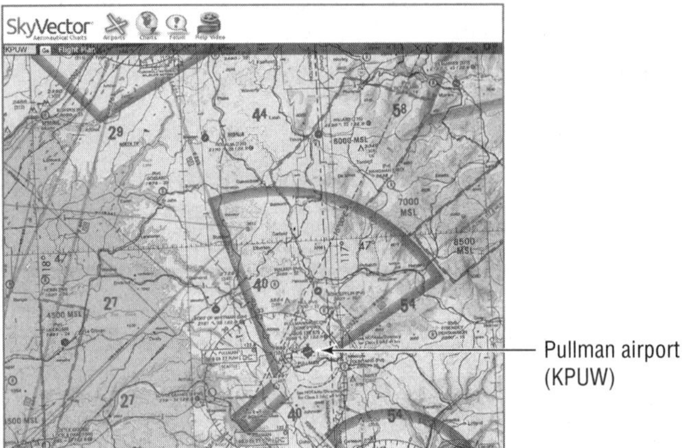

Figure 16-4: The area around Pullman, WA, on the Seattle sectional chart as shown on SkyVector.

Situations and Flights

This lesson uses the following files for X-Plane and FSX:

- X-Plane: `Wiley-SBT-PrivatePilot-Lesson-03.sit`
- FSX: `Wiley-SBT-PrivatePilot-Lesson-03.flt`

CROSS-REFERENCE **For more information about using Situations (X-Plane) and Flights (FSX), see Chapter 10.**

Tips for This Lesson

Here are a few suggestions to help you get the most from this lesson:

- Shrink or hide the instrument panel for most of this flight. Check your altimeter occasionally to verify that you remain at 3,500 ft. (within ±100 ft.) during the rectangular course.
- Practice flying the rectangular course with both left and right turns. It's usually harder to fly ground reference maneuvers with right turns, because you must look across the cockpit.

- When you are ready to fly toward KPUW, compare the view from the cockpit and the indications of the compass and heading indicator with your aircraft's position as shown on the interactive map in your simulation. In addition, compare that display with the area around Pullman on the Seattle sectional chart (available as a PDF file at this book's website or online at `http://SkyVector.com`).

What-Ifs

This is another short flight, but flying a ground reference maneuver can distract you. Try not to obsess about the rectangular pattern. In addition, consider the following:

- What are the best procedures to follow if you become disoriented and need to return to the vicinity of the Pullman airport?
- What should you do if another airplane approaches the area where you're practicing? Aerial applicators (usually known as "crop dusters") frequently operate in rural areas.

Objectives and Desired Outcome Grading Sheet

SCENARIO ACTIVITIES	SCENARIO SUB-ACTIVITIES	DESIRED OUTCOME
Practice flying the rectangular course, one of the ground reference maneuvers.	–	Practice
Learn the basic features of a sectional chart.	Identify and describe the information provided about KPUW.	Discuss/Explain
Learn how to orient yourself and practice basic navigation by comparing the view of the scenery in X-Plane or FSX with other sources of information.	When you're ready to return to Pullman, use the heading indicator and the interactive map and the Seattle sectional chart to help you navigate to the airport.	Practice

CHAPTER 17

Private Pilot Lesson 4: A Short Cross-Country Flight

As in the generic FITS syllabus, this lesson involves a short flight to a nearby town so that you can tour a manufacturing plant.

Scenario

This is a quick flight, but it gives you the opportunity to learn about essential procedures and skills that you should apply whenever you fly. As you cruise toward your destination, you should frequently consider how you would deal with various situations, such as unexpected changes in the weather, problems with the airplane, or distractions caused by passengers.

Objectives

The primary goals of this flight are:

- Making a normal takeoff and climb to cruise altitude (see Figure 17-1)
- Completing a short cross-country flight to practice aircraft control and basic navigation (pilotage) skills.

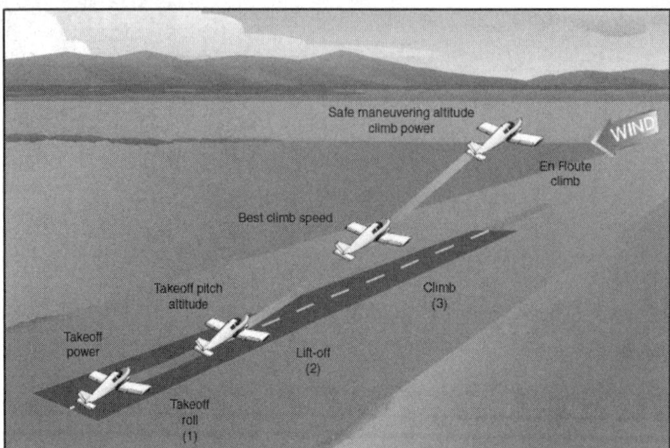

Figure 17-1: A normal takeoff and climb as shown in Figure 5-1 of the *Airplane Flying Handbook*

Secondary goals include introducing:

- The basics of aircraft performance and weight and balance calculations
- The basics of obtaining a preflight briefing
- The information in the Airport/Facilities Directory (A/FD) and related resources

You should also use this short flight to practice the basics of risk assessment and aeronautical decision making (ADM).

Completion Standards

The detailed goals for this lesson are outlined in the table at the end of this chapter. In general, before moving on to the next lesson, you should understand:

- The procedures for a normal takeoff and climb
- The fundamental concepts of aircraft performance and weight-and-balance
- The basic procedure for obtaining a preflight weather briefing
- How to find information about airports in the A/FD

You can also evaluate your performance by reviewing the *Airplane Flying Handbook* for information about common errors (in the sections about normal takeoffs).

References and Resources

To prepare for this lesson, review the following references and resources. The AOPA Air Safety Institute publications are valuable supplements to the official information in the FAA references.

TITLE	CHAPTER/SECTION	TOPIC/NOTES
Pilot's Handbook of Aeronautical Knowledge	Chapter 4, "Aerodynamics of Flight"	Weight and Balance (p. 4-35)
	Chapter 9, "Weight and Balance"	Review all sections
	Chapter 10, "Aircraft Performance"	Review all sections in pages 10-1–10-13
	Chapter 12, "Aviation Weather Services"	Aviation Weather Reports (p. 12-6) and Aviation Forecasts (p. 12-10)
	Chapter 15, "Navigation"	Measurement of Direction (p. 15-5) and Effect of Wind (p. 15-9)
Airplane Flying Handbook	Chapter 5, "Takeoff and Departure Climbs"	Review pages 5-1–5-4
Private Pilot Practical Test Standards	Task IV A: Normal and Crosswind Takeoff and Climb	Page 1-10
	Task VII: Navigation	Page 1-24
AOPA ASI Safety Advisor *Mastering Takeoffs and Landings*	–	–
AOPA ASI Safety Advisor *Operations at Nontowered Airports*	–	–

CROSS-REFERENCE **For more information about the references and resources that complement the lessons in this book, see Chapter 2.**

Preflight Briefing

This lesson begins with your Cessna 172 at Martin Field (S95) at College Place, WA (a small town just southwest of Walla Walla). Perform a normal takeoff and climb to a cruising altitude of 4,500 ft. You should climb straight ahead and fly a heading of 230° to Hermiston, OR (KHRI), a distance of about 38 nm, as shown in Figure 17-2. The flight will last about 25 minutes, including the time to climb to your cruising altitude, descend, and enter the traffic pattern at KHRI.

It's not necessary to fly the complete traffic pattern and land at KHRI, but you're welcome to try if you like.

Location and Weather

The lesson begins with your Skyhawk ready for takeoff from runway 23 at Martin Field (S95). The skies are mostly clear with light winds from the southwest all along your route.

NOTE **The chart shown in Figure 17-2 shows the course and distance from S95 to KHRI as depicted on SkyVector. For this and future flights, you can use the flight plan feature on SkyVector to draw course lines on interactive virtual charts and to show distance and flight time information in the Flight Plan box. To learn more about using the flight plan feature on SkyVector, see the help video at that website.**

Figure 17-2: The course from Martin Field to Hermiston as shown on the Seattle sectional chart on SkyVector

Situations and Flights

This lesson uses the following files for X-Plane and FSX:

- X-Plane: `Wiley-SBT-PrivatePilot-Lesson-04.sit`
- FSX: `Wiley-SBT-PrivatePilot-Lesson-04.flt`

CROSS-REFERENCE **For more information about using Situations (X-Plane) and Flights (FSX), see Chapter 10.**

Tips for This Lesson

Here are a few suggestions to help you get the most from this lesson:

- The simulated weather is set for this flight, but it's a useful exercise to obtain and review real-time weather information before each flight.
- Practice getting weather information using online sources such as the Aviation Digital Data Service (ADDS) and Aviation Weather Center (AWC), and at unofficial resources for pilots such as NavMonster. You can find links to these resources at this book's website.
- Information about airports in the A/FD is provided at this book's website or online at `http://SkyVector.com`, `http://AirNav.com`, and similar sites.
- Use the view features in X-Plane and FSX to shrink or hide the instrument panel as you fly so that you get a better view of the landscape.
- Review the guidance about flying techniques in Chapters 11 and 12 of this book. The configuration tables for the Cessna 172 can help you quickly establish and maintain stable climb, cruise, and descent conditions.
- Soon after you reach cruise altitude, you should see the Columbia River ahead and to the right. Compare its appearance in X-Plane or FSX to its depiction on the sectional chart.
- Use the interactive map in X-Plane or FSX occasionally to help you track your position. The interactive map is especially helpful as you approach the Hermiston airport.
- As you approach Cold Springs (a lake northeast of KHRI), begin a descent to 1,440 ft. (the traffic pattern altitude at KHRI). The lake should be clearly visible in either X-Plane or FSX.

- Plan to fly about two miles south of the airport so that you can enter the left-hand traffic pattern for runway 22.
- As you approach KHRI, in X-Plane you should see a pair of small white lights that can help you spot the runway at KHRI. In FSX, you should see a pair of red lights. These lights are a *visual approach slope indicator* (VASI), which is available at many airports.

What-Ifs

This is a typical short flight, but you shouldn't become complacent about the weather, navigation, or your passengers. Keep the following considerations in mind as you fly toward KHRI:

- What available resources (including the autopilot) can you use to help you manage all of the tasks involved in flying the airplane?
- Frequently consider how you should respond to a passenger who needs assistance, a change in the weather, or other unexpected circumstances.
- For an additional challenge, assume that a passenger asks you to make a short detour for sightseeing along the Columbia River. Can you safely and confidently change course, enjoy the sights, and then resume the flight to KHRI? Or should you stick to the original plan?

Objectives and Desired Outcome Grading Sheet

SCENARIO ACTIVITIES	SCENARIO SUB-ACTIVITIES	DESIRED OUTCOME
Practice performing a normal takeoff and climb.	–	Practice
Understand the basic process for obtaining information about the weather.	Use official and supplementary web resources to get weather reports and forecasts.	Describe/Practice
Understand how to obtain information about the airports you intend to use.	Use the A/FD and unofficial resources to learn airports along your route.	Describe/Practice
Understand the fundamentals of aircraft performance and weight-and-balance calculations.	Review the information and procedures described in the *Pilot's Handbook of Aeronautical Knowledge.*	Describe/Practice

CHAPTER

18

Private Pilot Lesson 5: Another Short Cross-Country Flight

This is another short flight, but it gives you the opportunity to practice essential procedures and skills that you should apply whenever you fly.

Scenario

As in the generic FITS syllabus, this lesson involves a flight to a nearby airport so that you can deliver an essential part to a shop that is restoring a classic car that you own. You are under pressure to get the part to the shop quickly. If you don't arrive today, the project will sit idle for at least a week.

As you cruise toward your destination, you should frequently consider how you would deal with various situations, such as unexpected changes in the weather, problems with the airplane, or other distractions.

Objectives

The primary goals of this flight are:

- Making a normal takeoff and climbing to cruise altitude
- Completing a short cross-country flight to practice aircraft control and basic navigation (pilotage) skills

Secondary goals include:

- Reviewing the basics of aircraft performance and weight-and-balance calculations (see Figure 18-1)
- Practicing the process for obtaining a preflight briefing
- Learning about NOTAMs, which provide current information about the status of airports, navigation aids, and other critical information
- Introducing the procedures for contacting a control tower

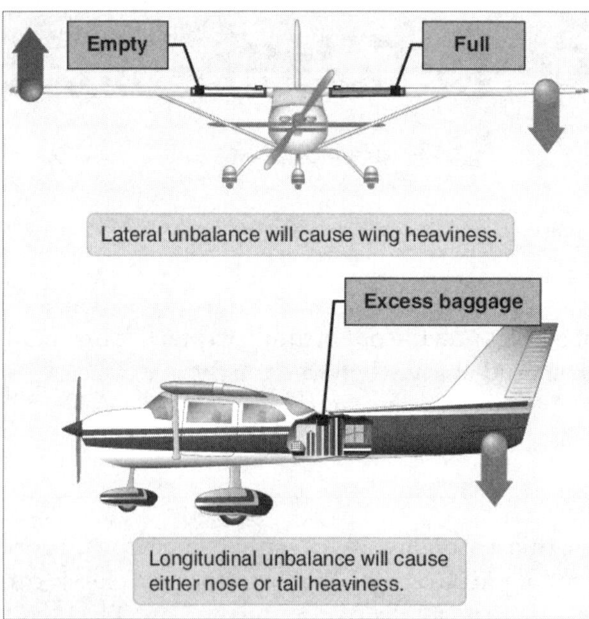

Figure 18-1: Some effects of improper aircraft loading, as shown in Figure 9-1 of the *Pilot's Handbook of Aeronautical Knowledge*

As in all lessons at this stage of your training, you should also use this short flight to practice the basics of risk assessment and aeronautical decision making (ADM).

Completion Standards

The detailed goals for this lesson are outlined in the table at the end of this chapter. In general, before moving on to the next lesson, you should understand:

- The procedures for a normal takeoff and climb

- The fundamental concepts of aircraft performance and weight-and-balance
- The basic procedures for obtaining a preflight briefing
- How to find information about airports in the A/FD

You can also evaluate your performance by reviewing the information about common errors associated with normal takeoffs on p. 5-4 of the *Airplane Flying Handbook*.

References and Resources

To prepare for this lesson, review the following references and resources. The AOPA Air Safety Institute publications are valuable supplements to the official information in the FAA references. The AOPA ASI Safety Advisors about airspace and operations at towered airports are especially helpful in preparing for this lesson.

TITLE	CHAPTER/SECTION	TOPIC/NOTES
Pilot's Handbook of Aeronautical Knowledge	Chapter 15, "Navigation"	Review
	Chapter 9, "Weight and Balance"	Review all sections
	Chapter 10, "Aircraft Performance"	Review all sections in pages 10-1–10-13
	Chapter 12, "Aviation Weather Services"	Weather Briefings (p. 12-5)
	Chapter 13, "Airport Operations"	Sources for Airport Data (p. 13-2) and Radio Communications (p. 13-11)
	Chapter 14, "Airspace"	Discussions of Class D on p. 13-13 and p. 14-9
Aeronautical Information Manual (AIM)	Chapter 4, Section 2	Radio Communications Phraseology and Techniques
Airplane Flying Handbook	Chapter 5, "Takeoff and Departure Climbs"	Review pages 5-1–5-4

Continued

(continued)

TITLE	CHAPTER/SECTION	TOPIC/NOTES
Aeronautical Chart Users Guide	Explanation of VFR Terms And Symbols	Review pages 1–3
	VFR Aeronautical Chart Symbols	Aeronautical Information: Airports (p. 11)
Risk Management Handbook	Chapter 6, "Single-Pilot Resource Management"	Review all sections
Private Pilot Practical Test Standards	Task 1 C: Weather Information	Page 1-2
	Task 1 D: Cross-Country Flight Planning	Page 1-2
	Task IV A: Normal and Crosswind Takeoff and Climb	Page 1-10
	Task IV B: Normal and Crosswind Approach and Landing	Page 1-11
	Task VII: Navigation	Page 1-24
AOPA ASI Safety Advisor *Mastering Takeoffs and Landings*	–	–
AOPA ASI Safety Advisor *Operations at Nontowered Airports*	–	–
AOPA ASI Safety Advisor *Operations at Towered Airports*	–	–
AOPA ASI Safety Advisor *Airspace for Everyone*	–	–
Using the Communications Radios	X-Plane Operations Manual	Controlling Instruments and Avionics with the Mouse (p. 65)
	FSX Learning Center	Using the Radios

CROSS-REFERENCE **For more information about the references and resources that complement the lessons in this book, see Chapter 2.**

Preflight Briefing

This lesson begins with your Cessna 172 ready for takeoff at the end of runway 23 at the Pullman, WA airport (KPUW). You plan to fly to Ephrata, WA (KEPH), a distance of about 105 nm, as shown in Figure 18-2. The estimated time en route is one hour, and you plan to cruise at 4,500 ft.

Perform a normal takeoff and climb to 4,500 ft. You should climb straight ahead for a couple of minutes and then turn right to a heading of 270° toward KEPH.

As you approach the Moses Lake airport (KMWH), you must contact the control tower for permission to fly through its Class D airspace. The air traffic control features in X-Plane and FSX aren't especially useful for training, but you can still tune the communication radios and, using the procedures described in the references for this lesson, practice communication techniques. You can assume that the tower at Moses Lake will clear you to fly through (transition) its airspace on your way to KEPH.

Location and Weather

The lesson begins with your Skyhawk ready for takeoff from runway 23 at Pullman, WA (KPUW). The skies are mostly clear with light winds from the southwest along your route.

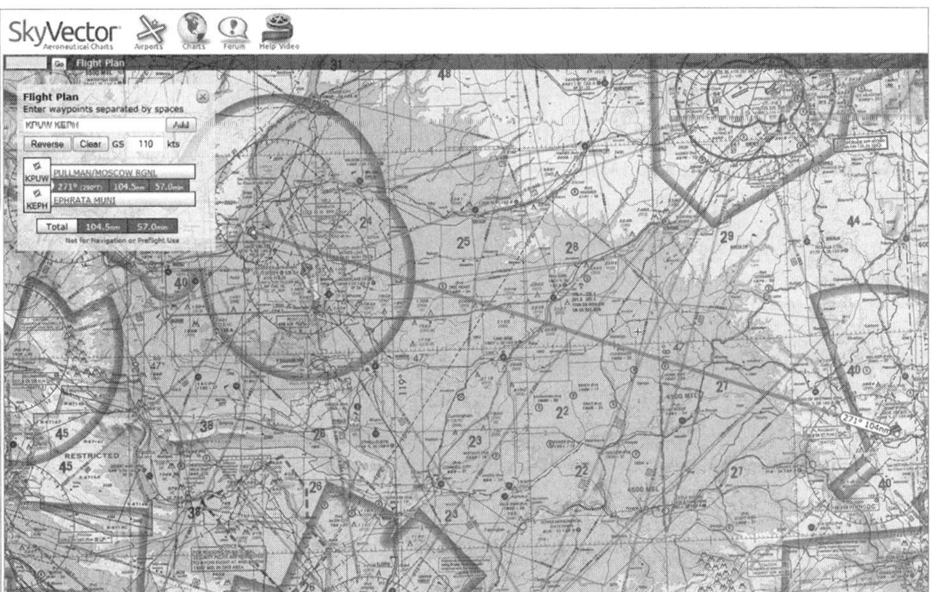

Figure 18-2: The course from KPUW to KEPH as shown on the Seattle sectional chart on SkyVector

NOTAMs

Notices to Airmen (NOTAMs) provide current information about the status of airports, navigation aids, and other critical information that isn't published on charts and airport guides. The NOTAM system was developed in the teletype age; and like many aspects of aviation, information about closed runways, temporary obstructions, air shows, and other potential hazards is presented in a standard format replete with arcane abbreviations.

Here are a couple of NOTAMs relevant to your flight to Ephrata:

- EPH 06/017 EPH AIRSPACE UNMANNED ROCKETS 2 NMR EPH319029 17000 AGL/BLW 1500-0500 DLY WEF 1106251500-1106270500
- EPH 06/010 EPH AIRSPACE AEROBATIC ACFT 6500/BLW 2 NMR 1500-0300 DLY TIL 1106270300

As you can probably tell from even a cursory reading, model rockets are being launched northeast of Ephrata, and aerobatic aircraft are practicing within a 2-nm radius of the airport.

To learn more about NOTAMs, see the references associated with this lesson.

Situations and Flights

This lesson uses the following files for X-Plane and FSX:

- X-Plane: `Wiley-SBT-PrivatePilot-Lesson-05.sit`
- FSX: `Wiley-SBT-PrivatePilot-Lesson-05.flt`

CROSS-REFERENCE **For more information about using Situations (X-Plane) and Flights (FSX), see Chapter 10.**

Tips for This Lesson

Here are a few suggestions to help you get the most from this lesson:

- As in previous lessons, practice getting weather information using online sources such as the Aviation Digital Data Service (ADDS) and Aviation Weather Center (AWC), and from unofficial resources for pilots such as NavMonster (`http://www.NavMonster.com/`).
- You can get information about airports via links to the A/FD provided at this book's website or online at `http://SkyVector.com`, `http://AirNav.com`, and similar sites.
- Use the interactive map in X-Plane or FSX occasionally to help you track your position. The interactive map is especially helpful as you approach KEPH.

- Review the sectional chart and try to identify useful checkpoints along your route. When flying an airplane like the Cessna 172, it's a good idea to establish checkpoints about every 20 nm, which translates to 10–15 minutes of flying time.
- Plan to fly about two miles south of KEPH so that you can enter the traffic pattern for runway 21. Follow the procedures for operating at a nontowered airport, and keep an eye out for aerobatic aircraft.

What-Ifs

Keep the following considerations in mind as you fly toward KEPH:

- What available resources (including the autopilot) can you use to help you manage all of the tasks involved in flying the airplane?
- Frequently consider how you should respond to a passenger who needs assistance, a change in the weather, or other unexpected circumstances.
- For an additional challenge, assume that about halfway to KEPH, clouds begin to obscure your path. You decide to return to KPUW. Can you reverse course and navigate back to Pullman?

Objectives and Desired Outcome Grading Sheet

SCENARIO ACTIVITIES	SCENARIO SUB-ACTIVITIES	DESIRED OUTCOME
Make a normal takeoff and climb.	–	Practice
Review the concepts and procedures for calculating weight and balance.	–	Describe/Practice
Practice gathering information for a preflight briefing.	Check current and forecast weather, NOTAMs, and review airport information.	Describe/Practice
Review the basics of Class D airspace.	Practice tuning the communication radios in your simulation.	Describe/Explain

CHAPTER 19

Private Pilot Lesson 6: A Trip to a Fly-In Breakfast

As in the generic FITS syllabus, this lesson involves a flight to a nearby airport — this time for a weekend fly-in breakfast.

Scenario

You're flying to a nearby airport for a fly-in breakfast and bringing a friend along. She wants to circle over Newman Lake, where her family has a cabin.

Objectives

The primary goals of this flight are:

- Making a normal takeoff and climbing to cruise altitude
- Completing a short cross-country flight to practice aircraft control and basic navigation (pilotage) skills
- Learning about and practicing steep turns (see Figure 19-1)
- Learning the fundamental principles of stalls and spins
- Understanding the risks involved in maneuvering flight

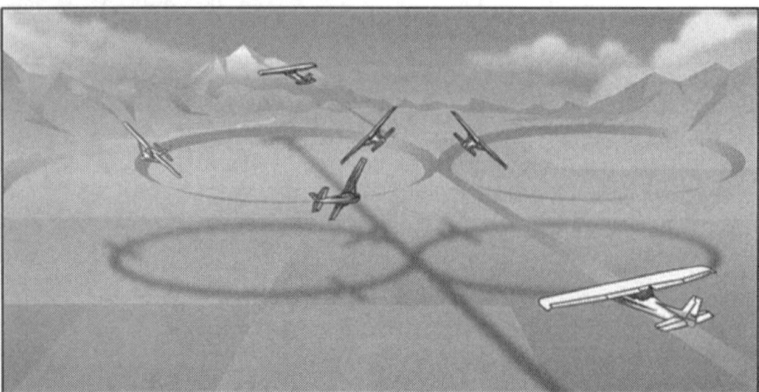

Figure 19-1: Steep turns as shown in Figure 9-1 from the *Airplane Flying Handbook*

Completion Standards

The detailed goals for this lesson are outlined in the table at the end of this chapter. In general, before moving on to the next lesson, you should understand the following:

- Basic principles of slow flight, stalls, and load factors
- Techniques for flying steep turns
- Fundamentals of determining takeoff and landing performance

References and Resources

To prepare for this lesson, review the following references and resources. The AOPA Air Safety Institute publications are valuable supplements to the official information in the FAA references.

TITLE	CHAPTER/SECTION	TOPIC/NOTES
Pilot's Handbook of Aeronautical Knowledge	Chapter 4, "Aerodynamics of Flight"	Stalls (p. 4-22) and Load Factors (p. 4-28)
	Chapter 9, "Weight and Balance"	Review all sections
	Chapter 10, "Aircraft Performance"	Climb Performance (p. 10-6) and Takeoff and Landing Performance (p. 10-11)
	Chapter 13, "Airport Operations"	Airport Markings and Signs (p. 13-4), Visual Approach Slope Indicator (VASI) (p. 13-7), Traffic Patterns (p. 13-20)

TITLE	CHAPTER/SECTION	TOPIC/NOTES
Airplane Flying Handbook	Chapter 4, "Slow Flight, Stalls, and Spins"	Review all sections
	Chapter 9, "Performance Maneuvers"	Steep Turns (p. 9-1)
Private Pilot Practical Test Standards	Task IV A: Normal and Crosswind Takeoff and Climb	Page 1-10
	Task IV B: Normal and Crosswind Approach and Landing	Page 1-11
	Task V: Performance Maneuvers	Steep Turns (p. 1-21)
	Task VIII: Slow Flight and Stalls	Page 1-26
AOPA ASI Safety Advisor *Mastering Takeoffs and Landings*	–	–
AOPA ASI Safety Advisor *Operations at Nontowered Airports*	–	Note the recommendations for exiting the traffic pattern
AOPA ASI Safety Advisor *Maneuvering Flight – Hazardous to Your Health?*	–	–
AOPA ASI Interactive Safety Course *Essential Aerodynamics: Stalls, Spins, and Safety*	–	–

CROSS-REFERENCE **For more information about the references and resources that complement the lessons in this book, see Chapter 2.**

Preflight Briefing

This lesson begins with your Cessna 172 ready for takeoff to the north from the Deer Park, WA, airport (KDEW). You plan to fly southeast to Coeur d'Alene, ID (KCOE), with a detour to overfly Newman Lake (see Figure 19-2). Total distance for this flight is about 29 nm. The estimated time en route, including an allowance for a couple of turns above the lake, is about 20 minutes. You plan to cruise at 5,500 ft.

When you arrive over Newman Lake, fly a few steep turns, both to the left and right.

Location and Weather

The lesson begins with your Skyhawk ready for takeoff from runway 34 at KDEW. The skies are mostly clear with light winds from the north along your route.

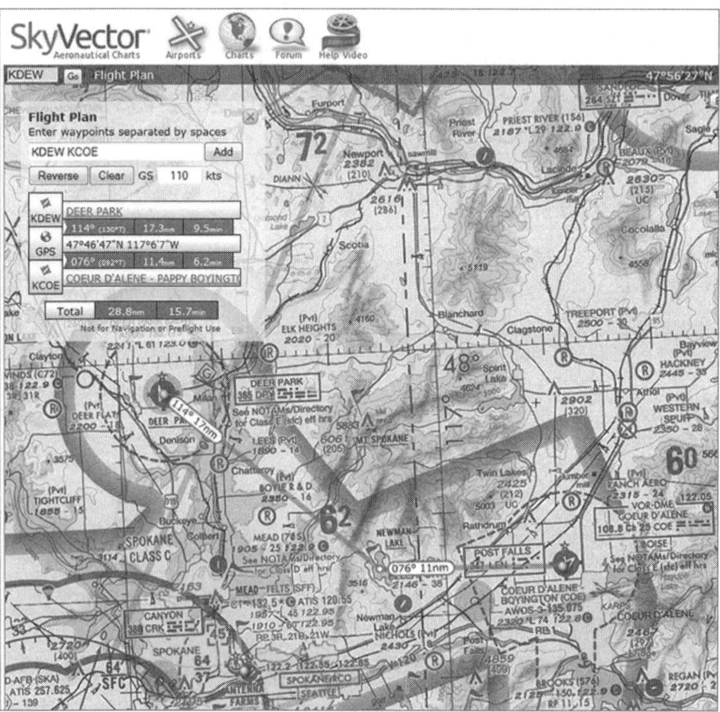

Figure 19-2: The course from KDEW to KCOE as shown on the Seattle sectional chart on SkyVector

Situations and Flights

This lesson uses the following files for X-Plane and FSX:

- X-Plane: `Wiley-SBT-PrivatePilot-Lesson-06.sit`
- FSX: `Wiley-SBT-PrivatePilot-Lesson-06.flt`

CROSS-REFERENCE **For more information about using Situations (X-Plane) and Flights (FSX), see Chapter 10.**

Tips for This Lesson

Here are a few suggestions to help you get the most from this lesson:

- Considering the information in the AOPA ASI Safety Advisor *Operations at Nontowered Airports*, what is the best way to depart the traffic pattern at KDEW and begin navigating toward Newman Lake?
- When flying the steep turns, shrink or hide the instrument panel and use the natural horizon to enter and fly the maneuver (see Figure 19-3).
- If the airplane starts to descend during a turn, shallow the bank before attempting to increase the pitch attitude.
- Review the common errors in the performance of steep turns in the *Airplane Flying Handbook.*

Figure 19-3: View from the pilot's seat during a steep turn in X-Plane

What-Ifs

Keep the following considerations in mind as you fly toward KCOE:

- How would you respond to your passenger's request to fly over the cabin at a low altitude?
- What would you do if your passenger asked you to change the bank angle so that she can get better pictures of the cabin?
- What would you do if the passenger opened her window to get better pictures?

Objectives and Desired Outcome Grading Sheet

SCENARIO ACTIVITIES	SCENARIO SUB-ACTIVITIES	DESIRED OUTCOME
Make a normal takeoff and climb.	–	Perform
Understand the principles of slow flight, steep turns, and stalls.	–	Describe/Explain
Fly power-off (approach) stalls.	–	Practice
Fly left and right 360° steep turns.	–	Practice

CHAPTER

20

Private Pilot Lesson 7: Ground Reference Maneuvers

As in the generic FITS syllabus, this lesson involves a flight to conduct an aerial survey of properties near an airport. The goal is to fly precise patterns over farm fields and roads. You must compensate for the effect of wind and maintain specific altitudes while maneuvering. At all times you also must keep a lookout for other aircraft and consider where you could make an emergency landing if your airplane experienced a mechanical failure.

Scenario

In this scenario you will take off from McMinnville, OR (KMMV), southwest of Portland, and fly northwest over the nearby farmland. After completing the ground reference maneuvers, you fly to the nearby airport at Aurora, OR (KUAO), join the appropriate traffic pattern, and land.

Objectives

The primary goals of this flight are:

- Practicing ground reference maneuvers: rectangular courses, S-turns across a road (see Figure 20-1), and turns around a point (see Figure 20-2)
- Reviewing and practicing fundamental flight maneuvers and basic navigation
- Reviewing traffic patterns and practicing the normal approach and landing

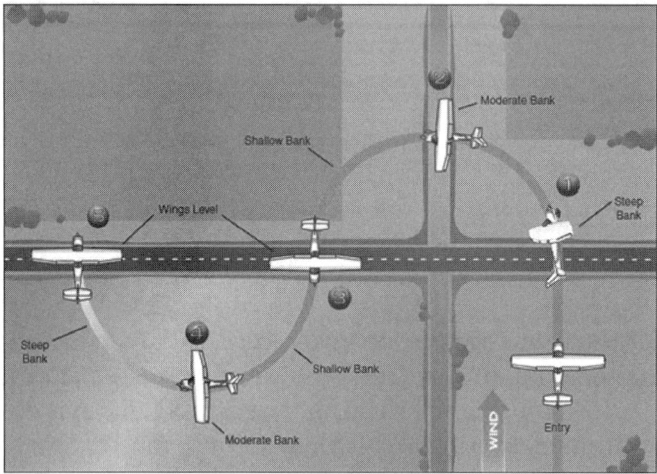

Figure 20-1: S-turns across a road, as shown in Figure 6-5 of the *Airplane Flying Handbook*

You have already practiced flying rectangular courses. Turns around a point and S-turns across a road are the other ground reference maneuvers that you may be required to fly during the private pilot practical test.

At this point in your training, you should also be able perform tasks that you've practiced in earlier lessons. In particular, you should be able to complete maneuvers at the Perform level of the FITS grading standards — that is, consistently within the limits established by the PTS.

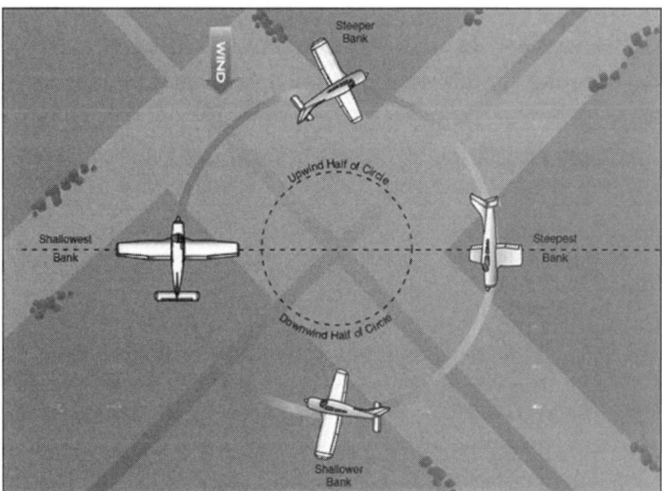

Figure 20-2: Turns around a point, as shown in Figure 6-6 of the *Airplane Flying Handbook*

Completion Standards

The detailed goals for this lesson are outlined in the table at the end of this chapter. In general, before moving on to the next lesson, you should be able to:

- Recognize and adjust for the effects of wind drift.
- Identify appropriate areas to conduct maneuvers at low altitudes.
- When flying new maneuvers, maintain altitude ±250 feet, roll out on the appropriate heading ±20 degrees, maintain bank angle within ±10 degrees, and fly at the appropriate airspeed within ±10 knots.

References and Resources

To prepare for this lesson, review the following references. The resources at the AOPA Flight Training website and the AOPA Air Safety Institute publications are valuable supplements to the official information in the FAA references.

TITLE	CHAPTER/SECTION	TOPIC/NOTES
Pilot's Handbook of Aeronautical Knowledge	Chapter 13, "Airport Operations"	Traffic Patterns (p. 13-10)
Airplane Flying Handbook	Chapter 6, "Ground Reference Maneuvers"	S-Turns Across a Road (p. 6-6), Turns Around a Point (p. 6-7)
	Chapter 7, "Airport Traffic Patterns"	Review all sections (p. 7-1)
	Chapter 8, "Approaches and Landings"	Normal Approach and Landing (p. 8-1–8-7)
Private Pilot Practical Test Standards	Task VI: Ground Reference Maneuvers	S-Turns (p. 1-22) and Turns Around a Point (p. 1-23)
	Task IV: Takeoffs, Landings, and Go-Arounds	Normal and Crosswind Takeoff and Climb (p. 1-10) and Normal and Crosswind Approach and Landing (p. 1-11)
AOPA ASI Safety Advisor *Operations at Nontowered Airports*	–	Note the recommendations for exiting and entering the traffic pattern.
AOPA ASI Safety Advisor *Mastering Takeoffs and Landings*	–	–
AOPA ASI Safety Advisor *Maneuvering Flight – Hazardous to Your Health?*	–	–
AOPA Flight Training website	Pre-Solo Flying Skills	Ground Reference Maneuvers
AOPA Flight Training magazine	April 2010	"Turns around a point"

CROSS-REFERENCE **For more information about the references and resources that complement the lessons in this book, see Chapter 2.**

Preflight Briefing

This lesson begins with your Cessna 172 ready for takeoff from runway 22 at McMinnville, OR (KMMV). You plan to fly over the farm fields northwest of the airport at 2,500 ft. and then fly several sequences of ground reference maneuvers (rectangular patterns, S-turns across a road, and turns around a point). You can use the boundaries and intersections of fields and roads as reference points. Take as much time as you like, and then fly to the Aurora, OR (KUAO) airport about 16 nm miles east-northeast of KMMV, join the traffic pattern, and land.

Location and Weather

The lesson begins with your Skyhawk on the ground at KMMV (see Figure 20-3). The skies are mostly clear with light winds from the southwest.

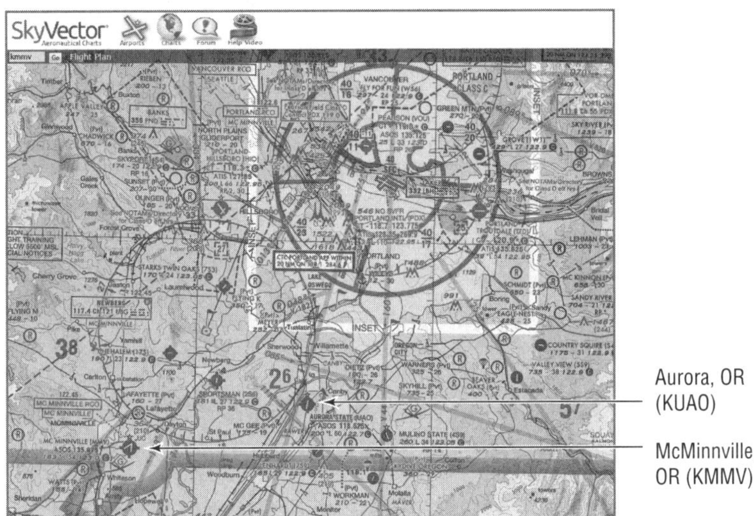

Figure 20-3: The area around KMMV, as shown on the Seattle sectional chart on SkyVector

Situations and Flights

This lesson uses the following files for X-Plane and FSX:

- X-Plane: `Wiley-SBT-PrivatePilot-Lesson-07.sit`
- FSX: `Wiley-SBT-PrivatePilot-Lesson-07.flt`

CROSS-REFERENCE **For more information about using Situations (X-Plane) and Flights (FSX), see Chapter 10.**

Tips for This Lesson

Here are a few suggestions to help you get the most from this lesson:

- Don't fixate on the ground reference points as you fly the maneuvers. Scan for other traffic and cross-check the instruments occasionally to verify your altitude and airspeed.

- Shrink or hide the instrument panel as you fly the ground reference maneuvers.
- Use the interactive map in X-Plane or FSX occasionally to help you track your position and to show your path over the ground. The ground tracks help you assess how well you've flown the ground reference maneuvers. The interactive map is also helpful when you finish the maneuvers and prepare to fly to KUAO.
- Use the A/FD information at `http://SkyVector.com` or other resources to determine the runway orientations and lengths, traffic pattern altitudes, and other critical data about KMMV and KUAO.

What-Ifs

Keep the following considerations in mind as you fly this scenario:

- Before you begin a ground reference maneuver, assess the general area and make sure you have located areas where you could make an off-airport landing if necessary.
- Fly precisely, but smoothly. If your flight path deviates substantially from the standard, stop the maneuver and set up for another try.

Objectives and Desired Outcome Grading Sheet

SCENARIO ACTIVITIES	SCENARIO SUB-ACTIVITIES	DESIRED OUTCOME
Make a normal takeoff and climb.	–	Perform
Fly rectangular courses.	–	Perform
Practice S-turns across a road.	–	Practice
Practice turns around a point.	–	Practice
Follow recommended procedures for seeing and avoiding other aircraft.	–	Perform
Follow recommended procedures for entering and flying the airport traffic pattern.	–	Perform
Fly a normal approach and landing.	–	Practice

CHAPTER

21

Private Pilot Lesson 8: Evening Flight

In the generic FITS syllabus, this lesson is flown in an FTD.

Scenario

You plan to meet a friend and make a late afternoon flight from Arlington, WA (KAWO) to Friday Harbor, WA (KFHR), for dinner (see Figure 21-1). You will meet at KAWO airport 5:00 p.m. sharp, and you must return no later than 8:00 p.m. The skies are cloudy with isolated rain showers.

In addition, when you check the airplane, you discover that only 15 gallons of fuel are in the tanks, and the fuel truck isn't available.

Figure 21-1: Approaching KFHR in X-Plane

Objectives

The primary goals of this flight are:

- Identifying and assessing the potential hazards of the proposed flight, and determining how the risks can be reduced or eliminated
- Learning how to set expectations when flying with passengers or meeting people at your destination
- Learning about the challenges associated with night flight
- Gathering information about services available at airports
- Expanding preflight planning skills, especially gathering and understanding information about the weather
- Reviewing flight planning, especially fuel requirements
- Reviewing and practicing fundamental flight maneuvers
- Reviewing and practicing normal takeoffs and landings

Completion Standards

The detailed goals for this lesson are outlined in the table at the end of this chapter. In general, before moving on to the next lesson, you should:

- Be able to collect and understand information about services available at airports.
- Understand the basic procedures for evaluating and mitigating risks associated with a flight.
- Understand the fundamentals of managing the fuel supply in your aircraft.
- Understand the process for obtaining a preflight weather briefing.
- Understand the major issues associated with flying at night.

References and Resources

To prepare for this lesson, review the following references and resources. The resources at the AOPA Flight Training website and the AOPA Air Safety Institute publications are valuable supplements to the official information in the FAA references.

TITLE	CHAPTER/SECTION	TOPIC/NOTES
Pilot's Handbook of Aeronautical Knowledge	Chapter 11, "Weather Theory"	Clouds (p. 11-15), Ceiling (p. 11-17), and Visibility (p. 11-18)
	Chapter 12, "Aviation Weather Services"	Weather Briefings (p. 12-5)
	Chapter 13, "Airport Operations"	Airport Lighting (p. 13-6) and Runway Lighting (p. 13-8)
	Chapter 14, "Airspace"	Class C Airspace (p. 14-2) and Basic VFR Weather Minimums (p. 14-7)
	Chapter 16, "Aeromedical Factors"	Vision in Flight (p. 16-17)
	Chapter 17, "Aeronautical Decision-Making"	Review all sections
Airplane Flying Handbook	Chapter 10, "Night Operations"	Review all sections
Private Pilot Practical Test Standards	Task I: Preflight Preparation	Cross-Country Flight Planning (p. 1-2)
Risk Management Handbook	Chapter 3, "Identifying and Mitigating Risk"	Review all sections
	Chapter 4, "Assessing Risk"	Review all sections
AOPA ASI Safety Advisor *Airspace for Everyone*	–	–
AOPA ASI interactive course *Say It Right: Mastering Radio Communication*	–	–
AOPA ASI Safety Advisor *Do the Right Thing – Decision Making for Pilots*	–	–
AOPA ASI Safety Advisor *Fuel Awareness*	–	–
AOPA ASI interactive course *Do the Right Thing: Decision Making for Pilots*	–	–
AOPA ASI interactive course *A Pilot's Guide to Flight Service*	–	–

CROSS-REFERENCE For more information about the references and resources that complement the lessons in this book, see Chapter 2.

Preflight Briefing

This lesson begins with your Cessna 172 ready for takeoff from the Arlington, WA airport (KAWO). You plan to fly northwest to Friday Harbor, WA (KFHR), a popular destination in the San Juan Islands. The straight-line distance for this flight is about 41 nm, and flight time is about 25 minutes, including time to climb to a cruising altitude of 4500 ft.

Note that the direct course for this flight passes directly through the Class C airspace around Naval Air Station Whidbey Island. If you follow that route — and you may not have enough fuel to fly around Whidbey's airspace — you must be familiar with the requirements for operating in Class C airspace.

Location and Weather

The lesson begins with your Skyhawk ready for takeoff from runway 34 at KAWO. A broken layer of clouds is reported at about 5,000 ft., all along your route (see Figure 21-2). Winds are generally from the north. As you approach KFHR, note that both runways 16 and 34 use a right-hand traffic pattern.

Figure 21-2: The course from KAWO to KFHR as shown on the Seattle sectional chart on SkyVector.

Situations and Flights

This lesson uses the following files for X-Plane and FSX:

- X-Plane: `Wiley-SBT-PrivatePilot-Lesson-08.sit`
- FSX: `Wiley-SBT-PrivatePilot-Lesson-08.flt`

CROSS-REFERENCE **For more information about using Situations (X-Plane) and Flights (FSX), see Chapter 10.**

Tips for This Lesson

Here are a few suggestions to help you get the most from this lesson:

- Review the regulations that specify the basic weather minimums for VFR flight (14 CFR 91.155).
- Review the procedures for operating in Class C airspace. You don't have to use the ATC features in X-Plane or FSX — just practice what you would say and the expected responses from ATC. The AOPA ASI interactive course *Say It Right: Mastering Radio Communication* offers excellent guidance.

What-Ifs

Keep the following considerations in mind as you fly toward KFHR:

- Weather for the route includes broken clouds at 5,000 ft. with isolated rain showers and areas of virga (rain that falls through the atmosphere but evaporates prior to striking the ground). How will you see and avoid rain showers and areas of reduced visibility after the sun sets?
- If flight at 4,500 ft. isn't advisable, what other cruise altitudes can you use?
- If you needed assistance from air traffic control during the flight, which facility would be best able to help, and how would you contact it?

Objectives and Desired Outcome Grading Sheet

SCENARIO ACTIVITIES	SCENARIO SUB-ACTIVITIES	DESIRED OUTCOME
Obtain and interpret a standard preflight weather briefing.	Use available web resources such as ADDS and NavMonster.	Describe/Practice
Estimate fuel required to complete a flight.	–	Describe/Practice
Collect information about services available at an airport.	–	Describe/Practice
Describe the major issues associated with flying at night.	–	Describe/Practice

CHAPTER

22

Private Pilot Lesson 9: Charity Flight

In the generic FITS syllabus, this lesson proposes a flight to an airport about 150 miles from your home field.

Scenario

This scenario involves a flight from Sanderson Field (KSHN) near Shelton, WA, to Newport, OR (KONP).

As in the FITS syllabus, you have a mission to fly. Assume that you are a volunteer pilot for a medical airlift program such as the Air Charity Network (aircharitynetwork.org) that transports patients and vital medical supplies, usually between airports that aren't served by the airlines. On this flight from KSHN (see Figure 22-1), you're carrying a perishable antivenin that must be delivered to Tillamook within two hours.

NOTE **To learn more about the many ways that general aviation (all types of flying except military and scheduled airline flights) supports communities with vital services, visit the website `www.gaservesamerica.com`, hosted by AOPA.**

Objectives

The primary goals of this flight are:

- Identifying and assessing the potential hazards of the proposed flight, and determining how the risks can be reduced or eliminated
- Gathering information about services available at airports
- Expanding preflight planning skills, especially gathering and understanding information about the weather
- Honing your basic navigation skills (pilotage)
- Reviewing and practicing normal takeoffs and landings

Figure 22-1: Your Cessna 172 on runway 23 at KSHN, as shown in FSX

Completion Standards

The detailed goals for this lesson are outlined in the table at the end of this chapter. In general, before moving on to the next lesson, you should:

- Be able to collect and understand information about services available at airports.
- Understand the basic procedures for evaluating and mitigating risks associated with a flight.

- Understand the fundamentals of managing the fuel supply in your aircraft.
- Understand the process for obtaining a preflight weather briefing.
- Understand the major issues associated with flying at night.

References and Resources

To prepare for this lesson, review the following references and resources. The resources at the AOPA Flight Training website and the AOPA Air Safety Institute publications are valuable supplements to the official information in the FAA references.

TITLE	CHAPTER/SECTION	TOPIC/NOTES
Pilot's Handbook of Aeronautical Knowledge	Chapter 11, "Weather Theory"	Fronts (p. 11-18–11-22)
	Chapter 12, "Aviation Weather Services"	Aviation Weather Reports (p. 12-6), Aviation Forecasts (p. 12-10)
	Chapter 13, "Airport Operations"	Airport Lighting (p. 13-6) and Runway Lighting (p. 13-8)
	Chapter 15, "Navigation"	Flight Diversion (p. 15-34)
	Chapter 16, "Aeromedical Factors"	Stress (p. 16-11), Fatigue (p. 16-12), Dehydration and Heatstroke (p. 16-12)
	Chapter 17, "Aeronautical Decision-Making"	Review all sections
Airplane Flying Handbook	Chapter 16 "Emergency Procedures"	Review all sections
General Aviation Pilot's Guide to Preflight Weather Planning	–	This handy pamphlet, published by the FAA, offers up-to-date tips about weather briefings.

Continued

(continued)

TITLE	CHAPTER/SECTION	TOPIC/NOTES
Private Pilot Practical Test Standards	Task I: Preflight Preparation	Cross-Country Flight Planning (p. 1-2)
AOPA ASI Safety Advisor *Volunteer Pilots: Recommendations for Enhanced Safety*	–	–
AOPA ASI Safety Advisor *Do the Right Thing – Decision Making for Pilots*	–	–
AOPA ASI Interactive Safety Course *Do the Right Thing: Decision Making for Pilots*	–	–
AOPA ASI Interactive Safety Course *A Pilot's Guide to Flight Service*	–	–

CROSS-REFERENCE **For more information about the references and resources that complement the lessons in this book, see Chapter 2.**

Preflight Briefing

This scenario begins with your Cessna 172 ready for takeoff from runway 23 at Sanderson Field (KSHN) near Shelton, WA, for a flight to Newport, OR (KONP), a direct distance of 164 nm. Your initial cruise altitude is 5,500 ft.

NOTE **The AOPA Air Safety Institute (formerly the Air Safety Foundation) offers a free AOPA ASF Flight Planner at the AOPA Flight Training website. This two-page form (PDF) helps you collect all the information that you need for a cross-country flight, and it includes an excellent template for a flight log to track your progress en route.**

Location and Weather

The flight from KSHN to KONP (see Figure 22-2) should require about 1 hour 30 minutes to complete, assuming light winds aloft. Reports and forecasts indicate good weather for a VFR flight will prevail along your route.

Figure 22-2: The course from KSHN to KONP as shown on the CF-16 WAC chart on SkyVector

Situations and Flights

This lesson uses the following files for X-Plane and FSX:

- X-Plane: `Wiley-SBT-PrivatePilot-Lesson-09.sit`
- FSX: `Wiley-SBT-PrivatePilot-Lesson-09.flt`

CROSS-REFERENCE **For more information about using Situations (X-Plane) and Flights (FSX), see Chapter 10.**

Tips for This Lesson

Here are a few suggestions to help you get the most from this lesson:

- Review the Seattle sectional chart or WAC chart to identify useful checkpoints for your flight.
- Carefully note and gather information about airports along the way that you can use as alternates should problems arise.
- You can accelerate the simulation during cruise flight (for more information, see the guides for X-Plane or FSX) to reduce the time required to complete the flight.

What-Ifs

This lesson includes the "Dice-Based Failure Scheme" described in Chapter 8. At any point during the flight, roll a die, draw a number from a hat, or use another method to select a random number between 1 and 6. Using Table 22-1, find the corresponding mechanical failure or problem to solve, and then take the appropriate action.

Use the tools described in Chapter 17, "Aeronautical Decision-Making," of the *Pilot's Handbook of Aeronautical Knowledge* to help you follow a logical process and use all available resources to resolve the issue. Use the table several times during the flight to test your ability to make good decisions and follow recommended procedures.

Table 22-1: Random Challenges for This Flight

NUMBER	RESULT
1	Low oil pressure
2	Fog reported at KONP
3	Low voltage light (alternator failure)
4	Unusual rate of fuel consumption (fuel leak)
5	Headwinds aloft much stronger than forecast
6	You are developing a headache

Objectives and Desired Outcome Grading Sheet

SCENARIO ACTIVITIES	SCENARIO SUB-ACTIVITIES	DESIRED OUTCOME
Obtain and interpret a standard preflight weather briefing.	Use available web resources such as ADDS and NavMonster.	Describe/Practice
Estimate the fuel required to complete a flight.	–	Describe/Practice
Collect information about services available at an airport.	–	Describe/Practice
Understand basic diversion and emergency procedures.	–	Describe/Practice

CHAPTER 23

Private Pilot Lesson 10: Crosswind Landings

In the generic FITS syllabus, this lesson proposes a flight to a nearby airport. It offers an opportunity to practice skills you've practiced in previous scenarios, and it introduces a new factor: crosswind landings.

Scenario

As in the FITS syllabus, you have an underlying purpose for the flight — a business meeting with an important client.

Objectives

The primary goals of this flight are:

- Applying knowledge and practice from previous lessons to hone your flying and decision-making skills
- Practicing crosswind landings (see Figure 23-1)

Figure 23-1: Crabbed approach, as shown in Figure 8-15 of the *Airplane Flying Handbook*

Completion Standards

The detailed goals for this lesson are outlined in the table at the end of this chapter. In general, before moving on to the next lesson, you should:

- Understand the procedures for evaluating and mitigating risks associated with a flight.
- Understand the process for obtaining a preflight weather briefing.
- Demonstrate your understanding of the techniques applicable to crosswind landings.

References and Resources

To prepare for this lesson, review the following references and resources. The resources at the AOPA Flight Training website and the AOPA Air Safety Institute publications are valuable supplements to the official information in the FAA references.

TITLE	CHAPTER/SECTION	TOPIC/NOTES
Pilot's Handbook of Aeronautical Knowledge	Chapter 12, "Aviation Weather Services"	Aviation Weather Reports (p. 12-6)
	Chapter 13, "Airport Operations"	Wind Direction Indicators (p. 13-10)
Airplane Flying Handbook	Chapter 8, "Approaches and Landings"	Crosswind Approach and Landing (p. 8-13)

TITLE	CHAPTER/SECTION	TOPIC/NOTES
Private Pilot Practical Test Standards	Task IV B: Normal and Crosswind Approach and Landing	p. 1-11
AOPA ASI Safety Advisor *Mastering Takeoffs and Landings*	–	–
AOPA ASI Safety Advisor *ASOS: Automated Surface Observing System*	–	–
AOPA ASI Safety Advisor *WeatherWise*	–	–
AOPA Flight Training website	Students: Solo Flying Skills	Crosswind landings
AOPA Live website	Cross-wind Landings	Video

CROSS-REFERENCE **For more information about the references and resources that complement the lessons in this book, see Chapter 2.**

Preflight Briefing

This scenario begins with your Cessna 172 in the air, a few miles northwest of the Tillamook, OR, airport (KTMK on current charts, listed as S47 in X-Plane and FSX). Like most airports located near a coastline, KTMK is often subject to crosswinds. You must choose the best runway for the conditions and apply the proper techniques to make a crosswind landing.

It's difficult to simulate and fly crosswind conditions in a PC-based simulation with typical flight yokes and joysticks, but you can still observe the effects of a crosswind and practice the basic procedures that you would use in a real crosswind landing. For example, you can fly in a crab to compensate for drift as you approach the runway; and if you turn off the automatic rudder features in your simulation, you can use the twist feature of a joystick to apply rudder and simulate a sideslip. Rudder pedals may help you understand how to apply the proper techniques. In the end, however, there's no substitute for practicing crosswind landings with an instructor in a real airplane.

Location and Weather

As the flight begins, you are a few miles northwest of KTMK (see Figure 23-2). The automated weather reported at the airport indicates winds from the southwest at about 8 knots. The autopilot is on.

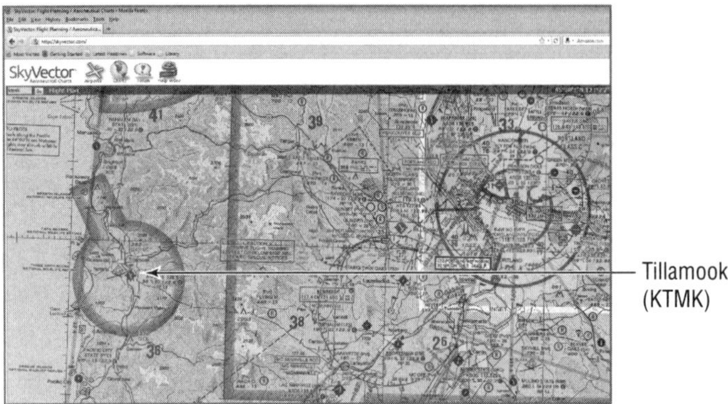

Figure 23-2: The area around KTMK as shown on the Seattle sectional chart on SkyVector

Situations and Flights

This lesson uses the following files for X-Plane and FSX:

- X-Plane: `Wiley-SBT-PrivatePilot-Lesson-10.sit`
- FSX: `Wiley-SBT-PrivatePilot-Lesson-10.flt`

CROSS-REFERENCE **For more information about using Situations (X-Plane) and Flights (FSX), see Chapter 10.**

Here are a few suggestions to help you get the most from this lesson:

- Review the airport information for KTMK on the Seattle sectional chart and in the A/FD.
- KTMK has two runways. Runway 1/19 is 2,910 ft. long. Runway 13/31 is 5,001 ft. long. Choose the best runway given the prevailing winds, your aircraft's performance, and your skills.
- Consider alternative airports if the winds suggest that landing may be difficult.
- If you want to test your crosswind landing skills, try using both runways, even if one would normally be the best choice given the winds.

- Note that the maximum demonstrated crosswind component for the Cessna 172 is 15 knots. This is not strictly a limitation — it is just the maximum value that the manufacturer demonstrated during flight testing — but it's often a good idea to consider it a practical limitation when attempting to land in strong crosswinds.

What-Ifs

You can also use the "Dice-Based Failure Scheme" described in Chapter 8 to add additional challenges for this flight.

At any point during the flight, roll a die, draw a number from a hat, or use another method to select a random number between 1 and 6. Using Table 23-1, find the corresponding problem to solve, and then take the appropriate action.

Table 23-1: Random Challenges for This Flight

NUMBER	RESULT
1	Runway 1/19 is blocked by equipment.
2	Runway 13/31 is blocked by equipment.
3	Wind increases to 25 knots from the west.
4	Weather at KTMK is below VFR minimums.
5	Divert to Scapoose, OR (KSPB).
6	Divert to Aurora, OR (KUAO).

Objectives and Desired Outcome Grading Sheet

SCENARIO ACTIVITIES	SCENARIO SUB-ACTIVITIES	DESIRED OUTCOME
Understand the procedures associated with crosswind landings.	–	Describe/Practice
Understand the resources available at an airport to help you determine wind direction and speed.	–	Describe/Explain

CHAPTER

24

Private Pilot Lesson 11: Preparation for Solo Flight

In the generic FITS syllabus, this lesson includes a short flight and a review of regulations and other requirements in preparation for solo flight. If you're involved in real flight training, you must complete a pre-solo written test administered and graded by your instructor, and meet several specific training requirements specified in 14 CFR Part 61, in particular §61.87. You must also understand key regulations in 14 CFR Part 91, the general operating rules.

Scenario

For the purposes of this book, you can review the relevant resources and references, and, as in the FITS syllabus, take a short practice flight to review what you've learned so far.

Objectives

The primary goals for this flight are:

- Applying knowledge and practice from previous lessons to hone your flying and decision-making skills
- Increasing your understanding of ground operations (see Figure 24-1)

Figure 24-1: The Cessna 172 in X-Plane leaving the runup area at Bremerton, WA (KPWT)

Completion Standards

The detailed goals for this lesson are outlined in the table at the end of this chapter. In general, before moving on to the next lesson, you should:

- Understand the requirements for student solo flights.
- Demonstrate the appropriate knowledge and skills required for solo flight as a student pilot.

References and Resources

To prepare for this lesson, review the following references and resources. The resources at the AOPA Flight Training website and the AOPA Air Safety Institute publications are valuable supplements to the official information in the FAA references.

TITLE	CHAPTER/SECTION	TOPIC/NOTES
Pilot's Handbook of Aeronautical Knowledge	Chapter 1, "Introduction to Flying"	The Student Pilot (p. 1-16–1-21)
	Chapter 13, "Airport Operations"	Review all sections
Airplane Flying Handbook	Chapter 2, "Ground Operations"	Review all sections
Private Pilot Practical Test Standards	Special Emphasis Areas	p. 5
AOPA ASI Safety Advisor *Instructor's Guide to the Pre-Solo Written Test*	–	–
AOPA ASI Interactive Safety Course: *Runway Safety*	–	–
AOPA Flight Training website	Students: Pre-Solo	Several topics cover FAQs and specific issues

CROSS-REFERENCE **For more information about the references and resources that complement the lessons in this book, see Chapter 2.**

Preflight Briefing

This scenario begins with your Cessna 172 on the ground at the Bremerton, WA, airport (KPWT), west of Seattle. KPWT (see Figure 24-2) is often used for student training. Complete your takeoff checks, take off from runway 19, fly to a practice area a few miles south of the airport, and review basic flight maneuvers. When you're ready to return, fly back to KPWT, enter the traffic pattern, and land.

Location and Weather

You have left the runup area and are holding short of runway 19 at KPWT. The automated weather reported at the airport indicates excellent VFR weather with light winds.

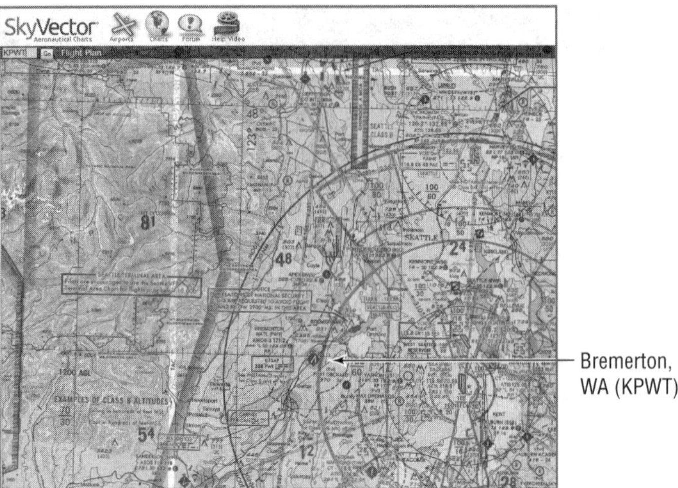

Figure 24-2: The area around KPWT as shown on the Seattle sectional chart on SkyVector

Situations and Flights

This lesson uses the following files for X-Plane and FSX:

- X-Plane: `Wiley-SBT-PrivatePilot-Lesson-11.sit`
- FSX: `Wiley-SBT-PrivatePilot-Lesson-11.flt`

CROSS-REFERENCE **For more information about using Situations (X-Plane) and Flights (FSX), see Chapter 10.**

Tips for This Lesson

Here are a few suggestions to help you get the most from this lesson:

- Review the airport information for KPWT on the Seattle sectional chart and in the A/FD at `http://SkyVector.com`.
- Review the procedures and recommendations described in the AOPA ASI Safety Advisor *Operations at Nontowered Airports.*
- Practice at least one ground reference maneuver, steep turns, slow flight, and approach (power-off) stalls. You can review the standards for all these maneuvers in the Private Pilot PTS.

What-Ifs

You can also use the "Dice-Based Failure Scheme" described in Chapter 8 to add additional challenges for this flight.

At any point during the flight, roll a die, draw a number from a hat, or use another method to select a random number between 1 and 6. Using Table 24-1, find the corresponding problem to solve and then take the appropriate action.

Table 24-1: Random Challenges for This Flight

NUMBER	RESULT
1	Runway 1/19 at KPWT is blocked by a disabled aircraft.
2	Several aircraft report that they are flying in the south practice area you intended to use.
3	A solid layer of clouds is moving in from the southwest.
4	Your engine begins to run roughly.
5	Divert to Shelton, WA (KSHN), southwest of KPWT.
6	Divert to Jefferson County, WA (0S9), north of KPWT.

Objectives and Desired Outcome Grading Sheet

SCENARIO ACTIVITIES	SCENARIO SUB-ACTIVITIES	DESIRED OUTCOME
Understand the procedures associated with crosswind landings.	–	Describe/Practice
Understand the resources available at an airport to help you determine wind direction and speed.	–	Describe/Explain

CHAPTER

25

Private Pilot Lesson 12: First Solo Flight

In the generic FITS syllabus, this lesson is your first supervised solo flight. In real flight training, your instructor watches from the ground as you make your first solo flight, which typically involves three laps around the traffic pattern.

Scenario

This scenario places you in the cockpit, ready to take off at Shelton, WA (KSHN), for three practice landings (see Figure 25-1).

Many student pilots obsess about the number of lessons and total flight hours they require before their first solo flight. Although every syllabus must include the first solo flight at some point, the actual number of lessons and hours of flight time required before that milestone vary considerably. If you fly regularly (at least 2–3 times per week) in a basic airplane from a quiet rural airport, you may be ready to fly alone after 10–12 hours of practice. More typically, student pilots accumulate 15–20 hours of instruction before they're ready to make their first solo flight.

Objectives

The primary goals for this flight are:

- Applying knowledge and practice from previous lessons to hone your flying and decision-making skills
- Increasing your understanding of ground operations

Figure 25-1: The Cessna 172 in FSX on runway 23 at Shelton, WA (KSHN)

Completion Standards

The detailed goals for this lesson are outlined in the table at the end of this chapter. In general, before moving on to the next lesson, you should:

- Understand the requirements for student solo flights.
- Demonstrate the appropriate knowledge and skills required for solo flight as a student pilot.

References and Resources

To prepare for this lesson, review the following references and resources. The resources at the AOPA Flight Training website and the AOPA Air Safety Institute publications are valuable supplements to the official information in the FAA references.

TITLE	CHAPTER/SECTION	TOPIC/NOTES
Pilot's Handbook of Aeronautical Knowledge	Chapter 1, "Introduction to Flying"	The Student Pilot (pp. 1-16–1-21)
	Chapter 13, "Airport Operations"	Review all sections
Airplane Flying Handbook	Chapter 2, "Ground Operations"	Review all sections
AOPA ASI Interactive Safety Course: *Runway Safety*	–	–
AOPA Flight Training website	Students: Pre-Solo	Several topics cover FAQs and specific issues

CROSS-REFERENCE For more information about the references and resources that complement the lessons in this book, see Chapter 2.

Preflight Briefing

This scenario begins with your Cessna 172 on the ground at the Sanderson Field airport (KSHN), southwest of Seattle. Fly the standard traffic pattern and make three landings.

Location and Weather

As the flight begins, you are lined up on runway 23 at KSHN (see Figure 25-2). The automated weather report from the AWOS at the airport indicates excellent VFR weather with light winds.

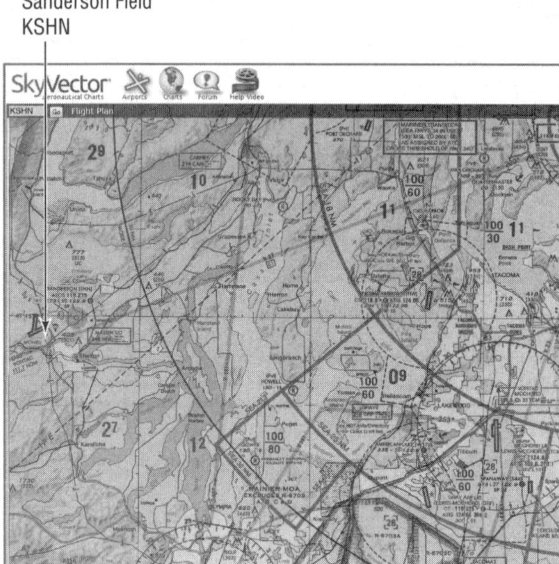

Figure 25-2: The area around KSHN as shown on the Seattle sectional chart on SkyVector

Situations and Flights

This lesson uses the following files for X-Plane and FSX:

- X-Plane: `Wiley-SBT-PrivatePilot-Lesson-12.sit`
- FSX: `Wiley-SBT-PrivatePilot-Lesson-12.flt`

CROSS-REFERENCE **For more information about using Situations (X-Plane) and Flights (FSX), see Chapter 10.**

Tips for This Lesson

Here are a few suggestions to help you get the most from this lesson:

- Review the airport information for KSHN on the Seattle sectional chart and in the A/FD at `http://SkyVector.com`.
- Review the procedures and recommendations described in the AOPA ASI Safety Advisor *Operations at Nontowered Airports*.
- Make all of your landings to a full stop and taxi back to runway 23 via the parallel taxiway before taking off again.

What-Ifs

The only "what-if" for this lesson is whether your instructor will follow an old tradition and cut the tail off your shirt when you taxi back after your final landing. Wise students wear old shirts as the time approaches for their first solo flight.

Objectives and Desired Outcome Grading Sheet

SCENARIO ACTIVITIES	SCENARIO SUB-ACTIVITIES	DESIRED OUTCOME
Understand the requirements for a first solo flight.	–	Describe/Explain
Fly a normal traffic pattern.	–	Perform
Fly a normal approach and landing.	–	Perform

CHAPTER

26

Private Pilot Lesson 13: Review of Basic Maneuvers

In the generic FITS syllabus, this lesson assumes you are an aircraft salesman. You're taking a short flight to demonstrate the key features of the airplane to a customer. You should use the flight to practice basic flight maneuvers, including slow flight, steep turns, stalls, and normal landings. Strive to fly the maneuvers smoothly and precisely, but don't show off. Remember, two of the most dangerous words in aviation are "watch this."

Scenario

In this scenario, you will fly from Pendleton, OR (KPDT), to Pasco, WA (KPSC), a distance of about 36 nm (see Figure 26-1). Both airports have control towers, and this is the first scenario that involves air traffic control.

Figure 26-1: The planned route from KPDT to KPSC as shown on the Seattle sectional chart on SkyVector

Objectives

The primary goals for this flight are:

- Applying knowledge and practice from previous lessons to hone your flying and decision-making skills
- Learning about operations at airports with control towers

Completion Standards

The detailed goals for this lesson are outlined in the table at the end of this chapter. In general, before moving on to the next lesson, you should:

- Be able to apply basic navigation skills on a short cross-country flight.
- Understand the fundamentals of operating at an airport with a control tower.

References and Resources

To prepare for this lesson, review the following references and resources. The resources at the AOPA Flight Training website and the AOPA Air Safety Institute publications are valuable supplements to the official information in the FAA references.

TITLE	CHAPTER/SECTION	TOPIC/NOTES
Pilot's Handbook of Aeronautical Knowledge	Chapter 13, "Airport Operations"	Review all sections
	Chapter 14, "Airspace"	Class D Airspace (p. 14-2)
Airplane Flying Handbook	Chapter 2, "Ground Operations"	Review all sections
Private Pilot Practical Test Standards	Task III: Airport and Seaplane Base Operations	p. 1-9
Aeronautical Information Manual (AIM)	Chapter 4, "Air Traffic Control"	Section 2. Radio Communications Phraseology and Techniques
AOPA ASI Safety Advisor *Operations at Towered Airports*	–	–
AOPA ASI Interactive Safety Course: *Say It Right: Mastering Radio Communication*	–	–

CROSS-REFERENCE **For more information about the references and resources that complement the lessons in this book, see Chapter 2.**

Preflight Briefing

This scenario begins with your Cessna 172 on the ground at the Pendleton, OR, airport (KPDT). The plan is to fly northwest to Pasco, WA (KPSC), a distance of about 36 nm, at a cruising altitude of 4,500 ft. After you practice basic flight maneuvers, plan to land on runway 21L at KPSC.

Location and Weather

As the flight begins, you are ready to take off from runway 25 at KPDT (see Figure 26-2). The automated weather reported at the airport indicates excellent VFR weather with light winds from the west.

Figure 26-2: The Cessna 172 in position on runway 25 at KPDT as shown in FSX

Situations and Flights

This lesson uses the following files for X-Plane and FSX:

- X-Plane: `Wiley-SBT-PrivatePilot-Lesson-12.sit`
- FSX: `Wiley-SBT-PrivatePilot-Lesson-12.flt`

CROSS-REFERENCE **For more information about using Situations (X-Plane) and Flights (FSX), see Chapter 10.**

Tips for This Lesson

Here are a few suggestions to help you get the most from this lesson:

- Review the airport information for KPDT and KPSC on the Seattle sectional chart and in the A/FD at `http://SkyVector.com`.
- Review the procedures and recommendations described in the AOPA ASI Safety Advisor *Operations at Towered Airports*.

What-Ifs

You can also use the "Dice-Based Failure Scheme" described in Chapter 8 to add additional challenges for this flight.

At any point during the flight, roll a die, draw a number from a hat, or use another method to select a random number between 1 and 6. Using Table 26-1, find the corresponding problem to solve, and then take the appropriate action.

Table 26-1: Random Challenges for This Flight

NUMBER	RESULT
1	Winds at KPSC increase to 25 knots.
2	You observe a large fire in a farmer's field south of KPSC.
3	Runway 21L at KPSC is blocked by a disabled aircraft.
4	Your engine begins to run rough.
5	Divert to Prosser, WA (S40).
6	Divert to Walla Walla, WA (KALW).

Objectives and Desired Outcome Grading Sheet

SCENARIO ACTIVITIES	SCENARIO SUB-ACTIVITIES	DESIRED OUTCOME
Follow procedures for operating airports with Class D airspace.	Review the purpose of an ATIS.	Describe/Practice
	Review procedures for contacting ground control and the tower.	Describe/Explain
Review procedures for operating at an airport with parallel runways.	–	Describe/Practice
Review basic flight maneuvers.	–	Perform
Review normal landings.	–	Perform
Review the fundamentals of aeronautical decision making.	–	Explain

CHAPTER

27

Private Pilot Lesson 14: Progress Assessment: Stage Check

In the generic FITS syllabus, this lesson is a progress assessment, often called a "stage check" in flight training.

Scenario

For this scenario, imagine that you are flying with a senior flight instructor who will test your knowledge and observe your flying skills. You should be able to demonstrate any flying skill practiced in earlier lessons, such as the steep turn shown in Figure 27-1.

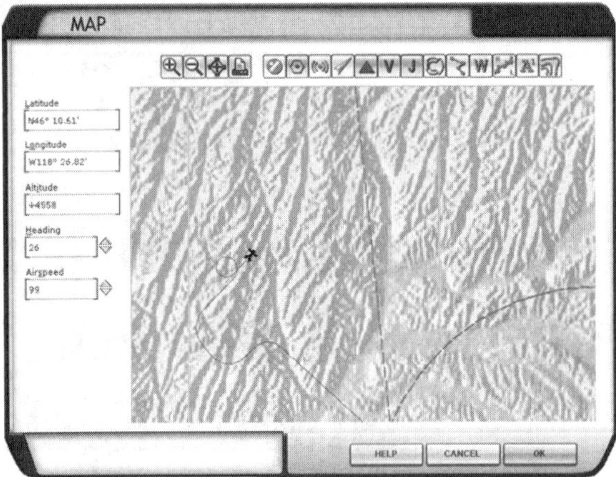

Figure 27-1: Your flight path after a steep turn, as shown on the interactive map in FSX

Objectives

The primary goal for this flight is:

- Applying knowledge and practice from previous lessons to demonstrate your flying and decision-making skills

Completion Standards

The detailed goals for this lesson are outlined in the table at the end of this chapter. In general, before moving on to the next lesson, you should meet the following standards, based on the generic FITS syllabus for this lesson and the PTS:

- During normal and crosswind takeoffs, maintain adequate directional control, use power properly, use proper control deflections to compensate for crosswinds, and lift off at a safe airspeed.
- While climbing, maintain airspeed within ±5 knots and use proper corrections for left-turning tendencies.
- In straight and level flight, maintain altitude within ±150 ft., heading within ±15 degrees, and airspeed within ±10 knots.

- During turns, establish the appropriate bank and maintain altitude within ±150 ft.
- Use power to establish a descent while maintaining airspeed within ±10 knots.
- During flight at various airspeeds and configurations, maintain altitude within ±150 ft., heading within ±15 degrees, and airspeed within ±10 knots.
- While conducting flight at slow airspeeds, maintain altitude within ±150 ft. and heading within ±20 degrees.
- When practicing stalls, recognize the indications of imminent and full stalls and recover promptly.
- During ground reference maneuvers, fly the appropriate ground track, bank no more than 45 degrees, correct for wind drift, and maintain altitude within ±150 ft. and airspeed within ±10 knots.
- During simulated emergencies, follow the recommended procedures while maintaining safe control of the airplane.
- Maintain continuous vigilance for other aircraft, especially in congested areas and when maneuvering.
- Use proper traffic pattern entry and departure procedures.
- While flying in the traffic pattern, maintain the recommended traffic pattern altitude within ±150 ft., recommended airspeeds within ±5 knots, and correct for wind drift.
- When performing go-arounds, maintain safe control of the aircraft at all times while following the recommended procedures.
- During normal and crosswind landings, make smooth, timely, and correct control applications during the final approach and the transition from approach to landing rollout.
- Touch down smoothly at approximate stalling speed, at or within 500 ft. beyond a specified point with no appreciable drift, and with the airplane's longitudinal axis aligned with the runway centerline.
- Maintain directional control, increasing aileron deflection into the wind, as necessary, during the after-landing roll.

References and Resources

To prepare for this lesson, review the following references and resources. The resources at the AOPA Flight Training website and the AOPA Air Safety Institute publications are valuable supplements to the official information in the FAA references.

TITLE	CHAPTER/SECTION	TOPIC/NOTES
Pilot's Handbook of Aeronautical Knowledge	Chapter 13, "Airport Operations"	Review all sections.
Airplane Flying Handbook	–	Review Chapters 1–8.
Private Pilot Practical Test Standards	–	Review all tasks associated with the activities in this lesson.

CROSS-REFERENCE **For more information about the references and resources that complement the lessons in this book, see Chapter 2.**

Preflight Briefing

This scenario begins with your Cessna 172 on the ground at the Walla Walla, WA, airport (KALW) ready for a local flight to demonstrate your knowledge and skills. After departing KALW, fly to the practice area north of the airport. Use the random challenges in the "What If" section of this chapter to help you practice a representative set of basic flying skills, and then return to KALW and land.

Location and Weather

You are ready to take off from runway 20 at KALW (see Figure 27-2). The weather at the airport indicates excellent VFR conditions with light winds from the southwest.

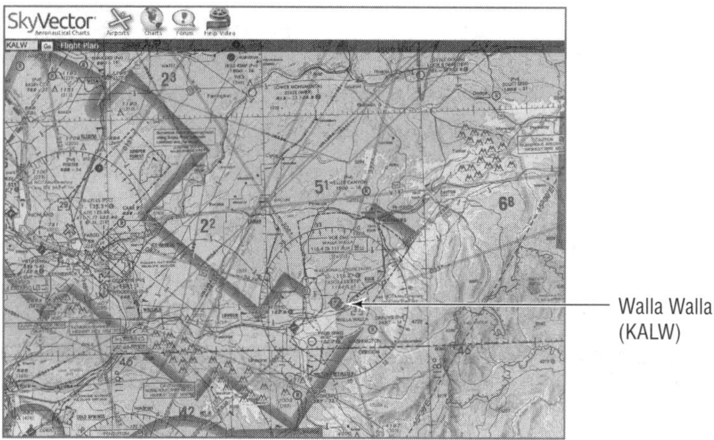

Figure 27-2: The area around KALW as shown on the Seattle sectional chart on SkyVector

Situations and Flights

This lesson uses the following files for X-Plane and FSX:

- X-Plane: `Wiley-SBT-PrivatePilot-Lesson-14.sit`
- FSX: `Wiley-SBT-PrivatePilot-Lesson-14.flt`

CROSS-REFERENCE **For more information about using Situations (X-Plane) and Flights (FSX), see Chapter 10.**

Tips for This Lesson

Here are a few suggestions to help you get the most from this lesson:

- Review the discussions of common errors that follow the detailed descriptions of each flight maneuver in the *Airplane Flying Handbook.*
- Periodically use the interactive map and replay features of X-Plane or FSX to verify how well you maintain altitude and heading as you fly.
- Review the descriptions of and standards for takeoffs, basic flight maneuvers, and landings in the Private Pilot PTS.

What-Ifs

You can also use the "Dice-Based Failure Scheme" described in Chapter 8 to help you simulate a real stage check.

At any point during the flight, roll a die, draw a number from a hat, or use another method to select a random number between 1 and 6. Using Table 27-1, find the corresponding task, and then fly the maneuver.

Table 27-1: Random Challenges for This Flight

NUMBER	RESULT
1	Rectangular course
2	Turns around a point
3	Slow flight
4	Departure stall
5	Approach stall
6	Steep turn

Objectives and Desired Outcome Grading Sheet

SCENARIO ACTIVITIES	SCENARIO SUB-ACTIVITIES	DESIRED OUTCOME
Normal takeoff	–	Perform
Basic flight maneuvers	–	Perform
Ground reference maneuvers	–	Perform
Stalls	–	Perform
Normal landing	–	Perform

CHAPTER 28

Private Pilot Lesson 15: Soft-Field Landings

As in the generic FITS syllabus, this lesson includes a short cross-county flight with a new challenge: landing on a runway that isn't paved.

Scenario

For this scenario, imagine that you are flying to a rural airport to attend a family reunion and picnic. The destination airport, Little Goose Lock and Dam (16W), is adjacent to the Snake River about 40 nm southwest of Pullman, WA (KPUW). It has a gravel runway, so you must use the proper techniques to make a soft-field landing and takeoff (see Figure 28-1).

Figure 28-1: Approaching 16W as shown in X-Plane

Objectives

The primary goals for this flight are:

- Applying knowledge and practice from previous lessons to demonstrate your basic navigation, flying, and decision-making skills
- Learning about soft-field takeoffs and landings. You should consider any runway that isn't paved a "soft field."

Completion Standards

The detailed goals for this lesson are outlined in the table at the end of this chapter. In general, before moving on to the next lesson, you should meet the following standards, based on the generic FITS syllabus for this lesson:

- Identify situations that require a go-around and promptly perform the maneuver using recommended procedures.
- Follow the appropriate procedures and use recommended techniques to perform soft-field takeoffs and landings.
- Perform basic flight maneuvers, pilotage, and operations at nontowered airports following recommended procedures.
- Perform appropriate emergency procedures as required.

References and Resources

To prepare for this lesson, review the following references and resources. The resources at the AOPA Flight Training website and the AOPA Air Safety Institute publications are valuable supplements to the official information in the FAA references.

TITLE	CHAPTER/SECTION	TOPIC/NOTES
Pilot's Handbook of Aeronautical Knowledge	Chapter 10, "Aircraft Performance"	Takeoff and Landing Performance (pp. 10-11–10-17)
Airplane Flying Handbook	Chapter 5, "Takeoff and Departure Climbs"	Soft/Rough-Field Takeoff and Climb (p. 5-10)
	Chapter 8, "Approaches and Landings"	Soft-Field Approach and Landing (p. 8-19) and Faulty Approaches and Landings (pp. 8-27–8-33)
	–	Go-Arounds (Rejected Landings) (p. 8-11)
	Chapter 16, "Emergency Procedures"	Review all sections
Private Pilot Practical Test Standards	Task IV: Takeoffs, Landings, and Go-Arounds	Tasks IV C (p. 1-12), D (p. 1-13), and L (p. 1-20)
	Task X: Emergency Operations	Tasks A, B, and C (pp. 1-32–1-33)
AOPA Air Safety Institute Safety Advisor *Mastering Takeoffs and Landings*	–	–
AOPA Air Safety Institute Safety Advisor *Emergency Procedures*	–	–

CROSS-REFERENCE **For more information about the references and resources that complement the lessons in this book, see Chapter 2.**

Preflight Briefing

This scenario begins with your Cessna 172 in the air after takeoff and climb from the Pullman, WA, airport (KPUW). You are on a short cross-country flight to Little Goose Lock and Dam airport (16W), a gravel strip along the Snake River, about 40 nm southwest of KPUW. Runway 7/25 at 16W is 3,400 ft. long, plenty long enough for your Cessna 172; but the A/FD entry for the airport includes the following remarks, which suggest that operating at 16W can be challenging:

- CTN: ARPT LCTD IN CANYON; ROLLING TERRAIN 700-800′ SOUTH RISING TO 750′; CANYON WALL 800′ SOUTH RISES STEEPLY TO 1800+′; NORTH WALL RISES TO 1600+′.
- CTC WASHINGTON STATE AVIATION DIVISION 360-651-6300 OR 1-800-552-0666 FOR FACILITY INFORMATION PRIOR TO USE.
- VEHICLES; PEDESTRIANS, AND ANIMALS ON & INVOF RY.
- CAUTION DENSITY ALTITUDE.
- HIGH TERRAIN SURROUNDS ARPT.
- STRONG WNDS POSSIBLE INSIDE CANYON.
- ARPT CLSD 1 OCT–1 JUN.

NOTE **Most of the abbreviations and phrases in the preceding remarks should be easy to understand in context, but if you need help, see *Contractions-JO7340.2B*, one of the official FAA handbooks available at this book's website.**

After you land at 16W, taxi back to the appropriate end of the runway, perform a soft-field takeoff, and return to KPUW.

Location and Weather

As the flight begins, you are about 30 miles from KPUW (see Figure 28-2). The weather at the airport indicates excellent VFR conditions with light winds from the southwest.

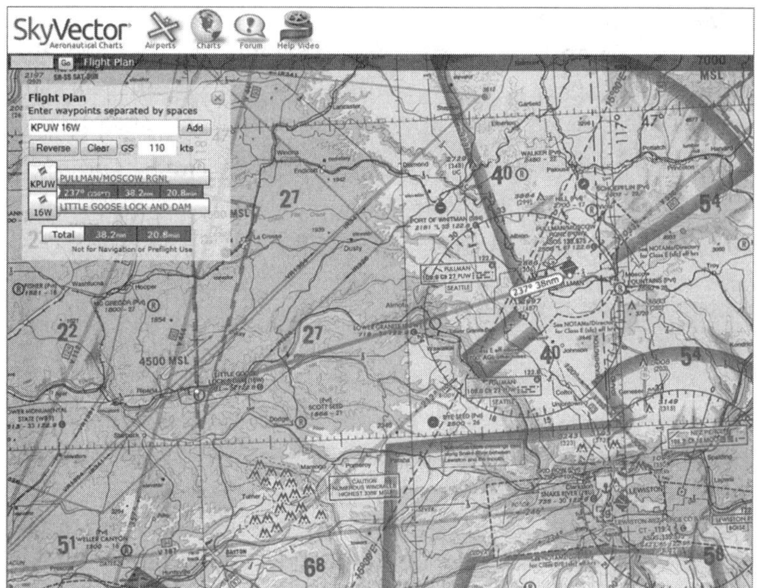

Figure 28-2: The direct route from KPUW to 16W as shown on the Seattle sectional chart on SkyVector

Situations and Flights

This lesson uses the following files for X-Plane and FSX:

- X-Plane: `Wiley-SBT-PrivatePilot-Lesson-15.sit`
- FSX: `Wiley-SBT-PrivatePilot-Lesson-15.flt`

CROSS-REFERENCE **For more information about using Situations (X-Plane) and Flights (FSX), see Chapter 10.**

Tips for This Lesson

Here are a few suggestions to help you get the most from this lesson:

- Review the airport information for 16W on the Seattle sectional chart and in the A/FD at `http://SkyVector.com`, especially the remarks in the A/FD.
- Use the interactive map in X-Plane or FSX to help you spot the airport as you approach 16W.

- Use Google Maps or Google Earth to get a bird's-eye view of Little Goose Lock and Dam airport and the surrounding area before you begin this scenario. Seeing the airport and the surrounding terrain will help you locate it from the air and plan your approach, landing, and takeoff.
- Note especially the information in "Faulty Approaches and Landings," in Chapter 8 of the *Airplane Flying Handbook.*
- Review the descriptions of and standards for the tasks associated with soft-field operations in the Private Pilot PTS.

What-Ifs

You can also use the "Dice-Based Failure Scheme" described in Chapter 8 to create additional challenges for this flight.

At any point during the flight, roll a die, draw a number from a hat, or use another method to select a random number between 1 and 6. Using Table 28-1, find the corresponding problem to solve, and then take the appropriate action.

Table 28-1: Random Challenges for This Flight

NUMBER	RESULT
1	Strong winds from the west at 16W
2	Strong winds from the east at 16W
3	Rough-running engine
4	Airsick passenger
5	Wispy, acrid-smelling smoke from instrument panel
6	Runway at 16W is blocked by disabled aircraft

Objectives and Desired Outcome Grading Sheet

SCENARIO ACTIVITIES	SCENARIO SUB-ACTIVITIES	DESIRED OUTCOME
Normal takeoff	–	Perform
Basic flight maneuvers	–	Perform
Airport traffic pattern	–	Perform
Soft-field landing	–	Perform

CHAPTER 29

Private Pilot Lesson 16: VOR Navigation

As in the generic FITS syllabus, this lesson includes a short cross-county flight that introduces flying solely by reference to instruments and navigation using VORs. Private pilots who do not have an instrument rating are not authorized to fly in instrument meteorological conditions (IMC) or under instrument flight rules (IFR), but during training they must practice and demonstrate basic instrument flying skills.

Scenario

For this scenario, imagine that you encounter marginal weather on a cross-country flight. You are soon surrounded by low clouds and rain showers that make it difficult to use the natural horizon to control the airplane (see Figure 29-1).

Figure 29-1: Marginal VFR weather as shown in X-Plane

Objectives

The primary goals for this flight are:

- Introducing maneuvering solely by reference to flight instruments
- Introducing the use of VOR navigation, especially identifying and tracking VOR radials
- Recognizing and recovering from unusual attitudes while flying on instruments
- Understanding and applying emergency procedures associated with instrument flying
- Honing aeronautical decision-making skills
- Enhancing your situational awareness

Completion Standards

The detailed goals for this lesson are outlined in the table at the end of this chapter. In general, before moving on to the next lesson, you should meet the following standards, based on the generic FITS syllabus for this lesson:

- Perform basic flight maneuvers solely by reference to instruments.
- Maintain altitude within ±200 feet, heading within ±30 degrees, and airspeed within ±10 knots while flying on instruments.

- Practice using radio aids for orientation, tracking and bracketing radials, and bearings.
- Perform appropriate emergency procedures as required.

References and Resources

To prepare for this lesson, review the following references and resources. The resources at the AOPA Flight Training website and the AOPA Air Safety Institute publications are valuable supplements to the official information in the FAA references.

TITLE	CHAPTER/SECTION	TOPIC/NOTES
Pilot's Handbook of Aeronautical Knowledge	Chapter 7, "Flight Instruments"	Review all topics
	Chapter 14, "Airspace"	Controlled Airspace (p. 14-1) and Basic VFR Weather Minimums (p. 14-7)
	Chapter 15, "Navigation"	Radio Navigation (pp. 15-21–15-34), especially Using the VOR, Tracking with VOR, Tips on Using the VOR, and Flight Diversion
Airplane Flying Handbook	Chapter 16, "Emergency Procedures"	Review all sections
Instrument Flying Handbook	Chapter 1, "Human Factors"	All topics pp.1-1–1-8
	Chapter 4, Section I, "Airplane Attitude Instrument Flying Using Analog Instrumentation"	Review all topics
	Chapter 5, Section I, "Airplane Basic Flight Maneuvers Using Analog Instrumentation"	All topics pp. 5-1–5-26 and Unusual Attitudes and Recoveries (pp. 5-26–5-28)
	Chapter 7, "Navigation Systems"	Very High Frequency Omnidirectional Range (VOR)

Continued

(continued)

TITLE	CHAPTER/SECTION	TOPIC/NOTES
Private Pilot Practical Test Standards	Task IX: Basic Instrument Maneuvers	Sections A–F (p. 1-29–1-31)
AOPA Air Safety Institute Safety Advisor *Emergency Procedures*	–	–
AOPA Air Safety Institute Safety Advisor *Say Intentions...When You Need ATCs Help*	–	–
AOPA Air Safety Institute Safety Advisor *Spatial Disorientation*	–	–
AOPA Air Safety Institute Safety Advisor *WeatherWise*	–	–
AOPA Air Safety Institute Safety Advisor *ASOS*	–	–
AOPA Air Safety Institute Safety Advisor *Do the Right Thing: Decision Making for Pilots*	–	–

CROSS-REFERENCE **For more information about the references and resources that complement the lessons in this book, see Chapter 2.**

Preflight Briefing

This scenario begins with your Cessna 172 in the air between Chehalis-Centralia, WA (KCLS), and Hillsboro, OR (KHIO). The area along the western slopes of the Cascade Range often experiences marginal weather that can trap pilots flying between the Seattle and Portland metropolitan areas.

As you continue south toward KHIO, tune and identify the Newburg VOR (UBG). Determine which radial you are on and track that radial toward UBG.

Fly several basic maneuvers using the instruments for reference, and then pause and maintain straight-and-level flight so that you can practice determining the radial you are on from UBG. Use the second VOR receiver in your airplane to tune and identify the Battleground VOR (BTG). Determine which radial you are on from that station, and plot your position on the Seattle sectional chart using the intersection of the radials from UBG and BTG.

Location and Weather

You are in the air north of the Columbia River (see Figure 29-2), flying south toward KHIO. The weather is marginal VFR (MVFR) with low clouds and rain showers. When the scenario begins, the autopilot is on.

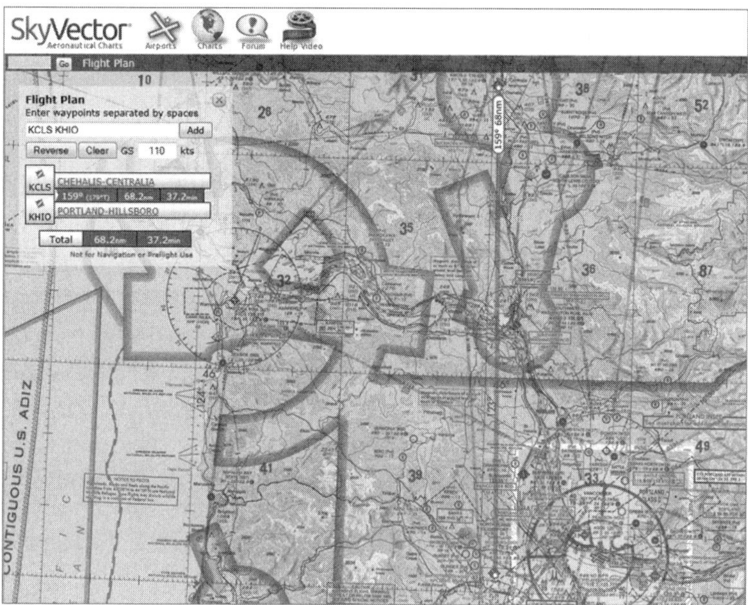

Figure 29-2: The direct route from KCLS to KHIO as shown on the Seattle sectional chart on SkyVector

Situations and Flights

This lesson uses the following files for X-Plane and FSX:

- X-Plane: `Wiley-SBT-PrivatePilot-Lesson-16.sit`
- FSX: `Wiley-SBT-PrivatePilot-Lesson-16.flt`

CROSS-REFERENCE **For more information about using Situations (X-Plane) and Flights (FSX), see Chapter 10.**

Tips for This Lesson

Here are a few suggestions to help you get the most from this lesson:

- Review "The Golden Rule of Flying" in Chapter 11 and the configuration tables in Chapter 12 of this book to help you establish and maintain specific flight conditions.

- Make sure that you understand the control-performance method of flying on instruments that is described in "Learning Methods" beginning on p. 4-2 in the *Instrument Flying Handbook*.
- The "Basic Instrument Flight Patterns" described on pp. 5–30 of the *Instrument Flying Handbook* are excellent exercises that can help you develop and hone your instrument flying skills. Don't be put off by the names of the specific patterns, which are based on common maneuvers in instrument flying. Instead, practice these patterns as if they were musical scales designed to improve your flying dexterity and prepare you for more complex tasks.
- Review the sections of the *X-Plane Operations Manual* or the FSX Learning Center that describe how to use the radios and VOR navigation equipment in your simulation.
- When you practice using the VOR system, check the interactive map occasionally in X-Plane or FSX to help you verify your position.
- To practice unusual attitudes, make sure the autopilot is off, close your eyes, attempt to turn left or right, and then, with your eyes still closed, try to return to straight-and-level flight. After 15–20 seconds, open your eyes, scan the flight instruments, and use the proper control inputs to return to straight-and-level flight. Try the same process with climbing and descending turns.

What-Ifs

You can also use the "Dice-Based Failure Scheme" described in Chapter 8 to create additional challenges for this flight.

At any point during the flight, roll a die, draw a number from a hat, or use another method to select a random number between 1 and 6. Using Table 29-1, find the corresponding problem to solve, and then take the appropriate action.

Table 29-1: Random Challenges for This Flight

NUMBER	RESULT
1	Solid clouds directly ahead block your path.
2	Solid clouds block your path ahead and west of your path.
3	Solid clouds block your path ahead and east of your path.
4	Solid clouds block the path north of your position.
5	You enter the clouds and lose all outside references.
6	The visibility reported at KHIO is 2 miles.

Objectives and Desired Outcome Grading Sheet

SCENARIO ACTIVITIES	SCENARIO SUB-ACTIVITIES	DESIRED OUTCOME
Fly basic maneuvers by reference to instruments.	Maintain straight-and-level and perform standard-rate turns and climbs and descents.	Practice
Fly the Basic Instrument Flight Patterns in Chapter 5 of the *Instrument Flying Handbook.*	–	Practice
VOR navigation	Identify and track VOR radials.	Practice
Diversion	Land at an alternate airport.	Perform
Recoveries from unusual attitudes	–	Practice

CHAPTER 30

Private Pilot Lesson 17: Maximum Performance Takeoffs and Landings

In the generic FITS syllabus, this lesson introduces maximum-performance takeoffs and landings, and reviews basic instrument flight maneuvers, recoveries from unusual attitudes, and aeronautical decision making.

Scenario

For this scenario, imagine that you will depart from Davenport, WA (68S), west of Spokane and fly to Wilson Creek, WA (5W1), to meet an important customer who is waiting to close a big deal (see Figure 30-1).

Both of the airports have runways less than 3,000 ft. long, well within the normal operating limits of the Cessna 172, but short enough to recommend the use of short-field (maximum performance) techniques. The flight is also in marginal VFR conditions, giving you an opportunity to practice your basic instrument flying and VOR navigation skills.

Figure 30-1: Ready to depart from runway 23 at 68S, as shown in FSX

Objectives

The primary goals for this flight are:

- Practicing maximum-performance takeoffs and landings
- Practicing maneuvering solely by reference to flight instruments
- Practicing VOR navigation
- Recognizing and recovering from unusual attitudes while flying on instruments
- Understanding and applying emergency procedures associated with instrument flying
- Honing aeronautical decision-making skills

Completion Standards

The detailed goals for this lesson are outlined in the table at the end of this chapter. In general, before moving on to the next lesson, you should meet the following standards, based on the generic FITS syllabus for this lesson:

- Maintain altitude within ±200 feet, heading within ±30 degrees, and airspeed within ±10 knots while flying on instruments and performing basic flight maneuvers solely by reference to instruments.
- Practice VOR navigation.

References and Resources

To prepare for this lesson, review the following references and resources. The resources at the AOPA Flight Training website and the AOPA Air Safety Institute publications are valuable supplements to the official information in the FAA references.

TITLE	CHAPTER/SECTION	TOPIC/NOTES
Pilot's Handbook of Aeronautical Knowledge	Chapter 7, "Flight Instruments"	Review all topics.
	Chapter 10, "Aircraft Performance"	Performance Charts (pp. 10-17–10-21), Landing Charts (p. 10-25)
	Appendix	C172R performance charts (pp. A-1–A-4)
	Chapter 15, "Navigation"	Radio Navigation (pp. 15-21–15-34), especially Using the VOR, Tracking with VOR, Tips on Using the VOR, and Flight Diversion
Airplane Flying Handbook	Chapter 5, "Takeoff and Departure Climbs"	Short-Field Takeoff and Maximum Performance Climb (p. 5-8)
	Chapter 8, "Approaches and Landings"	Short Field Approach and Landing (p. 8-17)
Instrument Flying Handbook	Chapter 4, Section I, "Airplane Attitude Instrument Flying Using Analog Instrumentation"	Review all topics.
	Chapter 5, Section I, "Airplane Basic Flight Maneuvers Using Analog Instrumentation"	All topics pp. 5-1–5-26 and Unusual Attitudes and Recoveries (pp. 5-26–5-28)
	Chapter 7, "Navigation Systems"	Very High Frequency Omnidirectional Range (VOR)

Continued

(continued)

TITLE	CHAPTER/SECTION	TOPIC/NOTES
Private Pilot Practical Test Standards	Task IV: Takeoffs, Landings, and Go-Arounds	Section E: Short-Field Takeoff and Maximum Performance Climb (p. 1-14) and F: Short-Field Approach and Landing (p. 1-15)
	Task IX: Basic Instrument Maneuvers	Sections A–F (pp. 1-29–1-31)
AOPA Air Safety Institute Safety Advisor *Spatial Disorientation*	–	–
AOPA Air Safety Institute Safety Advisor *Do the Right Thing: Decision Making for Pilots*	–	–

CROSS-REFERENCE For more information about the references and resources that complement the lessons in this book, see Chapter 2.

Preflight Briefing

This scenario begins with your Cessna 172 ready to depart runway 23 at Davenport, WA (68S), for a flight to Wilson Creek, WA (5W1), about 40 nm to the southwest (see Figure 30-2).

Use the VOR at Ephrata (EPH) to help guide you to 5W1. To practice basic instrument flight maneuvers, assume that you must deviate north or south of the direct course to avoid areas of restricted visibility. As described in Lesson 17, you can also practice recoveries from unusual attitudes by closing your eyes, attempting to maneuver, and then checking your instruments.

Location and Weather

You are on runway 23 at 68S ready to take off for 5W1. The weather is marginal VFR with rain showers and low clouds en route.

Figure 30-2: The direct route from 68S to 5W1 as shown on the Seattle sectional chart on SkyVector

Situations and Flights

This lesson uses the following files for X-Plane and FSX:

- X-Plane: `Wiley-SBT-PrivatePilot-Lesson-17.sit`
- FSX: `Wiley-SBT-PrivatePilot-Lesson-17.flt`

CROSS-REFERENCE **For more information about using Situations (X-Plane) and Flights (FSX), see Chapter 10.**

Tips for This Lesson

Here are a few suggestions to help you get the most from this lesson:

- When you practice using the VOR system, check the interactive map occasionally in X-Plane or FSX to help you verify your position.
- As you practice basic instrument flight maneuvers, use the autopilot occasionally to observe how it establishes and maintains banks, leads the roll out from turns, and adjusts pitch for climbs and descents.

- Review "The Golden Rule of Flying" in Chapter 11 and the configuration tables in Chapter 12 of this book to help you establish and maintain specific flight conditions.
- Make sure that you understand the control-performance method of flying on instruments that is described in "Learning Methods" beginning on p. 4-2 in the *Instrument Flying Handbook*.
- The "Basic Instrument Flight Patterns" described on p. 5-30 of the *Instrument Flying Handbook* are excellent exercises that can help you develop and hone your instrument flying skills. Don't be put off by the names of the specific patterns, which are based on common maneuvers in instrument flying. Instead, practice these patterns as if they were musical scales designed to improve your flying dexterity and prepare you for more complex tasks.

What-Ifs

You can also use the "Dice-Based Failure Scheme" described in Chapter 8 to create additional challenges for this flight.

At any point during the flight, roll a die, draw a number from a hat, or use another method to select a random number between 1 and 6. Using Table 30-1, find the corresponding problem to solve, and then take the appropriate action.

Table 30-1: Random Challenges for This Flight

NUMBER	RESULT
1	Solid clouds directly ahead block your path.
2	Solid clouds block your path ahead and north of your path.
3	Solid clouds block your path ahead and south of your path.
4	Solid clouds block the path east of your position.
5	You enter the clouds and lose all outside references.
6	The visibility reported at KEPH is 2 miles.

Objectives and Desired Outcome Grading Sheet

SCENARIO ACTIVITIES	SCENARIO SUB-ACTIVITIES	DESIRED OUTCOME
Practice a short-field take-off and landing.	–	Practice
Fly basic maneuvers by reference to instruments.	Maintain straight-and-level flight and perform standard-rate turns and climbs and descents.	Practice
Fly the Basic Instrument Flight Patterns in Chapter 5 of the *Instrument Flying Handbook.*	–	Practice
VOR navigation	Identify and track VOR radials.	Practice
Diversion	Land at an alternate airport.	Perform
Recoveries from unusual attitudes	–	Practice

CHAPTER

31

Private Pilot Lesson 18: Flight in Marginal Weather

In the generic FITS syllabus, this lesson involves a cross-country flight in marginal weather to deliver a vaccine to a rural airport.

Scenario

Imagine that you have departed Hillsboro, OR (KHIO), near Portland, en route to Hoquiam, WA (KHQM), as shown in Figure 31-1. To ensure good reception of VOR signals, you plan a route via the Astoria, OR VOR (AST).

Because you're in a simulation, you don't have worry about the regulations that govern IFR flight, and you'll make most of this trip in the virtual clouds so that you can gain experience using the flight instruments and VOR navigation system. In real-world flight training, your instructor could file an IFR flight plan and supervise you as you gained experience flying in the clouds.

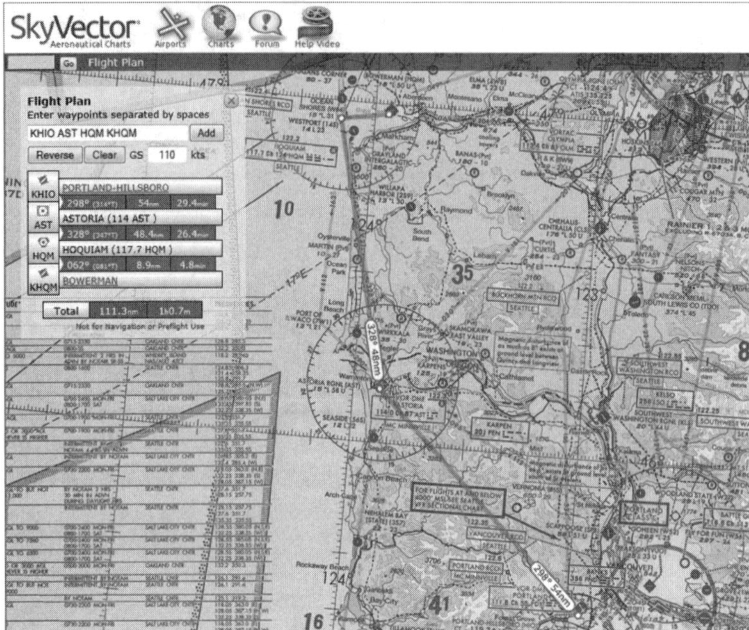

Figure 31-1: The planned route KHIO-AST-KHQM on the CF-16 WAC chart as shown on SkyVector

Objectives

The primary goals for this flight are:

- Practicing maneuvering solely by reference to flight instruments
- Practicing VOR navigation
- Recognizing and recovering from unusual attitudes while flying on instruments
- Understanding and applying emergency procedures associated with instrument flying
- Honing aeronautical decision-making skills

Completion Standards

The detailed goals for this lesson are outlined in the table at the end of this chapter. In general, before moving on to the next lesson, you should meet the following standards, based on the generic FITS syllabus for this lesson:

- Maintain altitude within ±200 ft., heading within ±30 degrees, and airspeed within ±10 knots while flying on instruments and performing basic flight maneuvers solely by reference to instruments.
- Use the VOR navigation system to determine your position, and track VOR radials.

References and Resources

To prepare for this lesson, review the following references and resources. The resources at the AOPA Flight Training website and the AOPA Air Safety Institute publications are valuable supplements to the official information in the FAA references.

TITLE	CHAPTER/SECTION	TOPIC/NOTES
Pilot's Handbook of Aeronautical Knowledge	Chapter 7, "Flight Instruments"	Review all topics.
	Chapter 10, "Aircraft Performance"	Performance Charts (pp. 10-17–10-21), Landing Charts (p. 10-25)
	Appendix	C172R performance charts (pp. A-1–A-4)
	Chapter 15, "Navigation"	Radio Navigation (pp. 15-21–15-34), especially Using the VOR, Tracking with VOR, Tips on Using the VOR, and Flight Diversion

Continued

(continued)

TITLE	CHAPTER/SECTION	TOPIC/NOTES
Instrument Flying Handbook	Chapter 4, Section I, "Airplane Attitude Instrument Flying Using Analog Instrumentation"	Review all topics.
	Chapter 5, Section I, "Airplane Basic Flight Maneuvers Using Analog Instrumentation"	Review all topics, pp. 5-1–5-26 and Unusual Attitudes and Recoveries (pp. 5-26–5-28).
	Chapter 7, "Navigation Systems"	Very High Frequency Omnidirectional Range (VOR)
Private Pilot Practical Test Standards	Task IX: Basic Instrument Maneuvers	Sections A–F (pp. 1-29–1-31)
AOPA Air Safety Institute Safety Advisor *Spatial Disorientation*	–	–
AOPA Air Safety Institute Safety Advisor *Do the Right Thing: Decision Making for Pilots*	–	–

CROSS-REFERENCE **For more information about the references and resources that complement the lessons in this book, see Chapter 2.**

Preflight Briefing

This scenario begins with your Cessna 172 about 30 nm northwest of KHIO, tracking inbound on the AST 120° radial (your course is 300°) at 4,000 ft. (see Figure 31-2). You are in the clouds, and you'll have to descend below them to land at KHQM. As the flight begins, the autopilot is on.

Track inbound to AST and then outbound on the AST 328° radial (which forms the V27 airway between AST and HQM) and inbound on the HQM 148° radial. About 10 minutes after you pass over the AST VOR, begin a stable descent on instruments to 2,500 ft. and maintain that altitude until you can see KHQM across the water to the northeast. Enter the traffic pattern and land.

Figure 31-2: The view of your cockpit instruments in FSX as this lesson begins

Location and Weather

You are between KHIO and AST. The weather is marginal VFR with rain showers and a solid cloud layer that begins at about 3,000 ft.

Situations and Flights

This lesson uses the following files for X-Plane and FSX:

- X-Plane: `Wiley-SBT-PrivatePilot-Lesson-18.sit`
- FSX: `Wiley-SBT-PrivatePilot-Lesson-18.flt`

CROSS-REFERENCE **For more information about using Situations (X-Plane) and Flights (FSX), see Chapter 10.**

Tips for This Lesson

Here are a few suggestions to help you get the most from this lesson:

- When you practice using the VOR system, check the interactive map occasionally in X-Plane or FSX to help you verify your position.
- Use radials from the OLM VOR to help you track your progress between AST and HQM.

What-Ifs

You can also use the "Dice-Based Failure Scheme" described in Chapter 8 to create additional challenges for this flight.

At any point during the flight, roll a die, draw a number from a hat, or use another method to select a random number between 1 and 6. Using Table 31-1, find the corresponding problem to solve, and then take the appropriate action.

Table 31-1: Random Challenges for This Flight

NUMBER	RESULT
1	Divert to Scappoose, OR (KSPB).
2	Divert to Olympia, WA (KOLM).
3	You see a low-voltage warning.
4	Rough-running engine
5	Vacuum system failure
6	The visibility reported at KHQM is 2 miles.

Objectives and Desired Outcome Grading Sheet

SCENARIO ACTIVITIES	SCENARIO SUB-ACTIVITIES	DESIRED OUTCOME
Practice a short-field takeoff and landing.	–	Practice
Fly basic maneuvers by reference to instruments.	Maintain straight-and-level flight and perform standard-rate turns and climbs and descents.	Practice
Fly the Basic Instrument Flight Patterns in Chapter 5 of the *Instrument Flying Handbook.*	–	Practice
VOR navigation	Identify and track VOR radials.	Practice
Diversion	Land at an alternate airport.	Perform
Recoveries from unusual attitudes	–	Practice

CHAPTER

32

Private Pilot Lesson 19: Solo Practice Flight

In the generic FITS syllabus, this lesson is a solo practice flight to a nearby airport. It's another opportunity to review and practice basic skills you learned in previous lessons.

Scenario

This scenario begins at the Bellingham, WA (KBLI) airport. You'll make a short (16 nm) scenic flight to the Orcas Island airport (KORS) in the San Juan Islands (see Figure 32-1).

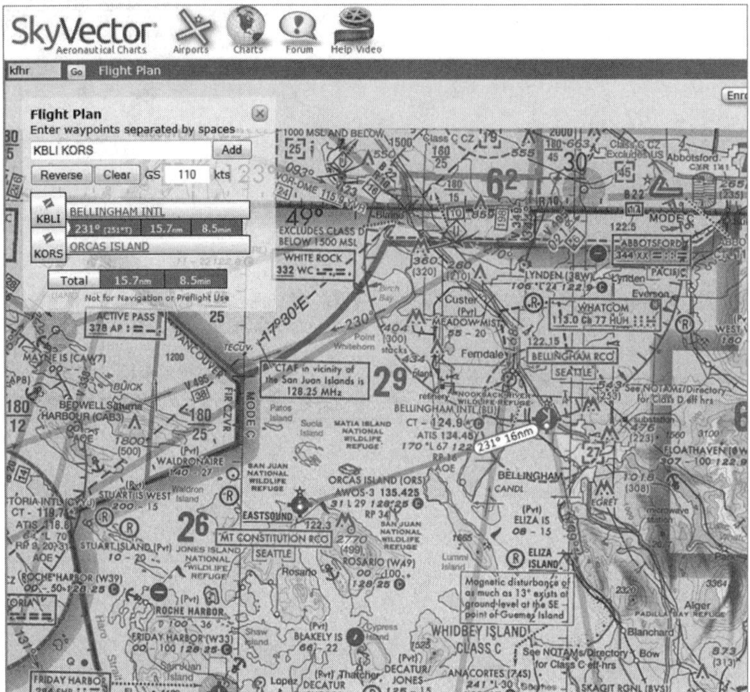

Figure 32-1: The planned route from KBLI to KORS on the Seattle sectional chart as shown on SkyVector

Objectives

The primary goals for this flight are practicing:

- All basic flying skills
- Pilotage
- VOR navigation
- Airport traffic patterns
- Short-field approach and landing

Completion Standards

The detailed goals for this lesson are outlined in the table at the end of this chapter. In general, before moving on to the next lesson, you should meet the following standards, based on the generic FITS syllabus for this lesson:

- During basic flight maneuvers, you should consistently meet the basic standards for a private pilot in the PTS — altitude ±100 ft. and heading ±10° during straight-and-level flight.
- When climbing or descending, you should level off at the target altitude within 100 ft. and roll out of turns within 10° of the intended heading.

References and Resources

To prepare for this lesson, review the following references and resources. The resources at the AOPA Flight Training website and the AOPA Air Safety Institute publications are valuable supplements to the official information in the FAA references.

TITLE	CHAPTER/SECTION	TOPIC/NOTES
Pilot's Handbook of Aeronautical Knowledge	Chapter 13, "Airport Operations"	Review all sections.
	Chapter 14, "Airspace"	Class D Airspace (p. 14-2) and Basic VFR Weather Minimums (p. 14-7)
Airplane Flying Handbook	Chapter 7, "Airport Traffic Pattern"	Review all sections.
	Chapter 8, "Approaches and Landings"	Short-Field Approach and Landing (p. 8-17)
Aeronautical Chart User's Guide	VFR Aeronautical Charts	–
	VFR Aeronautical Chart Symbols	–

Continued

(continued)

TITLE	CHAPTER/SECTION	TOPIC/NOTES
AOPA Air Safety Institute Safety Advisor *Operations at Towered Airports*	–	–
AOPA Air Safety Institute Safety Advisor *Operations at Nontowered Airports*	–	–
AOPA Air Safety Institute Safety Advisor *Mastering Takeoffs and Landings*	–	–

CROSS-REFERENCE **For more information about the references and resources that complement the lessons in this book, see Chapter 2.**

Preflight Briefing

This scenario begins with your Cessna 172 ready to depart runway 34 at KBLI. Take off and use standard procedures to exit the traffic pattern and turn southwest toward KORS. Follow the recommended practices for joining the appropriate traffic pattern at Orcas Island and make a short-field landing.

You should use pilotage to track your progress toward KORS, but the Whatcom VOR (HUH) north of KBLI provides a helpful reference (KORS is on the 203° radial from HUH).

Note that this flight includes an over-water leg. Consider how that fact might affect your choice of cruise altitude and route.

Location and Weather

The weather for this flight is good VFR with light winds from the north.

Situations and Flights

This lesson uses the following files for X-Plane and FSX:

- X-Plane: `Wiley-SBT-PrivatePilot-Lesson-19.sit`
- FSX: `Wiley-SBT-PrivatePilot-Lesson-19.flt`

CROSS-REFERENCE **For more information about using Situations (X-Plane) and Flights (FSX), see Chapter 10.**

Tips for This Lesson

Here are a few suggestions to help you get the most from this lesson:

- This flight begins at an airport with a control tower. Review the procedures for operating in Class D airspace and at towered airports.
- Pay attention to the note on the sectional chart about communications in the San Juan Islands and to the information about KORS (see Figure 32-2).
- Note that the runway at KORS is 2,900 ft. long.
- Use Google Earth to preview the terrain around KORS.
- It's easy to confuse one island for another. Use all available resources to confirm your position, even on a short flight like this.

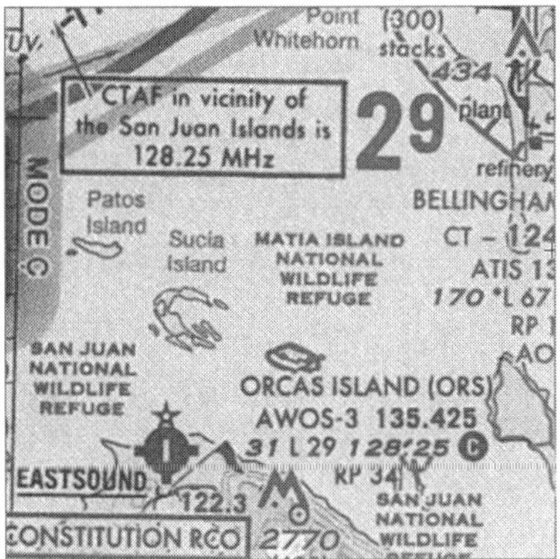

Figure 32-2: Information about KORS on the sectional chart

What-Ifs

You can also use the "Dice-Based Failure Scheme" described in Chapter 8 to create additional challenges for this flight.

At any point during the flight, roll a die, draw a number from a hat, or use another method to select a random number between 1 and 6. Using Table 32-1, find the corresponding problem to solve, and then take the appropriate action.

Table 32-1: Random Challenges for This Flight

NUMBER	RESULT
1	A thin layer of fog rolls in at KBLI, visibility is 2 miles.
2	A thin layer of fog rolls in at KORS, visibility is 2 miles.
3	Divert to KFHR.
4	Divert to S31.
5	Divert to KBVS.
6	Divert to KAWO.

Objectives and Desired Outcome Grading Sheet

SCENARIO ACTIVITIES	SCENARIO SUB-ACTIVITIES	DESIRED OUTCOME
Practice a short-field takeoff and landing.	–	Practice
VOR navigation	Identify and track VOR radials.	Practice
Diversion	Land at an alternate airport.	Perform

CHAPTER

33

Private Pilot Lesson 20: Long Cross-Country Flight

In the generic FITS syllabus, this lesson is a long cross-country flight required as part of private pilot training. It also introduces the effects of high-density altitude operations. As on all cross-country flights, you should have a plan B should weather, mechanical problems, or other issues arise en route.

Scenario

This scenario begins at the Bend, OR (KBDN), airport (FSX uses the old airport designator, S07). You will make a round-robin flight to Pendleton, OR (KPDT), Richland, WA (KRLD), and back to KBDN, a total distance of about 335 nm (see Figure 33-1). Note the restricted areas along the south side of the Columbia River. At typical Cessna 172 cruising speed, the flight requires about 3 hours (for suggestions about how to reduce or break up the flying time in your simulation, see "Tips for This Lesson").

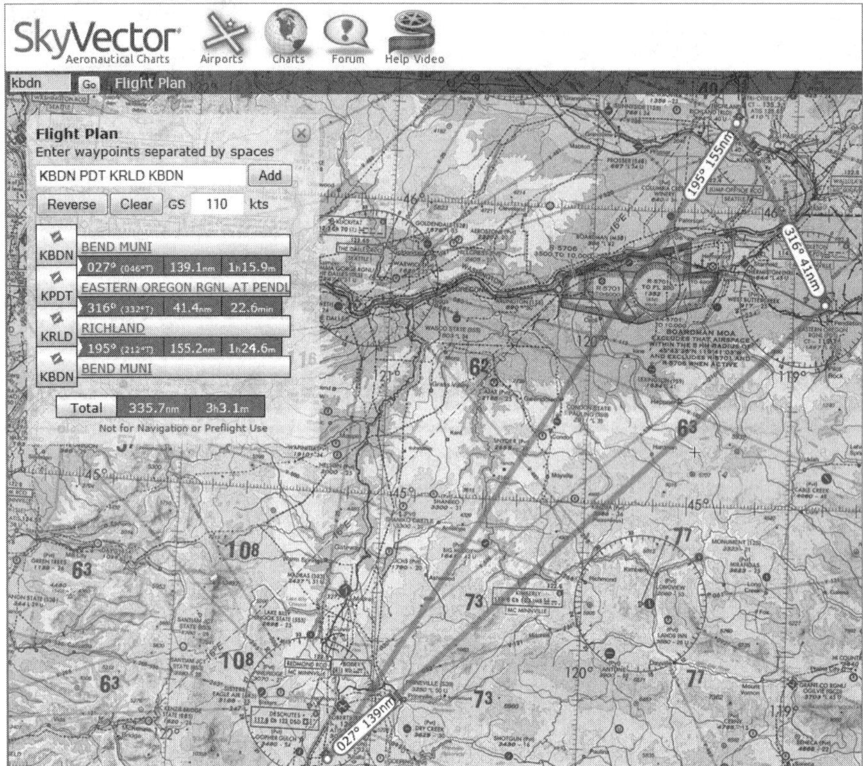

Figure 33-1: The direct route KBDN-KPDT-KRLD-KBDN on the CF-16 WAC chart as shown on SkyVector

Objectives

The primary goals for this flight are practicing:

- All basic flying skills
- Pilotage
- VOR navigation
- Procedures for obtaining a complete preflight briefing
- Diversion and emergency procedures

Completion Standards

The detailed goals for this lesson are outlined in the table at the end of this chapter. In general, before moving on to the next lesson, you should meet the following standards, based on the generic FITS syllabus for this lesson:

- Understand how to gather and interpret information about airports, VORs, and airspace on aeronautical charts.
- Collect and apply information in the A/FD about the airports you intend to use.
- Understand the process for obtaining a complete preflight briefing.

References and Resources

To prepare for this lesson, review the following references and resources. The resources at the AOPA Flight Training website and the AOPA Air Safety Institute publications are valuable supplements to the official information in the FAA references.

TITLE	CHAPTER/SECTION	TOPIC/NOTES
Pilot's Handbook of Aeronautical Knowledge	Chapter 10, "Aircraft Performance"	Review all sections in pp. 10-1–10-26.
	Chapter 12, "Aviation Weather Services"	Review all sections in pp. 12-1–12-18.
	Chapter 14, "Airspace"	Special Use Airspace (p. 14-3)
	Chapter 15, "Navigation"	Review all sections.
Airplane Flying Handbook	Chapter 16, "Emergency Procedures"	Review all sections.
Aeronautical Chart User's Guide	VFR Aeronautical Charts	–
	VFR Aeronautical Chart Symbols	–
AOPA Air Safety Institute Safety Advisor *Airspace for Everyone*	–	–

Continued

(continued)

TITLE	CHAPTER/SECTION	TOPIC/NOTES
AOPA Air Safety Institute Safety Interactive Safety Course *Know Before You Go: Navigating Today's Airspace*	–	–
AOPA Air Safety Institute Safety Advisor *WeatherWise*	–	–
X-Plane Operations Guide	Save/Load Situation	–
FSX Learning Center	All About Flights	–

CROSS-REFERENCE **For more information about the references and resources that complement the lessons in this book, see Chapter 2.**

Preflight Briefing

This scenario begins with your Cessna 172 ready to depart runway 34 at KBDN. Take off and use standard procedures to exit the traffic pattern and turn northwest toward KPDT. As noted in "Tips for This Lesson," you may want to deviate from the direct route for one or more legs to fly via charted airways or VOR to VOR, especially on the last leg from KRLD to KBDN.

Location and Weather

The weather for this flight is good VFR with winds from the northwest all along your route. Note, however, that it's a warm summer day, with surface temperatures in the 80s (about 30°C). The high-density altitude will affect your airplane's performance.

Situations and Flights

This lesson uses the following files for X-Plane and FSX:

- X-Plane: `Wiley-SBT-PrivatePilot-Lesson-20.sit`
- FSX: `Wiley-SBT-PrivatePilot-Lesson-20.flt`

CROSS-REFERENCE **For more information about using Situations (X-Plane) and Flights (FSX), see Chapter 10.**

Tips for This Lesson

Here are a few suggestions to help you get the most from this lesson:

- Download the *AOPA Air Safety Foundation Flight Planner*, a handy flight log and form for recording weather, NOTAMs, and related information. A link is at this book's website.
- The direct courses shown in Figure 33-1 may not be the easiest to follow, and you can't fly through the restricted areas southwest of KRLD. Consider adjusting the route to fly directly to and from VORs or via charted Victor airways, at least until you are in the vicinity of the airports where you intend to land (see Figure 33-2). How can you best adjust the last leg to avoid the restricted areas?
- If you don't want to fly the entire trip in real time or in one sitting, you can accelerate the simulation en route or, at any point during the flight, save your position as a Situation (X-Plane) or Flight (FSX) so that you can resume the trip later. You can also use the interactive map in your simulation to move your airplane along the intended route of flight.
- When you practice using the VOR system, check the interactive map occasionally in X-Plane or FSX to help you verify your position.
- Use the A/FD information at SkyVector.com or other resources on the web to learn more about the airports along your route, including the best alternatives should you need to divert.
- The weather for this flight is set to help you understand the effects of high-density altitude on aircraft performance; but practice using web resources to get a real-time weather briefing and NOTAMs for this flight. If you are a real pilot, you can use DUAT for an official preflight briefing.

Figure 33-2: En route to KPDT as shown in FSX

What-Ifs

You can also use the "Dice-Based Failure Scheme" described in Chapter 8 to create additional challenges for this flight.

At any point during the flight, roll a die, draw a number from a hat, or use another method to select a random number between 1 and 6. Using Table 33-1, find the corresponding problem to solve, and then take the appropriate action.

Table 33-1: Random Challenges for This Flight

NUMBER	RESULT
1	Divert to KALW.
2	Divert to KDLS.
3	Rough-running engine
4	Smoke and haze ahead reduce visibility to ~ 3 miles.
5	Wind at KPSC gusting to 25 knots
6	Thunderstorms reported SW of KPDT.

Objectives and Desired Outcome Grading Sheet

SCENARIO ACTIVITIES	SCENARIO SUB-ACTIVITIES	DESIRED OUTCOME
Learn about the effects of high-density altitude on aircraft performance.	–	Describe/Explain
Practice takeoffs, climbs, and landings in high-density altitude conditions.	–	Practice
VOR navigation	Identify and track VOR radials.	Practice
Review types of airspace.	Emphasize special use airspace (SUA).	Describe
Diversion	Land at an alternative airport.	Perform

CHAPTER

34

Private Pilot Lesson 21: Cross-Country Night Flight

In the generic FITS syllabus, this lesson is another multi-leg, cross-country flight that ends at night.

Scenario

This scenario begins at the Medford, OR (KMFR), airport at twilight. You plan to fly to Roseburg, OR (KRBG), and then on to Corvallis, OR (KCVO), a total distance of about 132 nm (see Figure 34-1). At typical Cessna 172 cruising speed, the flight requires about 1 hour and 15 minutes.

You have one passenger on the first leg, and you plan to pick up another friend at Roseburg before continuing to Corvallis.

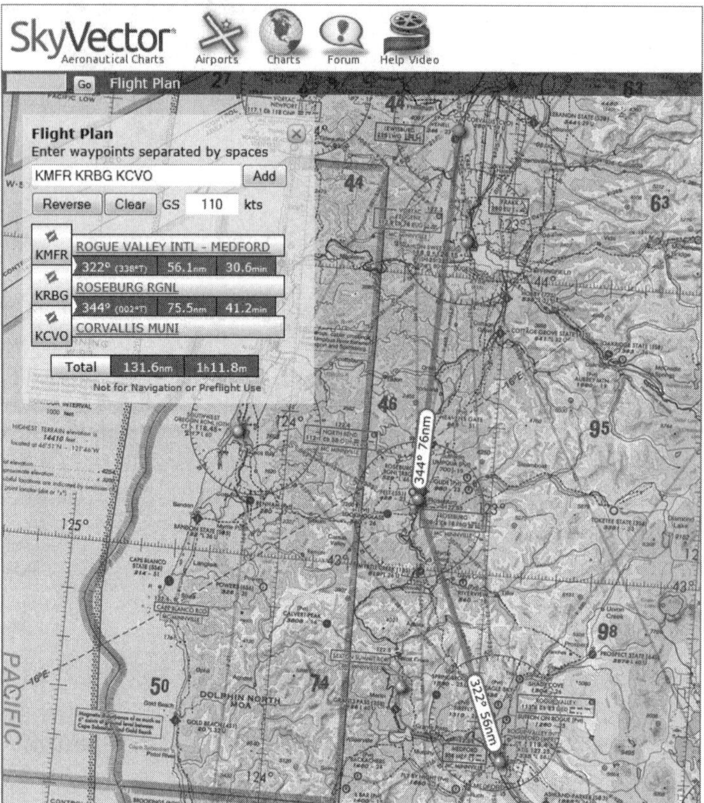

Figure 34-1: The direct route KMFR-KRBG-KCVO on the CF-16 WAC chart as shown on SkyVector

Objectives

The primary goals for this flight are practicing:

- All basic flying skills
- Night-flying procedures
- Pilotage
- VOR navigation
- Procedures for obtaining a complete preflight briefing
- Diversion and emergency procedures

Completion Standards

The detailed goals for this lesson are outlined in the table at the end of this chapter. In general, before moving on to the next lesson, you should meet the following standards, based on the generic FITS syllabus for this lesson:

- Understand how to gather and interpret information about airports, VORs, and airspace on aeronautical charts.
- Collect and apply information in the A/FD about the airports you intend to use.
- Understand the process for obtaining a complete preflight briefing.
- Understand the requirements for challenges involved in night flying.
- Apply techniques for instrument flying to night flying.

References and Resources

To prepare for this lesson, review the following references and resources. The resources at the AOPA Flight Training website and the AOPA Air Safety Institute publications are valuable supplements to the official information in the FAA references.

TITLE	CHAPTER/SECTION	TOPIC/NOTES
Pilot's Handbook of Aeronautical Knowledge	Chapter 12, "Aviation Weather Services"	Review all sections in pp. 12-1–12-18.
	Chapter 13, "Airport Operations"	Airport Lighting (pp. 13-6–13-9)
	Chapter 15, "Navigation"	Review all sections.
	Chapter 16, "Aeromedical Factors"	Review all sections, especially Vision in Flight (pp. 16-17–16-19).
Airplane Flying Handbook	Chapter 10, "Night Operations"	Review all sections.
	Chapter 16, "Emergency Procedures"	Review all sections.
Aeronautical Chart User's Guide	VFR Aeronautical Charts	–
	VFR Aeronautical Chart Symbols	–
AOPA Air Safety Institute Safety Advisor *WeatherWise*	–	–

CROSS-REFERENCE For more information about the references and resources that complement the lessons in this book, see Chapter 2.

Preflight Briefing

This scenario begins with your Cessna 172 ready to depart runway 32 at KMFR. Take off and use standard procedures to exit the traffic pattern and turn northwest toward KRBG. As noted in "Tips for This Lesson," you may want to deviate from the direct route for one or more legs to fly via charted airways or VOR to VOR.

Location and Weather

The weather for this flight is good VFR with light winds from the northwest along your route.

Situations and Flights

This lesson uses the following files for X-Plane and FSX:

- X-Plane: `Wiley-SBT-PrivatePilot-Lesson-21.sit`
- FSX: `Wiley-SBT-PrivatePilot-Lesson-21.flt`

CROSS-REFERENCE For more information about using Situations (X-Plane) and Flights (FSX), see Chapter 10.

Tips for This Lesson

Here are a few suggestions to help you get the most from this lesson:

- Download the *AOPA Air Safety Foundation Flight Planner*, a handy flight log and form for recording weather, NOTAMs, and related information. A link is at this book's website.
- The direct courses shown in Figure 34-1 may not be the easiest to follow, especially at night. Consider adjusting the route to fly directly to and from VORs or via charted Victor airways, at least until you are in the vicinity of the airports where you intend to land.
- Note the high terrain around both KMFR and KRBG. Consider your airplane's performance and the weather when choosing the best route to fly (see Figure 34-2).
- If you don't want to fly the entire trip in real time or in one sitting, you can accelerate the simulation en route or, after landing at the end of each

leg, save your position as a Situation (X-Plane) or Flight (FSX) so that you can resume the trip later. You can also use the interactive map in your simulation to move your airplane along the intended route of flight.

- When you practice using the VOR system, check the interactive map occasionally in X-Plane or FSX to help you verify your position.
- Use the A/FD information at SkyVector.com or other resources on the web to learn more about the airports along your route, including the best alternatives should you need to divert.
- The weather for this flight is set; but practice using web resources to get a real-time weather briefing and NOTAMs for this flight. If you are a real pilot, you can use DUAT for an official preflight briefing.

Figure 34-2: Typical turbulence patterns in the mountains, as shown in Figure 11-1 from the *Pilot's Handbook of Aeronautical Knowledge*

What-Ifs

You can also use the "Dice-Based Failure Scheme" described in Chapter 8 to create additional challenges for this flight.

At any point during the flight, roll a die, draw a number from a hat, or use another method to select a random number between 1 and 6. Using Table 34-1, find the corresponding problem to solve, and then take the appropriate action.

Table 34-1: Random Challenges for This Flight

NUMBER	RESULT
1	Rough-running engine
2	Low-voltage indication
3	Divert to KEUG.
4	Divert to KONP.
5	Emergency at KCVO closes the airport.
6	Passenger is ill.

Objectives and Desired Outcome Grading Sheet

SCENARIO ACTIVITIES	SCENARIO SUB-ACTIVITIES	DESIRED OUTCOME
Practice night flying procedures.	Takeoffs, climbs, en route navigation, and landings	Perform
VOR navigation	Identify and track VOR radials.	Practice
Diversion	Navigate to and land at an alternative airport.	Perform

CHAPTER

35

Private Pilot Lesson 22: Flight Planning and Navigation Practice

In the generic FITS syllabus, this lesson is another multi-leg, cross-country flight to practice flight planning (including weight-and-balance calculations), navigation, and basic flying skills. It also introduces basic GPS navigation.

Scenario

This scenario begins at the Nampa, ID (KMAN), airport near Boise (X-Plane and FSX use the old airport identifier, S67). You plan to fly to Baker City, OR (KBKE), and then on to Walla Walla, WA (KALW), a total direct distance of about 172 nm (see Figure 35-1). At typical Cessna 172 cruising speed, the flight requires about 1 hour and 35 minutes.

As in the FITS syllabus, assume that you are carrying two rear-seat passengers and video cameras. The passengers weigh 120 and 150 lbs. Their equipment weighs 30 lbs.

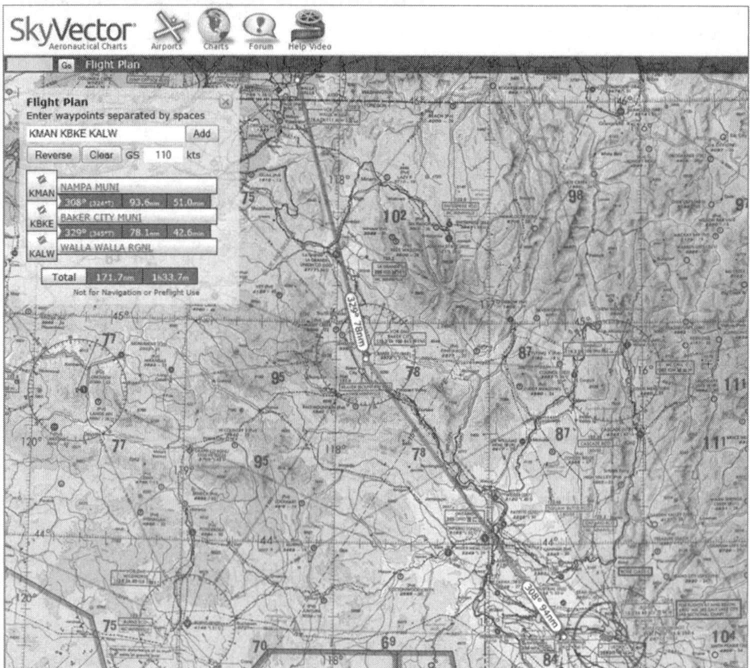

Figure 35-1: The direct route KMAN-KBKE-KALW on the CF-16 WAC chart as shown on SkyVector

Objectives

The primary goals for this flight are practicing:

- Weight and balance and performance calculations
- All basic flying skills
- Takeoffs and landings (including short-field and soft-field procedures)
- Pilotage
- VOR navigation
- Basic GPS navigation
- Procedures for obtaining a complete preflight briefing
- Diversion and emergency procedures

Completion Standards

The detailed goals for this lesson are outlined in the table at the end of this chapter. In general, before moving on to the next lesson, you should meet the following standards, based on the generic FITS syllabus for this lesson:

- Understand how to gather and interpret information about airports, VORs, and airspace on aeronautical charts.
- Collect and apply information in the A/FD about the airports you intend to use.
- Understand the process for obtaining a complete preflight briefing.
- Understand the basic procedures for using GPS under VFR.

References and Resources

To prepare for this lesson, review the following references and resources. The resources at the AOPA Flight Training website and the AOPA Air Safety Institute publications are valuable supplements to the official information in the FAA references.

TITLE	CHAPTER/SECTION	TOPIC/NOTES
Pilot's Handbook of Aeronautical Knowledge	Chapter 9, "Weight and Balance"	Review all sections.
	Chapter 12, "Aviation Weather Services"	Review all sections in pp. 12-1–12-18.
	Chapter 15, "Navigation"	Review all sections, especially Global Positioning System (p. 15-32) and Lost Procedures (p. 15-34).
Airplane Flying Handbook	Chapter 5, "Takeoff and Departure Climbs"	Review all sections.
Advanced Avionics Handbook	Chapter 3, "Navigation"	Review all sections in pp. 3-1–3-28.
Aeronautical Information Manual	1-1-19 Global Positioning System (GPS)	Note especially 1-1-19 b, VFR Use of GPS.

Continued

(continued)

TITLE	CHAPTER/SECTION	TOPIC/NOTES
Aeronautical Chart User's Guide	VFR Aeronautical Charts	–
	VFR Aeronautical Chart Symbols	–
AOPA Air Safety Institute Safety Advisor *GPS from the Ground Up*	–	–
AOPA Air Safety Institute interactive course *GPS for VFR Operations*	–	–
AOPA Air Safety Institute Interactive Safety Course *VFR GPS Guide: Garmin 430/530*	–	–
X-Plane Operations Manual	GPS Navigation	–
FSX Learning Center	Using the GPS	–

CROSS-REFERENCE **For more information about the references and resources that complement the lessons in this book, see Chapter 2.**

Preflight Briefing

This scenario begins with your Cessna 172 ready to depart runway 29 at KMAN. Take off and use standard procedures to exit the traffic pattern and turn northwest toward KBKE as you climb to an appropriate VFR cruising altitude. As noted in "Tips for This Lesson," you may want to deviate from the direct route for one or more legs to fly via charted airways or VOR to VOR.

Practice short-field and soft-field takeoff and landing procedures at the airports you visit during this flight.

Location and Weather

The weather for this flight is good VFR with light winds from the northwest along your route from KMAN to KALW.

Situations and Flights

This lesson uses the following files for X-Plane and FSX:

- X-Plane: `Wiley-SBT-PrivatePilot-Lesson-22.sit`
- FSX: `Wiley-SBT-PrivatePilot-Lesson-22.flt`

CROSS-REFERENCE **For more information about using Situations (X-Plane) and Flights (FSX), see Chapter 10.**

Tips for This Lesson

Here are a few suggestions to help you get the most from this lesson:

- Can you carry your passengers and their equipment and fill the fuel tanks in your Skyhawk? If not, consider how you will get fuel at the airports on your route.
- Download the *AOPA Air Safety Foundation Flight Planner*, a handy flight log and form for recording weather, NOTAMs, and related information. A link is at this book's website.
- The direct courses shown in Figure 35-1 may not be the best route to follow given terrain and other factors. Consider adjusting the route to fly directly to and from VORs or via charted Victor airways, at least until you are in the vicinity of the airports where you intend to land (see Figure 35-2).
- If you don't want to fly the entire trip in real time or in one sitting, you can accelerate the simulation en route or, after landing at the end of each leg, save your position as a Situation (X-Plane) or Flight (FSX) so that you can resume the trip later. You can also use the interactive map in your simulation to move your airplane along the intended route of flight.
- When you practice using the VOR system, check the interactive map occasionally in X-Plane or FSX to help you verify your position.
- Use the A/FD information at SkyVector.com or other resources on the web to learn more about the airports along your route, including the best alternatives should you need to divert.
- The weather for this flight is set; but practice using web resources to get a real-time weather briefing and NOTAMs for this flight. If you are a real pilot, you can use DUAT for an official preflight briefing.
- The GPS in X-Plane does not simulate as many features as the comparable unit in FSX. As noted in Chapter 1, add-on simulations of GPS navigators are available for both X-Plane and FSX.

Figure 35-2: Approaching KBKE as shown in FSX

What-Ifs

You can also use the "Dice-Based Failure Scheme" described in Chapter 8 to create additional challenges for this flight.

At any point during the flight, roll a die, draw a number from a hat, or use another method to select a random number between 1 and 6. Using Table 35-1, find the corresponding problem to solve, and then take the appropriate action.

Table 35-1: Random Challenges for This Flight

NUMBER	RESULT
1	Rough-running engine
2	Low-voltage indication
3	Divert to the best suitable airport.
4	Divert to KPDT.
5	Gusty winds at KALW
6	Passenger is ill.

Objectives and Desired Outcome Grading Sheet

SCENARIO ACTIVITIES	SCENARIO SUB-ACTIVITIES	DESIRED OUTCOME
Weight-and-balance calculations	–	Practice
Basic navigation skills	–	Perform
Practice takeoffs, climbs, and landings.	Soft-field and short-field procedures	Practice
VOR navigation	Identify and track VOR radials.	Practice
GPS navigation	Practice using GPS for VFR navigation.	Practice
Diversion	Navigate to and land at an alternate airport.	Perform

CHAPTER

36

Private Pilot Lesson 23: Night Cross-Country Flight

In the generic FITS syllabus, this lesson is a dual cross-country flight at night. You are taking your partner to a romantic dinner, and you want the flight to be a special occasion.

Scenario

This scenario begins at the Bremerton, WA (KPWT) airport just after sundown. You plan to fly to Friday Harbor, WA (KFHR), where you can walk into town for dinner at a waterfront restaurant. The direct distance is about 63 nm (see Figure 36-1). At typical Cessna 172 cruising speed, the flight requires about 35 minutes, far less than the hours required to drive to a ferry terminal, cross the Strait of Juan de Fuca, and then return.

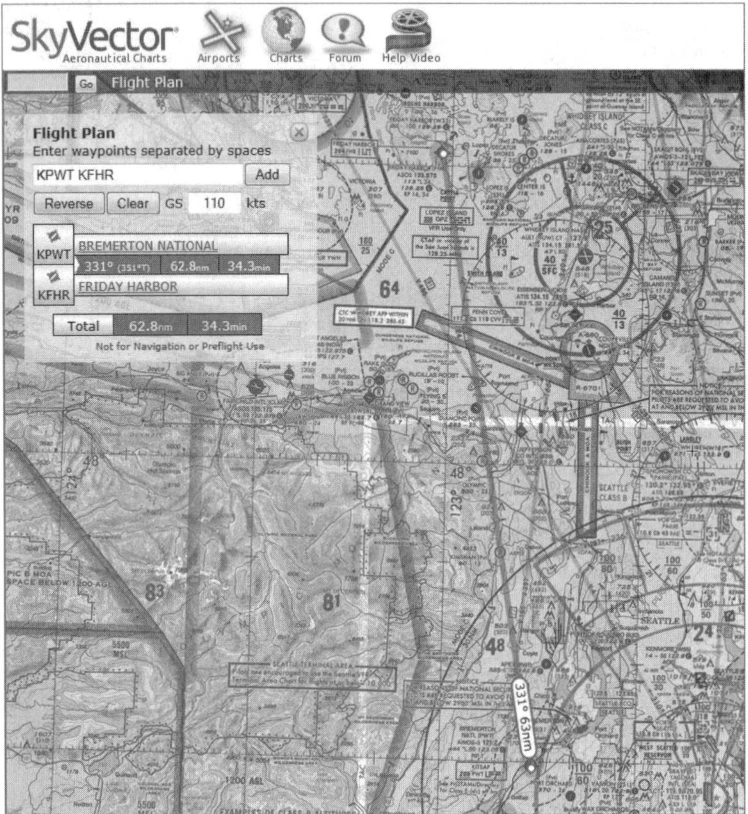

Figure 36-1: The direct route KPWT-KFHR on the Seattle sectional chart as shown on SkyVector

Objectives

The primary goals for this flight are practicing:

- All basic flying skills
- Night-flying procedures
- Pilotage
- VOR navigation
- Procedures for obtaining a complete preflight briefing
- Diversion and emergency procedures
- Aeronautical decision making

Completion Standards

The detailed goals for this lesson are outlined in the table at the end of this chapter. In general, before moving on to the next lesson, you should meet the following standards, based on the generic FITS syllabus for this lesson:

- Understand how to gather and interpret information about airports, VORs, and airspace on aeronautical charts.
- Know how to choose an appropriate route given terrain, time of day, length of over-water segments, airspace, and other factors.
- Understand the process for obtaining a complete preflight briefing.
- Understand the challenges involved in night flying.
- Understand how techniques for instrument flying can help you during night flights.

References and Resources

To prepare for this lesson, review the following references and resources. The resources at the AOPA Flight Training website and the AOPA Air Safety Institute publications are valuable supplements to the official information in the FAA references.

TITLE	CHAPTER/SECTION	TOPIC/NOTES
Pilot's Handbook of Aeronautical Knowledge	Chapter 13, "Airport Operations"	Airport Lighting (pp. 13-6–13-9)
	Chapter 15, "Navigation"	Review all sections.
	Chapter 16, "Aeromedical Factors"	Review all sections, especially Vision in Flight (pp. 16-17–16-19).
Airplane Flying Handbook	Chapter 10, "Night Operations"	Review all sections.
	Chapter 16, "Emergency Procedures"	Review all sections.
Aeronautical Chart User's Guide	VFR Aeronautical Charts	–
	VFR Aeronautical Chart Symbols	–

Continued

(continued)

TITLE	CHAPTER/SECTION	TOPIC/NOTES
AOPA Air Safety Institute Safety Advisor *Airspace for Everyone*	–	–
AOPA Air Safety Institute Interactive Safety Course *Do The Right Thing: Decision Making for Pilots*	–	–
AOPA Air Safety Institute Interactive Safety Course *VFR GPS Guide: Garmin 430/530*	–	–

CROSS-REFERENCE **For more information about the references and resources that complement the lessons in this book, see Chapter 2.**

Preflight Briefing

This scenario begins with your Cessna 172 ready to depart runway 01 at KPWT. Take off and use standard procedures to exit the traffic pattern and turn toward KFHR.

Location and Weather

The weather for this flight is good VFR with light winds from the northwest along your route.

Situations and Flights

This lesson uses the following files for X-Plane and FSX:

- X-Plane: `Wiley-SBT-PrivatePilot-Lesson-23.sit`
- FSX: `Wiley-SBT-PrivatePilot-Lesson-23.flt`

CROSS-REFERENCE **For more information about using Situations (X-Plane) and Flights (FSX), see Chapter 10.**

Tips for This Lesson

Here are a few suggestions to help you get the most from this lesson:

- Download the *AOPA Air Safety Foundation Flight Planner*, a handy flight log and form for recording weather, NOTAMs, and related information. A link is at this book's website.
- The direct course shown in Figure 36-1 may not be the easiest to follow, especially at night. Consider adjusting the route to fly directly to and from VORs or via charted Victor airways, at least until you are in the vicinity of the airports where you intend to land.
- Especially when flying over water, beware of illusions (see Figure 36-2).
- When you practice using the VOR system, check the interactive map occasionally in X-Plane or FSX to help you verify your position.
- Use the A/FD information at `http://SkyVector.com` or other resources on the web to learn more about the airports along your route, including the best alternatives should you need to divert.
- The weather for this flight is set; but practice using web resources to get a real-time weather briefing and NOTAMs for this flight. If you are a real pilot, you can use DUAT for an official preflight briefing.

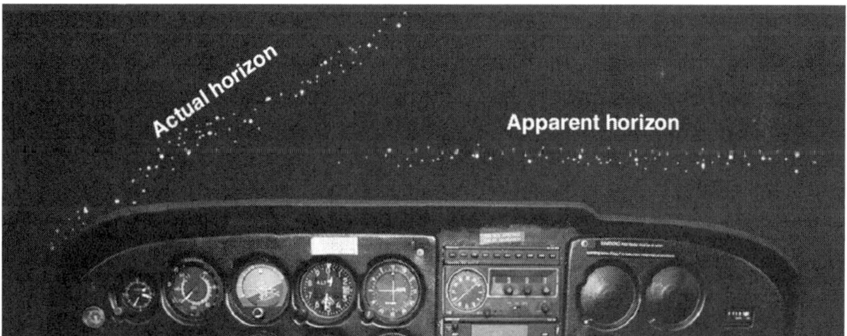

Figure 36-2: False horizon illusion at night, as shown in Figure 16-15 of the *Pilot's Handbook of Aeronautical Knowledge*

What-Ifs

You can also use the "Dice-Based Failure Scheme" described in Chapter 8 to create additional challenges for this flight.

At any point during the flight, roll a die, draw a number from a hat, or use another method to select a random number between 1 and 6. Using Table 36-1, find the corresponding problem to solve, and then take the appropriate action.

Table 36-1: Random Challenges for This Flight

NUMBER	RESULT
1	Rough-running engine
2	Low-voltage indication
3	Divert to KPAE.
4	Divert to KBVS.
5	Emergency at KFHR closes the airport.
6	Passenger is ill.

Objectives and Desired Outcome Grading Sheet

SCENARIO ACTIVITIES	SCENARIO SUB-ACTIVITIES	DESIRED OUTCOME
Identify controlled airspace along your route.	Review the requirements for operating in Class C airspace and MOAs.	Explain
VOR navigation	Identify and track VOR radials.	Practice
Night flying	Understand the challenges and hazards associated with night flying.	Explain/Practice
Diversion	Navigate to and land at an alternate airport.	Perform

CHAPTER

37

Private Pilot Lesson 24: Night Freight Run

In the generic FITS syllabus, this lesson is a dual cross-country flight at night. It assumes that you're flying a freight route that requires several stops. You're under pressure from the boss to complete the flight efficiently and on time. (Of course, as a private pilot, you can't fly for hire, but this exercise helps you understand the pressures that all pilots can feel during a flight.)

Scenario

This scenario involves a round-robin flight from Pasco, WA (KPSC), to Lewiston, ID (KLWS), and Spokane International Airport (KGEG) before returning to KPSC. The direct distance is about 270 nm (see Figure 37-1). At typical Cessna 172 cruising speed, the flight requires about 2 hours and 30 minutes of flying time. To help you focus on the main objectives for this lesson, the flight begins with your Skyhawk in the air between KPSC and KLWS.

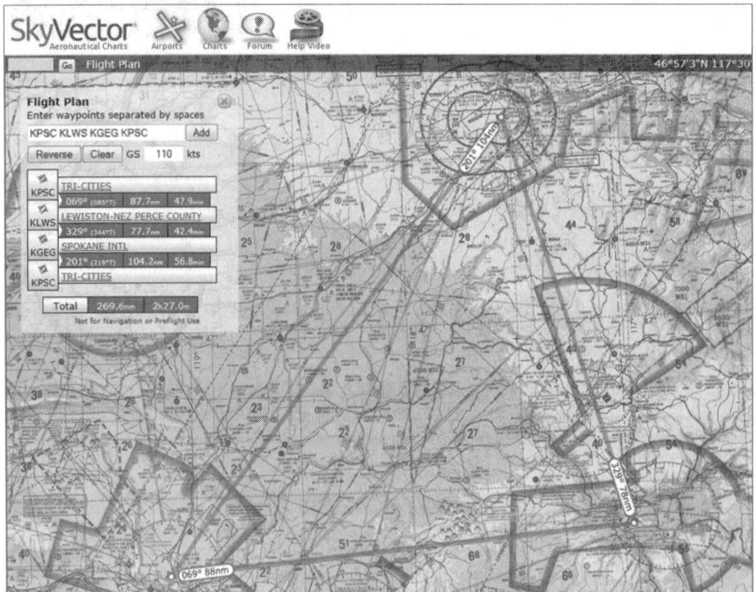

Figure 37-1: The direct route KPSC-KLWS-KGEG on the Seattle sectional chart as shown on SkyVector

Objectives

The primary goals for this flight are practicing:

- All basic flying skills
- Night-flying procedures
- VOR navigation
- Basic GPS navigation
- Procedures for obtaining a complete preflight briefing
- Diversion and emergency procedures
- Aeronautical decision making

Completion Standards

The detailed goals for this lesson are outlined in the table at the end of this chapter. In general, before moving on to the next lesson, you should meet the following standards, based on the generic FITS syllabus for this lesson:

- Understand how to gather and interpret information about airports, VORs, and airspace on aeronautical charts.
- Choose an appropriate route given the terrain, time of day, airspace, and other factors.
- Collect and apply information in the A/FD about the airports you intend to use.
- Understand the process for obtaining a complete preflight briefing.
- Understand the challenges involved in night flying.
- Apply techniques for instrument flying to night flying.
- Practice VOR and GPS navigation.

References and Resources

To prepare for this lesson, review the following references and resources. The resources at the AOPA Flight Training website and the AOPA Air Safety Institute publications are valuable supplements to the official information in the FAA references.

TITLE	CHAPTER/SECTION	TOPIC/NOTES
Pilot's Handbook of Aeronautical Knowledge	Chapter 13, "Airport Operations"	Airport Lighting (pp. 13-6–13-9)
	Chapter 15, "Navigation"	Review all sections.
	Chapter 16, "Aeromedical Factors"	Review all sections, especially Vision in Flight (pp. 16-17–16-19).
Airplane Flying Handbook	Chapter 10, "Night Operations"	Review all sections.
	Chapter 16, "Emergency Procedures"	Review all sections.
Aeronautical Chart User's Guide	VFR Aeronautical Charts	–
	VFR Aeronautical Chart Symbols	–

Continued

(continued)

TITLE	CHAPTER/SECTION	TOPIC/NOTES
AOPA Air Safety Institute Interactive Safety Course *Do The Right Thing: Decision Making for Pilots*	–	–
AOPA Air Safety Institute Interactive Safety Course *GPS for VFR Operations*	–	–
AOPA Air Safety Institute Interactive Safety Course *VFR GPS Guide: Garmin 430/530*	–	–

CROSS-REFERENCE **For more information about the references and resources that complement the lessons in this book, see Chapter 2.**

Preflight Briefing

This scenario begins with your Cessna 172 approaching KLWS. Use the VOR receivers and GPS to determine your position. Make a normal descent and landing at KLWS, and then continue the flight to KGEG. As noted in "Tips for This Lesson," you may want to deviate from the direct route to fly via charted airways or VOR to VOR.

Location and Weather

The weather for this flight is VFR with an overcast cloud layer at 6,000 ft. and light winds from the southwest along your route. Visibility is restricted to less than 10 miles in haze.

Situations and Flights

This lesson uses the following files for X-Plane and FSX:

- X-Plane: `Wiley-SBT-PrivatePilot-Lesson-24.sit`
- FSX: `Wiley-SBT-PrivatePilot-Lesson-24.flt`

CROSS-REFERENCE **For more information about using Situations (X-Plane) and Flights (FSX), see Chapter 10.**

Tips for This Lesson

Here are a few suggestions to help you get the most from this lesson:

- Download the *AOPA Air Safety Foundation Flight Planner*, a handy flight log and form for recording weather, NOTAMs, and related information. A link is at this book's website.
- The direct courses shown in Figure 37-1 may not be the easiest to follow, especially at night. Consider adjusting the route to fly directly to and from VORs or via charted Victor airways, at least until you are in the vicinity of the airports where you intend to land. Review the notes, obstructions, and terrain near KLWS (see Figure 37-2) and consider how they may affect your descent to and departure from Lewiston.
- If you don't want to fly the entire trip in real time or in one sitting, you can accelerate the simulation en route or, after landing at the end of each leg, save your position as a Situation (X-Plane) or Flight (FSX) so that you can resume the trip later. You can also use the interactive map in your simulation to move your airplane along the intended route of flight.
- When you practice using the VOR system, check the interactive map occasionally in X-Plane or FSX to help you verify your position.
- Use the A/FD information at `http://SkyVector.com` or other resources on the web to learn more about the airports along your route, including the best alternatives should you need to divert.
- The weather for this flight is set; but practice using web resources to get a real-time weather briefing and NOTAMs for this flight. If you are a real pilot, you can use DUAT for an official preflight briefing.

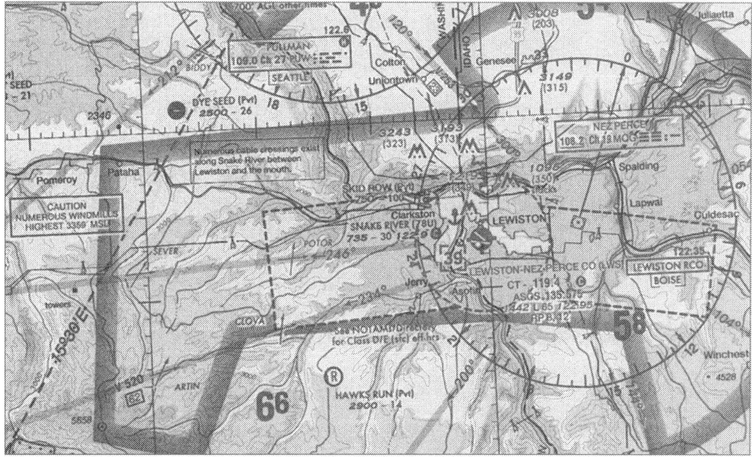

Figure 37-2: The area around Lewiston, ID as shown on the Seattle sectional chart

What-Ifs

You can also use the "Dice-Based Failure Scheme" described in Chapter 8 to create additional challenges for this flight.

At any point during the flight, roll a die, draw a number from a hat, or use another method to select a random number between 1 and 6. Using Table 37-1, find the corresponding problem to solve, and then take the appropriate action.

Table 37-1: Random Challenges for This Flight

NUMBER	RESULT
1	Rough-running engine
2	Low-voltage indication
3	Divert to KPUW.
4	Divert to KEPH.
5	Construction at KGEG closes runway 3-21.
6	Passenger is ill.

Objectives and Desired Outcome Grading Sheet

SCENARIO ACTIVITIES	SCENARIO SUB-ACTIVITIES	DESIRED OUTCOME
Practice all skills associated with night flying.	–	Practice
VOR navigation	Identify and track VOR radials.	Practice
Use basic instrument flying skills to help you maintain precise control.	–	Practice
Diversion	Navigate to and land at an alternative airport.	Perform

CHAPTER

38

Private Pilot Lesson 25: Cross-Country Flight in Marginal VFR

In the generic FITS syllabus, this lesson is a dual flight to demonstrate that you have mastered the tasks in the private pilot PTS for cross-country flight. You are flying to an important business meeting, so there's considerable pressure to arrive on time, but the weather along the route is marginal VFR.

Scenario

This scenario involves a flight from Troutdale, OR (KTTD), to Astoria, OR (KAST). The direct distance is about 72 nm (see Figure 38-1). At typical Cessna 172 cruising speed, the flight requires about 40 minutes of flying time.

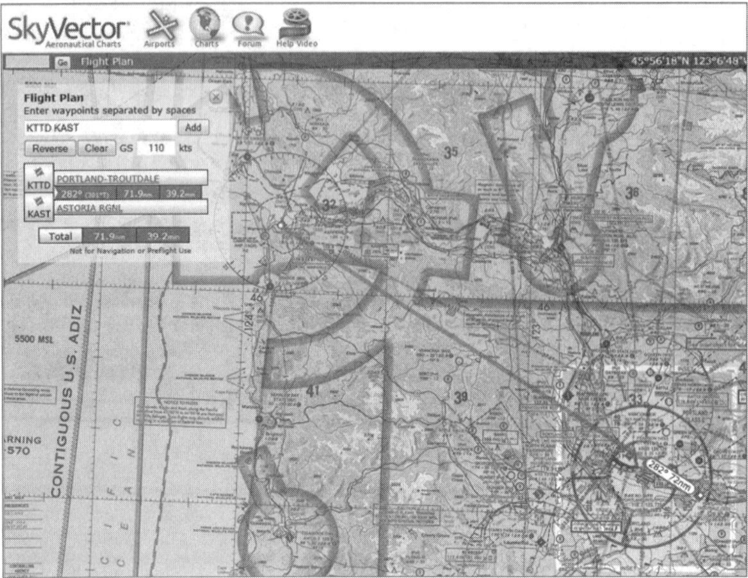

Figure 38-1: The direct route KTTD-KAST on the Seattle sectional chart as shown on SkyVector

Objectives

The primary goals for this flight are practicing:

- All basic flying skills
- VOR navigation
- Basic GPS navigation
- Procedures for obtaining a complete preflight briefing
- Diversion and emergency procedures
- Aeronautical decision making

Completion Standards

The detailed goals for this lesson are outlined in the table at the end of this chapter. In general, before moving on to the next lesson, you should meet the following standards, based on the generic FITS syllabus for this lesson:

- Understand how to gather and interpret information about airports, VORs, and airspace on aeronautical charts.
- Understand the process for obtaining a complete preflight briefing.
- Collect and apply information in the A/FD about the airports you intend to use.
- Use all available information to choose the most appropriate route given the terrain, time of day, airspace, and other factors.
- Use VOR and GPS equipment to navigate accurately.
- Understand the requirements for operating in various types of airspace.

References and Resources

To prepare for this lesson, review the following references and resources. The resources at the AOPA Flight Training website and the AOPA Air Safety Institute publications are valuable supplements to the official information in the FAA references.

TITLE	CHAPTER/SECTION	TOPIC/NOTES
Pilot's Handbook of Aeronautical Knowledge	Chapter 13, "Airport Operations"	–
	Chapter 15, "Navigation"	Review all sections.
Airplane Flying Handbook	–	–
Aeronautical Chart User's Guide	VFR Aeronautical Charts	–
	VFR Aeronautical Chart Symbols	–
AOPA Air Safety Institute Safety Advisor *WeatherWise*	–	–
AOPA Air Safety Institute Safety Advisor *Airspace for Everyone*	–	–

CROSS-REFERENCE **For more information about the references and resources that complement the lessons in this book, see Chapter 2.**

Preflight Briefing

This scenario begins with your Cessna 172 on the ground at KTTD. With the surrounding Class C airspace and nearby airports in mind, take off and proceed toward KAST.

Location and Weather

The weather for this flight is marginal VFR with an overcast cloud layer at about 4,000 ft., scattered rain shows, and light winds from the southwest along your route. Visibility is restricted to less than 10 miles.

Situations and Flights

This lesson uses the following files for X-Plane and FSX:

- X-Plane: `Wiley-SBT-PrivatePilot-Lesson-25.sit`
- FSX: `Wiley-SBT-PrivatePilot-Lesson-25.flt`

CROSS-REFERENCE **For more information about using Situations (X-Plane) and Flights (FSX), see Chapter 10.**

Tips for This Lesson

Here are a few suggestions to help you get the most from this lesson:

- Download the *AOPA Air Safety Foundation Flight Planner*, a handy flight log and form for recording weather, NOTAMs, and related information. A link is at this book's website.
- The direct course shown in Figure 38-1 may not be the best route to follow. Consider adjusting your flight path to fly directly to and from VORs or via charted Victor airways, at least until you are in the vicinity of the airports where you intend to land.
- For more detailed information about operating near Portland International Airport (KPDX), review the Portland inset on the Seattle sectional chart (see Figure 38-2).

- When you practice using the VOR system, check the interactive map occasionally in X-Plane or FSX to help you verify your position.
- Use the A/FD information at `http://SkyVector.com` or other resources on the web to learn more about the airports along your route, including the best alternatives should you need to divert.
- The weather for this flight is set; but practice using web resources such as `http://NavMonster.com` to get a real-time weather briefing and NOTAMs for this flight. If you are a real pilot, you can use DUAT for an official preflight briefing.

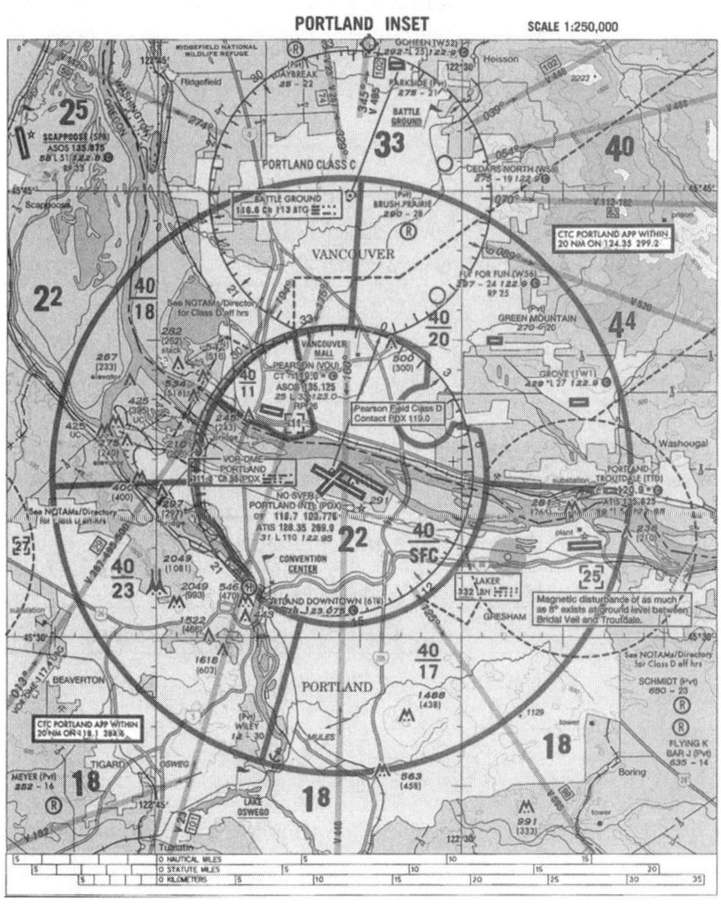

Figure 38-2: Portland inset on the Seattle sectional chart

What-Ifs

You can also use the "Dice-Based Failure Scheme" described in Chapter 8 to create additional challenges for this flight.

At any point during the flight, roll a die, draw a number from a hat, or use another method to select a random number between 1 and 6. Using Table 38-1, find the corresponding problem to solve, and then take the appropriate action.

Table 38-1: Random Challenges for This Flight

NUMBER	RESULT
1	Rough-running engine
2	Low-voltage indication
3	Divert to KHIO.
4	Divert to KSPB.
5	The ceiling at KAST lowers to 800 ft.
6	Wind at KAST is gusting to 25 knots.

Objectives and Desired Outcome Grading Sheet

SCENARIO ACTIVITIES	SCENARIO SUB-ACTIVITIES	DESIRED OUTCOME
Obtain a complete weather briefing.	Use the information to choose the best route and alternatives.	Explain/Describe
VOR navigation	Identify and track VOR radials.	Practice
GPS navigation	–	Practice
Diversion	Navigate to and land at an alternative airport.	Perform

CHAPTER 39

Private Pilot Lesson 26: Cross-Country Flight: Progress Check

In the generic FITS syllabus, this lesson is a progress check to assess your skills in planning and completing a typical cross-country flight.

Scenario

This scenario involves a flight from Boeing Field (KBFI) in Seattle, WA, across the Cascade Range to Yakima, WA (KYKM). The distance via Victor airways is about 113 nm (see Figure 39-1). At typical Cessna 172 cruising speed, the flight requires about 1 hour and 10 minutes of flying time.

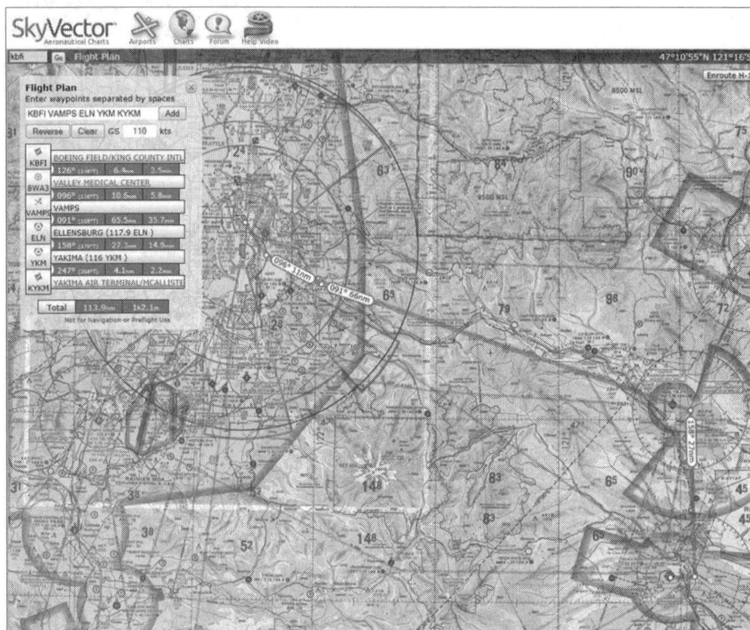

Figure 39-1: The route KBFI-VAMPS-ELN-YKM-KYKM on the Seattle sectional chart, as shown on SkyVector

Objectives

The primary goals for this flight are demonstrating proficiency in:

- Obtaining a complete preflight briefing
- Preflight planning
- All basic flying skills
- VOR navigation
- Basic GPS navigation
- Applying diversion and emergency procedures
- Aeronautical decision making

Completion Standards

The detailed goals for this lesson are outlined in the table at the end of this chapter. In general, before moving on to the next lesson, you should meet the following standards, based on the generic FITS syllabus for this lesson:

- Understand how to gather and interpret information about airports, VORs, and airspace on aeronautical charts.
- Understand the process for obtaining a complete preflight briefing.
- Collect and apply information in the A/FD about the airports you intend to use.
- Use all available information to choose the most appropriate route given the terrain, time of day, airspace, and other factors.
- Use VOR and GPS equipment to navigate accurately.
- Understand the requirements for operating in various types of airspace.

References and Resources

To prepare for this lesson, review the following references and resources. The resources at the AOPA Flight Training website and the AOPA Air Safety Institute publications are valuable supplements to the official information in the FAA references.

TITLE	CHAPTER/SECTION	TOPIC/NOTES
Pilot's Handbook of Aeronautical Knowledge	Chapter 10, "Aircraft Performance"	Review all sections.
	Chapter 12, "Aviation Weather Services"	Review all sections.
	Chapter 15, "Navigation"	Review all sections.
Instrument Flying Handbook	Chapter 7, "Navigation Systems"	Review all sections, pp. 7-1–7-19.
Aeronautical Chart User's Guide	VFR Aeronautical Charts	–
	VFR Aeronautical Chart Symbols	–
AOPA Air Safety Institute Safety Advisor *Mountain Flying*	–	–

CROSS-REFERENCE **For more information about the references and resources that complement the lessons in this book, see Chapter 2.**

Preflight Briefing

This scenario begins with your Cessna 172 on the ground at KBFI, ready to depart to the southeast. The route depicted in Figure 39-1 includes an initial leg to join V2-298, the low-altitude airway between SEA, ELN, and YKM. You can, of course, choose a different route.

Location and Weather

The weather for this flight is VFR with an overcast cloud layer at about 7,500 ft., scattered rain shows, and light winds from the southwest along your route. Visibility is restricted to less than 10 miles (see Figure 39-2).

Figure 39-2: Crossing the Cascade Range as shown in FSX

Situations and Flights

This lesson uses the following files for X-Plane and FSX:

- X-Plane: `Wiley-SBT-PrivatePilot-Lesson-26.sit`
- FSX: `Wiley-SBT-PrivatePilot-Lesson-26.flt`

CROSS-REFERENCE For more information about using Situations (X-Plane) and Flights (FSX), see Chapter 10.

Tips for This Lesson

Here are a few suggestions to help you get the most from this lesson:

- Download the *AOPA Air Safety Foundation Flight Planner*, a handy flight log and form for recording weather, NOTAMs, and related information. A link is at this book's website.
- When you practice using the VOR system, check the interactive map occasionally in X-Plane or FSX to help you verify your position.
- Use the A/FD information at `http://SkyVector.com` or other resources on the web to learn more about the airports along your route, including the best alternatives should you need to divert.
- The weather for this flight is set; but practice using web resources such as `http://NavMonster.com` to get a real-time weather briefing and NOTAMs for this flight. If you are a real pilot, you can use DUAT for an official preflight briefing.
- Note that sometimes you must zig and zag to avoid airspace and obstacles. The best route often isn't a straight line between point of departure and destination (see Figure 39-3).

Figure 39-3: The initial legs from KBFI that avoid airspace conflicts and join V-2-298 at VAMPS intersection, as shown on SkyVector

What-Ifs

You can also use the "Dice-Based Failure Scheme" described in Chapter 8 to create additional challenges for this flight.

At any point during the flight, roll a die, draw a number from a hat, or use another method to select a random number between 1 and 6. Using Table 39-1, find the corresponding problem to solve, and then take the appropriate action.

Table 39-1: Random Challenges for This Flight

NUMBER	RESULT
1	Rough-running engine
2	Low-voltage indication
3	Divert to KELN.
4	Divert to KEPH.
5	The ceiling at KYKM lowers to 800 ft.
6	The ceiling over the Cascades lowers to 6,500 ft.

Objectives and Desired Outcome Grading Sheet

SCENARIO ACTIVITIES	SCENARIO SUB-ACTIVITIES	DESIRED OUTCOME
Preflight planning	Obtain a complete weather briefing.	Practice
Choose an appropriate route.	–	Practice
VOR navigation	Identify and track VOR radials.	Practice
GPS navigation	–	Practice
Diversion	Navigate to and land at an alternative airport.	Perform

CHAPTER

40

Private Pilot Lesson 27: Long Solo Cross-Country Flight

In the generic FITS syllabus, this lesson is the long solo, cross-country flight required before you can take the practical test for the private pilot certificate.

Scenario

This scenario involves a round-robin cross-country flight from Bellingham, WA (KBLI), around the Olympic Peninsula to Hoquiam, WA (KHQM), and back to KBLI. You plan to stop at William Fairchild International (KCLM) before continuing to another landing at KHQM. The airport at Shelton, WA (KSHN), is both a checkpoint and a potential alternate airport on the last leg. The distance for the route, as shown in Figure 40-1, is about 330 nm. At typical Cessna 172 cruising speed, the flight requires about 3 hours. As noted in previous lessons, you can divide the flight into several sessions.

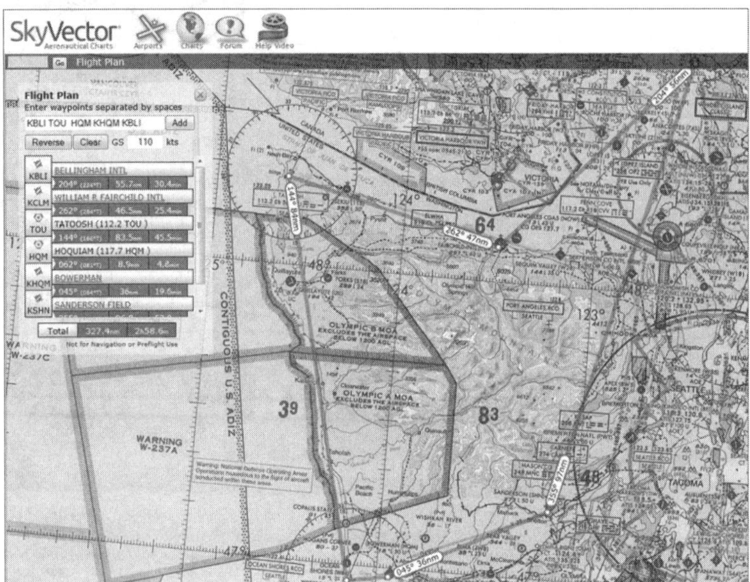

Figure 40-1: The planned route KBLI-KCLM-TOT-HQM-KHQM-KSHN-KBLI on the Seattle sectional chart, as shown on SkyVector

Objectives

The primary goals for this flight are demonstrating proficiency in:

- Obtaining a complete preflight briefing
- Preflight planning
- All basic flying skills
- VOR navigation
- Basic GPS navigation
- Applying diversion and emergency procedures
- Aeronautical decision making

Completion Standards

The detailed goals for this lesson are outlined in the table at the end of this chapter. In general, before moving on to the next lesson, you should meet the following standards, based on the generic FITS syllabus for this lesson:

- Understand how to gather and interpret information about airports, VORs, and airspace on aeronautical charts.
- Understand the process for obtaining a complete preflight briefing.
- Choose an appropriate route given the terrain, over-water legs, airspace, and other factors.
- Collect and apply information in the A/FD about the airports you intend to use.
- Practice VOR and GPS navigation.
- Make appropriate decisions en route considering the weather, fuel state, and other factors.

References and Resources

To prepare for this lesson, review the following references and resources. The resources at the AOPA Flight Training website and the AOPA Air Safety Institute publications are valuable supplements to the official information in the FAA references.

TITLE	CHAPTER/SECTION	TOPIC/NOTES
Pilot's Handbook of Aeronautical Knowledge	Chapter 10, "Aircraft Performance"	Review all sections.
	Chapter 12, "Aviation Weather Services"	Review all sections.
	Chapter 15, "Navigation"	Review all sections.
Instrument Flying Handbook	Chapter 7, "Navigation Systems"	Review all sections, pp. 7-1–7-19.
Aeronautical Chart User's Guide	VFR Aeronautical Charts	–
	VFR Aeronautical Chart Symbols	–

Continued

(continued)

TITLE	CHAPTER/SECTION	TOPIC/NOTES
Risk Management Handbook	–	Review all sections.
AOPA Air Safety Institute Safety Advisor *Do the Right Thing: Decision Making for Pilots*	–	–
AOPA Air Safety Institute Interactive Safety Course *ASI Flight Risk Evaluator*	–	–

CROSS-REFERENCE **For more information about the references and resources that complement the lessons in this book, see Chapter 2.**

Preflight Briefing

This scenario begins with your Cessna 172 on the ground at KBLI, ready to depart to the south. The first leg to KCLM takes you over the San Juan Islands and close to Canadian airspace (see Figure 40-2). Use VORs and landmarks to remain on the U.S. side of the border and to fly the best route across the Strait of Juan de Fuca.

Figure 40-2: Cruising over the San Juan Islands as shown in X-Plane

Location and Weather

The weather for this flight is good VFR with scattered clouds at 7,500 ft. and light winds from the southwest along your route.

Situations and Flights

This lesson uses the following files for X-Plane and FSX:

- X-Plane: `Wiley-SBT-PrivatePilot-Lesson-27.sit`
- FSX: `Wiley-SBT-PrivatePilot-Lesson-27.flt`

CROSS-REFERENCE For more information about using Situations (X-Plane) and Flights (FSX), see Chapter 10.

Tips for This Lesson

Here are a few suggestions to help you get the most from this lesson:

- Download the *AOPA Air Safety Foundation Flight Planner*, a handy flight log and form for recording weather, NOTAMs, and related information. A link is at this book's website.
- It's easy to confuse the islands in the San Juan Islands chain. Check your progress frequently on the chart.
- When you practice using the VOR system, check the interactive map occasionally in X-Plane or FSX to help you verify your position.
- Use the A/FD information at `http://SkyVector.com` or other resources on the web to learn more about the airports along your route, including the best alternatives should you need to divert.
- The weather for this flight is set; but practice using web resources such as `http://NavMonster.com` to get a real-time weather briefing and NOTAMs for this flight. If you are a real pilot, you can use DUAT for an official preflight briefing.

What-Ifs

You can also use the "Dice-Based Failure Scheme" described in Chapter 8 to create additional challenges for this flight.

At any point during the flight, roll a die, draw a number from a hat, or use another method to select a random number between 1 and 6. Using Table 40-1, find the corresponding problem to solve, and then take the appropriate action.

Table 40-1: Random Challenges for This Flight

NUMBER	RESULT
1	Rough-running engine
2	Low-voltage indication
3	Divert to KOLM.
4	Divert to KPAE.
5	The ceiling at KHQM lowers to 800 ft.
6	The ceiling in the Puget Sound area drops to 3,000 ft.

Objectives and Desired Outcome Grading Sheet

SCENARIO ACTIVITIES	SCENARIO SUB-ACTIVITIES	DESIRED OUTCOME
Preflight planning	Obtain a complete weather briefing.	Practice
	Choose appropriate routes.	Practice
VOR navigation	Identify and track VOR radials.	Practice
GPS navigation	–	Practice
Diversion	Navigate to and land at an alternative airport.	Perform

CHAPTER 41

Private Pilot Lesson 28: Preparation for the Practical Test

In the generic FITS syllabus, this lesson is a progress check (often called a "stage check") to assess the skills required to pass the practical test for the private pilot certificate. The basic objectives, references, and completion standards for the final three scenarios in this syllabus are similar, but the locations, weather, and other circumstances vary.

Scenario

This scenario involves a local flight near Hillsboro, OR (KHIO), west of Portland (see Figure 41-1), in good VFR weather. Use this lesson to focus on basic flight maneuvers, ground reference maneuvers, and abnormal conditions and emergencies.

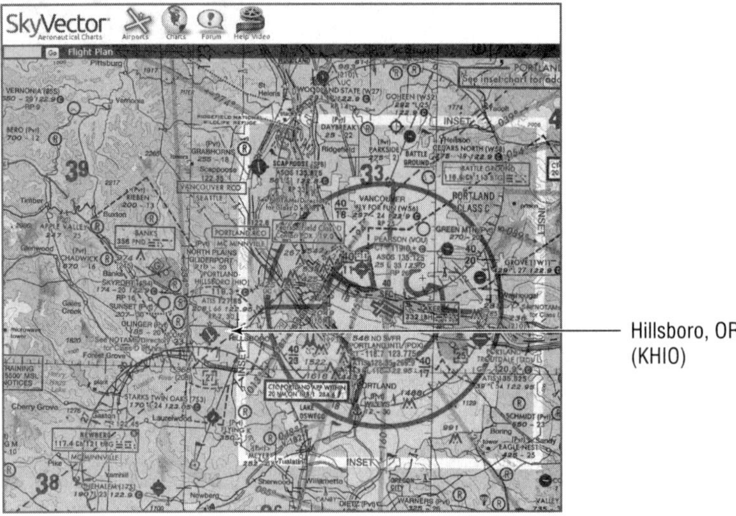

Figure 41-1: The area around KHIO on the Seattle sectional chart as shown on SkyVector

Objectives

The primary goals for this flight are demonstrating proficiency in:

- All tasks described in the private pilot PTS, especially Task V: Performance Maneuver, Task VI: Ground Reference Maneuvers, Task VIII: Slow Flight and Stalls, and Task X: Emergency Operations
- Application of the principles of aeronautical decision making as described in the *Risk Management Handbook*
- Following abnormal and emergency procedures

Completion Standards

The detailed goals for this lesson are outlined in the table at the end of this chapter. In general, before moving on to the next lesson, you should meet the following standards, based on the generic FITS syllabus for this lesson:

- Understand how to gather and interpret information about terrain, airports, navigation aids, and airspace on aeronautical charts.
- Understand the practical test standards.

- Perform the tasks outlined in the objectives to the standards described in the PTS.
- Demonstrate your ability to apply the principles of risk management and aeronautical decision making during preflight planning and while in the cockpit (see Figure 41-2).

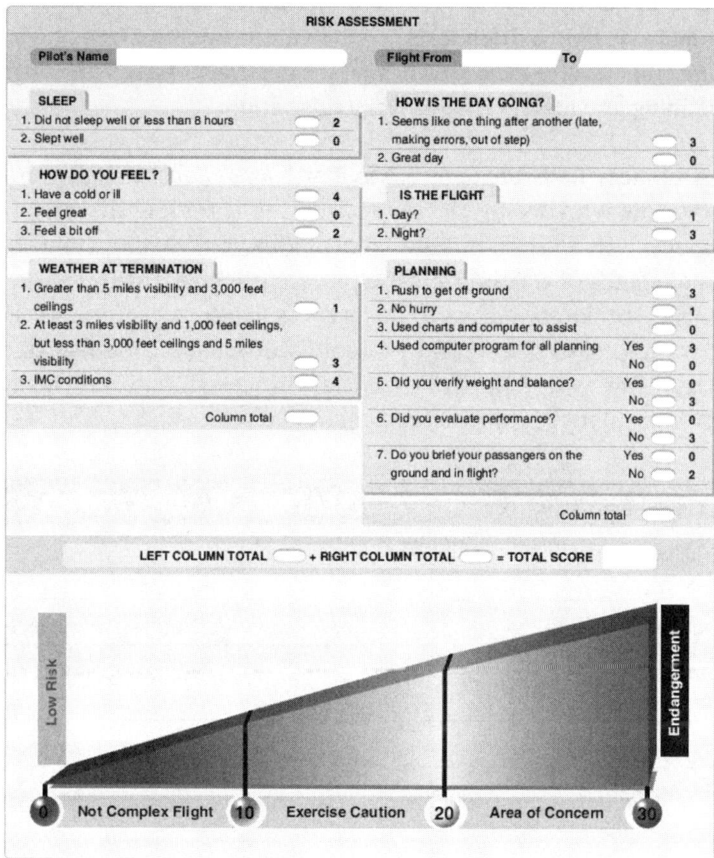

RISK ASSESSMENT

Pilot's Name ______ Flight From ______ To ______

SLEEP	
1. Did not sleep well or less than 8 hours	2
2. Slept well	0

HOW DO YOU FEEL?	
1. Have a cold or ill	4
2. Feel great	0
3. Feel a bit off	2

WEATHER AT TERMINATION	
1. Greater than 5 miles visibility and 3,000 feet ceilings	1
2. At least 3 miles visibility and 1,000 feet ceilings, but less than 3,000 feet ceilings and 5 miles visibility	3
3. IMC conditions	4

Column total ______

HOW IS THE DAY GOING?	
1. Seems like one thing after another (late, making errors, out of step)	3
2. Great day	0

IS THE FLIGHT	
1. Day?	1
2. Night?	3

PLANNING		
1. Rush to get off ground		3
2. No hurry		1
3. Used charts and computer to assist		0
4. Used computer program for all planning	Yes	3
	No	0
5. Did you verify weight and balance?	Yes	0
	No	3
6. Did you evaluate performance?	Yes	0
	No	3
7. Do you brief your passangers on the ground and in flight?	Yes	0
	No	2

Column total ______

LEFT COLUMN TOTAL ______ + RIGHT COLUMN TOTAL ______ = TOTAL SCORE ______

Figure 41-2: The risk assessment tool from Figure 4-2 in the *Risk Management Handbook*

References and Resources

To prepare for this lesson, review the following references and resources. The resources at the AOPA Flight Training website and the AOPA Air Safety Institute publications are valuable supplements to the official information in the FAA references.

The Flight Test Prep section of the AOPA Flight Training website offers several helpful resources for pilots at this stage of flight training, including interactive courses and quizzes that can help you determine if you're ready for the private pilot practical test.

CROSS-REFERENCE **Sporty's Pilot Shop (`www.sportys.com/PilotShop`) offers examples of questions from FAA computer-based knowledge tests (known informally as the "written tests") online at the Sporty's Free Study Buddy website. This service from Sporty's (and similar web-based offerings from other training providers) requires free registration.**

The AOPA Air Safety Institute Safety Advisor *Pilot's Guide to the Flight Review* is intended for pilots who are preparing for the flight review that most pilots must complete every two years, but it also provides good background for students in the final stages of training for the private pilot certificate.

Another AOPA ASI Safety Advisor, *Instructor's Guide to the Pre-Solo Written Test*, intended to help instructors and pre-solo students, is also useful at this stage of your training as a review of essential information about the aircraft you fly, key FAA regulations, and related matters.

TITLE	CHAPTER/SECTION	TOPIC/NOTES
Private Pilot Airplane Practical Test Standards	All tasks	–
Risk Management Handbook	–	Reference as necessary
Pilot's Handbook of Aeronautical Knowledge	–	Reference as necessary
Airplane Flying Handbook	–	Reference as necessary
Aeronautical Information Manual	–	Reference as necessary
AOPA Air Safety Institute Safety Advisor *Pilot's Guide to the Flight Review*	–	–
AOPA Air Safety Institute Safety Advisor *Instructor's Guide to the Pre-Solo Written Test*	–	–

CROSS-REFERENCE **For more information about the references and resources that complement the lessons in this book, see Chapter 2.**

Preflight Briefing

This scenario begins in the air north of KHIO so that you can practice basic flight maneuvers before descending to review ground-reference maneuvers. When you finish practicing, return to KHIO and make a normal landing.

Location and Weather

The weather for this flight is VFR, with high clouds and light winds.

Situations and Flights

This lesson uses the following files for X-Plane and FSX:

- X-Plane: `Wiley-SBT-PrivatePilot-Lesson-28.sit`
- FSX: `Wiley-SBT-PrivatePilot-Lesson-28.flt`

CROSS-REFERENCE For more information about using Situations (X-Plane) and Flights (FSX), see Chapter 10.

Tips for This Lesson

Here are a few suggestions to help you get the most from this lesson:

- Review the introduction to *Private Pilot PTS*, in particular the Special Emphasis Areas and the topics on page 10.
- Include several "what-ifs" from the following section to add realism to this lesson. During an actual private pilot practical test, the examiner will simulate at least one abnormal situation or emergency, and you will also be expected to demonstrate your ability to cope with distractions and unexpected circumstances, such as changes in the weather.
- Use the A/FD information at `http://SkyVector.com` or other resources on the web to learn more about the airports in the area, including the best alternatives should you need to divert.
- The weather for this flight is set, but practice using web resources such as `http://NavMonster.com` to get a real-time weather briefing and NOTAMs for this flight. If you are a real pilot, you can use DUAT for an official preflight briefing.

What-Ifs

You can also use the "Dice-Based Failure Scheme" described in Chapter 8 to create additional challenges for this flight.

At any point during the flight, roll a die, draw a number from a hat, or use another method to select a random number between 1 and 6. Using Table 41-1, find the corresponding problem to solve, and then take the appropriate action.

Table 41-1: Random Challenges for This Flight

NUMBER	RESULT
1	Rough-running engine
2	Low-voltage indication
3	Acrid smoke emerging from the instrument panel
4	Engine failure
5	The ceiling at KHIO lowers to 800 ft.
6	The visibility at KHIO drops to 2 miles.

Objectives and Desired Outcome Grading Sheet

SCENARIO ACTIVITIES	SCENARIO SUB-ACTIVITIES	DESIRED OUTCOME
Review *Private Pilot PTS*	Understand the PTS concept, private pilot tasks, testing procedures and performance standards.	Describe/Explain
Basic flight maneuvers	–	Perform
Ground reference maneuvers	–	Perform
Simulated abnormal/ emergency procedures	–	Perform
Diversion	Navigate to and land at an alternate airport.	Perform

CHAPTER

42

Private Pilot Lesson 29: Further Preparation for the Practical Test

In the generic FITS syllabus, this lesson is a ground session to assess your readiness to take the practical test for the private pilot certificate. As noted in Chapter 41, the basic objectives, references, and completion standards for the final three scenarios in this syllabus are similar, but the locations, weather, and other circumstances vary.

PC-based simulation adds an interactive component to ground lessons, and this scenario involves a short cross-country flight from Deer Park, WA (KDEW) to Coeur d'Alene (KCOE) in marginal VFR weather to help you review navigation, aeronautical decision making, and emergency procedures (see Figure 42-1).

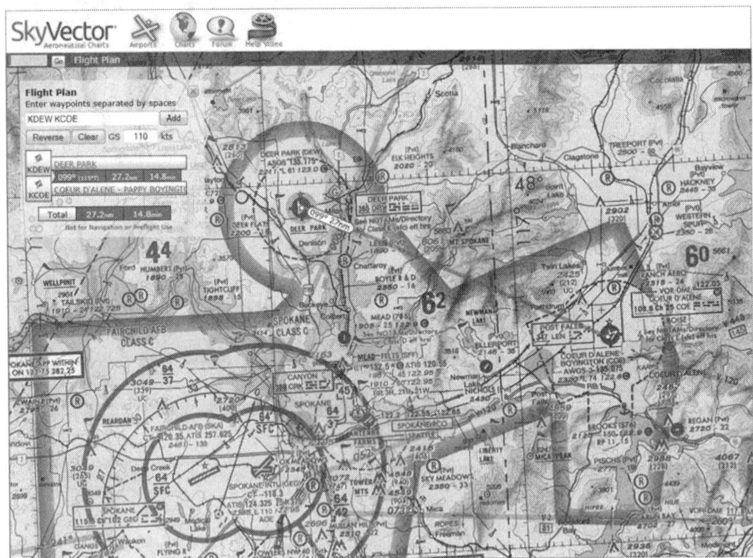

Figure 42-1: The direct route from KDEW to KCOE on the Seattle sectional chart as shown on SkyVector

Objectives

The primary goals for this flight are demonstrating proficiency in:

- All tasks described in the *Private Pilot PTS,* especially Task I: Preflight Preparation, Task VII: Navigation, and Task X: Emergency Operations
- Application of the principles of aeronautical decision making as described in the *Risk Management Handbook*

Completion Standards

The detailed goals for this lesson are outlined in the table at the end of this chapter. In general, before moving on to the next lesson, you should meet the following standards, based on the generic FITS syllabus for this lesson:

- Understand how to gather and interpret information about terrain, airports, navigation aids, and airspace on aeronautical charts.
- Understand the practical test standards.
- Perform pilotage and VOR navigation.
- Demonstrate your ability to apply the principles of risk management and aeronautical decision making during preflight planning and while in the cockpit.

References and Resources

To prepare for this lesson, review the following references and resources. The resources at the AOPA Flight Training website and the AOPA Air Safety Institute publications are valuable supplements to the official information in the FAA references.

You may want to review the "References and Resources" section of Chapter 41 for additional sources of information that can help you determine if you're ready for the private pilot practical test.

TITLE	CHAPTER/SECTION	TOPIC/NOTES
Private Pilot Airplane Practical Test Standards	All tasks	–
Risk Management Handbook	–	Reference as necessary
Pilot's Handbook of Aeronautical Knowledge	–	Reference as necessary
Airplane Flying Handbook	–	Reference as necessary
Aeronautical Information Manual	–	Reference as necessary
AOPA Air Safety Institute Safety Advisor *Do the Right Thing – Decision Making for Pilots*	–	–
AOPA Air Safety Institute Safety Advisor *Mastering Takeoffs and Landings*	–	–

CROSS-REFERENCE **For more information about the references and resources that complement the lessons in this book, see Chapter 2.**

Preflight Briefing

This scenario begins in the air south of KDEW so that you can practice pilotage and VOR before joining the traffic pattern at KCOE and making a normal landing. After landing at KCOE, practice the following tasks:

- Short-field (maximum performance) takeoff and landing
- Soft-field takeoff and landing
- Go-around
- Aborted takeoff

Location and Weather

The weather for this flight is marginal VFR, with an overcast layer of clouds at about 4,000 ft. Visibility is less than 10 miles (see Figure 42-2).

Figure 42-2: The view from the X-Plane Cessna 172 cockpit en route to KCOE

Situations and Flights

This lesson uses the following files for X-Plane and FSX:

- X-Plane: `Wiley-SBT-PrivatePilot-Lesson-29.sit`
- FSX: `Wiley-SBT-PrivatePilot-Lesson-29.flt`

CROSS-REFERENCE **For more information about using Situations (X-Plane) and Flights (FSX), see Chapter 10.**

Tips for This Lesson

Here are a few suggestions to help you get the most from this lesson:

- Review the introduction to the *Private Pilot PTS*, in particular the Special Emphasis Areas and the topics on page 10.
- Include several "what-ifs" from the following section to add realism to this lesson. During an actual private pilot practical test, the examiner will simulate at least one abnormal situation or emergency, and you will also be expected to demonstrate your ability to cope with distractions and unexpected circumstances, such as changes in the weather.
- Use the A/FD information at `http://SkyVector.com` or other resources on the web to learn more about the airports in the area, including the best alternatives should you need to divert.
- The weather for this flight is set, but practice using web resources such as `http://NavMonster.com` to get a real-time weather briefing and NOTAMs for this flight. If you are a real pilot, you can use DUAT for an official preflight briefing.

What-Ifs

You can also use the "Dice-Based Failure Scheme" described in Chapter 8 to create additional challenges for this flight.

At any point during the flight, roll a die, draw a number from a hat, or use another method to select a random number between 1 and 6. Using Table 42-1, find the corresponding problem to solve, and then take the appropriate action.

Table 42-1: Random Challenges for This Flight

NUMBER	RESULT
1	Rough-running engine
2	Low-voltage indication
3	Acrid smoke emerging from the instrument panel
4	Engine failure
5	A passenger is upset.
6	The visibility at KCOE drops to 2 miles.

Objectives and Desired Outcome Grading Sheet

SCENARIO ACTIVITIES	SCENARIO SUB-ACTIVITIES	DESIRED OUTCOME
Review the *Private Pilot PTS.*	Understand the PTS concept, private pilot tasks, testing procedures, and performance standards.	Describe/Explain
Pilotage	–	Perform
VOR navigation	Use cross-radials to fix your position; intercept and track radials.	Perform
Simulated abnormal/ emergency procedures	–	Perform
Takeoffs and landings	Practice normal, short-field, and soft-field takeoffs and landings, plus go-arounds and aborted takeoffs.	Perform
Diversion	Navigate to and land at an alternate airport.	Perform

CHAPTER 43

Private Pilot Lesson 30: The Private Pilot Practical Test

In the generic FITS syllabus, this lesson is the private pilot practical test. This is your opportunity to practice any of the tasks in the private pilot PTS in the context of a short cross-country flight.

A typical private pilot practical test (also known as a "check ride") involves an oral examination that lasts about two hours, and a flight test that usually requires about 90 minutes of flying time. The examiner (typically a designated pilot examiner, not an FAA inspector), must prepare a "plan of action," a representative sample of the tasks from the PTS. The FAA strongly encourages examiners to use scenarios, not just a series of isolated tasks, to assess the candidate's ability to operate safely as a pilot. The examiner is also required to create realistic distractions and to pose simulated abnormal conditions and emergencies to evaluate your ability to cope with the unexpected.

Scenario

For this scenario, assume that the examiner has asked you to plan a flight from Hermiston, OR (KHRI) to Felts Field (KSFF) at Spokane, WA (see Figure 43-1). The direct distance between the airports is about 137 nm; and at typical Cessna 172 cruising speed, the flight requires about 1 hour and 15 minutes of flying time.

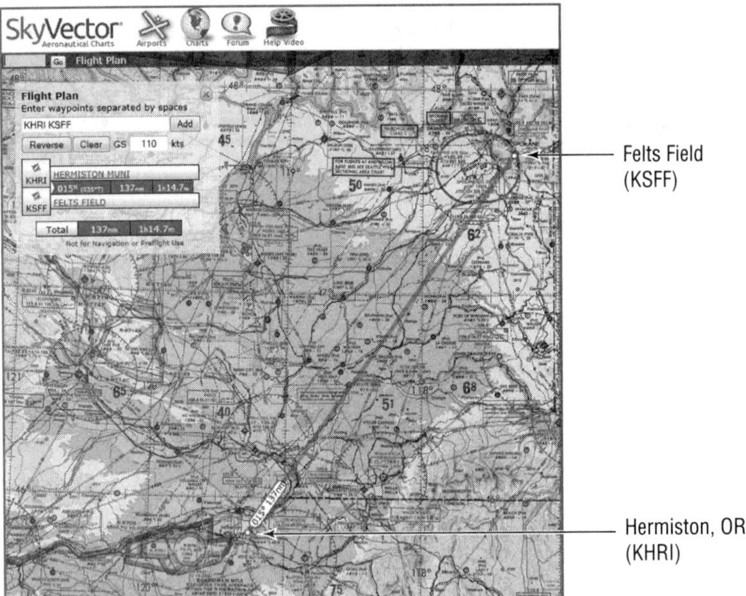

Figure 43-1: The direct route from KHRI to KSFF on the CF-16 WAC chart as shown on SkyVector

Objectives

The primary goal for this flight is earning a private pilot certificate based on your ability to demonstrate proficiency in:

- All tasks described in the *Private Pilot PTS*
- Application of the principles of aeronautical decision making as described in the *Risk Management Handbook*

Completion Standards

The completion standards for this scenario are clearly stated in the PTS. They include demonstrating knowledge of special emphasis areas such as stall/spin awareness and collision avoidance (see p. 5). As you fly the specific maneuvers in the PTS (see p. 8), you should always:

- Perform the tasks specified in the areas of operation for the certificate or rating sought within the approved standards.
- Demonstrate mastery of the aircraft with the successful outcome of each task performed never seriously in doubt.
- Demonstrate satisfactory proficiency and competency within the approved standards.
- Demonstrate sound judgment.

According to the PTS (see p. 9), the following lapses typically cause candidates to fail the practical test:

- Any action or lack of action by the applicant that requires corrective intervention by the examiner to maintain safe flight
- Failure to use proper and effective visual scanning techniques to clear the area before and while performing maneuvers
- Consistently exceeding tolerances stated in the objectives for the tasks
- Failure to take prompt corrective action when tolerances are exceeded

References and Resources

The official references for the practical test are outlined in the introduction to the PTS (see p. 3). You can find more detailed descriptions in Chapter 13 of this book. You may also want to review the "References and Resources" section of Chapter 41 for more information about additional sources that can help you determine if you're ready for the private pilot practical test.

CROSS-REFERENCE **For more information about the references and resources that complement the lessons in this book, see Chapter 2.**

Preflight Briefing

This scenario begins with your airplane ready to depart KHRI. A typical practical test might include the following tasks in roughly this sequence:

- Simulated short-field (maximum performance) or soft-field takeoff
- Climb and initial leg of a cross-country flight
- Basic flight maneuvers by reference to instruments
- Diversion
- Ground reference maneuvers
- Steep turns, slow flight, stalls
- Simulated emergency
- Return to the departure airport to demonstrate one or more landings, go-arounds, and related procedures

Location and Weather

The weather for this flight is VFR with an overcast layer of clouds at about 5,500 ft. Visibility is about 10 miles (see Figure 43-2).

Figure 43-2: The view from the FSX Cessna 172 cockpit en route to KSFF

Situations and Flights

This lesson uses the following files for X-Plane and FSX:

- X-Plane: `Wiley-SBT-PrivatePilot-Lesson-30.sit`
- FSX: `Wiley-SBT-PrivatePilot-Lesson-30.flt`

CROSS-REFERENCE **For more information about using Situations (X-Plane) and Flights (FSX), see Chapter 10.**

Tips for This Lesson

Here are a few suggestions to help you get the most from this lesson:

- Carefully review the Private Pilot PTS — in particular, the Special Emphasis Areas and the topics on pages 10 and 1-ix.
- Review the Examiner's Practical Test Checklist on page 1-xi of the PTS. It shows the specific tasks that you may be required to perform during the flight test.
- Complete the *AOPA Air Safety Institute Flight Planner* (link available at this book's website at `www.wiley.com/go/flightsimulatortraining`) for the planned flight from KHRI to KSFF.
- Include several "what-ifs" from the following section to add realism to this lesson. During an actual private pilot practical test, the examiner simulates at least one abnormal situation or emergency; and you are expected to demonstrate your ability to cope with distractions and unexpected circumstances, such as changes in the weather and mechanical problems with the aircraft.
- Use the A/FD information at `http://SkyVector.com` or other resources on the web to learn more about the airports in the area, including the best alternatives should you need to divert.
- The weather for this flight is set, but practice using web resources such as `http://NavMonster.com` to get a real-time weather briefing and NOTAMs for this flight. If you are a real pilot, you can use DUAT for an official preflight briefing.

What-Ifs

You can also use the "Dice-Based Failure Scheme" described in Chapter 8 to create additional challenges for this flight.

At any point during the flight, roll a die, draw a number from a hat, or use another method to select a random number between 1 and 6. Using Table 39-1, find the corresponding problem to solve, and then take the appropriate action.

Table 39-1: Random Challenges for This Flight

NUMBER	RESULT
1	Passenger is upset/anxious.
2	Rough-running engine
3	Acrid smoke emerging from the instrument panel
4	Visibility at KSFF drops to 2 miles in haze.
5	Rain showers obscure the direct route to KSFF.
6	Low-voltage reading (alternator failure)

Objectives and Desired Outcome Grading Sheet

SCENARIO ACTIVITIES	SCENARIO SUB-ACTIVITIES	DESIRED OUTCOME
Oral exam	FARs, privileges and limitations of a private pilot, ADM, and preflight planning	Perform/Manage/Decide
Flight test	Maneuvers and procedures in the PTS	Perform/Manage/Decide

Part V

Instrument Rating Scenarios

In This Part

CHAPTER

44

Introduction to the Instrument Rating Syllabus: Background and Resources for IFR Lessons

The scenarios that follow guide you through a training program to add an instrument rating to a private pilot certificate in a single-engine airplane. The syllabus consisting of 17 lessons covers ground and flight training and preparation for the practical test. Lesson 18 gives you an opportunity to fly a typical IFR practical test.

The lessons and scenarios are based on the *FITS Generic Instrument Airplane Rating Syllabus* published in August 2007. It is one of the documents available in the Generic Curriculums and Curriculum Guides section of the FAA/Industry Training Standards (FITS) website.

For the purposes of this book, the lessons are adapted for use with X-Plane and FSX, as described in Chapters 3 and 9. For example, in the FITS syllabus, some of the lessons are ground sessions. However, you can take to the virtual skies in X-Plane or FSX to see the concepts in action as you review the background information in FAA training handbooks and other sources. Even lessons that focus on learning about the instruments and cockpit controls begin in the air. Of course, if you're involved in flight training, you should follow your instructor's guidance when using a PC-based simulation to supplement your training.

During flight training for the instrument rating, students spend most of their flight time "under the hood," that is, wearing a view-limiting device such as a visor or goggles that restricts the view beyond the cockpit and requires the student to focus on the instrument panel (see Figure 44-1). PC-based simulations, of course, can reproduce a range of realistic weather, and most of the scenarios that follow begin in simulated instrument meteorological conditions (IMC) that restrict or eliminate the outside view.

Figure 44-1: The instrument panel of a Beechcraft Bonanza manufactured in the late 1980s

IFR flying is primarily a mental game. You're constantly solving a puzzle — confirming the aircraft's attitude and position, juggling instructions from ATC, referring to charts, and asking "What's next?"

The reward? After flying into the clouds just after takeoff, you fly hundreds of miles and then see the runway emerge from the mist moments before you touch down (see Figure 44-2).

Figure 44-2: Breaking out at minimums on an instrument approach as seen in FSX

What Is an Instrument Rating?

Adding an instrument rating to the private pilot certificate sharpens your skills and makes personal and business flying more practical. Training for the IFR "ticket" is also the next step in a typical private pilot's education. (Although it's possible to earn a commercial pilot certificate without an instrument rating, most pilots get an instrument rating before they begin training for the commercial certificate.) Without an instrument rating, you must operate within the limits set by 14 CFR §91.155 "Basic VFR weather minimums." In general, that rule requires flight visibility of at least 3 miles and a ceiling of at least 1,000 ft. above ground level. With an instrument rating, you can fly in the clouds and make approaches to many airports when the flight visibility is as low as one-half mile.

An instrument rating also qualifies you to fly at and above 18,000 ft. (that is, in Class A airspace); and if you plan to fly complex and high-performance aircraft, your insurance company may require that you have an instrument rating even if you want to fly only under VFR.

Basic Requirements

The legal minimums required to earn an instrument rating are spelled out in the FAA regulations, specifically 14 CFR Part 61, §61.65, "Instrument rating requirements." The prerequisites include:

- At least a private pilot certificate
- Ground training on the subjects related to flying under IFR, including:
  - Federal Aviation Regulations
  - Information that applies to flight operations under IFR in the *Aeronautical Information Manual*
  - Air traffic control systems and procedures for instrument flight operations
  - IFR navigation and approaches by use of navigation systems
  - Use of IFR en route and instrument approach procedure charts
  - Procurement and use of aviation weather reports and forecasts and the elements of forecasting weather trends
  - Safe and efficient operation of aircraft under instrument flight rules and conditions
  - Recognition of critical weather situations
  - Aeronautical decision making and judgment
  - Crew resource management, including crew communication and coordination

- Flight experience that includes:
  - 50 hours of cross-country flight time as pilot in command
  - 40 hours of actual or simulated instrument time, including at least 15 hours of instruction from an instrument flight instructor
  - At least one instructional cross-country flight of at least 250 nm that includes three different types of approaches

The regulations allow credit for using flight simulators, flight training devices, and aviation training devices. For example, you can count 10 hours of instruction in an approved ATD toward the 40 hours of required instrument time.

Essential References

The instrument rating lessons that follow rely on a set of key references (see Figure 44-3) that are available in PDF versions at the website for this book.

Figure 44-3: Essential resources for the instrument rating

These resources include:

- *Instrument Flying Handbook* (FAA-H-8083-15A), which focuses on the knowledge and skills required for earning an instrument rating
- *Instrument Procedures Handbook* (FAA-H-8261-1A), which expands on the fundamental skills and procedures described in the *Instrument Flying Handbook* and includes detailed coverage of instrument charts and procedures for IFR takeoff, departure, cruise, arrival, approach, and landing

- *Advanced Avionics Handbook* (FAA-H-8083-6), a guide to modern cockpit displays and navigation systems
- *Aeronautical Chart User's Guide, 9th Edition*, a detailed key to IFR charts
- *Aeronautical Information Manual* (AIM), updated semiannually
- *Pilot/Controller Glossary*, which complements the AIM
- *Instrument Rating Practical Test Standards for Airplane* (FAA-S-8081-4E), effective January 2010. You can find a complete list of references for all the tasks included in the instrument rating PTS on page 3 of that booklet.
- *Aviation Weather* (AC 00-6A), which explains weather theory
- *Aviation Weather Services* (AC 00-45G), a guide to the reports, forecasts, and other preflight and inflight weather resources available to pilots

The *Pilot's Handbook of Aeronautical Knowledge* and the *Airplane Flying Handbook*, introduced in the syllabus for the private pilot certificate, are also useful resources, as is *Air Force Manual 11-217, Instrument Flight Procedures*, the U.S. Air Force equivalent of the *Instrument Flying Handbook*.

You may want to review the following additional references from the FAA, available for download from this book's website:

- *General Aviation Pilot's Guide Preflight Planning, Weather Self-Briefings, and Weather Decision Making*
- *Instrument Proficiency Check (IPC) Guidance*

Resources from the AOPA Air Safety Institute

Most of the lessons that follow refer to supplemental publications, such as Safety Advisors published by the AOPA Air Safety Institute. These free booklets, available for download as PDFs from the AOPA ASI website, include:

- *Single-Pilot IFR*
- *Spatial Disorientation*
- *Weather Wise*
- *Aircraft Icing*
- *Aircraft Deicing and Anti-icing Equipment*

The AOPA ASI also offers many free interactive courses on its website. Several of these courses are valuable for IFR pilots, including:

- *Do the Right Thing: Decision Making for Pilots*
- *Weather Wise: Precipitation and Icing*

- *Weather Wise: Ceiling and Visibility*
- *Weather Wise: Air Masses and Fronts*
- *GPS for IFR Operations*
- *IFR Insights: Regulations*
- *IFR Insights: Charts*
- *Single-Pilot IFR*

CROSS-REFERENCE **You can find details about many free references and resources for pilots and virtual aviators in Chapter 2.**

IFR Charts

The instrument rating lessons rely on IFR charts that omit most information about terrain and ground features (after all, you're presumed to be flying in or above the clouds) in favor of detail about routes, minimum altitudes, navigation aids, and other data vital to pilots flying under IFR. These charts include:

- Low-altitude en route charts that, as the name implies, are used primarily for planning and reference as you cruise between the departure and arrival airports (see Figure 44-4)
- Departure and approach charts, often called *plates*. These charts, typically formatted to fit easily on a kneeboard or yoke clip for quick reference, are used during climb after takeoff and for the final stages of approach and landing (see Figure 44-5).

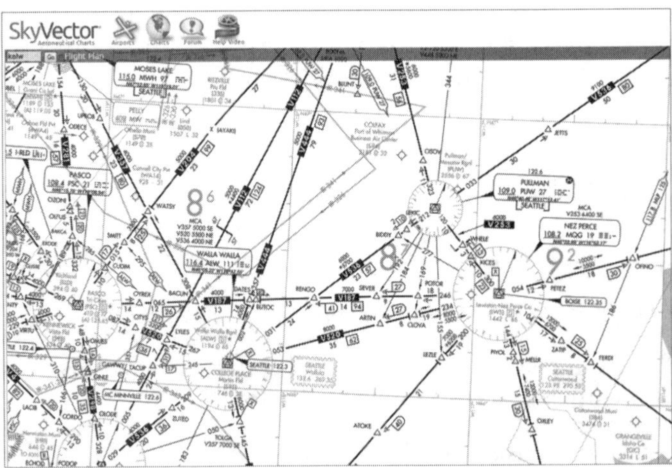

Figure 44-4: Part of a typical low-altitude en route chart published by FAA AeroNav Services, as shown on SkyVector

The IFR charts reproduced in this book are based on the editions published by FAA AeroNav Services. You can download PDF versions of the current editions of the charts from the FAA AeroNav Services website, and copies of the examples used in this book are also available at this book's website.

To learn about the terms and symbols used on charts published by FAA AeroNav Services, see the *Aeronautical Chart User's Guide, 9th Edition*. A PDF version of that handbook is available at this book's website.

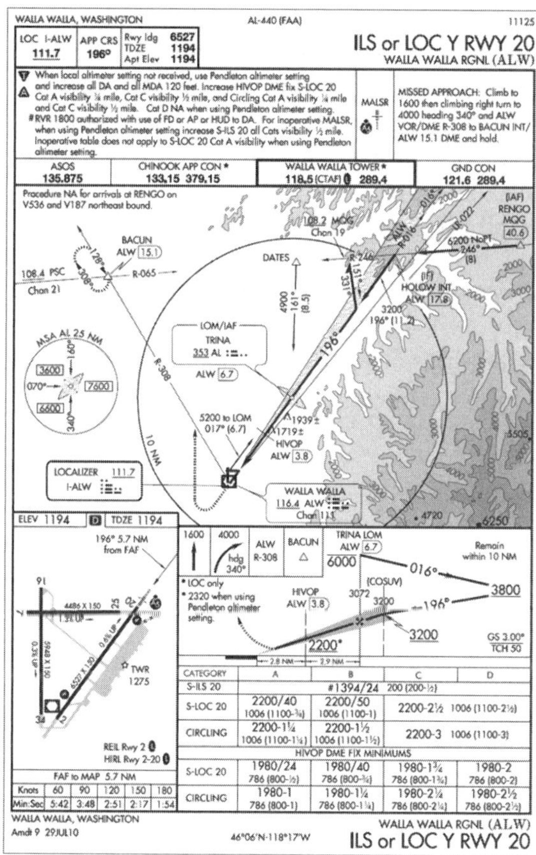

Figure 44-5: A typical instrument approach plate published by FAA AeroNav Services

Many instrument-rated pilots, including most airline pilots, use charts published by Jeppesen, which offers a range of packages by subscription. You can learn more about Jeppesen products by visiting the company's website (`www.jeppesen.com`).

Today, IFR pilots are rapidly adopting tablet computers like the Apple iPad, and aviation-specific software such as ForeFlight and WingX, to display charts and other information. These applications are excellent tools for use with PC-based simulations.

Important X-Plane Limitations

Before you begin using X-Plane for IFR practice, note that the basic Cessna 172 in X-Plane has a few key limitations:

- No distance-measuring equipment (DME)
- Limited GPS features
- No altitude preselect for the autopilot

Unless you add plug-ins (free or commercial products that you can find via the X-Plane website), you can't fly IFR procedures that require DME or GPS-based departures and approaches. The GPS in X-Plane is the equivalent of a unit approved only for en route navigation. You can use the GPS in X-Plane as a substitute for DME when tracking to and from VORs and to fly DME arcs, provided the current direct-to waypoint in the GPS corresponds to the appropriate ground-based navigation aid.

The basic autopilot in the X-Plane Cessna 172 can fly headings and track navigation signals (from the GPS, a VOR, or a localizer/ILS). It can also hold the current altitude and track an ILS glideslope. However, you cannot preselect an altitude or set a specific rate of climb or descent for it to fly.

Important FSX Limitations

The simulation of the Garmin 500-series GPS in FSX offers some RNAV (GPS) approaches, but many procedures in the simulation are out of date, and they usually don't correspond to current approach charts. In particular, the GPS in FSX does not support approaches with vertical guidance (APV). These procedures are available only in GPS units that use the Wide Area Augmentation System (WAAS). As noted in Chapter 1, you can buy add-on features that provide more current databases and additional features.

The autopilot in FSX reproduces most of the features of a typical Bendix/King unit installed in many single-engine airplanes. In addition to the features supported in the X-Plane autopilot, it includes altitude preselect, and you can set a rate of climb or descent (in feet per minute).

RNAV (GPS) Approaches

Because the basic versions of X-Plane and FSX do not simulate current GPS-based approaches, the scenarios in this book focus on procedures that rely on ground-based navigation aids. If you use FSX, you may find that you can substitute RNAV (GPS) procedures for some of the approaches in the instrument-rating syllabus. However, be aware that the details stored in the GPS database may not correspond to the information on the current RNAV (GPS) charts for that procedure.

Current Approach Information

As noted in Chapter 1, the databases of navigation aids and airports in X-Plane and FSX are not current. Many of the changes that require real-world pilots to update charts and navigation databases every 28 days are minor. Other updates add, eliminate, or substantially change vital information, especially details that affect instrument approach procedures.

Nevertheless, even if some details (for example, the minimum descent altitude or decision altitude) have changed since X-Plane and FSX were last updated, you can probably still fly the procedures in the simulation. Just use the latest values on the chart. Even if the published courses used for VOR, localizer, or ILS procedures have changed, you can still fly many approaches and practice techniques that apply to general types of procedures.

The IFR Syllabus

Like the generic FITS syllabus for the instrument rating, the IFR lessons in this book are organized into two stages:

- Stage I introduces and refines basic attitude instrument (BAI) flying skills and reinforces aeronautical decision making and risk management.
- Stage II applies basic skills to the full range of tasks required to fly under IFR during all phases of flight. It also includes abnormal conditions and emergencies relevant to IFR flight.

NOTE **Appendix B, "Instrument Training Lesson Guide," of the *Instrument Flying Handbook* describes another generic syllabus that can help you get an overview of the training required for the instrument rating.**

As described in Chapter 9, each lesson includes specific objectives, recommends background reading and practice, and provides a grading grid that helps you evaluate your knowledge and skills.

The lessons follow the logical progression in the FITS syllabus, but you can, of course, skip or repeat scenarios and fly them in any sequence.

Keep in mind that the first lessons may be useful even if you're already an IFR pilot, have experience with FSX or X-Plane, or are switching from one simulation to the other. They help you review key features of the simulations, as described in Chapters 6 and 7, and they give you a chance to practice fundamental flying skills so that you can become comfortable with the controls and "flying" qualities of the simulation installed on your computer.

CHAPTER

45

IFR Lesson 1: Basic Attitude Instrument Flying

Imagine that you have inadvertently flown into the clouds and must maintain positive control of the airplane, a scenario known to aviation safety experts as "continued VFR flight into IMC." This situation leads to many accidents, either through loss of control of the airplane or a crash into terrain or obstacles. The latter situation, known as *controlled flight into terrain* (CFIT), remains a major concern of the FAA, the airlines, and the general aviation community.

Surprisingly, accidents involving inadvertent flight into instrument meteorological conditions claim many instrument-rated pilots. Even these pilots, who have been trained to fly by reference to instruments, may be unprepared for the loss of visual references. Startled, they lose control or try to duck under the clouds and then collide with terrain or obstacles such as antennas and water towers (see Figure 45-1).

Figure 45-1: Loss of visual references in low clouds and rain

Scenario

This scenario, like Lesson 16 of the private pilot syllabus, introduces the basics of flying by reference to instruments. Unlike that earlier lesson, however, this flight begins with your airplane in the clouds so that you can practice basic flight maneuvers solely by reference to the flight instruments.

Objectives

The primary goals for this flight are:

- Developing the critical skills of instrument cross-check and interpretation
- Maneuvering solely by reference to flight instruments
- Recognizing and recovering from unusual attitudes while flying on instruments

> An unusual attitude is an airplane attitude not normally required for instrument flight. Unusual attitudes may result from a number of conditions, such as turbulence, disorientation, instrument failure, confusion, preoccupation with flight deck duties, carelessness in cross-checking, errors in instrument interpretation, or lack of proficiency in aircraft control.
>
> Instrument Flying Handbook, p. 5-26

This lesson is the most important session in the instrument rating syllabus. Basic instrument flying skills are the foundation of everything that follows. You may find it helpful to return to this scenario periodically as you work toward the instrument rating.

NOTE **Chapter 4 of the *Instrument Flying Handbook* describes two fundamental approaches to attitude instrument flying. The "control and performance instrument" concept, advocated by the U.S. Air Force and many instrument instructors, is often easier to understand and apply in the cockpit than the "primary and supporting instrument" method, the topic of several questions on the FAA knowledge test for the instrument rating. The fundamental goal of each method — precise control of an aircraft by reference to instruments — is the same.**

Completion Standards

The detailed goals for this lesson are outlined in the table at the end of this chapter. In general, before moving on to the next lesson, you should meet the following standards, based on the generic FITS syllabus and the instrument rating PTS. These goals include:

- Demonstrating knowledge of the elements related to attitude instrument flying during straight-and-level flight, climbs, turns, and descents
- Using proper instrument cross-check and interpretation techniques and applying the appropriate pitch, bank, power, and trim corrections
- Maintaining altitude within ±100 ft. during level flight, headings within ±10°, airspeed within ±10 knots, and bank angles within ±5° during turns

References and Resources

To prepare for this lesson, review the following references and resources. The resources at the AOPA Air Safety Institute are valuable supplements to the official information in the FAA references.

TITLE	CHAPTER/SECTION	TOPIC/NOTES
Instrument Flying Handbook	Chapter 1, "Human Factors"	Review all topics pp.1-1–1-8
	Chapter 3, "Flight Instruments"	Review all topics pp. 3-1–3-21 and Required Navigation Instrument System Inspection (p. 3-34)
	Chapter 4, Section I, "Airplane Attitude Instrument Flying Using Analog Instrumentation"	Review all topics
	Chapter 5, Section I, "Airplane Basic Flight Maneuvers Using Analog Instrumentation"	Review all topics pp. 5-1–5-26, Unusual Attitudes and Recoveries (pp. 5-26–5-28), and Basic Instrument Flight Patterns (p. 5-30)
Instrument Rating Practical Test Standards	Task IV: Flight by Reference to Instruments	Review all sections.
AOPA Air Safety Institute Safety Advisor *Spatial Disorientation*	–	–
AOPA Air Safety Institute Interactive Safety Course *Weather Wise: Ceiling and Visibility*	–	–
AOPA Air Safety Institute Interactive Safety Course *Accident Case Study: VFR into IMC*	–	–

CROSS-REFERENCE **For more information about the references and resources that complement the lessons in this book, see Chapter 2.**

Preflight Briefing

This scenario begins with your Cessna 172 in the air between the Walla Walla (ALW) and Pullman (PUW) VORs in eastern Washington. You can use those navigation aids to help you track your position as you practice basic instrument flight maneuvers. The autopilot is on with the HDG and ALT hold features active.

Practice basic flight maneuvers and the instrument flight patterns described in Chapter 5 of the *Instrument Flying Handbook:*

- Racetrack pattern
- Standard 45° procedure turn
- Teardrop patterns

Note that during these exercises, you shouldn't try to compensate for the wind. Later, when you are tracking navigation signals and flying holding patterns, you'll adjust to fly the appropriate ground tracks.

Earlier editions of the *Instrument Flying Handbook* described two additional instrument flight patterns, Pattern A (see Figure 45-2) and Pattern B (see Figure 45-3), that are excellent exercises to help you develop and fine-tune the instrument flying skills you will need later in your training. Practice them during this lesson.

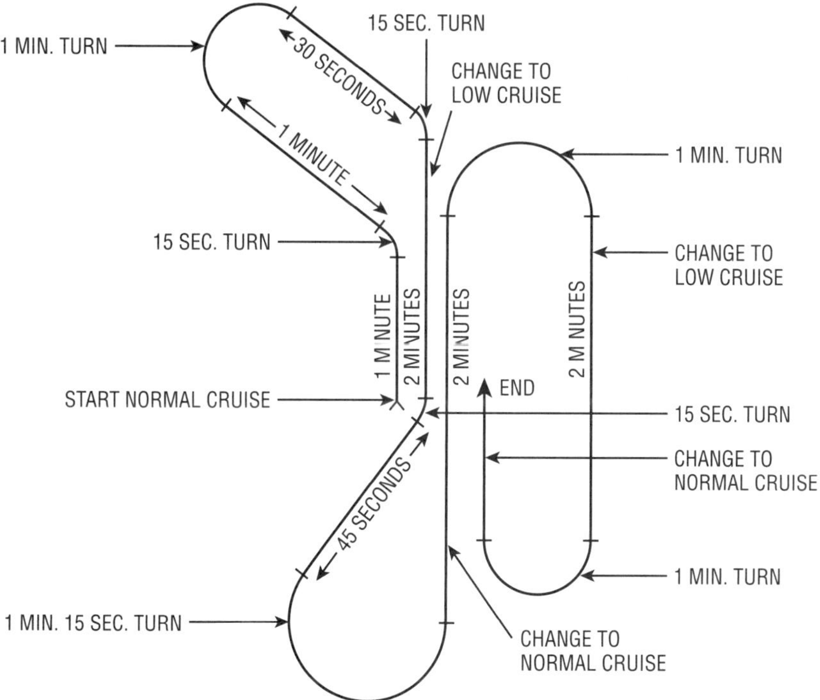

Figure 45-2: Basic instrument flight Pattern A

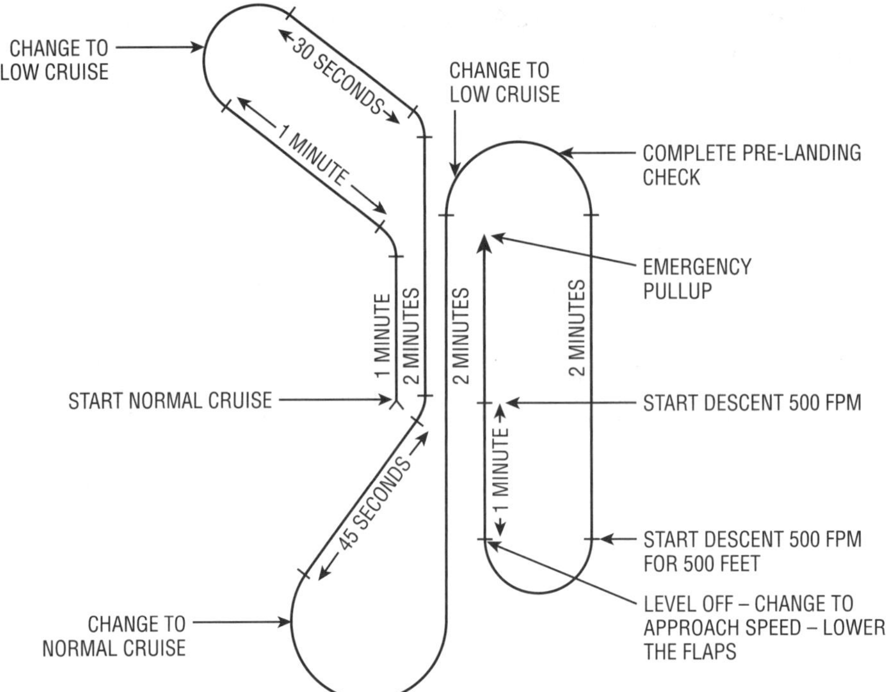

Figure 45-3: Basic instrument flight Pattern B

Air Force Manual 11-217: Instrument Flight Procedures (the U.S. Air Force equivalent to the *Instrument Flying Handbook*), describes several variations on another useful exercise for aspiring instrument pilots, the vertical S.

The basic vertical S (S-A) is a continuous series of climbs and descents flown at a specific rate while maintaining a constant heading. For example, from straight-and-level flight at 3,500 ft. on a heading of 090°, establish a climb at 500 feet per minute, climb 1,000 ft., and then transition smoothly to a descent at 500 feet per minute. You must increase power to initiate the climb and reduce power to start the descent. You can use the configuration tables in Chapter 12 to help you establish and maintain stable climbs and descents. Repeat this sequence a few times, and then level off at your original altitude.

Vertical S-B (see Figure 45-4) follows the same sequence as vertical S-A, except that you establish and maintain a constant angle of bank (20°–30° of bank works well for this exercise) during each climb and descent.

The C and D variations of the vertical S add complexity — for example, a change in bank direction each time you transition from level flight, a climb, or a descent. You can also change the initial conditions for the maneuver — for example, by starting in a low-speed cruise configuration. For more information about these maneuvers, see Chapter 2, "Instrument Flight Maneuvers — Fixed Wing," in *Air Force Manual 11-217: Instrument Flight Procedures*, one of the references available as a PDF at this book's website.

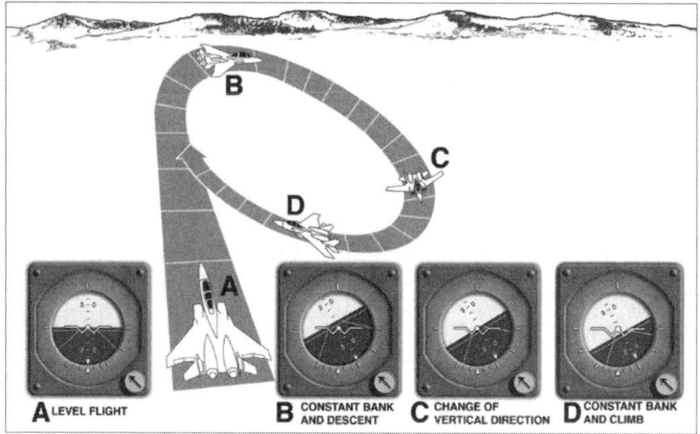

Figure 45-4: The vertical S-B as illustrated in Figure 2.6 of *Air Force Manual 11-217: Instrument Flight Procedures*

Location and Weather

As mentioned earlier, this scenario begins in the air with your Cessna 172 between the Walla Walla (ALW) and Pullman (PUW) VORs (see Figure 45-5). The bases of the clouds in the area are at about 2,500 ft.

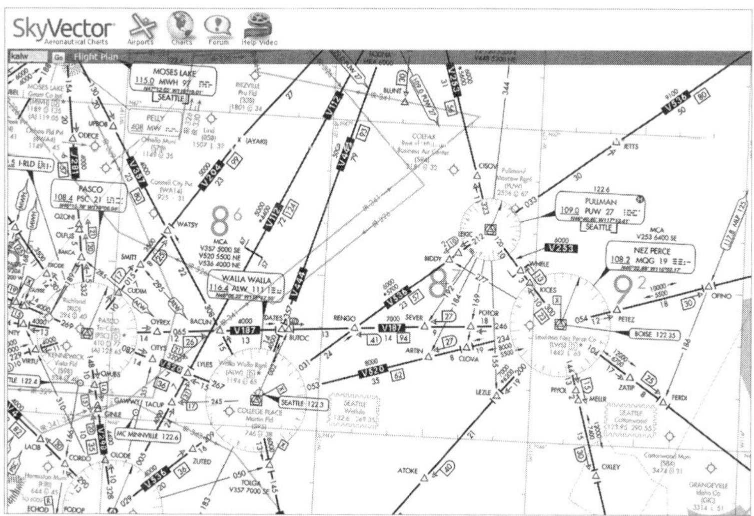

Figure 45-5: The area around Walla Walla, WA (KALW), on the L-13 IFR en route chart as shown on SkyVector

Situations and Flights

This lesson uses the following files for X-Plane and FSX:

- X-Plane: `Wiley-SBT-IFR-Lesson-01.sit`
- FSX: `Wiley-SBT-IFR-Lesson-01.flt`

CROSS-REFERENCE **For more information about using Situations (X-Plane) and Flights (FSX), see Chapter 10.**

Tips for This Lesson

Here are a few suggestions to help you get the most from this lesson:

- Review the information in Chapter 11 about options for changing the view of the instrument panel in X-Plane or FSX.
- Review Chapter 12, especially "Flying Tips" and the configuration tables for the simulation that you use.
- Carefully review Chapters 4 and 5 of the *Instrument Flying Handbook*. You must understand and master the fundamental skills of instrument cross-check, interpretation, and control before you try to juggle all the tasks involved in flying instrument procedures.
- Check the interactive map in X-Plane or FSX periodically as you practice basic instrument flight maneuvers. You can check your position relative to airports and navigation aids, and you can see how well your actual track matches the ideal flight path.
- You may find it helpful to use the autopilot initially. With the autopilot on, you can observe bank angles, pitch attitudes, and changes in airspeed as you turn, climb, and descend. You can also experiment with the throttle to see how changes in power affect airspeed and rate of climb and descent. With those experiments and the configuration tables in Chapter 12 in mind, you can try to match the instrument indications when you fly manually.
- To practice recoveries from unusual attitudes, just close your eyes and try to roll into left and right turns, climbs, and descents. After 20–30 seconds of maneuvering, open your eyes and use the proper recovery techniques.

What-Ifs

You can use the "Dice-Based Failure Scheme" described in Chapter 8 to create additional challenges for this flight. For the IFR lessons, if the random number results in the failure of a system or component, use the system failure options in X-Plane or FSX to create a realistic simulation of the problem.

At any point during the flight, roll a die, draw a number from a hat, or use another method to select a random number between 1 and 6. Using Table 45-1, find the corresponding problem to solve, and then take the appropriate action.

Table 45-1: Random Challenges for This Flight

NUMBER	RESULT
1	Vacuum system failure
2	Attitude indicator failure
3	Low-voltage indication
4	Pilot tube blocked
5	Static system blocked
6	Heading indicator failure

Objectives and Desired Outcome Grading Sheet

SCENARIO ACTIVITIES	SCENARIO SUB-ACTIVITIES	DESIRED OUTCOME
Basic instrument flight maneuvers	Instrument flight patterns	Practice
Constant rate climbs and descents	–	Practice
Constant airspeed climbs and descents	–	Practice
Recoveries from unusual attitudes	–	Practice

CHAPTER 46

IFR Lesson 2: Basic Attitude Instrument Flying

This lesson is similar to the second lesson in the FITS syllabus for the instrument rating.

Scenario

This scenario is another opportunity to practice basic instrument flying skills. However, it adds a challenge: After practicing a series of instrument flight patterns, you must determine your position relative to the Walla Walla VOR (ALW), and then track a VOR radial inbound to the station (see Figure 46-1).

Figure 46-1: Intercepting the 340° radial inbound to ALW as shown in FSX

Objectives

The primary goals for this flight are:

- Honing the critical skills of instrument cross-check and interpretation
- Increasing your precision while maneuvering solely by reference to flight instruments
- Intercepting and tracking VOR radials while flying solely by reference to the instruments

Completion Standards

The detailed goals for this lesson are outlined in the table at the end of this chapter. In general, before moving on to the next lesson, you should meet the following standards, based on the generic FITS syllabus and the instrument rating PTS:

- Demonstrate knowledge of the elements related to attitude instrument flying during straight-and-level flight, climbs, turns, and descents.
- Use proper instrument crosscheck and interpretation techniques and apply the appropriate pitch, bank, power, and trim corrections.
- Maintain altitude within ±100 ft. during level flight, headings within ±10°, airspeed within ±10 knots, and bank angles within ±5° during turns.
- Intercept and track VOR radials, allowing no more than three-quarter-scale deflection of the course deviation indicator (CDI) while tracking.

References and Resources

To prepare for this lesson, review the following references and resources. The resources at the AOPA Air Safety Institute are valuable supplements to the official information in the FAA references.

TITLE	CHAPTER/SECTION	TOPIC/NOTES
Instrument Flying Handbook	Chapter 3, "Flight Instruments"	Review all topics pp. 3-1–3-21 and Required Navigation Instrument System Inspection (p. 3-34)
	Chapter 4, Section I, "Airplane Attitude Instrument Flying Using Analog Instrumentation"	Review all topics
	Chapter 5, Section I, "Airplane Basic Flight Maneuvers Using Analog Instrumentation"	Review all topics pp. 5-1–5-26 and Basic Instrument Flight Patterns (p. 5-30)
Aeronautical Chart User's Guide	IFR Aeronautical Charts: Explanation of IFR Enroute Terms and Symbols	–
Instrument Rating Practical Test Standards	Task IV: Flight by Reference to Instruments	Review all sections.
	Task V: Navigation Systems	A: Intercepting and Tracking Navigation Systems (p. 1-8)

CROSS-REFERENCE For more information about the references and resources that complement the lessons in this book, see Chapter 2.

Preflight Briefing

Practice basic flight maneuvers and the instrument flight patterns described in Chapter 5 of the *Instrument Flying Handbook* and in Chapter 45.

When you finish flying several of the patterns, determine which radial you are on from the ALW VOR and track it inbound until you reach the station.

Location and Weather

This scenario begins in the air. Your Cessna 172 is between the Walla Walla (ALW) and Pullman (PUW) VORs (see Figure 46-2). The bases of the clouds in the area are at about 2,500 ft.

The autopilot is on, with the HDG and ALT hold features active.

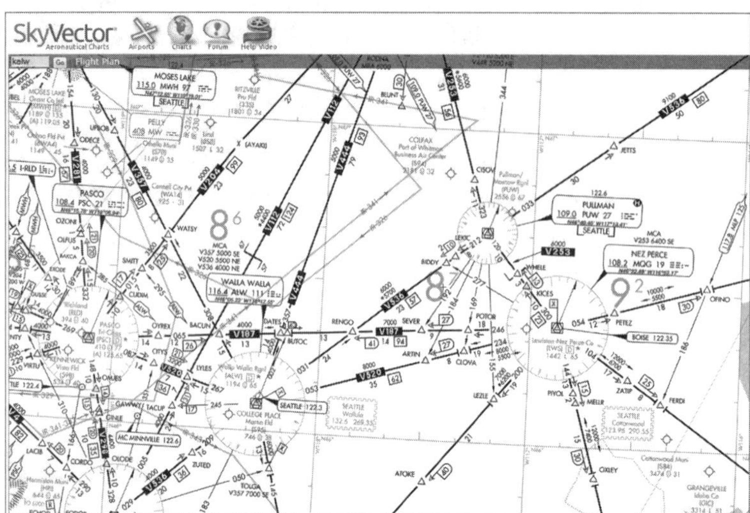

Figure 46-2: The area around Walla Walla, WA (KALW) on the L-13 IFR en route chart as shown on SkyVector

Situations and Flights

This lesson uses the following files for X-Plane and FSX:

- X-Plane: `Wiley-SBT-IFR-Lesson-02.sit`
- FSX: `Wiley-SBT-IFR-Lesson-02.flt`

CROSS-REFERENCE For more information about using Situations (X-Plane) and Flights (FSX), see Chapter 10.

Tips for This Lesson

Here are a few suggestions to help you get the most from this lesson:

- Review the information in Chapter 11 about options for changing the view of the instrument panel in X-Plane and FSX.

- Review Chapter 12, especially "Flying Tips" and the configuration tables for the simulation that you use.
- Check the interactive map in X-Plane or FSX periodically as you practice basic instrument flight maneuvers and as you track inbound to the VOR at ALW.

What-Ifs

You can also use the "Dice-Based Failure Scheme" described in Chapter 8 to create additional challenges for this flight. For the IFR lessons, if the random number results in the failure of a system or component, use the system failure options in X-Plane or FSX to create a realistic simulation of the problem.

At any point during the flight, roll a die, draw a number from a hat, or use another method to select a random number between 1 and 6. Using Table 46-1, find the corresponding problem to solve, and then take the appropriate action.

Table 46-1: Random Challenges for This Flight

NUMBER	RESULT
1	Vacuum system failure
2	Attitude indicator failure
3	Low-voltage indication
4	Pilot tube blocked
5	Static system blocked
6	Heading indicator failure

Objectives and Desired Outcome Grading Sheet

SCENARIO ACTIVITIES	SCENARIO SUB-ACTIVITIES	DESIRED OUTCOME
Basic instrument flight maneuvers	Instrument flight patterns	Practice
Intercepting and tracking VOR radials	–	Practice
Constant airspeed climbs and descents	–	Practice

CHAPTER

47

IFR Lesson 3: Partial-Panel Flight

Now that you have learned and practiced the skills needed for basic instrument maneuvers, you must also learn to fly when important equipment fails.

Most aircraft used in primary instrument training are still equipped with attitude indicators and other instruments that rely on gyroscopes that are spun by air. A vacuum pump supplies the air that blows through the instrument. When that pump fails, one or more important instruments become unreliable and you must rely on other instruments.

The electronics in most new aircraft can also fail. Such "glass cockpit" aircraft are typically equipped with backup mechanical instruments to help you maintain control when the primary flight displays are inoperative.

Simulations are excellent tools for introducing and practicing such "partial-panel" flying.

Scenario

Like the third lesson in the FITS syllabus for the instrument rating, this scenario introduces basic instrument flight maneuvers when some instruments are inoperative or displaying false indications (see Figure 47-1).

Figure 47-1: Flying with a failed vacuum system as shown in X-Plane

Objectives

The primary goals for this flight are:

- Honing the critical skills of instrument cross-check and interpretation
- Practicing basic flight maneuvers with some instruments inoperative

Completion Standards

The detailed goals for this lesson are outlined in the table at the end of this chapter. In general, before moving on to the next lesson, you should meet the following standards, based on the generic FITS syllabus and the instrument rating PTS. These goals include:

- Using proper instrument cross-check and interpretation techniques and applying the appropriate pitch, bank, power, and trim corrections, including when flying with inoperative or malfunctioning instruments (partial panel)
- Maintaining altitude within ±100 feet during level flight, headings within ±10°, airspeed within ±10 knots, and bank angles within ±5° during turns

References and Resources

To prepare for this lesson, review the following references and resources. The resources at the AOPA Air Safety Institute are valuable supplements to the official information in the FAA references.

TITLE	CHAPTER/SECTION	TOPIC/NOTES
Instrument Flying Handbook	Chapter 3, "Flight Instruments"	Review all topics, pp. 3-1–3-21
	Chapter 4, Section I, "Airplane Attitude Instrument Flying Using Analog Instrumentation"	Review all topics.
	Chapter 5, Section I, "Airplane Basic Flight Maneuvers Using Analog Instrumentation"	Review all topics, pp. 5-1–5-26, Unusual Attitudes and Recoveries (pp. 5-26–5-28), and Basic Instrument Flight Patterns (p. 5-30)
	Chapter 11, "Emergency Operations"	Review all topics pp. 11-3–11-8
Instrument Rating Practical Test Standards	Task IV: Flight by Reference to Instruments	Review all sections.
	Task VII: Emergency Operations	D: Approach with Loss of Primary Flight Instrument Indicators (p. 1-17)
Aeronautical Chart User's Guide	IFR Aeronautical Charts: Explanation of IFR Enroute Terms and Symbols	–
AOPA *Flight Training magazine*	"Partial-Panel Emergencies" in the September 1998 issue	–

CROSS-REFERENCE **For more information about the references and resources that complement the lessons in this book, see Chapter 2.**

Preflight Briefing

This scenario begins with your Cessna 172 in the air northwest of the VOR at Olympia, WA (OLM). The autopilot is off, and the vacuum system has failed. The simulation is paused; press the P key to start flying.

Practice basic flight maneuvers and the instrument flight patterns described in Chapter 5 of the *Instrument Flying Handbook* and in Chapter 46 of this book.

When you finish flying several of the patterns, determine which radial you are on from the OLM VOR and track it inbound until you reach the station.

NOTE In real-world IFR flying, if important equipment fails you must notify air traffic control (see 14 CFR §91.187, "Operation under IFR in controlled airspace: Malfunction reports," and AIM 5-3-3, "Additional Reports").

Location and Weather

This scenario begins in the air. Your Cessna 172 is northwest of OLM (see Figure 47-2). The bases of the clouds in the area are at about 2,000 ft.

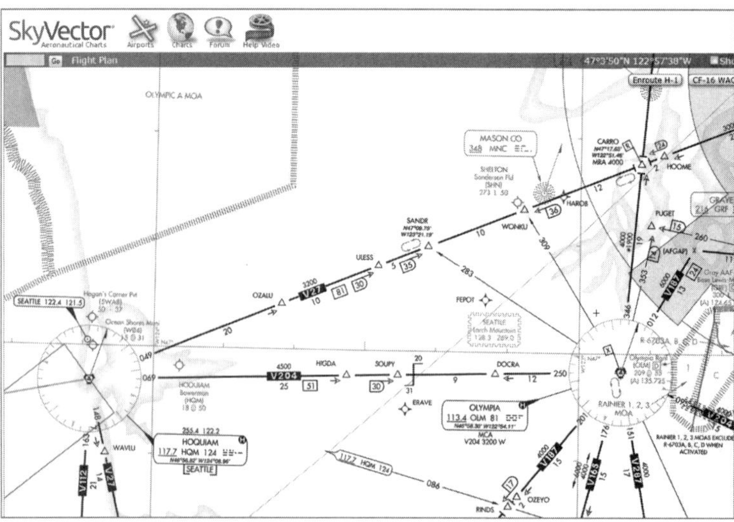

Figure 47-2: The area around Olympia, WA (OLM), on the L-1 IFR en route chart as shown on SkyVector

Situations and Flights

This lesson uses the following files for X-Plane and FSX:

- X-Plane: `Wiley-SBT-IFR-Lesson-03.sit`
- FSX: `Wiley-SBT-IFR-Lesson-03.flt`

CROSS-REFERENCE For more information about using Situations (X-Plane) and Flights (FSX), see Chapter 10.

Tips for This Lesson

Here are a few suggestions to help you get the most from this lesson:

- Review Chapter 12, especially "Flying Tips" and the configuration tables for the simulation that you use. Knowing the pitch, power, and configuration required for various conditions makes partial-panel flying much easier and safer.
- When flying a real airplane, instrument pilots often carry a pad of sticky notes to keep track of important information. They're also handy temporary instrument covers that can help you avoid serious distractions caused by inoperative instruments. When flying X-Plane or FSX, you can cover a failed attitude indicator by placing a sticky note on the screen.

What-Ifs

You can use the "Dice-Based Failure Scheme" described in Chapter 8 to create additional challenges for this flight. For the IFR lessons, if the random number results in the failure of a system or component, use the system failure options in X-Plane or FSX to create a realistic simulation of the problem.

At any point during the flight, roll a die, draw a number from a hat, or use another method to select a random number between 1 and 6. Using Table 47-1, find the corresponding problem to solve, and then take the appropriate action.

Table 47-1: Random Challenges for This Flight

NUMBER	RESULT
1	Vacuum system failure
2	Attitude indicator failure
3	Low-voltage indication
4	Pilot tube blocked
5	Static system blocked
6	Heading indicator failure

Objectives and Desired Outcome Grading Sheet

SCENARIO ACTIVITIES	SCENARIO SUB-ACTIVITIES	DESIRED OUTCOME
Basic instrument flight maneuvers	Instrument flight patterns	Practice
Intercepting and tracking VOR radials	Applying proper correction to maintain a course, allowing no more than 3/4-scale deflection of the CDI.	Practice
Constant airspeed climbs and descents	–	Practice
Recoveries from unusual attitudes	–	Practice
Basic flight maneuvers with inoperative instruments	–	Practice

CHAPTER 48

IFR Lesson 4: Partial-Panel Instrument Flight

Chapter 47 introduced the fundamentals of partial-panel flying. Now it's time to practice how to handle additional challenges that can arise when you try to maintain control after primary instruments fail.

Scenario

Like the fourth lesson in the FITS syllabus for the instrument rating, this scenario reviews partial-panel instrument flying skills and introduces recoveries from unusual attitudes while flying with inoperative instruments (see Figure 48-1).

Figure 48-1: A steep spiral with an inoperative attitude indicator as shown in FSX

Objectives

The primary goals for this flight are:

- Honing partial-panel skills while flying basic instrument flight maneuvers
- Learning to recognize and recover from nose-high and nose-low unusual attitudes while flying with inoperative instruments

Completion Standards

The detailed goals for this lesson are outlined in the table at the end of this chapter. In general, before moving on to the next lesson, you should meet the following standards, based on the generic FITS syllabus and the instrument rating PTS. These goals include:

- Maintaining altitude within ±100 ft. during level flight, headings within ±10°, airspeed within ±10 knots, and bank angles within ±5° during turns while flying with inoperative instruments
- Recognizing and recovering promptly from unusual attitudes while flying with inoperative instruments

References and Resources

To prepare for this lesson, review the following references and resources. The resources at the AOPA Air Safety Institute are valuable supplements to the official information in the FAA references.

TITLE	CHAPTER/SECTION	TOPIC/NOTES
Instrument Flying Handbook	Chapter 3, "Flight Instruments"	Review all topics, pp. 3-1–3-21
	Chapter 4, Section I, "Airplane Attitude Instrument Flying Using Analog Instrumentation"	Review all topics.
	Chapter 5, Section I, "Airplane Basic Flight Maneuvers Using Analog Instrumentation"	Review all topics, pp. 5-1–5-26, Unusual Attitudes and Recoveries (pp. 5-26–5-28), and Basic Instrument Flight Patterns (p. 5-30)
	Chapter 11, "Emergency Operations"	Review all topics, pp. 11-3–11-8
Instrument Rating Practical Test Standards	Task VII: Emergency Operations	D: Approach with Loss of Primary Flight Instrument Indicators (p. 1-17)
AOPA *Flight Training magazine*	"Partial-Panel Emergencies" in the September 1998 issue	–

CROSS-REFERENCE For more information about the references and resources that complement the lessons in this book, see Chapter 2.

Preflight Briefing

This scenario begins with your Cessna 172 in the air northeast of the VOR at Astoria, OR (AST). You are in the clouds and on a heading to intercept V187 and fly southwest toward AST. However, the attitude indicator has failed. Practice partial-panel instrument flying skills as you intercept the airway and proceed toward AST. Try a few turns, climbs, and descents (the basic instrument flight patterns described in previous chapters are also good exercises) to practice maneuvering with an inoperative attitude indicator.

When you're ready to practice recoveries from unusual attitudes, close your eyes and attempt to make a series of turns, climbs, and descents. After 20–30 seconds, open your eyes and attempt to recover smoothly and accurately from the resulting unusual attitude.

NOTE **In real-world IFR flying, if important equipment fails you must notify air traffic control (see 14 CFR §91.187, "Operation under IFR in controlled airspace: Malfunction reports," and AIM 5-3-3, "Additional Reports").**

Location and Weather

This scenario begins in the air. Your Cessna 172 is northeast of AST (see Figure 48-2). The bases of the clouds in the area are at about 2,000 ft.

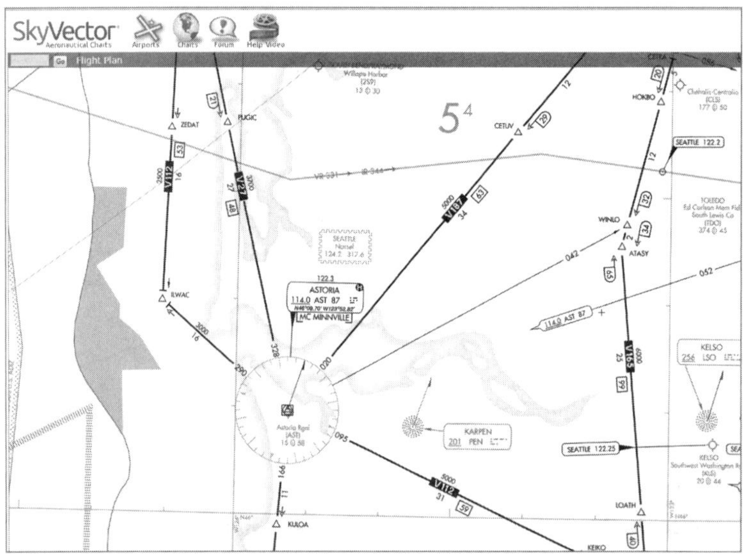

Figure 48-2: The area around Astoria, OR, on the L-1 en route chart as shown on SkyVector

Situations and Flights

This lesson uses the following files for X-Plane and FSX:

- X-Plane: `Wiley-SBT-IFR-Lesson-04.sit`
- FSX: `Wiley-SBT-IFR-Lesson-04.flt`

CROSS-REFERENCE **For more information about using Situations (X-Plane) and Flights (FSX), see Chapter 10.**

Tips for This Lesson

Here are a few suggestions to help you get the most from this lesson:

- Review Chapter 12, especially "Flying Tips" and the configuration tables for the simulation that you use. Knowing the pitch, power, and configuration required for various conditions makes partial-panel flying much easier and safer.
- Note the specific recommendations for recovering from nose-high and nose-low unusual attitudes, and review the common errors pilots make when recovering from unusual attitudes as described in the *Instrument Flying Handbook* (p. 5-28).
- When flying a real airplane, instrument pilots often carry a pad of sticky notes to keep track of important information. They're also handy temporary instrument covers that can help you avoid serious distractions caused by inoperative instruments. When flying X-Plane or FSX, you can cover a failed attitude indicator by placing a sticky note on the screen.

What-Ifs

You can also use the "Dice-Based Failure Scheme" described in Chapter 8 to create additional challenges for this flight. For the IFR lessons, if the random number results in the failure of a system or component, use the system failure options in X-Plane or FSX to create a realistic simulation of the problem.

At any point during the flight, roll a die, draw a number from a hat, or use another method to select a random number between 1 and 6. Using Table 48-1, find the corresponding problem to solve, and then take the appropriate action.

Table 48-1: Random Challenges for This Flight

NUMBER	RESULT
1	Vacuum system failure
2	Attitude indicator failure
3	Low-voltage indication
4	Pilot tube blocked
5	Static system blocked
6	Heading indicator failure

Objectives and Desired Outcome Grading Sheet

SCENARIO ACTIVITIES	SCENARIO SUB-ACTIVITIES	DESIRED OUTCOME
Practice basic instrument flight maneuvers.	Instrument flight patterns	Perform
Fly constant airspeed climbs and descents.	–	Perform
Review basic flight maneuvers with inoperative instruments.	Instrument flight patterns	Perform
Practice recoveries from unusual attitudes with inoperative instruments.	–	Practice

CHAPTER

49

IFR Lesson 5: Holding Procedures

Air traffic controllers use several techniques and procedures to separate aircraft that are flying under IFR. Sometimes, however, too many airplanes converge on an airport, and ATC must direct pilots to hold until there's room to accommodate each airplane in sequence.

For many pilots, learning and mastering holding procedures is among the most challenging phases of training for the instrument rating. Fortunately, holding is a skill best learned and honed in an FTD — or a PC-based simulation.

Scenario

Like the fifth lesson in the FITS syllabus for the instrument rating, this scenario is another opportunity to practice basic instrument flying skills and tracking of VOR radials as part of a typical cross-country flight — but there's a twist. While you are en route to the Astoria, OR (KAST) airport, air traffic control informs you that the Coast Guard is recovering a search and rescue aircraft. You must hold (see Figure 49-1) until it is safely on the ground.

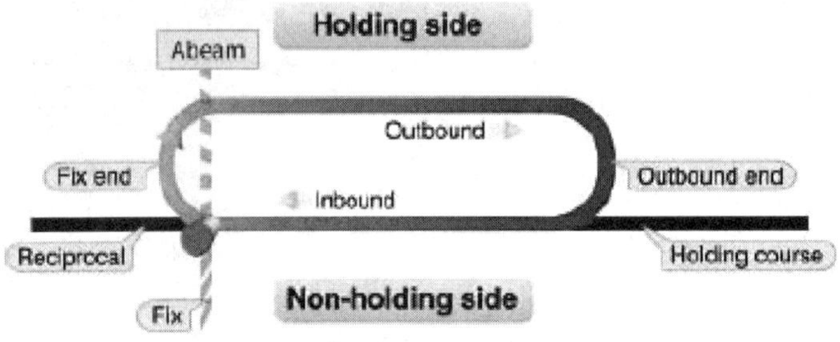

Figure 10-4. *Standard Holding Pattern—No Wind.*

Figure 49-1: A standard holding pattern, as shown in Figure 10-4 of the *Instrument Flying Handbook*

Objectives

The primary goals for this flight are:

- Honing basic instrument flying skills
- Accurately intercepting and tracking VOR radials
- Practicing holding procedures at a VOR

Completion Standards

The detailed goals for this lesson are outlined in the table at the end of this chapter. In general, before moving on to the next lesson, you should meet the following standards, based on the generic FITS syllabus and the instrument rating PTS. These goals include:

- Maintaining altitude within ±100 ft. during level flight, headings within ±10°, airspeed within ±10 knots, and bank angles within ±5° during turns
- Changing to the holding airspeed when three minutes or less from, but prior to arriving at, the holding fix
- Describing and using an entry procedure that ensures the aircraft remains within the holding pattern

- Recognizing arrival at the holding fix and initiating prompt entry into the holding pattern
- Complying with ATC reporting requirements
- Using the proper timing criteria
- Using proper wind correction procedures to maintain the desired pattern and to arrive over the fix as close as possible to a specified time
- Using moving maps and other graphical navigation displays, if installed, to monitor position
- Demonstrating an appropriate level of single-pilot resource management skills

References and Resources

To prepare for this lesson, review the following references and resources. The resources at the AOPA Air Safety Institute are valuable supplements to the official information in the FAA references.

TITLE	CHAPTER/SECTION	TOPIC/NOTES
Instrument Flying Handbook	Chapter 10, "IFR Flight"	Holding Procedures (pp. 10-9–10-12)
	Appendix A, "Clearance Shorthand"	–
Instrument Procedures Handbook	Chapter 3, "En Route Operations"	Holding Procedures (pp. 3-23–3-25)
AIM	5–3–7 "Holding"	–
Instrument Rating Practical Test Standards	Task III: Air Traffic Control Clearances and Procedures	C: Holding Procedures
	Task VII: Emergency Operations	D: Approach with Loss of Primary Flight Instrument Indicators (p. 1-17)
AOPA Air Safety Institute Safety Advisor *Single-Pilot IFR*	–	–

CROSS-REFERENCE **For more information about the references and resources that complement the lessons in this book, see Chapter 2.**

Preflight Briefing

This scenario begins with your Cessna 172 in the air near the VOR at Astoria, OR (AST). You are in the clouds and on a heading to intercept V187 and fly southwest toward AST. The autopilot is on, with the heading and altitude hold modes active.

Intercept the airway and track it inbound to AST.

Your holding instructions are as follows:

- Hold northeast of AST on the 020° radial, right turns. Expect further clearance in 45 minutes.

When you have completed three laps around the holding pattern, depart AST to the northwest on V27. If you use the "what-ifs" later in this chapter to practice other holding patterns, restart the Situation or Flight each time.

Location and Weather

This scenario begins in the air. Your Cessna 172 is northeast of AST (see Figure 49-2). The bases of the clouds in the area are at about 2,000 ft.

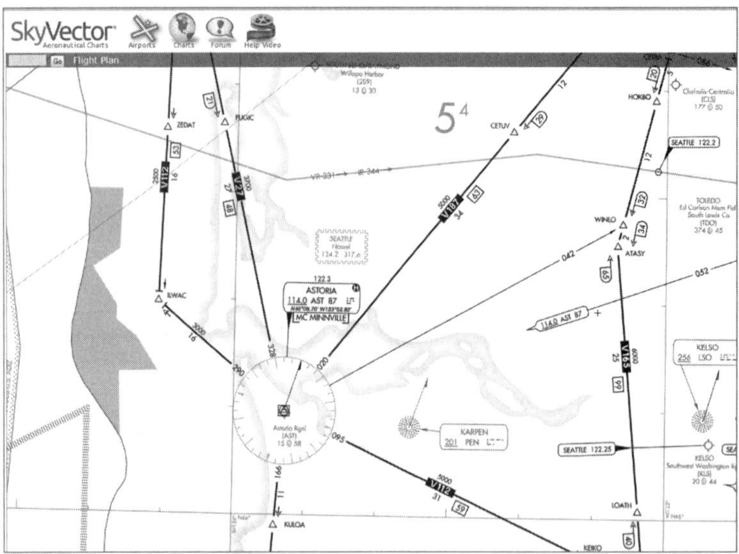

Figure 49-2: The area around Astoria, OR, on the L-1 en route chart as shown on SkyVector

Situations and Flights

This lesson uses the following files for X-Plane and FSX:

- X-Plane: `Wiley-SBT-IFR-Lesson-05.sit`
- FSX: `Wiley-SBT-IFR-Lesson-05.flt`

CROSS-REFERENCE **For more information about using Situations (X-Plane) and Flights (FSX), see Chapter 10.**

Tips for This Lesson

Here are a few suggestions to help you get the most from this lesson:

- Use the Low-Speed Cruise/Initial Approach Speed configuration described in Chapter 12 for flying holding patterns. Delay is the point of holding, so maintaining cruise speed is counterproductive. Reducing speed may mean fewer trips around the holding pattern, and operating at a lower power setting also conserves fuel.
- Use the interactive map in your simulation to help you orient yourself to the assigned holding pattern.
- When you start practicing holding patterns, use the autopilot with the heading mode active so that you can concentrate on visualizing the entry and the holding pattern.
- Take your time. Simulation is the ideal tool for practicing skills like flying holding patterns. If you get confused or want to repeat entering and flying a hold, restart the Situation or Flight.

What-Ifs

You can use the "Dice-Based Failure Scheme" described in Chapter 8 to create additional challenges for this flight. In this case, use the random numbers to practice entering and flying a variety of holding patterns as if they were assigned by ATC. You can restart the flight each time to practice approaching the VOR and entering the hold.

At any point during the flight, roll a die, draw a number from a hat, or use another method to select a random number between 1 and 6. Using Table 49-1, find the corresponding problem to solve, and then take the appropriate action.

Table 49-1: Random Challenges for This Flight

NUMBER	RESULT
1	Hold NE on the AST 020° radial, right turns.
2	Hold NW on the AST 328° radial, right turns.
3	Hold SE on the AST 095° radial, right turns.
4	Hold south on the AST 166° radial, right turns.
5	Hold NE on the AST 020° radial, left turns.
6	Hold SE on the AST 095° radial, left turns.

Objectives and Desired Outcome Grading Sheet

SCENARIO ACTIVITIES	SCENARIO SUB-ACTIVITIES	DESIRED OUTCOME
Intercept and track VOR radials.	Apply proper correction to maintain a course, allowing no more than ¾-scale deflection of the CDI.	Perform
Enter and fly holding patterns.	Fly the appropriate recommended entry method to a variety of holding patterns.	Describe/Practice

CHAPTER

50

IFR Lesson 6: Non-Precision Approach

The previous lessons in this syllabus have prepared you for the primary goal of flying under IFR — landing when the weather prevents visual approaches.

Scenario

The sixth lesson in the FITS syllabus for the instrument rating introduces a nonprecision approach (an approach without vertical guidance), followed by a missed approach and a holding pattern. The lesson also includes a procedure turn (a course reversal) to begin the approach. All of those maneuvers are combinations of the basic instrument flight patterns that you practiced in previous lessons.

This scenario follows that basic sequence. Assume you have an important meeting at the Boeing factory at Paine Field (KPAE) near Everett, WA. NOTAMs tell you the only procedure you can fly is the VOR RWY 16R approach (see Figure 50-1). Because the wind is from the north, you should expect to use the circling minimums for this approach, which are a ceiling of 1,100 ft. (494 ft. above the runway) and 1 mile visibility.

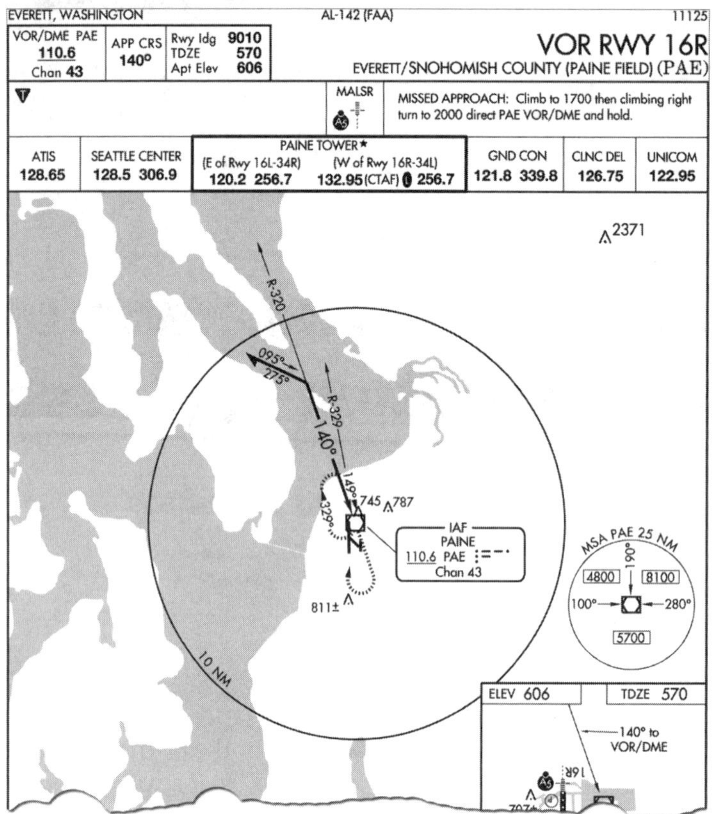

Figure 50-1: An excerpt of the VOR RWY 16R approach chart at KPAE

NOTE **You can find detailed descriptions of the symbols and terminology used on instrument approach charts in Chapter 8 of the *Instrument Flying Handbook* and Chapter 5 of the *Instrument Procedures Handbook.***

Objectives

The primary goals for this flight are:

- Honing VOR tracking skills
- Learning about instrument approach charts
- Flying a complete instrument approach procedure, including a procedure turn (see Figure 50-2)
- Understanding and flying a missed approach procedure
- Practicing holding procedures at a VOR

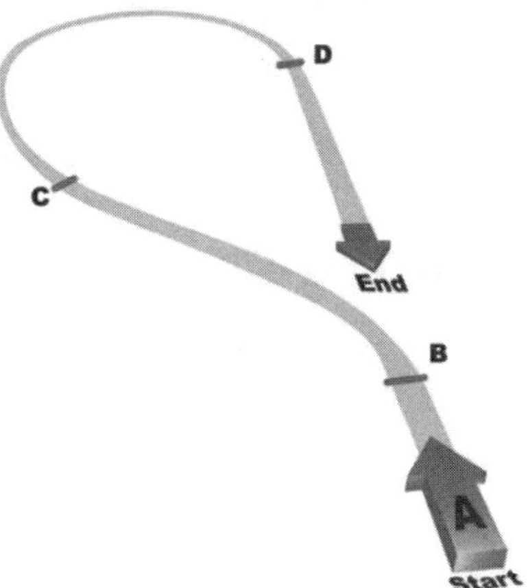

Figure 50-2: A standard procedure turn as shown in Figure 5-42 of the *Instrument Flying Handbook*

Completion Standards

The detailed goals for this lesson are outlined in the table at the end of this chapter. In general, before moving on to the next lesson, you should meet the following standards, based on the generic FITS syllabus and the instrument rating PTS. These goals, which apply to most instrument approach procedures, include:

- Selecting, tuning, identifying, and confirming the operational status of navigation equipment to be used for the approach procedure
- Maintaining, prior to beginning the final approach segment, altitude within ±100 ft., heading within ±10° and allowing less than ¾-scale deflection of the course deviation indicator (CDI), and maintaining airspeed within ±10 knots
- Establishing a stabilized approach profile with a rate of descent and track that ensures arrival at the minimum descent altitude (MDA) prior to reaching the missed approach point (MAP)
- While on the final approach segment, allowing no more than a ¾-scale deflection of the CDI and maintaining airspeed within ±10 knots of the appropriate speed
- Maintaining the MDA, when reached, within +100 ft., –0 ft. to the MAP

- Executing the missed approach procedure (MAP) when the required visual references are not distinctly visible and identifiable at the missed approach point
- Using moving maps and other graphical navigation displays, if installed, to monitor position, track, wind drift, and other parameters to maintain the desired flight path
- Demonstrating an appropriate level of single-pilot resource management skills

References and Resources

To prepare for this lesson, review the following references and resources. The resources at the AOPA Air Safety Institute are valuable supplements to the official information in the FAA references.

TITLE	CHAPTER/SECTION	TOPIC/NOTES
Instrument Flying Handbook	Chapter 5, "Section I Airplane Basic Flight Maneuvers Using Analog Instrumentation"	Procedure Turn (pp. 5-30–5-31) and Circling Approach Patterns (p. 5-32)
	Chapter 8, "The National Airspace System"	Instrument Approach Procedure (IAP) Charts (pp. 8-12–8-18)
	Chapter 10, "IFR Flight"	Holding Procedures (pp. 10-9–10-12), Approaches (pp. 10-12–10-14), Circling Approaches (p. 10-20), IAP Minimums (p. 10-21), Missed Approaches (p. 10-21)
Instrument Procedures Handbook	Chapter 5, "Approaches"	Approach Chart Formats (p. 5-7), Instrument Approach Procedure Briefing (p. 5-26), Instrument Approach Procedure Segments (pp. 5-36–5-42), VOR Approach (p. 5-59)

TITLE	CHAPTER/SECTION	TOPIC/NOTES
AIM	5–3–7 "Holding"	–
	5–4–5 "Instrument Approach Procedure Charts"	–
	5–4–7 "Instrument Approach Procedures"	Note paragraph J, "Pilot Operational Considerations When Flying Nonprecision Approaches"
	5–4–9 "Procedure Turn and Hold–in–lieu of Procedure Turn"	–
Instrument Rating Practical Test Standards	VI: Area of Operation: Instrument Approach Procedures	A. Task: Nonprecision Approach
AOPA Air Safety Institute Safety Advisor *Single-Pilot IFR*	–	–
AOPA Air Safety Institute Interactive Safety Course *IFR Insights: Charts*	–	–

CROSS-REFERENCE **For more information about the references and resources that complement the lessons in this book, see Chapter 2.**

Preflight Briefing

This scenario begins with your Cessna 172 in the air southwest of Paine Field (KPAE). You are in the clouds and cleared direct to the PAE VOR to fly the VOR RWY 16R approach. The autopilot is on, with the heading and altitude hold modes active.

Track inbound and cross PAE at 2000. Fly the complete approach, including the procedure turn and, if necessary, the missed approach procedure and holding pattern at PAE, as published on the VOR RWY 16R approach chart. This scenario is complete when you have landed or flown two laps in the holding pattern at PAE.

CROSS-REFERENCE You can find the instrument approach chart for this and other procedures used in the lessons in the document `IFR_Charts.pdf`, available at this book's website.

Location and Weather

This scenario begins in the air. Your Cessna 172 is southwest of KPAE (see Figure 50-3). The bases of the clouds in the area are at about 1000 ft. and the flight visibility is about 1 mile. The wind is from the north. If you see the runway at or before the missed approach point, fly the circle-to-land procedure by entering close-in left downwind for runway.

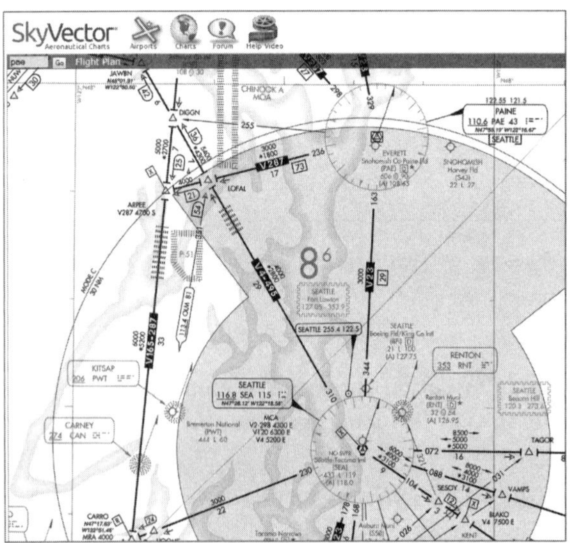

Figure 50-3: The area around KPAE on the L-1 en route chart as shown on SkyVector

Situations and Flights

This lesson uses the following files for X-Plane and FSX:

- X-Plane: `Wiley-SBT-IFR-Lesson-06.sit`
- FSX: `Wiley-SBT-IFR-Lesson-06.flt`

CROSS-REFERENCE For more information about using Situations (X-Plane) and Flights (FSX), see Chapter 10.

Tips for This Lesson

Here are a few suggestions to help you get the most from this lesson:

- Use the briefing section at the top of the approach chart to help you verify the essential information required to fly the approach and missed approach procedure.
- Use the Low-Speed Cruise/Initial Approach Speed configuration described in Chapter 12 for flying the initial stages of the approach. Use other examples in that chapter to help you set up stable configurations for the remaining phases of the approach.
- Use the interactive map in your simulation to help you orient yourself throughout the procedure.
- Use the replay and review features in X-Plane or FSX to check how well you tracked the courses and maintained the appropriate altitudes during the flight.
- As noted in Chapter 45, the basic Cessna 172 in X-Plane does not include distance-measuring equipment (DME), but you can specify the PAE VOR as the direct-to GPS waypoint to substitute for DME while flying the approach.

What-Ifs

You can use the "Dice-Based Failure Scheme" described in Chapter 8 to create additional challenges for this flight. At any point during the flight, roll a die, draw a number from a hat, or use another method to select a random number between 1 and 6. Using Table 50-1, find the corresponding problem to solve, and then take the appropriate action. If the challenge is a failure of an aircraft system or instrument, use the failure options in X-Plane or FSX to replicate the problem.

Table 50-1: Random Challenges for This Flight

NUMBER	RESULT
1	Vacuum system failure
2	Visibility reported at KPAE drops to one-half mile.
3	ATC requires you to hold at PAE as shown on the chart before you can begin the approach.
4	ATC requires you to hold at east of LOFAL intersection on V287 at 4,000 ft.
5	The ceiling reported at KPAE drops to 800 ft.
6	Runway 16R is reported as blocked just after you turn inbound from the procedure turn.

Objectives and Desired Outcome Grading Sheet

SCENARIO ACTIVITIES	SCENARIO SUB-ACTIVITIES	DESIRED OUTCOME
Understand the key information on VOR RWY 16R approach chart.	–	Describe/Explain
Complete a pre-approach briefing based on the VOR RWY 16R approach chart.	–	Describe/Practice
Fly the complete VOR RWY 16R approach within the standards outlined in the PTS.	–	Practice
Understand the rules and procedures governing circle-to-land procedures.	–	Describe/Explain
Understand the elements of a missed approach procedure.	–	Describe/Explain

CHAPTER

51

IFR Lesson 7: IFR Departures and Localizer Approach

The seventh lesson in the FITS syllabus for the instrument rating introduces IFR departure procedures and includes a short cross-country flight that ends with another type of nonprecision approach, a localizer-only procedure.

Scenario

This scenario follows the basic pattern in the FITS syllabus. Imagine that you are flying a friend from Corvallis, OR (KCVO), to pick up her airplane, which has undergone a major avionics upgrade at a shop at Aurora, OR (KUAO). It's Friday afternoon, and you need to get to the shop before it closes for the weekend, because your friend expects to depart for an important business trip on Sunday evening.

The flight includes following a standard instrument departure procedure (see Figure 51-1) and flying a localizer-based instrument approach (see Figure 51-2).

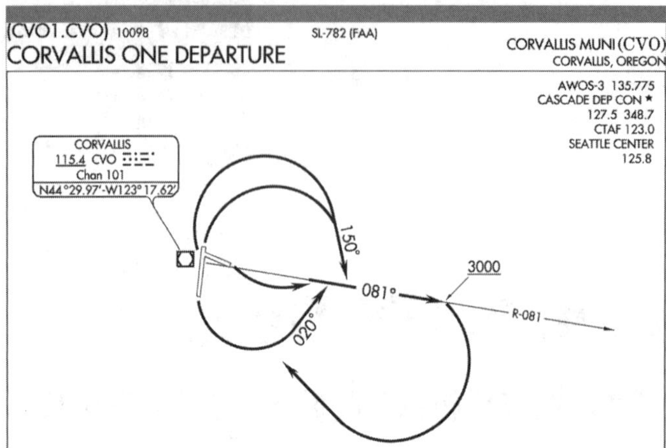

Figure 51-1: Part of the CORVALLIS ONE departure procedure for KCVO

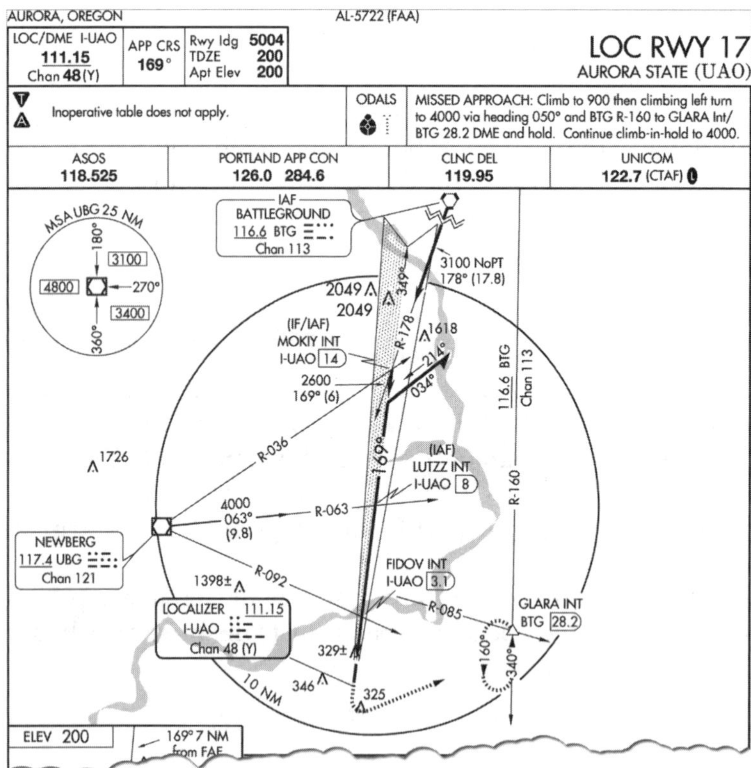

Figure 51-2: Part of the LOC RWY 17 approach chart for KUAO

NOTE **You can find detailed descriptions of the symbols and terminology used on instrument procedure charts in Chapter 8 of the *Instrument Flying Handbook* and Chapter 5 of the *Instrument Procedures Handbook.***

Objectives

The primary goals for this flight are:

- Learning about and practicing IFR departure procedures
- Practicing IFR flight along airways
- Flying a complete instrument approach, including a procedure turn, based on a localizer
- Understanding and flying a missed approach procedure
- Practicing missed-approach holding procedures

The LOC RWY 17 approach at KUAO challenges your ability to use VOR radials to identify key points along the final approach path and to navigate to and fly the missed approach holding pattern, especially in the basic X-Plane Cessna 172, which is not equipped with DME.

Completion Standards

The detailed goals for this lesson are outlined in the table at the end of this chapter. In general, before moving on to the next lesson, you should meet the following standards, based on the generic FITS syllabus and the instrument rating PTS. These goals, which apply to most instrument approach procedures, include:

- Maintaining, prior to beginning the final approach segment, altitude within ±100 ft., heading within ±10° and allowing less than ¾-scale deflection of the course deviation indicator (CDI), and maintaining airspeed within ±10 knots
- Establishing a stabilized approach profile with a rate of descent and track that ensures arrival at the minimum descent altitude (MDA) prior to reaching the missed approach point (MAP)
- While on the final approach segment, allowing no more than a ¾-scale deflection of the CDI and maintaining airspeed within ±10 knots of the appropriate speed
- Maintaining the MDA, when reached, within +100 ft., –0 ft. to the MAP

- Executing the missed approach procedure (MAP) when the required visual references are not distinctly visible and identifiable at the missed approach point
- Using moving maps and other graphical navigation displays, if installed, to monitor position, track, wind drift, and other parameters to maintain the desired flight path
- Demonstrating an appropriate level of single-pilot resource management skills

References and Resources

To prepare for this lesson, review the following references and resources. The resources at the AOPA Air Safety Institute are valuable supplements to the official information in the FAA references.

TITLE	CHAPTER/SECTION	TOPIC/NOTES
Instrument Flying Handbook	Chapter 7, "Navigation Systems"	Instrument Approach Systems (p. 7-37), Localizer (p. 7-38), ILS Function (p. 7-42)
	Chapter 8, "The National Airspace System"	Instrument Approach Procedure (IAP) Charts (pp. 8-12–8-18)
	Chapter 10, "IFR Flight"	Clearances (p. 10-3), Departure Procedures (p. 10-5), Holding Procedures (pp. 10-9–10-12), Approaches (pp. 10-12–10-14), IAP Minimums (p. 10-21), Missed Approaches (p. 10-21)
	Appendix A "Clearance Shorthand"	–
Instrument Procedures Handbook	Chapter 2, "Takeoffs and Departures"	Departure Procedures (pp. 2-12–2-34)
	Chapter 5, "Approaches"	Approach Chart Formats (p. 5-7), Instrument Approach Procedure Briefing (p. 5-26), Instrument Approach Procedure Segments (pp. 5-36–5-42), Localizer Approaches (p. 5-63)

TITLE	CHAPTER/SECTION	TOPIC/NOTES
AIM	Chapter 4, "Air Traffic Control"	4-4-1 "Clearance," 4-4-2 "Clearance Prefix," 4-4-3 "Clearance Items," 4-4-4 "Amended Clearances," 4-4-7, "Pilot Responsibility upon Clearance Issuance," 4-4-10 "Adherence to Clearance"
	Chapter 5, "Air Traffic Procedures"	5-1-8 "Flight Plan – Domestic IFR Flights"
	–	5-2-7 "Departure Control," 5-2-8 "Instrument Departure Procedures – DP and SID"
	–	5—3—7 "Holding"
	–	5—4—7 "Instrument Approach Procedures"
	–	5—4—5 "Instrument Approach Procedure Charts"
	–	5—4—9 "Procedure Turn and Hold—in—lieu of Procedure Turn"
FAA Regulations	14 CFR Part 91	Instrument Flight Rules: §91.167–§91.187
Risk Management Handbook	–	Review all sections.
Instrument Rating Practical Test Standards	III. Air Traffic Control Clearances and Procedures	–
	VI. Instrument Approach Procedures	A. Task: Nonprecision Approach
AOPA Air Safety Institute Interactive Safety Course *IFR Insights: Charts*	–	–

CROSS-REFERENCE **For more information about the references and resources that complement the lessons in this book, see Chapter 2.**

Preflight Briefing

This scenario begins with your Cessna 172 on the ground at Corvallis, OR (KCVO), ready to depart from runway 17 and fly to Aurora, OR (KUAO). You'll make the entire flight in instrument meteorological conditions (IMC).

CROSS-REFERENCE **You can find the IFR procedure charts for this lesson in `IFR_Charts.pdf`, available at this book's website.**

IFR Clearance

Cleared to KUAO via CORVALLIS ONE departure, V495, UBG, maintain 4000, departure control frequency 127.5, squawk 4200.

NOTE **Many IFR pilots use the sequence C-R-A-F-T to record an IFR clearance. The letters denote the following:**

- **Clearance limit: Usually your destination airport, but possibly an en route fix, such as a VOR**
- **Route: The combination of departure procedures, radar vectors, navigation aids, airways, fixes, and arrival procedures that define the path air traffic control (ATC) expects you fly**
- **Altitude: The initial altitude or cruise altitude ATC expects you to maintain**
- **Frequency: The first frequency that you should use to contact ATC after takeoff**
- **Transponder: The four-digit code ("squawk") that you enter into the transponder**

Location and Weather

This scenario begins with your Cessna 172 on runway 17 at KCVO (see Figure 51-3). The bases of the clouds throughout the area are at about 900 ft., and the flight visibility below the ceiling is about 1 mile. The wind is out of the south at approximately 10 knots.

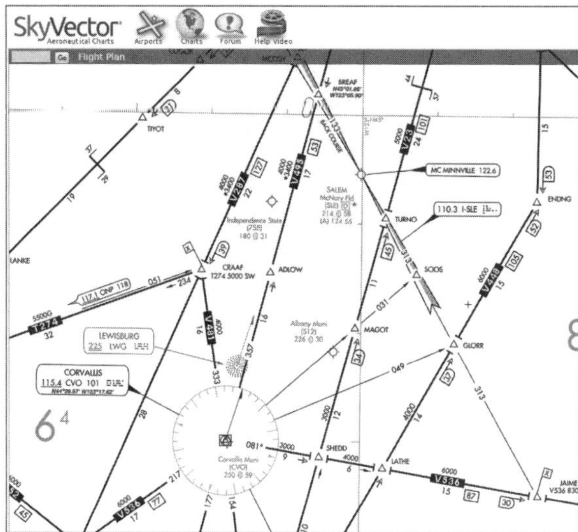

Figure 51-3: The area around KCVO on the L-1 en route chart as shown on SkyVector

Situations and Flights

This lesson uses the following files for X-Plane and FSX:

- X-Plane: `Wiley-SBT-IFR-Lesson-07.sit`
- FSX: `Wiley-SBT-IFR-Lesson-07.flt`

CROSS-REFERENCE **For more information about using Situations (X-Plane) and Flights (FSX), see Chapter 10.**

Tips for This Lesson

Here are a few suggestions to help you get the most from this lesson:

- After taking off and joining V495 northbound, restart the Situation or Flight and practice flying the same departure procedure using different runways at KCVO.
- Use the configurations described in Chapter 12 to help you establish and maintain stable climb, cruise, and approach settings for each phase of the flight.

- Use the interactive map in your simulation to help you orient yourself throughout the flight.
- Use the replay and review features in X-Plane or FSX to check how well you tracked the courses and maintained altitude during the flight.
- As noted in Chapter 45, the basic Cessna 172 in X-Plane does not include distance measuring equipment (DME), but throughout this lesson you can specify VORs as direct-to GPS waypoints to substitute for DME.

What-Ifs

You can use the "Dice-Based Failure Scheme" described in Chapter 8 to create additional challenges for this flight.

At any point during the flight, roll a die, draw a number from a hat, or use another method to select a random number between 1 and 6. Using the following table, find the corresponding problem to solve, and then take the appropriate action. If the challenge is a failure of an aircraft system or instrument, use the failure options in X-Plane or FSX to replicate the problem.

Table 51-1: Random Challenges for This Flight

NUMBER	RESULT
1	Vacuum system failure.
2	Visibility reported at KUAO drops to ½ mile.
3	ATC requires you to hold at UBG as published on the en route chart (that is, on the 183° radial).
4	Return to KCVO and fly either the VOR-A or ILS RWY 17 approach.
5	The ceiling reported at KUAO drops to 700 ft.
6	Runway 17 at KUAO is reported blocked just after you turn inbound after completing the procedure turn.

Objectives and Desired Outcome Grading Sheet

SCENARIO ACTIVITIES	SCENARIO SUB-ACTIVITIES	DESIRED OUTCOME
Understand the key regulations that apply to IFR flight.	–	Describe/Explain
Understand the key elements of IFR departure procedures.	–	Describe/Explain
Understand the key information on the KUAO LOC RWY17 approach chart.	–	Describe/Explain
Complete a pre-approach briefing based on the KUAO LOC RWY17 approach chart.	–	Describe/Practice
Fly the complete KUAO LOC RWY17 approach within the standards outlined in the PTS.	–	Practice
Understand the elements of the missed approach procedure at KUAO.	–	Describe/Explain

CHAPTER

52

IFR Lesson 8: ILS Approach

The eighth lesson in the FITS syllabus for the instrument rating introduces the instrument landing system (ILS) approach and reviews IFR en route procedures. The ILS is the primary precision approach in use today. A precision approach provides both lateral and vertical guidance. Typical minimums for an ILS approach are a 200-ft. ceiling and ½ mile visibility (see Figure 52-1).

NOTE **The FAA is rapidly publishing new GPS-based approaches, including procedures that provide vertical guidance. Technically, approaches with LPV and LNAV/VNAV guidance to decision altitudes do not meet the international definition of a "precision" approach, but as a practical matter they are almost identical to an ILS. In fact, the FAA allows you to substitute such approaches with vertical guidance (APV) for an ILS when you take the practical test for an instrument rating.**

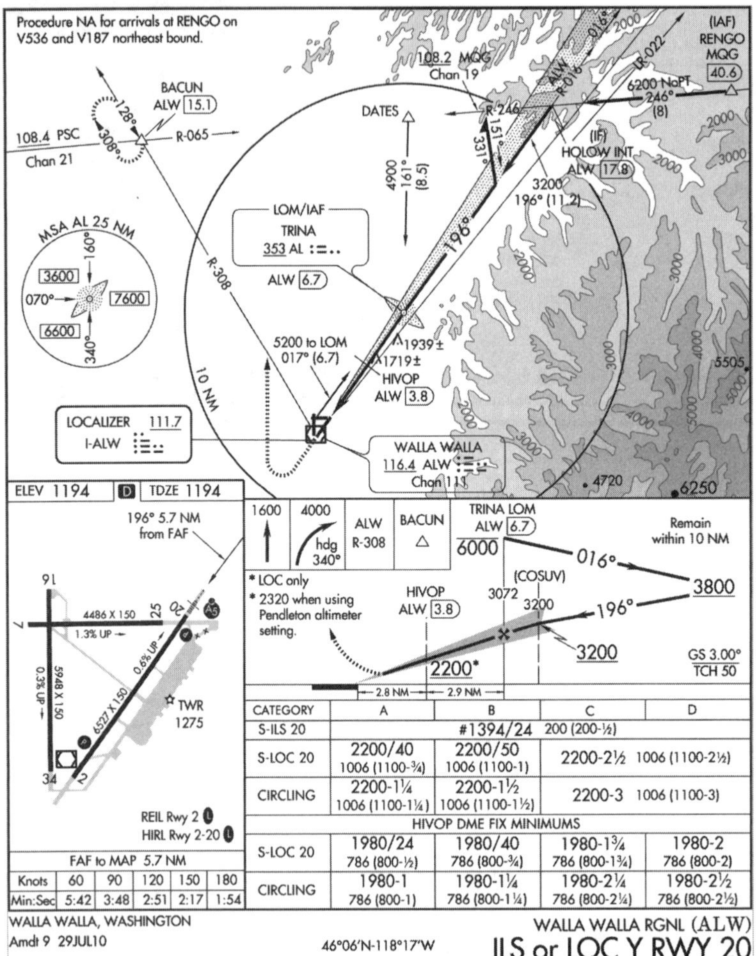

CATEGORY	A	B	C	D
S-ILS 20	#1394/24 200 (200-½)			
S-LOC 20	2200/40 1006 (1100-¾)	2200/50 1006 (1100-1)	2200-2½ 1006 (1100-2½)	
CIRCLING	2200-1¼ 1006 (1100-1¼)	2200-1½ 1006 (1100-1½)	2200-3 1006 (1100-3)	
HIVOP DME FIX MINIMUMS				
S-LOC 20	1980/24 786 (800-½)	1980/40 786 (800-¾)	1980-1¾ 786 (800-1¾)	1980-2 786 (800-2)
CIRCLING	1980-1 786 (800-1)	1980-1¼ 786 (800-1¼)	1980-2¼ 786 (800-2¼)	1980-2½ 786 (800-2½)

Figure 52-1: Part of the chart for the ILS or LOC Y RWY 20 approach at KALW

Scenario

For this scenario, imagine that you are en route to Walla Walla, WA (KALW), to meet friends for a class reunion at Whitman College and to explore the area's wineries. You need to arrive at KALW by 6:00 p.m. to make sure you don't miss the opening celebration.

NOTE **You can find detailed descriptions of the symbols and terminology used on instrument procedure charts in Chapter 8 of the *Instrument Flying Handbook* and Chapter 5 of the *Instrument Procedures Handbook*.**

Objectives

The primary goals for this flight are:

- Practicing IFR flight along airways
- Learning about and flying charted transitions ("feeder routes" and "terminal routes") to instrument approaches
- Flying an ILS approach

Completion Standards

The detailed goals for this lesson are outlined in the table at the end of this chapter. In general, before moving on to the next lesson, you should meet the following standards, based on the generic FITS syllabus and the instrument rating PTS. These goals, which apply to most instrument approach procedures, include:

- Maintaining, prior to beginning the final approach segment, altitude within ±100 ft., heading within ±10° and allowing less than ¾-scale deflection of the course deviation indicator (CDI), and maintaining airspeed within ±10 knots
- Maintaining a stabilized final approach, from the final approach fix to decision altitude (DA) and allowing no more than ¾-scale deflection of either the glideslope or localizer indications, and maintaining the target airspeed within ±10 knots
- Immediately initiating the missed approach when at the DA and the required visual references for the runway are not unmistakably visible and identifiable
- Transitioning to a normal landing approach only when the aircraft is in a position from which a descent to a landing on the runway can be made at a normal rate of descent using normal maneuvering
- Maintaining localizer and glideslope within ¾-scale deflection of the indicators during the visual descent from DA to a point over the runway where glideslope must be abandoned to accomplish a normal landing

References and Resources

To prepare for this lesson, review the following references and resources. The resources at the AOPA Air Safety Institute are valuable supplements to the official information in the FAA references.

TITLE	CHAPTER/SECTION	TOPIC/NOTES
Instrument Flying Handbook	Chapter 7, "Navigation Systems"	Instrument Approach Systems (p. 7-37), Localizer (p. 7-38), ILS Function (p. 7-42)
	Chapter 8, "The National Airspace System"	Instrument Approach Procedure (IAP) Charts (pp. 8-12–8-18)
	Chapter 10, "IFR Flight""	Approaches (pp. 10-12–10-14), IAP Minimums (p. 10-21)
Instrument Procedures Handbook	Chapter 5, "Approaches"	Approach Chart Formats (p. 5-7), Instrument Approach Procedure Briefing (p. 5-26), Instrument Approach Procedure Segments (pp. 5-36–5-42), ILS Approaches (pp. 5-50–5-52)
AIM	Chapter 1, "Air Navigation"	1-1-9 Instrument Landing System
	Chapter 5, "Air Traffic Procedures"	5—4—7 "Instrument Approach Procedures" and 5—4—5 "Instrument Approach Procedure Charts"
Instrument Rating Practical Test Standards	VI. Instrument Approach Procedures	B. Task: Precision Approach
AOPA Air Safety Institute Interactive Safety Course *IFR Insights: Charts*	–	–

CROSS-REFERENCE For more information about the references and resources that complement the lessons in this book, see Chapter 2.

Preflight Briefing

Assume that you departed from Felts Field (KSFF) at Spokane, WA, where good VFR weather prevails. This scenario begins with your Cessna 172 in the air near RENGO intersection, northeast of KALW, where clouds and fog have settled over the area (see Figure 52-2). Fly the published transition route from RENGO to intercept the ILS approach to runway 20.

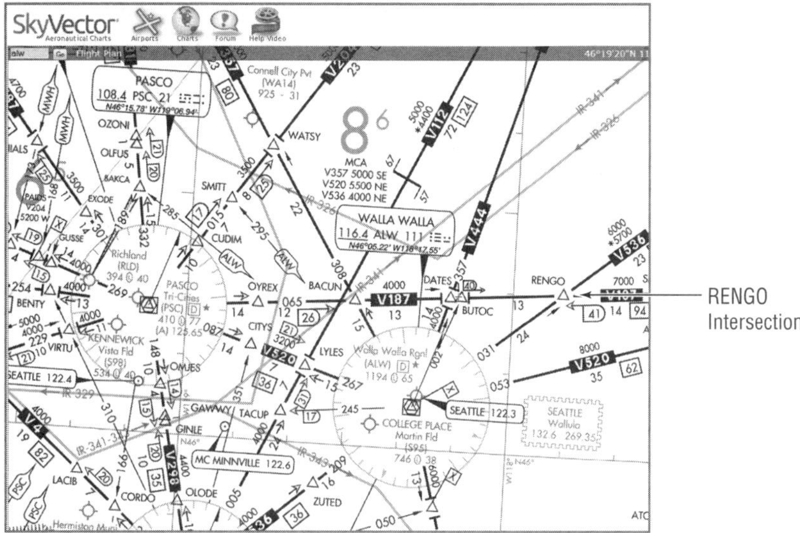

Figure 52-2: The area around KALW on the L-13 en route chart as shown on SkyVector

CROSS-REFERENCE You can find the IFR procedure charts for this lesson in `IFR_Charts.pdf`, available at this book's website.

Clearance

Cross RENGO at or above 6200. Cleared for the ILS Yankee runway 20 approach. Contact the tower at TRINA.

Location and Weather

This scenario begins with your Cessna 172 at 7,000 ft., just east of the RENGO intersection. The bases of the clouds throughout the area are at about 1,500 ft., and the flight visibility below the ceiling is about 1 mile. The wind is out of the southwest at approximately 10 knots.

Situations and Flights

This lesson uses the following files for X-Plane and FSX:

- X-Plane: `Wiley-SBT-IFR-Lesson-08.sit`
- FSX: `Wiley-SBT-IFR-Lesson-08.flt`

CROSS-REFERENCE **For more information about using Situations (X-Plane) and Flights (FSX), see Chapter 10.**

Tips for This Lesson

Here are a few suggestions to help you get the most from this lesson:

- Use the briefing section at the top of the approach chart to help you verify the essential information required to fly the approach and missed approach procedure.
- Use the configurations described in Chapter 12 to help you establish and maintain stable climb, cruise, and approach settings for each phase of the flight.
- Use the interactive map in your simulation to help you orient yourself throughout the flight.
- Use the replay and review features in X-Plane or FSX to check how well you tracked the courses and maintained altitude during the flight.
- As noted in Chapter 45, the basic Cessna 172 in X-Plane does not include distance measuring equipment (DME), but throughout this lesson you can specify VORs as direct-to waypoints in the GPS to substitute for DME.
- You can also use this scenario to practice the VOR RWY 16 approach at KALW.

What-Ifs

You can use the "Dice-Based Failure Scheme" described in Chapter 8 to create additional challenges for this flight.

At any point during the flight, roll a die, draw a number from a hat, or use another method to select a random number between 1 and 6. Using Table 52-1, find the corresponding problem to solve, and then take the appropriate action. If the challenge is a failure of an aircraft system or instrument, use the failure options in X-Plane or FSX to replicate the problem.

Table 52-1: Random Challenges for This Flight

NUMBER	RESULT
1	Vacuum system failure
2	Visibility reported at KALW drops to ¼ mile
3	ATC requires you to hold north of ALW on the 340° radial, right turns, maintain 6,000 ft., for 15 minutes before you are cleared for the full ILS approach.
4	The ILS at KALW is reported out of service.
5	Runway 20 is blocked.
6	The glideslope for the RWY 20 ILS is reported out of service.

Objectives and Desired Outcome Grading Sheet

SCENARIO ACTIVITIES	SCENARIO SUB-ACTIVITIES	DESIRED OUTCOME
Understand the key regulations that apply to IFR flight.	–	Describe/Explain
Understand the key information on the KALW ILS or LOC Y RWY 20 approach chart.	–	Describe/Explain
Complete a pre-approach briefing based on the KALW ILS or LOC Y RWY 20 approach chart.	–	Describe/Practice
Fly the KALW ILS or LOC Y RWY 20 approach within the standards outlined in the PTS.	–	Practice
Understand the elements of the missed approach procedure for the KALW ILS or LOC Y RWY 20.	–	Describe/Explain

CHAPTER

53

IFR Lesson 9: IFR Cross-Country

The ninth lesson in the FITS syllabus for the instrument rating focuses on cross-country flights under IFR. It includes a three-leg IFR flight with different types of approaches at each airport. The lesson is designed to give you a realistic workout during an IFR flight.

Scenario

This scenario follows that pattern with a round-robin flight from Astoria, OR (KAST), to Olympia, WA (KOLM), then to Hoquiam, WA (KHQM), and finally back to KAST (see Figure 53-1). The flight plan includes a dogleg to CARRO intersection after KOLM to give you the option to practice an approach at Shelton, WA (KSHN). The total distance for the flight is about 220 nm, and at typical Cessna 172 cruise speed requires about 2 hours of flying time, not counting the time required to fly approaches.

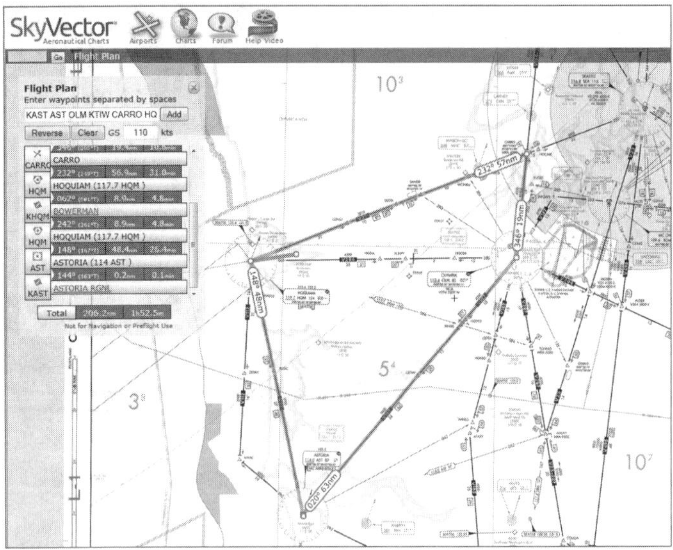

Figure 53-1: The route KAST-AST-OLM-KOLM-CARRO-HQM-KHQM-HQM-AST-KAST on the L-1 en route chart as shown on SkyVector

The lesson also introduces two concepts that deserve special attention:

- DME arcs
- ADF navigation and NDB approaches

DME Arcs

Many instrument approach procedures include DME arcs as feeder routes and transitions at the beginning of an approach (see Figure 53-2).

To learn about DME arcs, see "DME Arc" in Chapter 7, "Navigation Systems," in the *Instrument Flying Handbook* (pp. 7-17–7-19).

As noted earlier, the basic Cessna 172 in X-Plane does not include distance measuring equipment (DME), but throughout this lesson you can specify the appropriate VOR as a direct-to waypoint in the GPS to substitute for DME.

The approach at KAST in this lesson gives you an opportunity to practice flying a DME arc. If you want to practice that skill before starting this scenario, you can use the Situation (X-Plane) or Flight (FSX) associated with Lesson 2 (Chapter 46) to practice intercepting and flying hypothetical DME arcs at various distances from the VORs at Walla Walla, WA (ALW) and Pasco, WA (PSC). As you practice flying DME arcs, check the interactive map in X-Plane or FSX periodically to verify how well you are tracking the arc you specified.

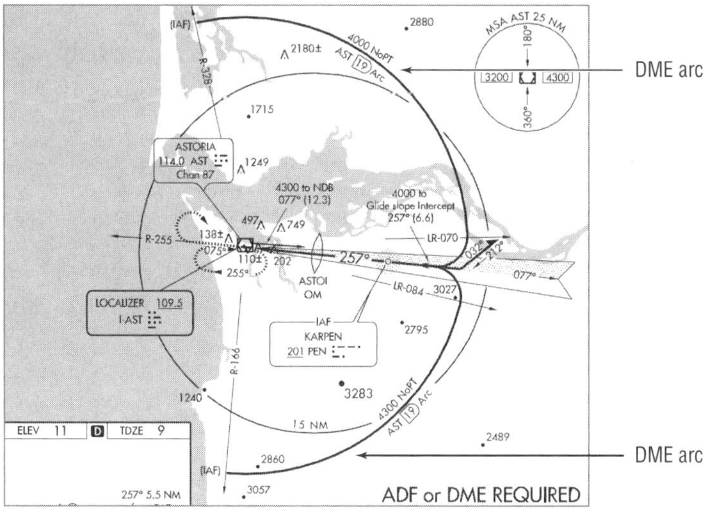

Figure 53-2: DME arcs on the ILS RWY 26 approach at KAST

Automatic Direction Finder (ADF)

Few new aircraft are equipped with automatic direction finder (ADF) receivers and indicators (see Figure 53-3); and in the U.S., most pilots fly approaches based on nondirectional beacons (NDBs) only during training or flight tests. For that reason, this is the only lesson in the IFR syllabus that includes the optional use of ADF.

Figure 53-3: A typical ADF indicator and receiver as shown in Figure 7-2 of the *Instrument Flying Handbook*

If ADF equipment is installed in your airplane, however, you must be able to use it when you take the practical test for the instrument rating. To help you learn about and practice using the ADF, this scenario includes a supplemental Situation (X-Plane) and Flight (FSX):

- X-Plane: `Wiley-SBT-IFR-ADF-Practice.sit`
- FSX: `Wiley-SBT-IFR-ADF-Practice.flt`

These setups place your simulated Cessna 172 in the sky near Shelton, WA (KSHN), so that you can practice ADF navigation by using the Mason County (MNC) and Carney (CAN) NDBs (see Figure 53-4).

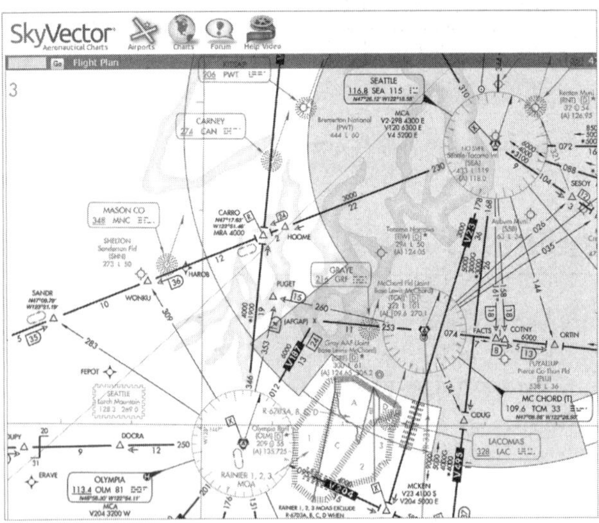

Figure 53-4: The area around KSHN on the L-1 en route chart as shown on SkyVector

To learn about using ADF, see "Nondirectional Radio Beacon (NDB)" in Chapter 7, "Navigation Systems," in the *Instrument Flying Handbook* (pp. 7-3–7-8). Additional information is available in "Automatic Direction Finder" in Chapter 15, "Navigation" in the *Pilot's Handbook of Aeronautical Knowledge* (p. 15-29).

While learning how to use the ADF, leave the autopilot on, with the altitude and heading features active. You can then fly the airplane by moving the bug on the heading indicator. As the airplane turns, you can observe the relationship between the aircraft's heading and the bearing pointer on the ADF indicator. You can also use this technique to practice intercepting and tracking bearings to and from the MNC and CAN beacons. Check the interactive map in X-Plane or FSX periodically to verify your position and to help you understand the relationship between the aircraft's heading and the bearing indicated by the ADF needle.

If you want to practice flying approaches based on NDBs, try the NDB or GPS-A approach at KSHN and the NDB RWY 1 approach at Bremerton, WA (KPWT). Both of those procedures include holding patterns based on the NDBs, and the ADF practice Situation or Flight noted earlier puts your airplane in position to fly those approaches.

Objectives

The primary goals for this lesson are:

- Practicing IFR procedures on typical cross-country flights, including standard instrument departures and en route navigation
- Flying several types of instrument approaches
- Practicing holding patterns

Completion Standards

The detailed goals for this lesson are outlined in the table at the end of this chapter. In general, before moving on to the next lesson, you should meet the standards in the relevant sections of the instrument rating PTS. The general standards include:

- During departures and en route flight, intercept, in a timely manner, all courses, radials, and bearings appropriate to the procedure, route, or clearance; maintain the applicable airspeed within ±10 knots; fly headings within ±10°; maintain altitude within ±100 ft; and track courses, radials, or bearings within ¾-scale deflection of the CDI.
- When tracking a DME arc, maintain the arc within ±1 nm.
- During approaches, meet the accuracy standards for nonprecision or precision approaches, as described in previous lessons and the instrument rating PTS.

References and Resources

To prepare for this lesson, review the following references and resources. The resources at the AOPA Air Safety Institute are valuable supplements to the official information in the FAA references.

TITLE	CHAPTER/SECTION	TOPIC/NOTES
Instrument Flying Handbook	Chapter 7, "Navigation Systems"	Nondirectional Radio Beacon (NDB), (pp. 7-3–7-8), DME Arc (pp. 7-17–7-19)
Pilot's Handbook of Aeronautical Knowledge	Chapter 15, "Navigation"	Automatic Direction Finder (p. 15-29)
Instrument Procedures Handbook	Chapter 2, "Takeoffs and Departures"	Review all topics.
	Chapter 3, "En Route Operations"	Review all topics.
	Chapter 4, "Arrivals"	Review all topics.
	Chapter 5, "Approaches"	Review all topics.
AIM	Chapter 5, "Air Traffic Procedures"	Sections 1–5
General Aviation Pilot's Guide to Preflight Weather Planning, Weather Self-Briefings, and Weather Decision Making	–	–
Instrument Rating Practical Test Standards	I. Preflight Preparation	Review all tasks.
	V. Navigation Systems	Review all tasks.
	VI. Instrument Approach Procedures	Review all tasks.
AOPA Air Safety Institute Safety Advisor *Single-Pilot IFR*	–	–
AOPA Air Safety Institute Interactive Safety Course *IFR Insights: Regulations*	–	–

CROSS-REFERENCE **For more information about the references and resources that complement the lessons in this book, see Chapter 2.**

Preflight Briefing

This lesson begins with your Cessna 172 ready to depart KAST on a three-leg flight to KOLM and KHQM before returning to KAST. Use the following sequence to complete this lesson:

- Depart runway 13, fly the ASTORIA ONE departure, and then proceed via V187 to OLM.
- Fly the ILS or LOC RWY 17 approach at KOLM. Fly the published missed approach procedure, and after one turn in the holding pattern at CERTA, return to the OLM VOR and track the 346° radial to CARRO intersection.
- Next, follow V27 to HQM and fly the VOR-RWY 6 approach to KHQM. If you land at KHQM, fly the published departure procedure for KHQM and, after reaching HQM, join V27 southeast bound to AST. Otherwise, fly the published missed approach procedure at KHQM.
- After entering the holding pattern at HQM, join V27 southeast bound toward AST. Join the 19 nm DME arc north of AST, fly the ILS RWY 26 approach, and then land at KAST.

If you want to practice using the ADF, insert the following step in your flight:

- After flying the approach at KOLM, proceed to CARRO, and fly the NDB or GPS-A approach at KSHN. After flying the missed approach procedure and returning to the MNC beacon, join V27 southwest bound to HQM.

CROSS-REFERENCE **You can find the IFR procedure charts for this lesson in `IFR_Charts.pdf`, available at this book's website.**

Clearance

For this lesson, assume that you have filed three flight plans, one for each leg of the journey. The clearances for each leg are as follows:

- Cleared to KOLM via the ASTORIA ONE departure, then V27 to OLM. Maintain 5000. Contact Seattle Center on 124.2. Squawk 4200.
- Cleared to KHQM via the YELM TWO departure, OLM, CARRO, V27 to HQM. Maintain 4000. Contact Seattle Departure on 121.1. Squawk 4200.
- Cleared to KAST via the published departure procedure, HQM, V27 to AST. Maintain 5000. Contact Seattle Center on 128.3. Squawk 4200.

Note that there is no charted departure procedure for KHQM. To depart under IFR from airports like KHQM, you can often follow a text obstacle departure procedure (ODP) published in the A/FD (see Figure 53-5),

HOQUIAM, WA
BOWERMAN
TAKE-OFF MINIMUMS: **Rwy 6**, 600-2 or std. with a min. climb of 260' per NM to 600.
DEPARTURE PROCEDURE: **Rwy 6**, climbing right turn heading 110°; **Rwy 24**, climb runway heading. **All aircraft** climb to 600 continue climb on course.

Figure 53-5: The ODP for KHQM described in the A/FD

Location and Weather

This scenario begins with your Cessna 172 ready to depart runway 13 at KAST. The bases of the clouds throughout the area are at about 500 ft., and the flight visibility below the ceiling is about 1 mile. The wind is out of the southwest at approximately 10 knots.

Situations and Flights

This lesson uses the following files for X-Plane and FSX:

- X-Plane: `Wiley-SBT-IFR-Lesson-09.sit`
- FSX: `Wiley-SBT-IFR-Lesson-09.flt`

Optional files for practicing ADF navigation:

- X-Plane: `Wiley-SBT-IFR-ADF-Practice.sit`
- FSX: `Wiley-SBT-IFR-ADF-Practice.flt`

CROSS-REFERENCE **For more information about using Situations (X-Plane) and Flights (FSX), see Chapter 10.**

Tips for This Lesson

Here are a few suggestions to help you get the most from this lesson:

- To speed up the en route portions of this lesson, use the interactive map in X-Plane or FSX to reposition your airplane on the appropriate airway a few miles from the next destination.
- Use the interactive map in your simulation to help you orient yourself throughout the flight.
- Use the replay and review features in X-Plane or FSX to check how well you tracked the courses and maintained altitude during the flight.
- If you want to divide this lesson into several sessions, pause the simulation at any point and save a new Situation (X-Plane) or Flight (FSX) so that you can quickly resume the flight from that position.

What-Ifs

You can use the "Dice-Based Failure Scheme" described in Chapter 8 to create additional challenges for this flight.

At any point during the flight, roll a die, draw a number from a hat, or use another method to select a random number between 1 and 6. Using Table 53-1, find the corresponding problem to solve, and then take the appropriate action. If the challenge is a failure of an aircraft system or instrument, use the failure options in X-Plane or FSX to replicate the problem.

Table 53-1: Random Challenges for This Flight

NUMBER	RESULT
1	Vacuum system failure
2	Hold as published at SANDR intersection about halfway between CARRO and HQM on V27. Proceed to HQM after three laps around the holding pattern.
3	Visibility at KOM drops to ¼ mile.
4	The ILS at KOLM is reported out of service.
5	Wind at KHQM shifts to 270° at 20 knots.
6	Approach lights at KAST are out of service.

Objectives and Desired Outcome Grading Sheet

SCENARIO ACTIVITIES	SCENARIO SUB-ACTIVITIES	DESIRED OUTCOME
Understand the key regulations that apply to IFR flight.	–	Describe/Explain
Complete a pre-approach briefing prior to flying each procedure.	–	Describe/Practice
Fly each approach within the standards outlined in the PTS.	–	Practice
Understand the requirements for including alternate airports under IFR.	–	Describe/Explain

CHAPTER

54

IFR Lesson 10: IFR Cross-Country

The tenth lesson in the FITS syllabus for the instrument rating focuses on a short IFR cross-country flight. The challenge in this scenario is a nagging problem with the airplane's electrical system.

Scenario

This scenario follows the basic sequence for an IFR flight with a trip from Eugene, OR (KEUG), to Newport, OR (KONP). Assume that your airplane has been in the maintenance shop at KEUG to address a problem with the alternator and you're ready to fly it home to KONP. It's a short flight — about 45 nm en route that will require about 25 minutes of flying time at typical Cessna 172 cruising speed. Unfortunately, the good weather expected for the flight hasn't materialized, and low ceilings persist across the entire route.

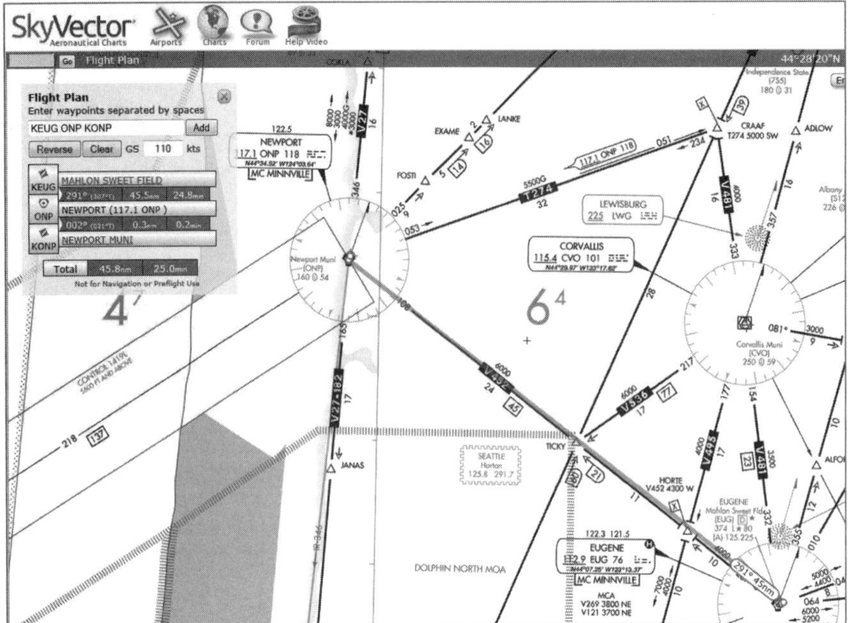

Figure 54-1: The route KEUG-ONP-KONP on the L-1 en route chart as shown on SkyVector

Objectives

The primary goals for this lesson are:

- Practicing IFR procedures on typical cross-country flights, including standard instrument departures and en route navigation
- Flying precision or nonprecision approaches
- Practicing emergency procedures, especially loss of communications with air traffic control

Completion Standards

The detailed goals for this lesson are outlined in the table at the end of this chapter. In general, before moving on to the next lesson, you should meet the standards in the relevant sections of the instrument rating PTS. The general standards include:

- During departures and en route flight, intercept, in a timely manner, all courses, radials, and bearings appropriate to the procedure, route, or clearance; maintain the applicable airspeed within ±10 knots; fly headings within ±10°; maintain altitude within ±100 ft.; and track courses, radials, or bearings within ¾-scale deflection of the CDI.

- Comply with the regulations and procedures that govern emergencies and loss of communication under IFR.
- While flying approaches, meet the appropriate accuracy standards for precision and nonprecision procedures as described in previous lessons and in the instrument rating PTS.

References and Resources

To prepare for this lesson, review the following references and resources. The resources at the AOPA Air Safety Institute are valuable supplements to the official information in the FAA references.

TITLE	CHAPTER/SECTION	TOPIC/NOTES
Instrument Flying Handbook	Chapter 10, "IFR Flight"	IFR Flight Plan (p. 10-2)
	Chapter 11, "Emergency Operations"	Aircraft System Malfunctions (p. 11-3), Communications/ Navigation System Malfunction (p. 11-8)
Instrument Procedures Handbook	Chapter 2, "Takeoffs and Departures"	Review all topics.
	Chapter 3, "En Route Operations"	Review all topics.
	Chapter 4, "Arrivals"	Review all topics.
	Chapter 5, "Approaches"	Review all topics.
AIM	Chapter 5, "Air Traffic Procedures"	Sections1–5 and Section 5–1–8 "Flight Plan (FAA Form 7233–1) – Domestic IFR Flights"
	Chapter 6, "Emergency Procedures"	6–4–1 "Two-way Radio Communications Failure"

Continued

(continued)

TITLE	CHAPTER/SECTION	TOPIC/NOTES
Federal Aviation Regulations (14 CFR Part 91)	§91.167: Fuel requirements for flight in IFR conditions and §91.169: IFR flight plan: Information required	Note the requirements for including an alternate airport in your flight plan.
	§91.185: IFR operations: Two-way radio communications failure	–
	§91.187: Operation under IFR in controlled airspace: Malfunction reports	–
General Aviation Pilot's Guide to Preflight Weather Planning, Weather Self-Briefings, and Weather Decision Making	–	–
Instrument Rating Practical Test Standards	I. Preflight Preparation	Review all tasks.
	V. Navigation Systems	Review all tasks.
	VI. Instrument Approach Procedures	Review all tasks.
AOPA Air Safety Institute Safety Advisor *Single-Pilot IFR*	–	–
AOPA Air Safety Institute Safety Advisor *Emergency Procedures*	–	–
AOPA Air Safety Institute Interactive Safety Course *IFR Insights: Regulations*	–	–

CROSS-REFERENCE **For more information about the references and resources that complement the lessons in this book, see Chapter 2.**

Preflight Briefing

This lesson begins with your Cessna 172 ready to depart KEUG for the short flight to KONP (see Figure 54-2).

Figure 54-2: Ready for takeoff at KEUG as seen from the cockpit of the Cessna 172 in FSX

Because the weather throughout the area is IMC, you must include an alternate airport in your IFR flight plan. Follow the sequence below for this flight:

- Fly the EUGENE EIGHT departure.
- When you reach the VOR at ONP, fly the full ILS or LOC RWY 16 approach or the VOR-A approach at KONP.
- Alternatively, when you reach ONP, proceed via V452 and V536 to CVO and fly either the ILS RWY 17 or VOR-A approach at KCVO.

CROSS-REFERENCE **You can find the IFR procedure charts for this lesson in `IFR_Charts.pdf`, available at this book's website.**

Clearance

For this lesson, assume that KCVO is your alternate airport.

- Cleared to KONP via the EUGENE EIGHT departure, V452 ONP. Maintain 6000. Contact Seattle Center on 125.8. Squawk 4200.
- After takeoff, at 3,000 ft., turn right to heading 345° and intercept V452 northwest toward ONP.

Location and Weather

This scenario begins with your Cessna 172 ready to depart runway 16R at KEUG. The bases of the clouds throughout the area are at about 500 ft., and the flight visibility below the ceiling is about 1 mile. The wind is out of the southwest at approximately 10 knots.

Situations and Flights

This lesson uses the following files for X-Plane and FSX:

- X-Plane: `Wiley-SBT-IFR-Lesson-10.sit`
- FSX: `Wiley-SBT-IFR-Lesson-10.flt`

CROSS-REFERENCE **For more information about using Situations (X-Plane) and Flights (FSX), see Chapter 10.**

Tips for This Lesson

Here are a few suggestions to help you get the most from this lesson:

- Review the requirements for alternate airports under IFR.
- Use the interactive map in your simulation to help you orient yourself throughout the flight and to review your flight path.
- After flying one of the approaches at KONP, restart the Situation or Flight, reposition your aircraft near ONP, and then fly the other procedure.
- If you want to practice using the ADF, fly the published missed approach procedure for the KNOP ILS RWY 16 and hold as published at the AGGET beacon.

What-Ifs

You can use the "Dice-Based Failure Scheme" described in Chapter 8 to create additional challenges for this flight.

At any point during the flight, roll a die, draw a number from a hat, or use another method to select a random number between 1 and 6. Using Table 54-1, find the corresponding problem to solve, and then take the appropriate action. If the challenge is a failure of an aircraft system or instrument, use the failure options in X-Plane or FSX to replicate the problem.

Table 54-1: Random Challenges for This Flight

NUMBER	RESULT
1	Vacuum system failure
2	Alternator failure
3	Communications failure en route to KONP
4	Weather at KONP is below the minimums for the ILS approach.
5	ATC requires you to hold on V452 southeast of TICKY intersection at 6000; expect three laps in the holding pattern.
6	The ILS at KONP is out of service.

Objectives and Desired Outcome Grading Sheet

SCENARIO ACTIVITIES	SCENARIO SUB-ACTIVITIES	DESIRED OUTCOME
Understand the key regulations that apply to IFR flight.	–	Describe/Explain
Understand the emergency procedures to be followed under IFR.	–	Explain/Perform
Understand the key information on the approach charts associated with this lesson.	–	Describe/Explain
Complete a pre-approach briefing for each approach used in this lesson.	–	Describe/Practice
Fly each approach within the standards outlined in the PTS.	–	Practice
Understand the elements of the missed approach procedures at the airports used in this lesson.	–	Describe/Explain

CHAPTER

55

IFR Lesson 11: IFR Cross-Country and Equipment Malfunctions

This lesson in the FITS syllabus for the instrument rating focuses on an IFR cross-country flight with malfunctions that test your ability to deal with equipment failures.

Scenario

This scenario follows the basic pattern for an IFR flight with a trip from Bend, OR (KBDN), to Pendleton, OR (KPDT). The flight begins in the air southwest of PDT on V536 (see Figure 55-1). Up to this point, the flight has progressed normally, but fog has materialized in the area, adding to the pressure you feel about an important meeting in Pendleton.

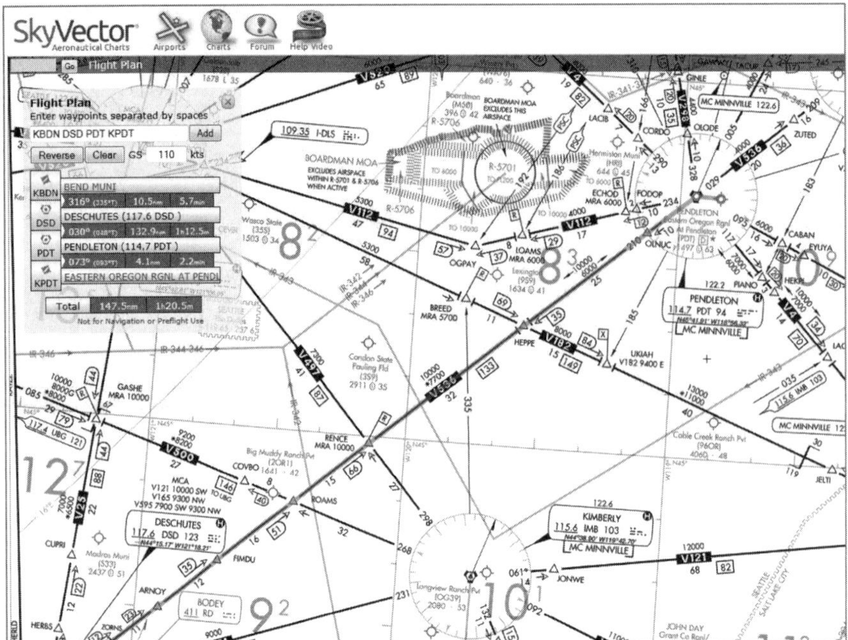

Figure 55-1: Part of the route from KBDN to KPDT on the L-13 en route chart as shown on SkyVector

Objectives

The primary goals for this lesson are:

- Practicing IFR procedures on typical cross-country flights
- Flying precision or nonprecision approaches
- Practicing flying DME arcs (see Figure 55-2)
- Practicing emergency procedures, including loss of primary flight instruments
- Developing skills in aeronautical decision making and single-pilot resource management

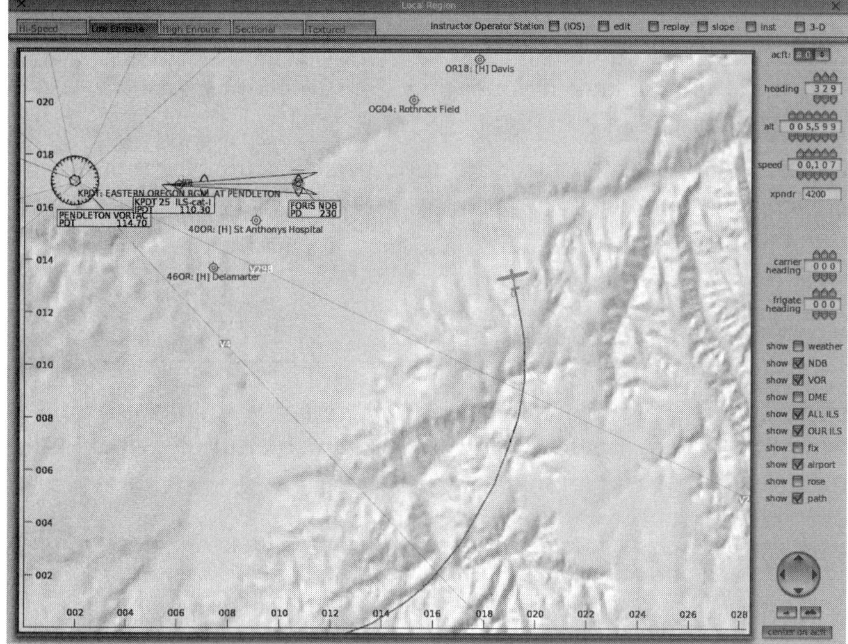

Figure 55-2: The Cessna's track on a DME arc while flying an approach at KPDT, as shown on the interactive map in X-Plane

Completion Standards

The detailed goals for this lesson are outlined in the table at the end of this chapter. In general, before moving on to the next lesson, you should meet the standards in the relevant sections of the instrument rating PTS. The general standards include:

- Apply the techniques and procedures described in the *Risk Management Handbook* during a typical IFR flight.
- During en route flight, intercept, in a timely manner, all courses, radials, and bearings appropriate to the procedure, route, or clearance; maintain the applicable airspeed within ±10 knots; fly headings within ±10°; maintain altitude within ±100 ft; and track courses, radials, or bearings within ¾-scale deflection of the CDI.

- Comply with the regulations and procedures that govern emergencies and loss of communication under IFR.
- Apply the appropriate techniques and skills to maintain control when essential equipment fails in flight.
- While flying approaches, meet the appropriate accuracy standards for precision and nonprecision procedures as described in previous lessons and in the instrument rating PTS.

References and Resources

To prepare for this lesson, review the following references and resources. The resources at the AOPA Air Safety Institute are valuable supplements to the official information in the FAA references.

TITLE	CHAPTER/SECTION	TOPIC/NOTES
Instrument Flying Handbook	Chapter 10, "IFR Flight"	IFR Flight Plan (p. 10-2)
	Chapter 11, "Emergency Operations"	Aircraft System Malfunctions (p. 11-3), Communications/ Navigation System Malfunction (p. 11-8)
Instrument Procedures Handbook	Chapter 3, "En Route Operations"	Review all topics.
	Chapter 4, "Arrivals"	Review all topics.
	Chapter 5, "Approaches"	Review all topics.
Risk Management Handbook	Chapter 5, "Aeronautical Decision Making"	–
	Chapter 6, "Single-Pilot Resource Management"	–
AIM	Chapter 6, "Emergency Procedures"	–
Federal Aviation Regulations (14 CFR Part 91)	§91.187: Operation under IFR in controlled airspace: Malfunction reports	–

TITLE	CHAPTER/SECTION	TOPIC/NOTES
Instrument Rating Practical Test Standards	V. Navigation Systems	—
	VI. Instrument Approach Procedures	—
	VII. Emergency Operations	—
AOPA Air Safety Institute Safety Advisor *Single-Pilot IFR*	—	—
AOPA Air Safety Institute Safety Advisor *Emergency Procedures*	—	—

CROSS-REFERENCE **For more information about the references and resources that complement the lessons in this book, see Chapter 2.**

Preflight Briefing

This lesson begins with your Cessna 172 in the air at 11,000 ft. near HEPPE intersection southwest of PDT on V536 (see Figure 55-3).

Figure 55-3: The view near HEPPE intersection from the cockpit of the Cessna 172 in X-Plane

You filed the following route from KBDN to KPDT, with KALW as your alternate.

- DSD V536 PDT

Fly either the ILS LOC/DME RWY 25 or VOR RWY 7 approach at KPDT. If you miss the approach, continue to ALW and fly the most appropriate approach at KALW.

CROSS-REFERENCE **You can find the IFR procedure charts for this lesson in `IFR_Charts.pdf`, available at this book's website.**

Clearance

ATC issued the following clearance before you departed KBDN:

- Cleared to KPDT via the BEND ONE departure, V546. Maintain 11,000. Contact Seattle Center on 128.15. Squawk 4200.

Location and Weather

This scenario begins with your Cessna 172 southwest of PDT. The bases of the clouds throughout the area are at about 500 ft., and the flight visibility below the ceiling is about 1 mile in fog. The wind is out of the southwest at approximately 10 knots.

Situations and Flights

This lesson uses the following files for X-Plane and FSX:

- X-Plane: `Wiley-SBT-IFR-Lesson-11.sit`
- FSX: `Wiley-SBT-IFR-Lesson-11.flt`

CROSS-REFERENCE **For more information about using Situations (X-Plane) and Flights (FSX), see Chapter 10.**

Tips for This Lesson

Here are a few suggestions to help you get the most from this lesson:

- Review the requirements for alternate airports under IFR.
- Review the fundamentals of instrument flying and the procedures for flying with inoperative flight instruments in Chapter 4 of the *Instrument Flying Handbook.*
- Use the interactive map in your simulation to help you orient yourself throughout the flight and to review your flight path.
- If you fly X-Plane, use the GPS to substitute for DME. Set an appropriate VOR as the direct-to waypoint.

What-Ifs

You can use the "Dice-Based Failure Scheme" described in Chapter 8 to create additional challenges for this flight.

At any point during the flight, roll a die, draw a number from a hat, or use another method to select a random number between 1 and 6. Using Table 55-1, find the corresponding problem to solve, and then take the appropriate action. If the challenge is a failure of an aircraft system or instrument, use the failure options in X-Plane or FSX to replicate the problem.

Table 55-1: Random Challenges for This Flight

NUMBER	RESULT
1	Vacuum system failure
2	Alternator failure
3	Weather at KPDT is below the minimums for the ILS approach.
4	You encounter ice at 7,000 ft. as you descend toward PDT.
5	ATC requires you to hold on V536 southwest of HEPPE intersection. Descend in the holding pattern to 7,000 ft. and then continue to PDT.
6	Ice is reported between PDT and ALW between 5,000 and 8,000 ft.

Objectives and Desired Outcome Grading Sheet

SCENARIO ACTIVITIES	SCENARIO SUB-ACTIVITIES	DESIRED OUTCOME
Understand the key regulations that apply to IFR flight.	–	Describe/Explain
Understand the emergency procedures to be followed under IFR.	–	Explain/Perform
Understand the key information on the approach charts associated with this lesson.	–	Describe/Explain
Complete a pre-approach briefing for each approach used in this lesson.	–	Describe/Practice
Fly each approach within the standards outlined in the PTS.	–	Practice
Understand the elements of the missed approach procedures at the airports used in this lesson.	–	Describe/Explain
Understand how to proceed to an alternate airport.	–	Explain/Perform

CHAPTER

56

IFR Lesson 12: IFR Cross-Country and Off-Airway Routes

This lesson in the FITS syllabus for the instrument rating focuses on an IFR cross-country flight. It continues practice in all phases of IFR flight, including off-airway routes.

Scenario

This scenario involves a flight from Eastsound Airport on Orcas Island, WA (KORS), to Port Angeles, WA (KCLM). You are a volunteer pilot for an organization that provides free transportation to people who need medical care, such as periodic visits for chemotherapy. This service is especially important for patients who live in isolated areas like the San Juan Islands.

For the reasons explained below, the best route to file for a flight in your Cessna 172 is probably similar to the path shown in Figure 56-1.

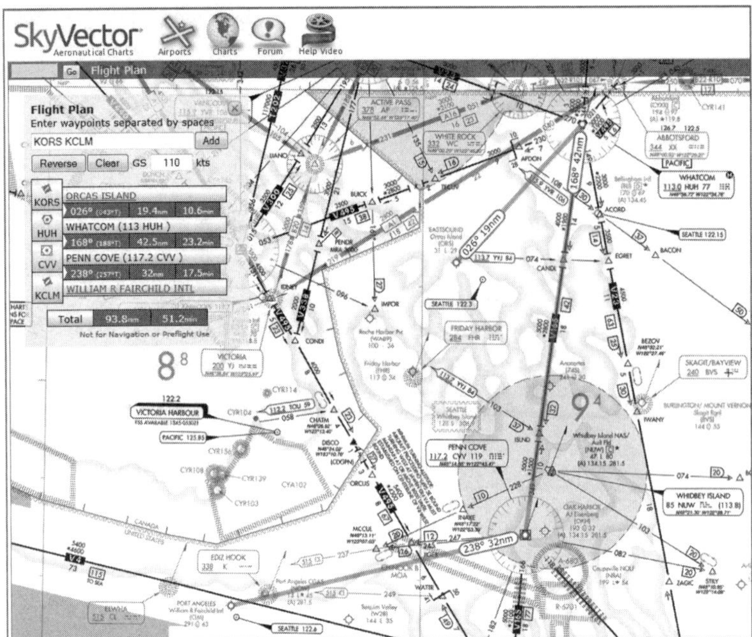

Figure 56-1: The route from KORS to KCLM as shown on the L-1 en route chart on SkyVector

Under IFR, this short flight presents two primary challenges. First, the IFR departure procedure at KORS sends you to the Whatcom VOR (HUH) before you can proceed on course (see Figure 56-2). In a real flight, you would probably receive radar vectors from Whidbey Approach or Victoria Terminal shortly after takeoff or, in an aircraft equipped with an IFR-approved GPS, a clearance to a fix along a more direct route. For the purposes of this exercise, however, fly the published departure procedure. This route also takes you toward Bellingham International Airport (KBLI), where several instrument approaches are available should you encounter problems during the early phase of the flight.

EASTSOUND, WA
ORCAS ISLAND (ORS)
AMDT 1 09351 (FAA)
TAKE-OFF MINIMUMS: **Rwy 16,** NA-Terrain. **Rwy 34,** 500-3 or std. w/ min. climb of 224' per NM to 600.
DEPARTURE PROCEDURE: **Rwy 34,** climbing right turn to 2000 to intercept HUH VORTAC R-210 to HUH VORTAC, then climb-in-hold (hold South, Left turns, 352° inbound) to cross HUH VORTAC at or above 3800 before proceeding on course.
NOTE: **Rwy 34,** trees beginning 330' from DER, 411' left of centerline, up to 120' AGL/139' MSL.

Figure 56-2: The published obstacle departure procedure for KORS

Second, the most direct route involves an over-water leg across the Strait of Juan de Fuca, something to be considered carefully in a single-engine airplane. After departing HUH, it makes sense to fly closer to land via V165 to CVV, which is also an initial approach fix (IAF) for the ILS or LOC RWY 08 approach at KCLM.

Objectives

The primary goals for this lesson are:

- Practicing IFR departure procedures, especially at airports without a control tower
- Flying complex instrument approaches
- Flying a course reversal that uses a holding pattern
- Developing skills in aeronautical decision making and single-pilot resource management
- Practicing emergency procedures

Completion Standards

The detailed goals for this lesson are outlined in the table at the end of this chapter. In general, before moving on to the next lesson, you should meet the standards in the relevant sections of the instrument rating PTS. The general standards include:

- Apply the techniques and procedures described in the *Risk Management Handbook* during a typical IFR flight.
- Understand when and how to include procedure turns when flying approaches.
- While flying approaches, meet the appropriate accuracy standards for precision and nonprecision procedures as described in previous lessons and the instrument rating PTS.

References and Resources

To prepare for this lesson, review the following references and resources. The resources at the AOPA Air Safety Institute are valuable supplements to the official information in the FAA references.

TITLE	CHAPTER/SECTION	TOPIC/NOTES
Instrument Flying Handbook	Chapter 10, "IFR Flight"	IFR Flight Plan (p. 10-2)
	Chapter 11, "Emergency Operations"	Aircraft System Malfunctions (p. 11-3), Communications/ Navigation System Malfunction (p. 11-8)
Instrument Procedures Handbook	Chapter 2, "Takeoffs and Departures"	Obstacle Departure Procedures (p. 2-18), Departures from Airports without an Operating Control Tower (p. 2-27)
	Chapter 3, "En Route Operations"	Review all topics.
	Chapter 4, "Arrivals"	Review all topics.
	Chapter 5, "Approaches"	Review all topics.
	Chapter 11, "Emergency Procedures"	Review all topics.
Risk Management Handbook	Chapter 5, "Aeronautical Decision Making"	–
	Chapter 6, "Single-Pilot Resource Management"	–
AIM	Chapter 5, "Air Traffic Procedures"	5–4–9 "Procedure Turn and Hold–in–Lieu of Procedure Turn"
Instrument Rating Practical Test Standards	V. Navigation Systems	–
	VI. Instrument Approach Procedures	–
AOPA Air Safety Institute Safety Advisor *Single-Pilot IFR*	–	–

CROSS-REFERENCE **For more information about the references and resources that complement the lessons in this book, see Chapter 2.**

Preflight Briefing

This lesson begins with your Cessna 172 ready to depart KORS to the north. Assume that you filed the following route:

- HUH-V165-CVV

When reaching CVV, fly the ILS or LOC RWY 8 approach at KCLM. Note that to reverse course at YUCSU, you must use the depicted holding pattern in lieu of a typical procedure turn (see Figure 56-3).

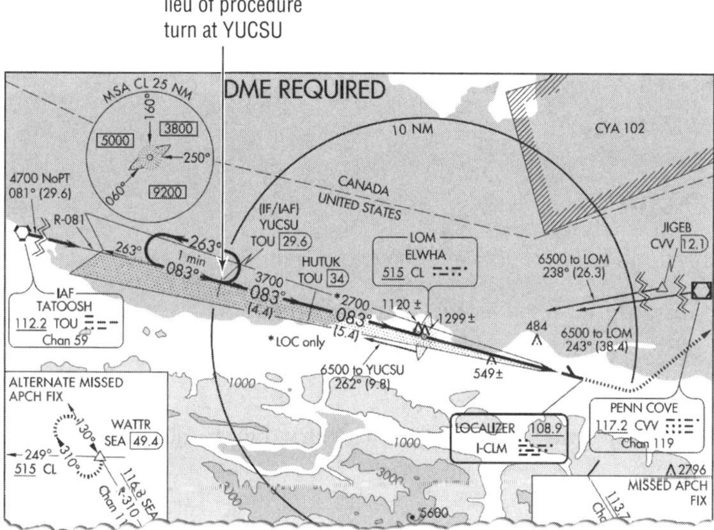

Figure 56-3: The holding pattern at YUCSU as shown on the chart for the ILS or LOC RWY 8 approach at KCLM

CROSS-REFERENCE **You can find the IFR procedure charts for this lesson in `IFR_Charts.pdf`, available at this book's website.**

Clearance

You have received the following clearance from Victoria Terminal:

- Cleared to KCLM via the published departure for runway 34 at KORS then as filed. Maintain 5,000. Contact Victoria Terminal on 132.7. Squawk 4200.

Location and Weather

You are ready to take off from runway 34 at KORS. The bases of the clouds throughout the area are at about 600 ft., and the flight visibility below the ceiling is about 1 mile in fog. The wind is out of the northeast at approximately 10 knots.

Situations and Flights

This lesson uses the following files for X-Plane and FSX:

- X-Plane: `Wiley-SBT-IFR-Lesson-12.sit`
- FSX: `Wiley-SBT-IFR-Lesson-12.flt`

CROSS-REFERENCE For more information about using Situations (X-Plane) and Flights (FSX), see Chapter 10.

Tips for This Lesson

Here are a few suggestions to help you get the most from this lesson:

- Review the requirements for alternate airports under IFR.
- Use the interactive map in your simulation to help you orient yourself throughout the flight and to review your flight path.
- If you fly X-Plane, use the GPS to substitute for DME. Set TOU as the direct-to waypoint.

What-Ifs

You can use the "Dice-Based Failure Scheme" described in Chapter 8 to create additional challenges for this flight.

At any point during the flight, roll a die, draw a number from a hat, or use another method to select a random number between 1 and 6. Using Table 56-1, find the corresponding problem to solve, and then take the appropriate action. If the challenge is a failure of an aircraft system or instrument, use the failure options in X-Plane or FSX to replicate the problem.

Table 56-1: Random Challenges for This Flight

NUMBER	RESULT
1	Vacuum system failure
2	Alternator failure
3	Weather at KCLM is below the minimums for the ILS approach.
4	Your #2 communications/navigation radio fails.
5	ATC requires you to hold north of CVV on the 349° radial at 5000. Continue after making three laps in the holding pattern.
6	You are unable to communicate with ATC.

Objectives and Desired Outcome Grading Sheet

Learning Objectives/Desired Outcome/Grade Sheet

SCENARIO ACTIVITIES	SCENARIO SUB-ACTIVITIES	DESIRED OUTCOME
Understand the emergency procedures to be followed under IFR.	–	Explain/Perform
Understand the procedures to follow after a communications failure.	–	Explain/Perform
Understand the key information on the approach charts associated with this lesson.	–	Describe/Explain
Complete a pre-approach briefing for each approach used in this lesson.	–	Describe/Practice
Fly each approach within the standards outlined in the PTS.	–	Practice
Understand the elements of the missed approach procedures at the airports used in this lesson.	–	Describe/Explain
Understand how to proceed to an alternate airport.	–	Explain/Perform

CHAPTER

57

IFR Lesson 13: Long IFR Cross-Country

This lesson in the FITS syllabus for the instrument rating is the so-called long cross-country flight required by the regulations that govern training for the instrument rating. This flight must cover at least 250 nm and include different types of approaches at three airports.

Scenario

This scenario involves a round-robin flight from Spokane, WA (KGEG), to Yakima, WA (KYM), Pasco, WA (KPSC), and then back to KGEG (see Figure 57-1). The distance as planned is about 324 nm, and at typical Cessna 172 cruising speed it requires about 3 hours to fly, not including time to complete the approaches.

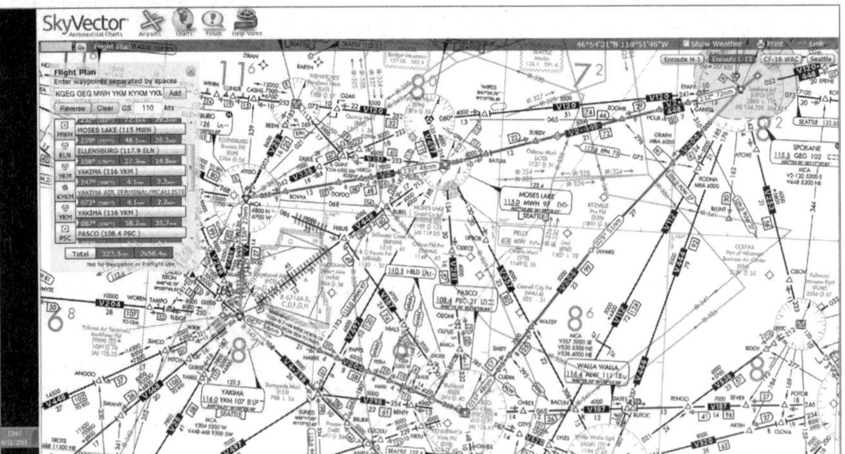

Figure 57-1: Route for the round-robin flight on the L-13 en route chart as shown on SkyVector

Assume that you are a physician who uses a personal aircraft to visit clinics throughout the Pacific Northwest to consult on cases that involve your specialty. The patients are too ill to travel, so you must go to them. Today, low clouds and fog cover the entire route.

Objectives

The primary goals for this lesson are:

- Meeting the requirement for a long cross-country flight during training for the instrument rating
- Practicing IFR departure procedures
- Flying a variety of complex instrument approaches (see Figure 57-2)
- Practicing DME arcs and holding
- Honing the skills involved in aeronautical decision making and single-pilot resource management
- Practicing partial-panel flying and the procedures for dealing with equipment failures

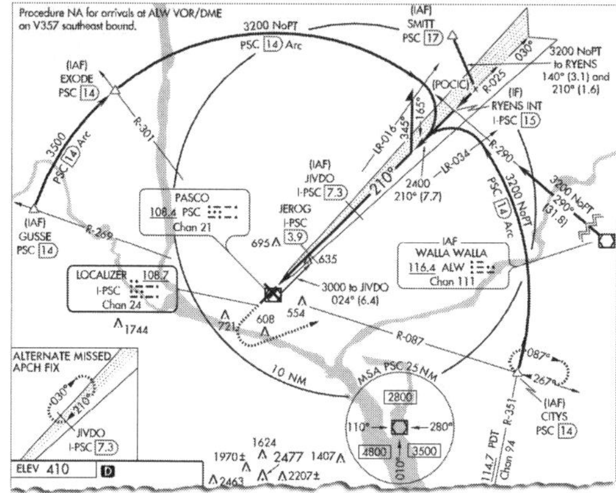

Figure 57-2: The busy plan view for the ILS or LOC/DME RWY 21R approach at KPSC

Completion Standards

The detailed goals for this lesson are outlined in the table at the end of this chapter. In general, before moving on to the next lesson, you should meet the standards in the relevant sections of the instrument rating PTS. The general standards include:

- Apply the techniques and procedures described in the *Risk Management Handbook* during a typical IFR flight.
- Plan and fly departure procedures according to the standards in the instrument rating PTS.
- While flying approaches, meet the appropriate accuracy standards for precision and nonprecision procedures as described in previous lessons and in the instrument rating PTS.

References and Resources

To prepare for this lesson, review the following references and resources. The resources at the AOPA Air Safety Institute are valuable supplements to the official information in the FAA references.

TITLE	CHAPTER/SECTION	TOPIC/NOTES
Instrument Flying Handbook	Chapter 10, "IFR Flight"	IFR Flight Plan (p. 10-2)
Instrument Procedures Handbook	Chapter 2, "Takeoffs and Departures"	–
	Chapter 3, "En Route Operations"	Review all topics.
	Chapter 5, "Approaches"	Review all topics.
Risk Management Handbook	Chapter 5, "Aeronautical Decision Making"	–
	Chapter 6, "Single-Pilot Resource Management"	–
Instrument Rating Practical Test Standards	V. Navigation Systems	–
	VI. Instrument Approach Procedures	–

CROSS-REFERENCE **For more information about the references and resources that complement the lessons in this book, see Chapter 2.**

Preflight Briefing

This lesson begins with your Cessna 172 ready to depart runway 7 at KGEG on the first segment of a three-leg flight to KYKM and KPSC before returning to KGEG.

Assume that you have filed the following routes for the three legs of this flight:

- GEG-V2-ELN-V25-YKM
- YKM-V204-PSC
- PSC-V204-GEG

This flight challenges you with several standard instrument departure procedures (SID) and a variety of instrument approaches, including the following:

- **KGEG:** SPOKANE ONE departure
- **KYKM:** ILS Z RWY 27 (but consider the ILS Y RWY 27)
- **KYKM:** GROMO TWO departure

- **KPSC:** ILS or LOC/DME RWY 21R
- **KPSC:** VOR/DME RWY 21R
- **KPSC:** TRI-CITIES FOUR departure
- **KGEG:** VOR RWY 3 approach

Consider the following NOTAMs that are valid for this flight:

- **KGEG:** Runway 3/21 is closed due to construction.
- **KPSC:** The glideslope for the ILS or LOC/DME RWY 21R is out of service.

CROSS-REFERENCE **You can find the IFR procedure charts for this lesson in `IFR_Charts.pdf`, available at this book's website.**

Clearance

You have received the following clearances for each leg of the flight:

- Cleared to KYKM via the SPOKANE ONE departure, as filed, maintain 8000. Contact departure on 123.75. Squawk 4200.
- Cleared to KPSC via the GROMO TWO departure, as filed, maintain 7000. Contact departure on 123.8. Squawk 4200.
- Cleared to KGEG via the TRI-CITIES departure, as filed, maintain 5000. Contact departure on 128.75. Squawk 4200.

Location and Weather

You are ready to take off from runway 7 at KGEG. The bases of the clouds throughout the area are at about 600 ft., and the flight visibility below the ceiling is about 1 mile in fog. The wind is out of the southwest at approximately 10 knots.

Situations and Flights

This lesson uses the following files for X-Plane and FSX:

- X-Plane: `Wiley-SBT-IFR-Lesson-13.sit`
- FSX: `Wiley-SBT-IFR-Lesson-13.flt`

CROSS-REFERENCE **For more information about using Situations (X-Plane) and Flights (FSX), see Chapter 10.**

Tips for This Lesson

Here are a few suggestions to help you get the most from this lesson:

- Review the fuel requirements for IFR flights. Consider whether you need to refuel at one or more airports along your route.
- Given the weather, what are the best alternate airports for your proposed flight?
- Use the interactive map in your simulation to help you orient yourself throughout the flight and to review your flight path.
- If you fly the X-Plane Cessna 172, use the GPS to substitute for DME. Consider how this limitation affects which approaches you can fly at KPSC.
- If you want to break up this scenario, save the Situation (X-Plane) or Flight (FSX) after you land at each airport (see Figure 57-3). To protect the original configurations, be sure to give unique names to these intermediate Situations or Flights.

Figure 57-3: At decision altitude on the ILS approach at KYKM as shown in FSX. It's often a good idea to take a break after flying a challenging approach.

What-Ifs

You can use the "Dice-Based Failure Scheme" described in Chapter 8 to create additional challenges for this flight.

At any point during the flight, roll a die, draw a number from a hat, or use another method to select a random number between 1 and 6. Using Table 57-1, find the corresponding problem to solve, and then take the appropriate action. If the challenge is a failure of an aircraft system or instrument, use the failure options in X-Plane or FSX to replicate the problem.

Table 57-1: Random Challenges for This Flight

NUMBER	RESULT
1	Vacuum system failure
2	Alternator failure
3	Weather at KYKM is below the minimums for the ILS approach.
4	ATC requires you to hold north at YKM as published on the ILS RWY 27 chart. Continue after making three laps in the holding pattern.
5	Before you can begin the approach at KPSC, ATC requires you to hold north of PSC on the 332° radial. Make three laps in the holding pattern before flying the approach.
6	You are unable to communicate with ATC.

Objectives and Desired Outcome Grading Sheet

SCENARIO ACTIVITIES	SCENARIO SUB-ACTIVITIES	DESIRED OUTCOME
Understand the procedures to follow after a communications failure.	–	Explain/Perform
Understand the key information on the approach charts associated with this lesson.	–	Describe/Explain
Complete a pre-approach briefing for each approach used in this lesson.	–	Describe/Practice
Fly each approach within the standards outlined in the PTS.	–	Practice
Understand the elements of the missed approach procedures at the airports used in this lesson.	–	Describe/Explain
Understand how to proceed to an alternate airport.	–	Explain/Perform

CHAPTER

58

IFR Lesson 14: Night IFR Flight

This lesson in the FITS syllabus involves another cross-country flight under IFR. Like the remaining lessons in the syllabus, it's an opportunity to hone the skills you've acquired.

This scenario, however, adds a twist that's not in the generic syllabus (or the regulations that govern instrument training) — IFR flight at night. Unfortunately, many IFR pilots get their first experience combining the challenges of night and IFR flying on their own.

Scenario

This scenario involves a late-night flight from Roseburg, OR (KRBG), to Hillsboro, OR (KHIO). You've had a long day of meetings followed by a dinner with clients in Roseburg, but you need to be back at work in Portland in the morning. The trip isn't long — about 150 nm and 1 hour 20 minutes at typical cruise speed (see Figure 58-1) — but this evening, clouds cover the entire route; and to add to the challenge, your passenger is a nervous flyer.

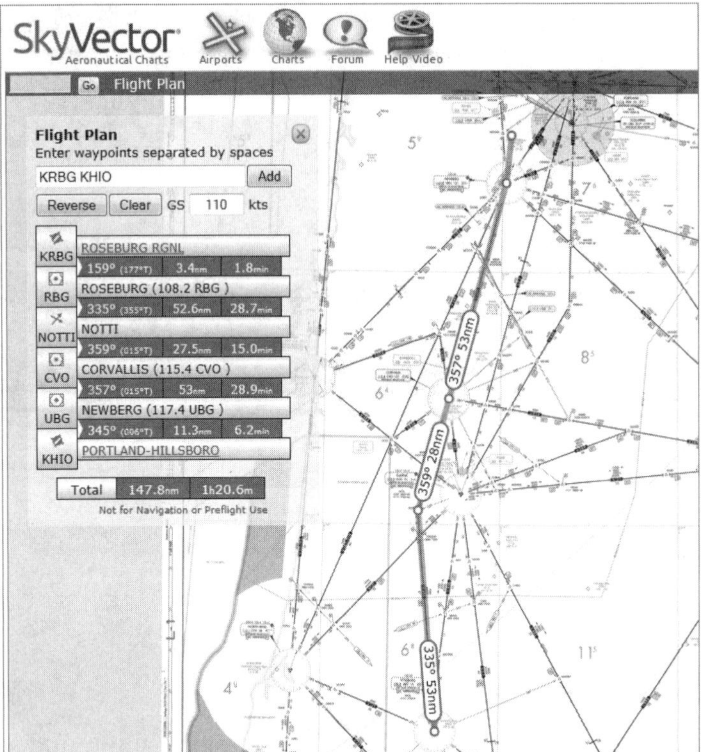

Figure 58-1: Route for the flight from KRBG to KHIO on the L-1 en route chart as shown on SkyVector

Objectives

The primary goals for this lesson are:

- Learning about the challenges of operating at night under IFR
- Practicing holding patterns — in this case, as part of a departure procedure
- Reviewing human factors — especially the limitations of night vision and the dangers of spatial disorientation
- Practicing IFR departure procedures
- Honing the skills involved in aeronautical decision making and single-pilot resource management

Completion Standards

The detailed goals for this lesson are outlined in the table at the end of this chapter. In general, before moving on to the next lesson, you should meet the standards in the relevant sections of the instrument rating PTS. The general standards include:

- Apply the techniques and procedures described in the *Risk Management Handbook* during a typical IFR flight.
- Plan and fly departure procedures according to the standards in the instrument rating PTS.
- While flying approaches, meet the appropriate accuracy standards for precision and nonprecision procedures as described in previous lessons and the instrument rating PTS.

References and Resources

To prepare for this lesson, review the following references and resources. The resources at the AOPA Air Safety Institute are valuable supplements to the official information in the FAA references.

TITLE	CHAPTER/SECTION	TOPIC/NOTES
Airplane Flying Handbook	Chapter 10, "Night Operations"	–
Instrument Flying Handbook	Chapter 1, "Human Factors"	–
Instrument Procedures Handbook	Chapter 2, "Takeoffs and Departures"	–
	Chapter 3, "En Route Operations"	–
	Chapter 5, "Approaches"	–
Risk Management Handbook	Chapter 5, "Aeronautical Decision Making"	–
	Chapter 6, "Single-Pilot Resource Management"	–

Continued

(continued)

TITLE	CHAPTER/SECTION	TOPIC/NOTES
Instrument Rating Practical Test Standards	–	Review all tasks.
AOPA Air Safety Institute *Terrain Avoidance Safety Brief*	–	–
AOPA Air Safety Institute *Safety Quiz Night Operations*	–	–
AOPA Air Safety Institute *Safety Quiz Airport Lighting: IFR*	–	–

CROSS-REFERENCE **For more information about the references and resources that complement the lessons in this book, see Chapter 2.**

Preflight Briefing

Roseburg lies in a valley, and at first glance, departing the airport doesn't appear too challenging; but a review of an approach chart (always a good idea when departing an airport under IFR) offers several hints that KRBG is surrounded by challenging terrain and obstacles (see Figure 58-2).

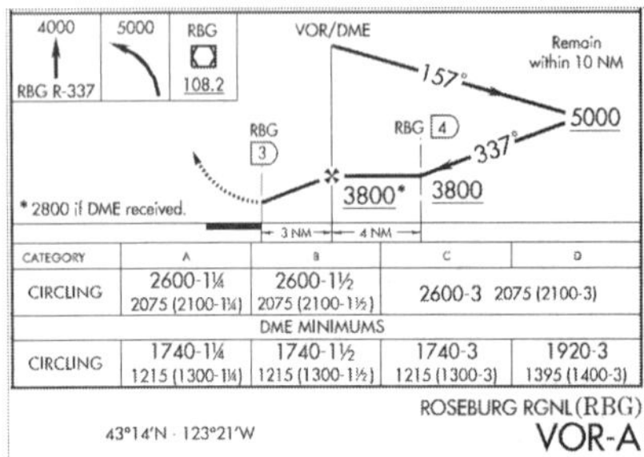

Figure 58-2: The minimums section of the VOR-A approach chart at KRBG

Note the high minimum descent altitude (MDA) for this approach — it's more than 2,000 ft. above the airport elevation. Even with DME, the MDA is 1,215 ft. above the airport.

The text for the obstacle departure procedure at KRBG confirms that obstacles are close at hand and tests your skill flying holding patterns (see Figure 58-3).

ROSEBURG, OR
ROSEBURG RGNL (RBG)
AMDT 6 10322 (FAA)
TAKE-OFF MINIMUMS: **Rwy 16**, 800-2 w/ min. climb of 460' per NM to 4500, or 2700-3 for climb in visual conditions. **Rwy 34**, 900-2 w/ min. climb of 400' per NM to 4000, or 2700-3 for climb in visual conditions.
DEPARTURE PROCEDURE: **Rwy 16**, climb direct RBG VOR/DME, continue climb in RBG VOR/DME holding pattern (Hold N, right turns, 163° inbound) to cross RBG VOR/DME at or above MEA/MCA for route of flight, or for climb in visual conditions cross Roseburg RGNL Airport southbound at or above 3100 then direct RBG VOR/DME, continue climb in RBG VOR/DME holding pattern (Hold N, right turns, 163° inbound) to cross RBG VOR/DME at or above MEA/MCA for route of flight. **Rwy 34**, climb heading 342° to 2900 before proceeding on course, or for climb in visual conditions cross Roseburg RGNL Airport southbound at or above 3100 then direct RBG VOR/DME, continue climb in RBG VOR/DME holding pattern (Hold N, right turns, 163° inbound) to cross RBG VOR/DME at or above MEA/MCA for route of flight.
NOTE: **Rwy 16**, pole and trees beginning 37' from DER, 186' right of centerline, up to 73' AGL/593' MSL. Pole and trees, beginning 52' from DER, 1' left of centerline, up to 100' AGL/559' MSL. Vehicles on road 266' from DER, 251' right of centerline, up to 15' AGL/513' MSL. **Rwy 34**, trees and bushes beginning 16' from DER, 48' right and left of centerline up to 100' AGL/1339' MSL. Ground 1065' from DER, 298' right of centerline, 608' MSL. Signs, poles and obstacle lights on poles beginning 640' from DER, 55' left of centerline, up to 60' AGL/894' MSL.

Figure 58-3: The obstacle departure procedure for KRBG

This lesson begins with your Cessna 172 ready to depart runway 16 at KRGB.

Assume that you have filed the following route for this flight:

- RBG-V495-UBG

CROSS-REFERENCE **You can find the IFR procedure charts for this lesson in `IFR_Charts.pdf`, available at this book's website.**

Clearance

You have received the following clearance:

- Cleared to KHIO via the published departure procedure, as filed, maintain 7000. Contact Seattle Center on 121.4. Squawk 4200.

Location and Weather

You are ready to take off on runway 16 at KRGB. The bases of the clouds throughout the area are at about 800 ft., and the flight visibility below the ceiling is about 1 mile. The wind is out of the southwest at approximately 10 knots.

Situations and Flights

This lesson uses the following files for X-Plane and FSX:

- X-Plane: `Wiley-SBT-IFR-Lesson-14.sit`
- FSX: `Wiley-SBT-IFR-Lesson-14.flt`

CROSS-REFERENCE **For more information about using Situations (X-Plane) and Flights (FSX), see Chapter 10.**

Tips for This Lesson

Here are a few suggestions to help you get the most from this lesson:

- To simulate the difficulty of operating in a dimly lit cockpit, fly this scenario in a dark room. Use a flashlight to illuminate charts.
- Given the weather and other factors, what are the best alternate airports for your proposed flight?
- Use the interactive map in your simulation to help you orient yourself throughout the flight and to review your flight path.
- If you fly the X-Plane Cessna 172, use the GPS to substitute for DME.

What-Ifs

You can use the "Dice-Based Failure Scheme" described in Chapter 8 to create additional challenges for this flight.

At any point during the flight, roll a die, draw a number from a hat, or use another method to select a random number between 1 and 6. Using Table 58-1, find the corresponding problem to solve, and then take the appropriate action. If the challenge is a failure of an aircraft system or instrument, use the failure options in X-Plane or FSX to replicate the problem.

Table 58-1: Random Challenges for This Flight

NUMBER	RESULT
1	Vacuum system failure
2	Alternator failure
3	Your passenger is ill.
4	ATC requires you to hold as published at BREAF intersection southwest of UBG. Make three laps in the holding pattern before proceeding.
5	The glideslope at KHIO is out of service.
6	You are unable to communicate with ATC.

Objectives and Desired Outcome Grading Sheet

SCENARIO ACTIVITIES	SCENARIO SUB-ACTIVITIES	DESIRED OUTCOME
Understand and apply the elements of departure procedures.	–	Explain/Perform
Understand the procedures to follow after a communications failure.	–	Explain/Perform
Complete a pre-approach briefing for each approach used in this lesson.	–	Describe/Practice
Fly each approach within the standards outlined in the PTS.	–	Practice
Understand how to proceed to an alternate airport.	–	Explain/Perform

CHAPTER

59

IFR Lesson 15: Night Approaches

This lesson in the FITS syllabus involves a cross-country flight and a radar approach. Because radar approaches are increasingly rare, and to avoid the complications of using the simulated ATC in X-Plane and FSX, this scenario provides another opportunity to practice conventional approaches at night.

NOTE **To learn more about radar approaches, see "Radar Approaches" (pp. 10-17–10-18) in the *Instrument Flying Handbook*.**

Scenario

This scenario involves a night flight in the vicinity of Walla Walla, WA (KALW), to give you opportunities to fly ILS, localizer, VOR, or NDB approaches (see Figure 59-1) at KALW, Pasco, WA (KPSC), or Richland, WA (KRLD).

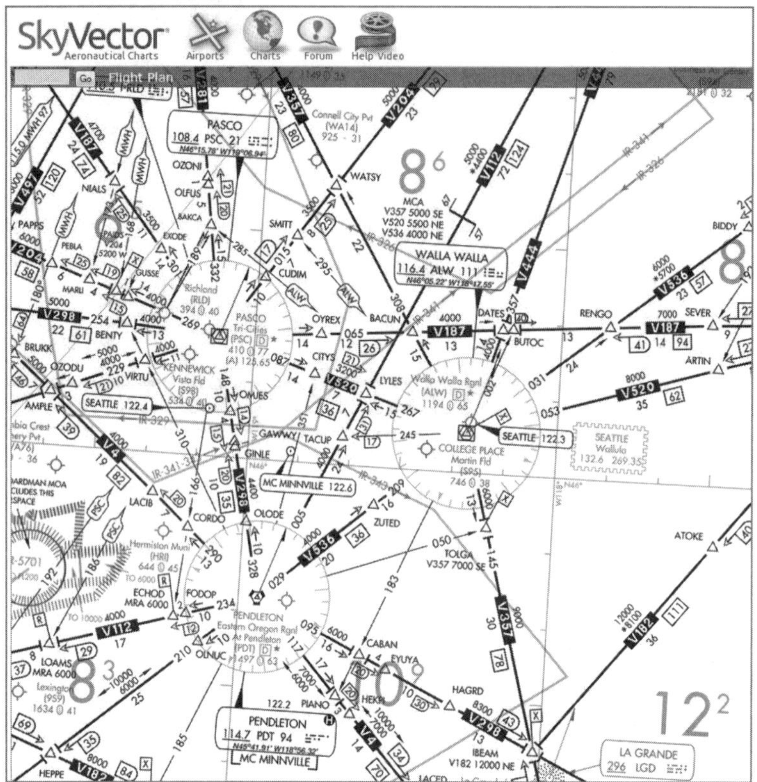

Figure 59-1: The area around KALW on the L-13 en route chart as shown on SkyVector

Objectives

The primary goals for this lesson are:

- Practicing the challenges of operating at night under IFR
- Flying a variety of instrument approaches, such as the ILS or LOC Y RWY 20 approach at KALW (see Figure 59-2)
- Practicing holding patterns
- Reviewing human factors — especially the limitations of night vision and the dangers of spatial disorientation
- Practicing missed approach procedures

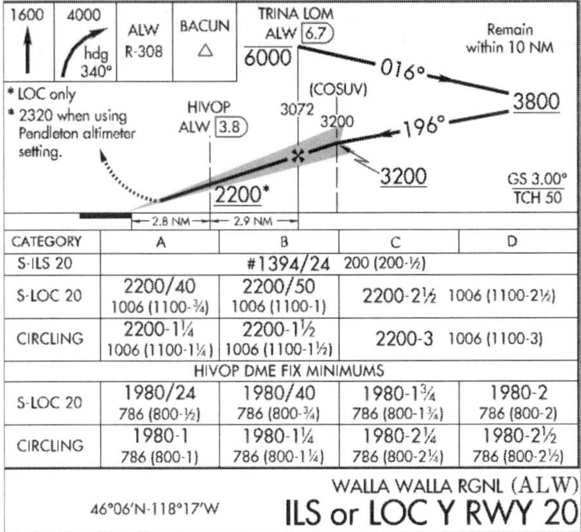

CATEGORY	A	B	C	D
S-ILS 20	#1394/24 200 (200-½)			
S-LOC 20	2200/40 1006 (1100-¾)	2200/50 1006 (1100-1)	2200-2½ 1006 (1100-2½)	
CIRCLING	2200-1¼ 1006 (1100-1¼)	2200-1½ 1006 (1100-1½)	2200-3 1006 (1100-3)	
HIVOP DME FIX MINIMUMS				
S-LOC 20	1980/24 786 (800-½)	1980/40 786 (800-¾)	1980-1¾ 786 (800-1¾)	1980-2 786 (800-2)
CIRCLING	1980-1 786 (800-1)	1980-1¼ 786 (800-1¼)	1980-2¼ 786 (800-2¼)	1980-2½ 786 (800-2½)

Figure 59-2: The complex minimums section of the chart for the KALW ILS or LOC Y RWY 20 approach

Completion Standards

The detailed goals for this lesson are outlined in the table at the end of this chapter. In general, before moving on to the next lesson, you should meet the standards in the relevant sections of the instrument rating PTS. The general standards include:

- While flying approaches, meet the appropriate accuracy standards for precision and nonprecision procedures as described in previous lessons and the instrument rating PTS.
- Fly missed approach procedures, including holds, according to the standards in the instrument rating PTS.

References and Resources

To prepare for this lesson, review the following references and resources. The resources at the AOPA Air Safety Institute are valuable supplements to the official information in the FAA references.

TITLE	CHAPTER/SECTION	TOPIC/NOTES
Airplane Flying Handbook	Chapter 10, "Night Operations"	–
Instrument Flying Handbook	Chapter 1, "Human Factors"	–
Instrument Procedures Handbook	Chapter 4, "Arrivals"	Cruise Clearance (p. 4-4)
	Chapter 5, "Approaches"	–
Risk Management Handbook	Chapter 3, "Identifying and Mitigating Risk"	–
Instrument Rating Practical Test Standards	–	Review all tasks.
AOPA Air Safety Institute Safety Quiz *Night Operations*	–	–
AOPA Air Safety Institute Safety Quiz *Airport Lighting: IFR*	–	–

CROSS-REFERENCE **For more information about the references and resources that complement the lessons in this book, see Chapter 2.**

Preflight Briefing

This lesson begins with your Cessna in the air between PSC and ALW. Proceed to ALW and then fly any of published approach procedures, followed by the appropriate missed approach procedure and hold.

After completing three laps in the holding pattern, fly another approach at KALW or join V520 to PSC and fly one of the approaches at KPSC or KRLD.

CROSS-REFERENCE **You can find the IFR procedure charts for this lesson in `IFR_Charts.pdf`, available at this book's website.**

Clearance

You have received the following clearance:

- Cleared to KALW via V520, cruise 7000.

NOTE **A *cruise clearance* "allow[s] a pilot to conduct flight at any altitude from the minimum IFR altitude up to and including the altitude specified in the clearance [and] authorizes a pilot to proceed to and make an approach at the destination airport" (*Instrument Flying Handbook, p. 4-4*).**

Location and Weather

You are cruising at 4,000 ft. on V520 northwest of ALW. The bases of the clouds throughout the area are at about 500 ft., and the flight visibility below the ceiling is about 1 mile. The wind is out of the southwest at approximately 10 knots.

Situations and Flights

This lesson uses the following files for X-Plane and FSX:

- X-Plane: `Wiley-SBT-IFR-Lesson-15.sit`
- FSX: `Wiley-SBT-IFR-Lesson-15.flt`

CROSS-REFERENCE **For more information about using Situations (X-Plane) and Flights (FSX), see Chapter 10.**

Tips for This Lesson

Here are a few suggestions to help you get the most from this lesson:

- To simulate the difficulty of operating in a dimly lit cockpit, fly this scenario in a dark room. Use a flashlight to illuminate charts like the one shown in Figure 59-3.
- Use the interactive map in your simulation to help you orient yourself throughout the flight and to review your flight path.
- If you fly the X-Plane Cessna 172, use the GPS to substitute for DME.

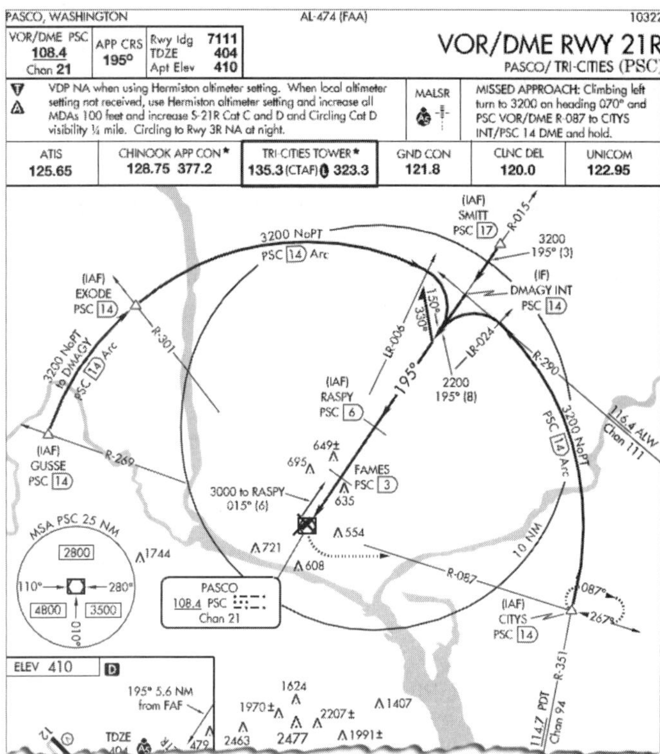

Figure 59-3: Consider the difficulty of noting the details on this chart for the VOR-DME approach at KPSC at night.

What-Ifs

You can use the "Dice-Based Failure Scheme" described in Chapter 8 to create additional challenges for this flight.

At any point during the flight, roll a die, draw a number from a hat, or use another method to select a random number between 1 and 6. Using Table 59-1, find the corresponding problem to solve, and then take the appropriate action. If the challenge is a failure of an aircraft system or instrument, use the failure options in X-Plane or FSX to replicate the problem.

Table 59-1: Random Challenges for This Flight

NUMBER	RESULT
1	Vacuum system failure
2	Alternator failure
3	ATC requires you to hold at BACUN as published on the KALW ILS or LOC Y RWY 20 approach chart.
4	ATC requires you to hold north of ALW on V444. Maintain 4000. Make three laps in the holding pattern before proceeding.
5	The glideslope at KALW is out of service.
6	The approach lights at KALW are out of service.

Objectives and Desired Outcome Grading Sheet

SCENARIO ACTIVITIES	SCENARIO SUB-ACTIVITIES	DESIRED OUTCOME
Understand the procedures to follow after a communications failure.	–	Explain/Perform
Complete a pre-approach briefing for each approach used in this lesson.	–	Describe/Practice
Fly each approach within the standards outlined in the PTS.	–	Practice

CHAPTER

60

IFR Lesson 16: Practical Test Preparation

The final lessons in the FITS instrument rating syllabus are designed to test your skills in preparation for the instrument rating practical test.

At this point in your training, you should be familiar with and able to fly all instrument procedures, including departures, arrivals, and approaches within the standards established in the instrument rating PTS.

This scenario begins with your Cessna 172 in the air near Corvallis, OR (KCVO), so that you can practice a variety of instrument approaches at KCVO and other airports (see Figure 60-1).

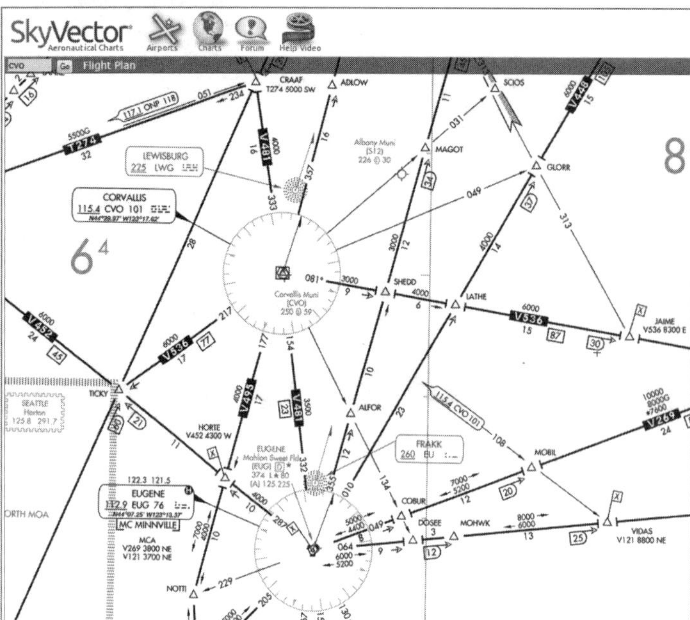

Figure 60-1: The area around KCVO on the L-1 en route chart as shown on SkyVector

Objectives

The primary goals for this lesson are:

- Practicing all elements of instrument approach procedures, including missed approach procedures
- Practicing holding patterns

Completion Standards

The detailed goals for this lesson are outlined in the table at the end of this chapter. In general, before moving on to the next lesson, you should meet the standards in the relevant sections of the instrument rating PTS. The general standards include:

- While flying approaches, meet the appropriate accuracy standards for precision and nonprecision procedures as described in previous lessons and the instrument rating PTS.
- Fly missed approach procedures, including holds, according to the standards in the instrument rating PTS.

References and Resources

To prepare for this lesson, review the following references and resources. The resources at the AOPA Air Safety Institute are valuable supplements to the official information in the FAA references.

TITLE	CHAPTER/SECTION	TOPIC/NOTES
Instrument Flying Handbook	Chapter 7, "Navigation Systems"	–
Instrument Procedures Handbook	Chapter 5, "Approaches"	–
Instrument Rating Practical Test Standards	–	Review all topics.

CROSS-REFERENCE For more information about the references and resources that complement the lessons in this book, see Chapter 2.

Preflight Briefing

This lesson begins with your Cessna in the air between EUG and CVO. Proceed to CVO and then fly any of published approach procedures at KCVO, followed by the appropriate missed approach procedure and hold (see Figure 60-2).

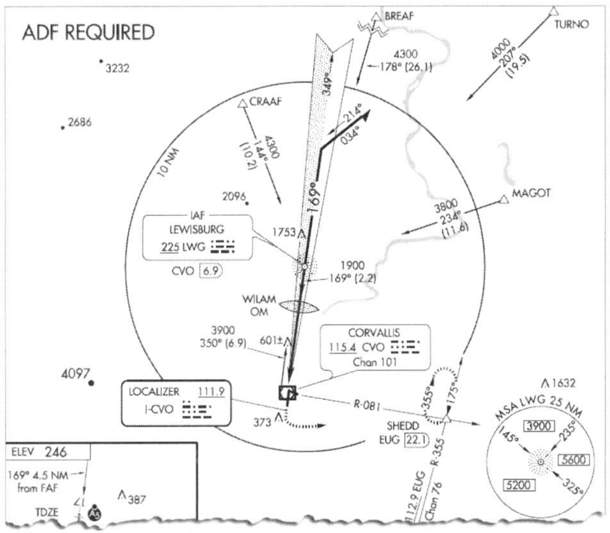

Figure 60-2: Plan view for the ILS RWY 17approach at KCVO

After completing three laps in the missed approach holding pattern, fly another approach at KCVO or proceed to UBG and fly an approach to KHIO or KUAO (see Figure 60-3).

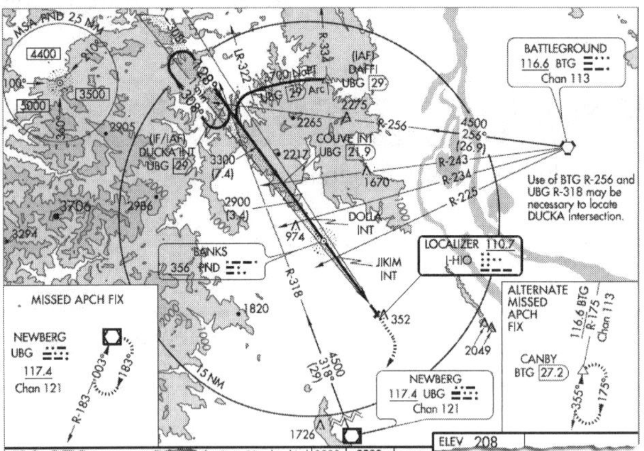

Figure 60-3: Complex plan view for the ILS or LOC RWY 12 approach at KHIO

CROSS-REFERENCE You can find the IFR procedure charts for this lesson in `IFR_Charts.pdf`, available at this book's website.

Clearance

You have received the following clearance:

- Cleared to KCVO via V481, cruise 4000.

Location and Weather

You are cruising at 5,000 ft. on V481 south of CVO. The bases of the clouds throughout the area are at about 600 ft., and the flight visibility below the ceiling is about 1 mile. The wind is out of the southwest at approximately 10 knots.

Situations and Flights

This lesson uses the following files for X-Plane and FSX:

- X-Plane: `Wiley-SBT-IFR-Lesson-16.sit`
- FSX: `Wiley-SBT-IFR-Lesson-16.flt`

CROSS-REFERENCE For more information about using Situations (X-Plane) and Flights (FSX), see Chapter 10.

Tips for This Lesson

Here are a few suggestions to help you get the most from this lesson:

- Use the interactive map in your simulation to help you orient yourself throughout the flight and to review your flight path.
- If you fly the X-Plane Cessna 172, use the GPS to substitute for DME.

What-Ifs

You can use the "Dice-Based Failure Scheme" described in Chapter 8 to create additional challenges for this flight.

At any point during the flight, roll a die, draw a number from a hat, or use another method to select a random number between 1 and 6. Using Table 60-1, find the corresponding problem to solve, and then take the appropriate action. If the challenge is a failure of an aircraft system or instrument, use the failure options in X-Plane or FSX to replicate the problem.

Table 60-1: Random Challenges for This Flight

NUMBER	RESULT
1	Vacuum system failure
2	Alternator failure
3	ATC requires you to hold at CVO on V481. Maintain 4000. Make three laps in the holding pattern before proceeding.
4	ATC requires you to hold north of CVO on V481. Maintain 4000. Make three laps in the holding pattern before proceeding.
5	The glideslope at KCVO is out of service.
6	The approach lights at KCVO are out of service.

Objectives and Desired Outcome Grading Sheet

SCENARIO ACTIVITIES	SCENARIO SUB-ACTIVITIES	DESIRED OUTCOME
Understand the procedures to follow after a communications failure.	–	Explain/Perform
Complete a pre-approach briefing for each approach used in this lesson.	–	Describe/Practice
Fly each approach within the standards outlined in the PTS.	–	Practice

CHAPTER

61

IFR Lesson 17: Practical Test Preparation

The final lessons in the FITS instrument rating syllabus are designed to test your skills in preparation for the instrument rating practical test.

At this point in your training, you should be familiar with and able to fly all instrument procedures, including departures, arrivals, and approaches within the standards established in the instrument rating PTS.

Scenario

This scenario challenges you with a complex departure procedure from Medford, OR (KMFR). If you can fly the BRUTE FIVE procedure (see Figure 61-1) consistently and smoothly within the PTS criteria, you have developed good instrument flying skills.

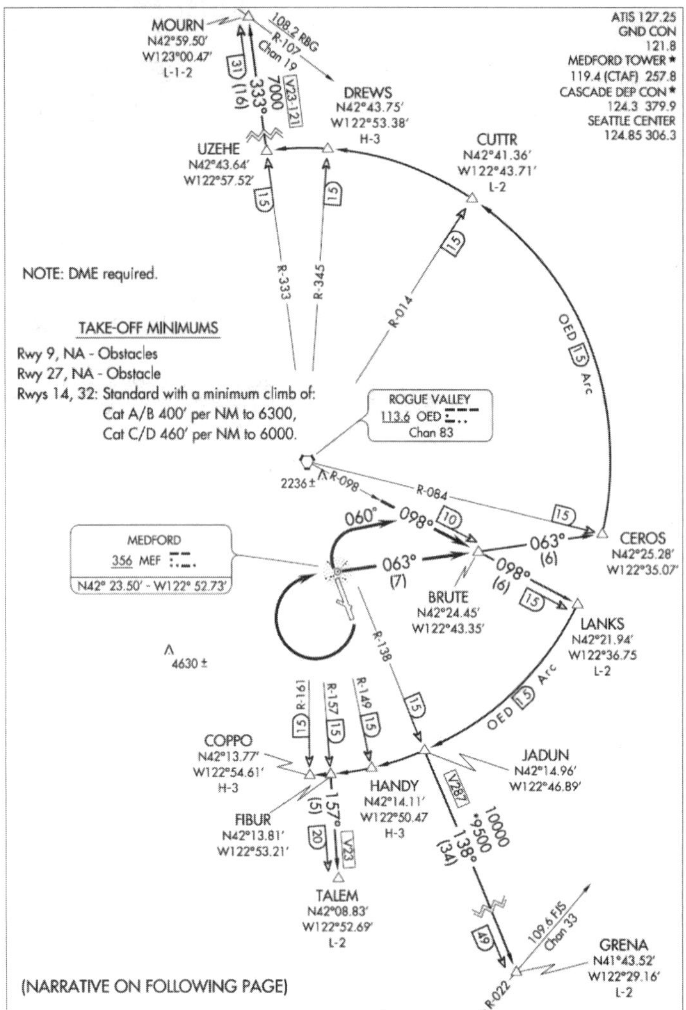

Figure 61-1: Plan view of the BRUTE FIVE departure procedure at KMFR

Objectives

The primary goals for this lesson are:

- Honing all your instrument flying skills in preparation for the instrument rating practical test
- Reviewing and practicing the elements related to flying standard instrument departure procedures

Completion Standards

The detailed goals for this lesson are outlined in the table at the end of this chapter. In general, before moving on to the next lesson, you should meet the standards in the relevant sections of the instrument rating PTS. The general standards include:

- While flying approaches, meet the appropriate accuracy standards for precision and nonprecision procedures as described in previous lessons and in the instrument rating PTS.
- Fly departure procedures within the standards in the instrument rating PTS.

References and Resources

To prepare for this lesson, review the following references and resources. The resources at the AOPA Air Safety Institute are valuable supplements to the official information in the FAA references.

TITLE	CHAPTER/SECTION	TOPIC/NOTES
Instrument Flying Handbook	Chapter 10, "Navigation Systems"	Departure Procedures (DPs) (p. 10-5)
Instrument Procedures Handbook	Chapter 2, "Takeoffs and Departures"	Review all topics.
	Chapter 5, "Approaches"	Review all topics.
Instrument Rating Practical Test Standards	–	Review all tasks.

CROSS-REFERENCE **For more information about the references and resources that complement the lessons in this book, see Chapter 2.**

Preflight Briefing

This lesson begins with your Cessna 172 on the ground at KMFR (see Figure 61-2). Fly the BRUTE FIVE departure procedure and the MOURN transition.

Figure 61-2: Your Cessna 172 ready to depart runway 14 at KMFR, as shown in FSX

When you reach MOURN intersection, reverse course via a standard holding pattern and then return to the Rogue Valley VOR (OED) via V23 and fly one of the following approaches at KMFR:

- VOR-A
- VOR/DME-C (if you use X-Plane, use the GPS to substitute for DME from OED)

For additional practice, restart this scenario and fly the BRUTE FIVE departure procedure and the TALEM transition, followed by the one of the VOR-based approaches at KMFR.

If you use FSX, you can also fly the following approaches at KMFR, which require reception of the DME from the localizer:

- ILS OR LOC/DME RWY 14
- LOC/DME BC-B

CROSS-REFERENCE **You can find the IFR procedure charts for this lesson in `IFR_Charts.pdf`, available at this book's website.**

Clearance

You have received the following clearance:

- Cleared to KMFR via the BRUTE FIVE departure, MOURN transition, V23 OED, maintain 7000.

Location and Weather

You are ready for takeoff from runway 14 at KMFR (see Figure 61-3). The bases of the clouds throughout the area are at about 500 ft., and the flight visibility below the ceiling is about 1 mile. The wind is out of the southwest at approximately 10 knots.

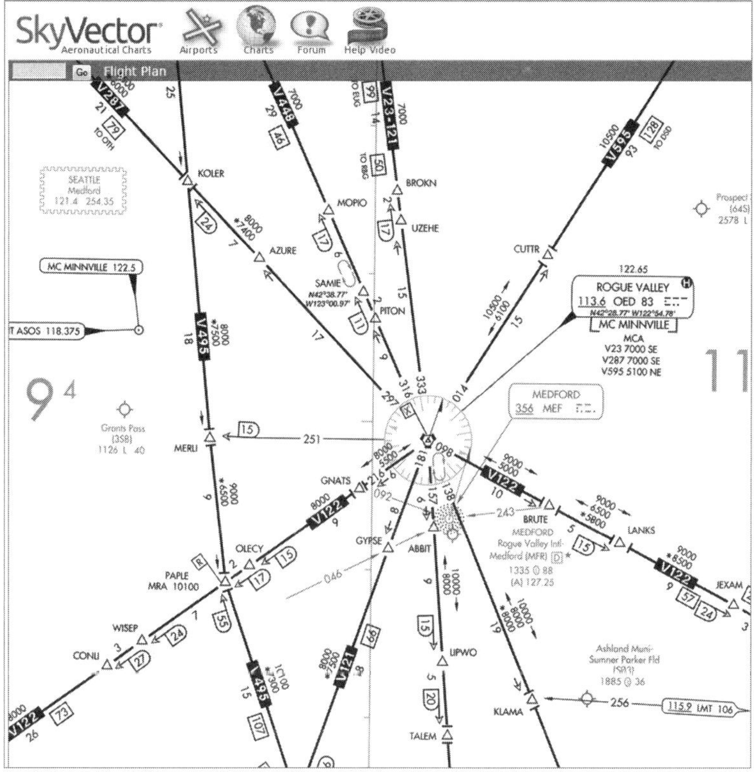

Figure 61-3: The area around KMFR on the L-2 en route chart as shown on SkyVector

Situations and Flights

This lesson uses the following files for X-Plane and FSX:

- X-Plane: `Wiley-SBT-IFR-Lesson-17.sit`
- FSX: `Wiley-SBT-IFR-Lesson-17.flt`

CROSS-REFERENCE **For more information about using Situations (X-Plane) and Flights (FSX), see Chapter 10.**

Tips for This Lesson

Here are a few suggestions to help you get the most from this lesson:

- If you fly X-Plane, specify OED as a direct-to waypoint to substitute for DME when you fly the arcs that are key parts of the departure procedure.
- The departure procedure requires the use of the ADF receiver or a GPS waypoint to track to and from the MEF nondirectional beacon. To test your ADF tracking skills, use the ADF.
- Use the interactive map in your simulation to help you orient yourself throughout the flight and to review your flight path.

What-Ifs

You can use the "Dice-Based Failure Scheme" described in Chapter 8 to create additional challenges for this flight.

At any point during the flight, roll a die, draw a number from a hat, or use another method to select a random number between 1 and 6. Using Table 61-1, find the corresponding problem to solve, and then take the appropriate action. If the challenge is a failure of an aircraft system or instrument, use the failure options in X-Plane or FSX to replicate the problem.

Table 61-1: Random Challenges for This Flight

NUMBER	RESULT
1	Vacuum system failure
2	Alternator failure
3	ATC clears you to hold at OED as published on the ILS or LOC/DME RWY 14 approach chart. Maintain 7000 and complete three laps in the hold.
4	If you are using FSX, fly the LOC/DME BC-B approach at KMFR.
5	If you are using X-Plane, fly the VOR-A approach at KMFR.
6	The visibility at KMFR drops to ¾ mile.

Objectives and Desired Outcome Grading Sheet

SCENARIO ACTIVITIES	SCENARIO SUB-ACTIVITIES	DESIRED OUTCOME
Understand the procedures to follow after a communications failure.	–	Explain/Perform
Complete a pre-approach briefing for each approach used in this lesson.	–	Describe/Practice
Fly each approach within the standards outlined in the PTS.	–	Perform

CHAPTER 62

IFR Lesson 18: IFR Practical Test

In the generic FITS syllabus, this lesson is the practical test for the instrument rating. This scenario is your opportunity to practice any of the tasks in the instrument rating PTS in the context of a short cross-country flight.

A typical instrument rating practical test (also known as a "check ride") involves an oral examination that lasts about two hours and a flight test that usually requires up to about two hours of flying time. According to the PTS, the examiner (usually a designated pilot examiner, not an FAA inspector), must prepare a "plan of action," a representative sample of the tasks from the PTS. The FAA requires examiners to use scenarios, not just a series of isolated tasks, to assess the candidate's ability to operate under IFR (see p. 5 of the PTS for the instrument rating). The examiner is also directed to create realistic distractions and to pose simulated abnormal conditions and emergencies to evaluate your ability to cope with the unexpected.

Scenario

For this scenario, assume that the examiner has asked you to plan a flight from Astoria, OR (KAST), to Hoquiam, WA (KHQM), to Olympia, WA (KOLM), and then back to KAST (see Figure 62-1). As planned, this flight is about 182 nm and requires about 1 hour 40 minutes flying time at typical Cessna 172 cruise speed.

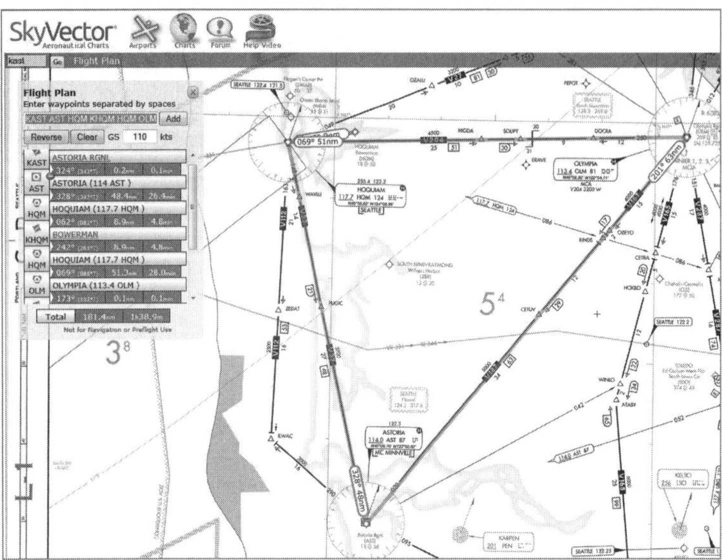

Figure 62-1: The route KAST-AST-HQM-KQHM-KHQM-OLM-KOLM-OLM-AST-KAST as shown on the L-1 en route chart on SkyVector

Objectives

The primary goal for this lesson is:

- Demonstrating your instrument flying skills according to the instrument rating PTS

Completion Standards

The completion standards for this scenario are clearly stated in the PTS. They include demonstrating knowledge of special emphasis areas (see p. 7). As you fly the specific tasks in the PTS (see p. 1-1), you should always:

- Perform the tasks specified in the areas of operation for the certificate or rating sought within the approved standards.

- Demonstrate mastery of the aircraft with the successful outcome of each task performed never seriously in doubt.
- Demonstrate satisfactory proficiency and competency within the approved standards.
- Demonstrate sound judgment.

The instrument rating PTS requires the examiner to evaluate your "ability throughout the practical test to use good aeronautical decision-making procedures in order to evaluate risks" (see p. 12-14).

According to the PTS (see p. 12), the following lapses typically cause candidates to fail the practical test:

- Any action or lack of action by the applicant that requires corrective intervention by the examiner to maintain safe flight
- Failure to use proper and effective visual scanning techniques to clear the area before and while performing maneuvers
- Consistently exceeding tolerances stated in the objectives for the tasks
- Failure to take prompt corrective action when tolerances are exceeded

In addition, the instrument rating PTS notes that:

> The applicant is expected to utilize an autopilot and/or flight management system (FMS), if properly installed, during the instrument practical test to assist in the management of the aircraft. The examiner is expected to test the applicant's knowledge of the systems that are installed and operative during the oral and flight portions of the practical test. The applicant will be required to demonstrate the use of the autopilot and/or FMS during one of the nonprecision approaches. The applicant is expected to demonstrate satisfactory automation management skills.
>
> Instrument Rating PTS, p. 8

References and Resources

The official references for the practical test are outlined in the introduction to the PTS (see p. 3). You can find more detailed descriptions of those references in Chapter 13 of this book.

CROSS-REFERENCE For more information about the references and resources that complement the lessons in this book, see Chapter 2.

Preflight Briefing

This scenario begins with your airplane ready to depart KAST.

A typical practical test might include the following tasks in roughly this sequence:

- Takeoff followed by an instrument departure procedure
- Climb and initial leg of a cross-country flight under IFR
- Instrument approach followed by a missed approach and hold at the first airport on the route
- Diversion
- Simulated emergency
- Return to the departure airport to demonstrate another type of approach with inoperative flight instruments, followed by a missed approach
- Third approach to a landing

CROSS-REFERENCE **You can find the IFR procedure charts for this lesson in `IFR_Charts.pdf`, available at this book's website.**

Clearance

You filed the following route:

- KAST-AST-V27-HQM-KQHM-HQM-V204-OLM-KOLM-OLM-V187-AST-KAST

You received the following clearance:

- Cleared to KHQM via the ASTORIA ONE departure, then as filed. Maintain 4000. Contact Seattle Center on 124.2. Squawk 4200.

Location and Weather

You are ready for takeoff from runway 13 at KAST (see Figure 62-2). The bases of the clouds throughout the area are at about 500 ft., and the flight visibility below the ceiling is about 1 mile. The wind is out of the southwest at approximately 10 knots.

Figure 62-2: Your Cessna 172 ready to depart KAST as shown in X-Plane

Situations and Flights

This lesson uses the following files for X-Plane and FSX:

- X-Plane: `Wiley-SBT-IFR-Lesson-18.sit`
- FSX: `Wiley-SBT-IFR-Lesson-18.flt`

CROSS-REFERENCE For more information about using Situations (X-Plane) and Flights (FSX), see Chapter 10.

Tips for This Lesson

Here are a few suggestions to help you get the most from this lesson:

- Carefully review the instrument rating PTS.
- Review the checklists for the applicant and the examiner on pages 1-iii and 1-V of the PTS.
- Complete the AOPA Air Safety Institute Flight Planner (link at this book's website) for the planned round-robin flight from KAST to KHQM, KOLM, and back to KAST.
- Include several "what-ifs" from the following section to add realism to this lesson. During an actual instrument rating practical test, the examiner simulates at least one abnormal situation or emergency, and you are expected to demonstrate your ability to cope with distractions and unexpected circumstances, such as changes in the weather and mechanical problems with the aircraft.
- Use the A/FD information at `http://SkyVector.com` or other resources on the web to learn more about the airports in the area, including the best alternates should you need to divert.

What-Ifs

You can use the "Dice-Based Failure Scheme" described in Chapter 8 to create additional challenges for this flight.

At any point during the flight, roll a die, draw a number from a hat, or use another method to select a random number between 1 and 6. Using Table 62-1, find the corresponding problem to solve, and then take the appropriate action. If the challenge is a failure of an aircraft system or instrument, use the failure options in X-Plane or FSX to replicate the problem.

Table 62-1: Random Challenges for This Flight

NUMBER	RESULT
1	Vacuum system failure
2	Alternator failure
3	You cannot communicate with ATC.
4	Return to KAST.
5	Divert to KSHN.
6	The number two communications and navigation receiver is inoperative.

Objectives and Desired Outcome Grading Sheet

SCENARIO ACTIVITIES	SCENARIO SUB-ACTIVITIES	DESIRED OUTCOME
Oral exam	FARs, ADM, preflight planning, IFR charts, emergency procedures	Perform/Manage/Decide
Flight test	Maneuvers and procedures in the PTS	Perform/Manage/Decide

Part

VI

Advanced Scenarios

In This Part

CHAPTER

63

Introduction to the Advanced Scenarios: Test Your Skills

The scenarios that follow are a reward for completing the lessons for the private pilot certificate and the instrument rating. They also give you opportunities to fly advanced aircraft that test and expand your flying abilities and knowledge — especially your instrument flying skills — in scenarios that resemble typical charter and business flights.

NOTE **The weather simulated in the advanced scenarios requires flight under IFR; but if you prefer to fly visually, use the weather options in X-Plane or FSX to clear the skies before you take off.**

These scenarios are based on the following aircraft included with the basic versions of X-Plane and FSX:

- Piper PA-46 Malibu (X-Plane), a turbocharged, pressurized single-engine airplane (see Figures 63-1 and 63-2)
- Beechcraft BE58 Baron (FSX), a twin-engine airplane (see Figures 63-3 and 63-4)

These aircraft are popular for personal and business flying, especially under IFR. They're fast, able to carry 4–5 passengers, and can fly longer distances than the Cessna 172. When flying the advanced scenarios, you can, of course, substitute any airplane that you have installed in your virtual hangar for X-Plane or FSX.

NOTE **If you use FSX and don't want to tangle with the difficulties involved in flying a twin-engine airplane, PC-based simulation gives you a terrific advantage. Unless you use the options to create failures, the virtual engines never quit. You can think of the Baron in FSX as a faster, heavier, single-engine Bonanza. If you do want to learn more about flying twins like the Baron, see Chapter 12, "Transition to Multiengine Airplanes," in the *Airplane Flying Handbook*.**

Figure 63-1: The Piper Malibu in X-Plane

Figure 63-2: Instrument panel of the Piper Malibu in X-Plane

Figure 63-3: The Beechcraft Baron in FSX

Figure 63-4: Main instrument panel of the Beechcraft Baron in FSX

Useful References

For general information about flying faster, more powerful airplanes, see Chapter 11, "Transition to Complex Airplanes," in the *Airplane Flying Handbook*. The following sections are especially helpful:

- Constant-Speed Propeller (p. 11-4)
- Turbocharging (p. 11-7)
- Retractable Landing Gear (p. 11-9)

You also need to learn about two instruments in aircraft equipped with piston engines that produce more than about 200 hp: the *manifold pressure gauge* and the *tachometer* (see Figures 63-5 and 63-6). You've seen the tachometer in the Cessna 172, but the manifold pressure (MP) gauge is new. The throttle sets MP; the propeller control selects propeller RPM. For more information about these instruments and controls, see "Adjustable-Pitch Propeller" (p. 6-6) in Chapter 6, "Aircraft Systems," in the *Pilot's Handbook of Aeronautical Knowledge.*

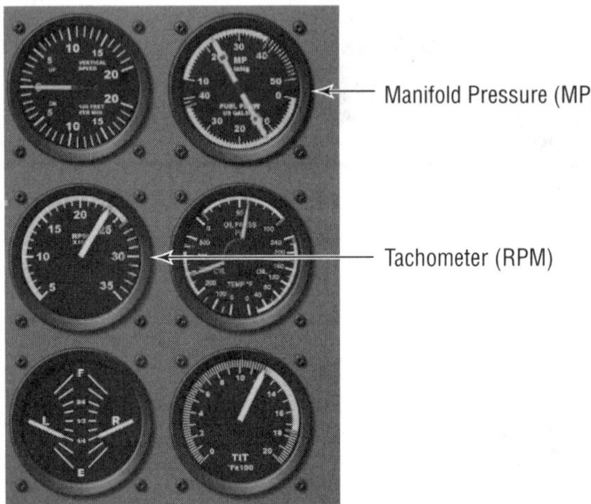

Figure 63-5: The manifold pressure gauge and tachometer in the X-Plane Malibu

Figure 63-6: The manifold pressure gauges and tachometers in the FSX Baron

To learn more about other advanced flight instruments in the Malibu and Baron, see:

- *Instrument Flying Handbook*, Chapter 3, "Flight Instruments," especially "Horizontal Situation Indicator (HSI)" on p. 3-22

For additional information about flying high-performance aircraft, see the following syllabi available at the FITS website:

- FITS Generic Commercial Airplane Multi Engine Land Syllabus
- FITS Generic Commercial Airplane Single Engine Land Syllabus
- FITS Generic Transition Syllabus

CROSS-REFERENCE **You can find details about many free references and resources for pilots and virtual aviators in Chapter 2.**

Flying Tips

The tables and illustrations that follow show how to apply the Golden Rule of Flying (see Chapter 11) to set pitch, power, and configuration to achieve stable flight for common situations in both the Malibu (X-Plane) and Baron (FSX). With these settings, you can quickly establish stable flight for situations such as normal cruise, climbs and descents, and instrument approaches, as described in Chapter 12.

NOTE **To help you become comfortable with any new aircraft, you may find it helpful to return to fly previous lessons that focus on fundamental flight maneuvers, substituting the new airplane for the Cessna 172.**

Configuration Tables

The following tables are guidelines for use with X-Plane and FSX. They're not a substitute for the information and procedures in the official aircraft flight manuals. It's also important to understand that larger, more powerful aircraft like the Malibu and Baron operate in a wider range of weights and speeds than a basic airplane like the Cessna 172. The tables are good starting points, but the speeds and rates of climb and descent that the aircraft achieve at a particular power setting vary according to weight and other factors.

NOTE **You can create your own configuration tables regardless of the type of airplane you fly. Use the autopilot to stabilize the airplane and observe how changes in pitch, power, and configuration affect indicated airspeed and rate of climb and descent.**

Piper Malibu: X-Plane Configurations

The following screen captures and tables show several configurations for the Piper Malibu as simulated in X-Plane. The basic power settings, configurations, and speeds are based on rules of thumb that an experienced instructor uses when flying and teaching in the Malibu.

En Route Climb

Figure 63-7 and Table 63-1 show typical Pitch-Power-Configuration values for an en route climb in the Piper Malibu in X-Plane. You should establish this configuration after reaching about 1,000 ft. above airport elevation.

Figure 63-7: En route climb configuration in the X-Plane Malibu

Table 63-1: En Route Climb in the X-Plane Malibu

ITEM	VALUE
Pitch	+5°
Power	MP: 35 / RPM: 2500
Landing gear	UP
Flaps	0°
Airspeed	120–130 KIAS
Rate of Climb	+500–800 fpm

Normal Cruise

Figure 63-8 and Table 63-2 show typical Pitch-Power-Configuration values for cruise in the Piper Malibu in X-Plane. You can use the same power settings for a normal descent; just adjust the pitch attitude to a few degrees nose-down and reduce power as necessary to control airspeed.

Figure 63-8: Cruise configuration in the X-Plane Malibu

Table 63-2: Cruise in the X-Plane Malibu

ITEM	VALUE
Pitch	+0°
Power	MP: 29.5 / RPM: 2400
Landing gear	UP
Flaps	0°
Airspeed	≈160 KIAS, but varies with altitude
Rate of Climb	0 fpm

Initial Approach

Figure 63-9 and Table 63-3 show typical Pitch-Power-Configuration values for initial approach in the Piper Malibu in X-Plane. You can ause these settings before intercepting the final approach course.

Figure 63-9: Initial approach configuration in the X-Plane Malibu

Tble 63-3: Initial Approach in the X-Plane Malibu

ITEM	VALUE
Pitch	+0°
Power	MP: 25 / RPM: 2400
Landing gear	UP
Flaps	10° (first detent)
Airspeed	120 KIAS
Rate of Climb	0 fpm

ILS Approach

Figure 63-10 and Table 63-4 show typical Pitch-Power-Configuration values for an ILS approach in the Piper Malibu in X-Plane.

Figure 63-10: ILS approach configuration in the X-Plane Malibu

Table 63-4: ILS Approach in the X-Plane Malibu

ITEM	VALUE
Pitch	+0°
Power	MP: 20 / RPM: 2300–2400
Landing gear	DOWN
Flaps	10° (first detent)
Airspeed	100–110 KIAS
Rate of Descent	500–700 fpm

Landing Configuration

Figure 63-11 and Table 63-5 show the configuration to use in the final stages of approach. Use the ILS numbers, but extend full flaps and then smoothly reduce the throttle to idle, timing the reduction to establish 90 KIAS over the threshold. After you set idle power, make sure that you advance the propeller control to maximum RPM so that full power is available if you need to go-around — that is, abort the landing and climb away for another attempt.

Figure 63-11: Landing configuration in the X-Plane Malibu

Table 63-5: Landing Configuration in the X-Plane Malibu

ITEM	VALUE
Pitch	-1° until flare
Power	MP: Reduce to idle / RPM: Maximum
Landing gear	DOWN
Flaps	DOWN
Airspeed	90 KIAS
Rate of Descent	500–700 fpm

FSX Configurations

The following screen captures and tables show several configurations for the Beechcraft Baron as simulated in FSX. The basic power settings, configurations, and speeds are based on rules of thumb used by many Baron pilots.

Note that two key features of the Baron cockpit, the engine controls (see Figure 63-12) and the avionics stack (see Figure 63-13), appear in supplementary windows. To display or hide these windows, click the corresponding icons on the main instrument panel. You can use the mouse to operate the controls in these supplementary windows just as you do in the main cockpit.

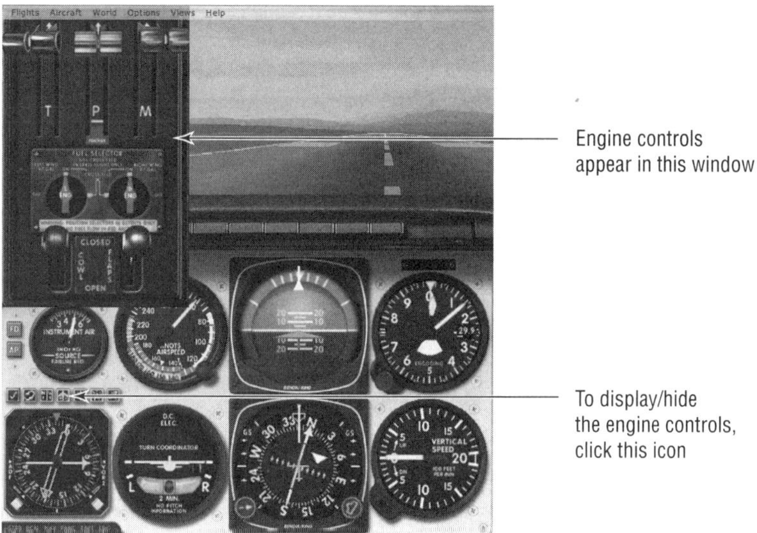

Figure 63-12: Engine controls window in the FSX Baron

Figure 63-13: Avionics window in the FSX Baron

En Route Climb

Figure 63-14 and Table 63-6 show typical Pitch-Power-Configuration values for an en route climb in the FSX Baron.

Figure 63-14: En route climb configuration in the FSX Baron

Table 63-6: En Route Climb in FSX Baron

ITEM	VALUE
Pitch	+5
Power	MP: Maximum available / RPM: 2500
Landing Gear	UP
Flaps	0°
Airspeed	120–140 KIAS
Rate of Climb	+800–1000 fpm

Normal Cruise

Figure 63-15 and Table 63-7 show typical Pitch-Power-Configuration values for normal cruise in the FSX Baron. Indicated airspeed decreases at higher altitudes. You can use the same power settings for a normal descent; just adjust the pitch attitude to a few degrees nose-down and reduce power as necessary to control airspeed as you descend.

Figure 63-15: Normal cruise configuration in the FSX Baron

Table 63-7: Normal Cruise in the FSX Cessna 172

ITEM	VALUE
Pitch	+0
Power	MP: 23 or maximum available / RPM: 2300
Landing Gear	UP
Flaps	0°
Airspeed	160 KIAS (decreases with altitude)
Rate of Climb	0 fpm

Initial Approach

Figure 63-16 and Table 63-8 show typical Pitch-Power-Configuration values for initial approach in the FSX Baron. Note that this configuration also results in an indicated airspeed below the limit (154 KIAS) for extending flaps to the approach setting. You can establish this configuration with the flaps up and then use the APR flap setting as you prepare to join the final approach course.

Figure 63-16: Initial approach configuration in the FSX Baron

Table 63-8: Low-Speed Cruise in the FSX Baron

ITEM	VALUE
Pitch	+1
Power	MP: 16–18 / RPM: 2300
Flaps	UP or APR
Airspeed	110–140 KIAS, depending on flap setting
Rate of Climb	0 fpm

ILS Approach

Figure 63-17 and Table 63-9 show typical Pitch-Power-Configuration values for flying an ILS approach at about 110 KIAS with APR flaps in the FSX Baron.

Figure 63-17: ILS approach configuration in the FSX Baron

Table 63-9: ILS Approach in the FSX Baron

ITEM	VALUE
Pitch	–1
Power	MP: 16–18 / RPM: 2300–2500
Landing gear	DOWN
Flaps	APR
Airspeed	110–120 KIAS
Rate of Descent	500–700 fpm

Landing Configuration

Figure 63-18 and Table 63-10 show the configuration to use in the final stages of approach in the FSX Baron. Use the basic ILS numbers, but extend full flaps and then smoothly reduce power to idle, timing the reduction to establish 100 KIAS over the threshold. After you set idle power, make sure that you advance the propeller controls to maximum RPM so that full power is available if you need to go-around. The landing flare over the runway should reduce speed to about 90 KIAS before touchdown.

Figure 63-18: Landing configuration in the FSX Baron

Table 63-10: Landing Configuration in the FSX Baron

ITEM	VALUE
Pitch	-1° until flare
Power	MP: Reduce to idle / RPM: Maximum
Landing gear	DOWN
Flaps	DOWN
Airspeed	100 KIAS, decreasing in the flare
Rate of Descent	500–700 fpm

CHAPTER 64

Advanced 1: Eugene, OR, to Olympia, WA

You are a volunteer pilot for an organization that provides free transportation for medical patients, organs for transplant, and caregivers. Your mission today is to fly a donated liver from a medical center in Eugene, OR (KEUG), to Olympia, WA (KOLM).

This trip of about 175 nm (see Figure 64-1) requires about an hour of flying time in either the Malibu (X-Plane) or the Baron (FSX).

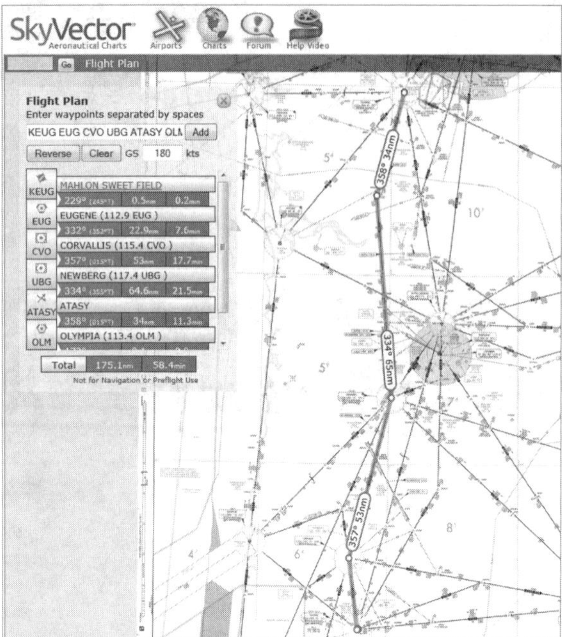

Figure 64-1: First part of the route from KEUG to KOLM on the L-1 en route chart as shown on SkyVector

Charts and Information

To prepare for this flight, review the following charts and other references. You can find the IFR procedure charts for this flight in `IFR_Charts.pdf`, available at this book's website. You can find Airport/Facility Directory (A/FD) information and online charts at `http://SkyVector.com`.

CHARTS	REFERENCES
KEUG airport diagram	A/FD: KEUG and KOLM
EUGENE EIGHT departure	
En route L-1 IFR chart	
Klamath Falls Sectional North	
Seattle Sectional North and South	
KOLM ILS RWY 17	
KOLM airport diagram	

CROSS-REFERENCE **For more information about the references and resources that complement this book, see Chapter 2.**

Preflight Briefing

This scenario begins with your aircraft ready to depart runway 16R at KEUG for the flight to KOLM (see Figure 64-2).

Figure 64-2: Ready for takeoff at KEUG as seen from the cockpit of the Baron in FSX

Because the weather throughout the area is IMC, you must include an alternate airport in your IFR flight plan. Follow the sequence below for this flight:

- Fly the EUGENE EIGHT departure. Reaching 3000, turn right direct to CVO, and then join the flight plan route.
- When you reach the Olympia (OLM) VOR, fly the full ILS RWY 17 approach at KOLM.

Clearance

For this lesson, assume that Boeing Field in Seattle (KBFI) is your alternate airport.

- Cleared to KOLM via the EUGENE EIGHT departure, V481 CVO, V495 UBG V165 OLM. Maintain 10,000. Contact Seattle Center on 125.8. Squawk 4200.

When you reach 3,000 ft. after takeoff, turn right to intercept V495 northwest toward CVO.

Weather

The bases of the clouds throughout the area are at about 500 ft., and the flight visibility below the ceiling is about 1 mile. The wind is out of the southwest at approximately 10 knots.

Situations and Flights

This lesson uses the following files for X-Plane and FSX:

- X-Plane: `Wiley-Advanced-01.sit`
- FSX: `Wiley-Advanced-01.flt`

CROSS-REFERENCE **For more information about using Situations (X-Plane) and Flights (FSX), see Chapter 10.**

What-Ifs

You can use the "Dice-Based Failure Scheme" described in Chapter 8 to create additional challenges for this flight.

At any point during the flight, roll a die, draw a number from a hat, or use another method to select a random number between 1 and 6. Using Table 64-1, find the corresponding problem to solve, and then take the appropriate action. If the challenge is a failure of an aircraft system or instrument, use the failure options in X-Plane or FSX to replicate the problem.

Table 64-1: Random Challenges for This Flight

NUMBER	RESULT
1	Vacuum system failure
2	Alternator failure
3	Communications failure en route to KOLM
4	Weather at KOLM is below the minimums for the ILS approach.
5	ATC requires you to hold as published at OLM. Make three turns in the holding pattern before continuing.
6	The ILS at KOLM is out of service.

CHAPTER 65

Advanced 2: Night Flight: Spokane, WA, to Walla Walla, WA

You have finished a full day of meetings in Spokane, and you have another series of appointments starting early tomorrow morning in Walla Walla, WA (KALW). To make the breakfast engagement, you need to make a night flight from Felts Field (KSFF) to KALW.

This trip of about 107 nm (see Figure 65-1) requires about 35 minutes of flying time in either the Malibu (X-Plane) or the Baron (FSX).

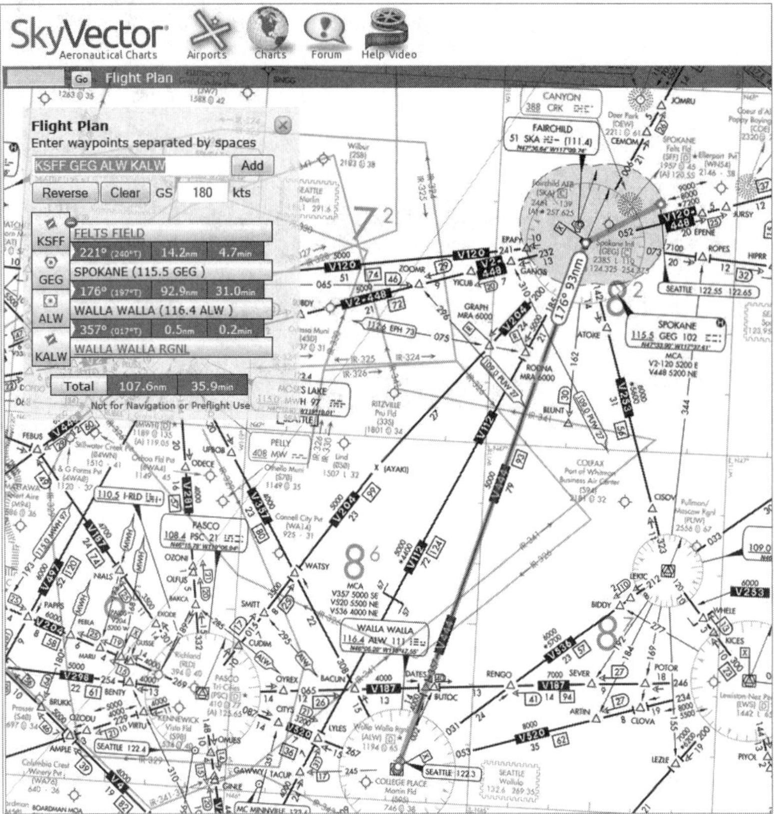

Figure 65-1: Route from KSFF to KALW on the L-13 en route chart as shown on SkyVector

Charts and Information

To prepare for this flight, review the following charts and other references. You can find the IFR procedure charts for this flight in `IFR_Charts.pdf`, available at this book's website. You can find Airport/Facility Directory (A/FD) information and online charts at `http://SkyVector.com`.

CHARTS	REFERENCES
KSFF and KALW airport diagrams	A/FD: KSFF and KALW
FELTS TWO departure	
En route L-13 IFR chart	
Seattle Sectional North and South	
KALW ILS or LOC Y RWY 20	

CROSS-REFERENCE **For more information about the references and resources that complement this book, see Chapter 2.**

Preflight Briefing

This lesson begins with your aircraft ready to depart runway 21R at KSFF for the flight to KALW (see Figure 65-2).

Figure 65-2: Ready for takeoff at KSFF as seen from the cockpit of the FSX Baron

Because the weather throughout the area is IMC, you must include an alternate airport in your IFR flight plan. Follow the sequence below for this flight:

- Fly the FELTS TWO departure. Upon reaching 5,500 ft., fly direct GEG and then join the flight plan route.
- When you reach the Walla Walla (ALW) VOR, fly the full ILS or LOC Y RWY 20 approach at KALW.

Clearance

For this lesson, assume that Pasco, WA (KPSC), is your alternate airport.

- Cleared to KALW via the FELTS TWO departure, GEG V444 ALW. Maintain 8000. Contact Spokane Departure on 133.35. Squawk 4200.

Weather

The bases of the clouds throughout the area are at about 500 ft., and the flight visibility below the ceiling is about 1 mile. The wind is out of the southwest at approximately 10 knots.

Situations and Flights

This lesson uses the following files for X-Plane and FSX:

- X-Plane: `Wiley-Advanced-02.sit`
- FSX: `Wiley-Advanced-02.flt`

CROSS-REFERENCE **For more information about using Situations (X-Plane) and Flights (FSX), see Chapter 10.**

What-Ifs

You can use the "Dice-Based Failure Scheme" described in Chapter 8 to create additional challenges for this flight.

At any point during the flight, roll a die, draw a number from a hat, or use another method to select a random number between 1 and 6. Using Table 65-1, find the corresponding problem to solve, and then take the appropriate action. If the challenge is a failure of an aircraft system or instrument, use the failure options in X-Plane or FSX to replicate the problem.

Table 65-1: Random Challenges for This Flight

NUMBER	RESULT
1	Vacuum system failure
2	Alternator failure
3	Communications failure en route to KALW
4	Weather at KALW is below the minimums for the ILS approach.
5	ATC requires you to hold north of ALW on V444. Make three turns in the holding pattern before continuing.
6	The ILS at KALW is out of service.

CHAPTER

66

Advanced 3: Boise, ID, to Redmond, OR

This flight from Boise, ID (KBOI) to Redmond, OR (KRDM) shows the advantages of flying a high-performance airplane in the mountainous terrain of the western U.S. The trip of about 235 nm (see Figure 66-1) requires about 1 hour and 20 minutes of flying time in either the Malibu (X-Plane) or the Baron (FSX).

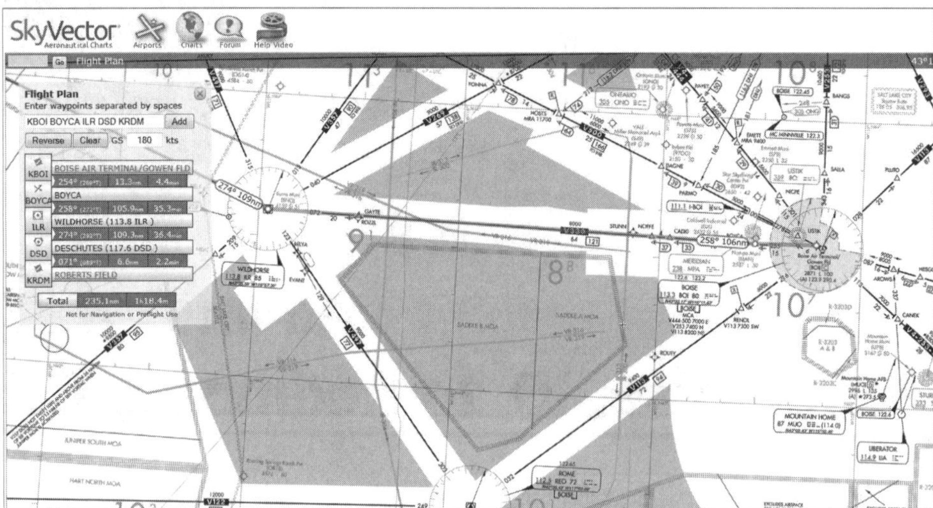

Figure 66-1: First part of the route from KBOI to KRDM on the L-11 en route chart as shown on SkyVector

Charts and Information

To prepare for this flight, review the following charts and other references. You can find the IFR procedure charts for this flight in `IFR_Charts.pdf`, available at this book's website. You can find Airport/Facility Directory (A/FD) information and online charts at `http://SkyVector.com`.

CHARTS	REFERENCES
KBOI and KRDM airport diagrams	A/FD: KBOI and KRDM
KBOI BOISE TWO departure	
En route L-11 IFR chart	
En route L-13 IFR chart	
Salt Lake City Sectional North	
Klamath Falls Sectional North	
KRDM ILS or LOC Y RWY 22	

CROSS-REFERENCE **For more information about the references and resources that complement this book, see Chapter 2.**

Preflight Briefing

This lesson begins with your aircraft ready to depart runway 28L at KBOI for the flight to KRDM.

Use the following sequence for this flight:

- Fly the BOISE TWO departure. Upon reaching 5,500 ft., turn left to join V330 and continue on the flight plan route.
- As you approach DSD, join the DSD 22 nm arc and fly the ILS or LOC Y RWY 22 approach at KRDM (see Figure 66-2).

Figure 66-2: Joining the DME arc from DSD as seen from the cockpit of the Malibu in X-Plane

Clearance

For this lesson, assume that Pendleton, OR (KPDT) is your alternate airport.

- Cleared to KRDM via the BOISE TWO departure, BOYCA, V330 ILR, V269 DSD. Maintain 12000. Contact Boise Departure on 119.6. Squawk 4200.

Weather

The bases of the clouds throughout the area are at about 500 ft., and the flight visibility below the ceiling is about 1 mile. The wind is out of the southwest at approximately 10 knots.

Situations and Flights

This lesson uses the following files for X-Plane and FSX:

- X-Plane: `Wiley-Advanced-03.sit`
- FSX: `Wiley-Advanced-03.flt`

CROSS-REFERENCE **For more information about using Situations (X-Plane) and Flights (FSX), see Chapter 10.**

What-Ifs

You can use the "Dice-Based Failure Scheme" described in Chapter 8 to create additional challenges for this flight.

At any point during the flight, roll a die, draw a number from a hat, or use another method to select a random number between 1 and 6. Using Table 66-1, find the corresponding problem to solve, and then take the appropriate action. If the challenge is a failure of an aircraft system or instrument, use the failure options in X-Plane or FSX to replicate the problem.

Table 66-1: Random Challenges for This Flight

NUMBER	RESULT
1	Vacuum system failure
2	Alternator failure
3	Communications failure en route to KRDM
4	Weather at KRDM is below the minimums for the ILS approach.
5	ATC requires you to hold south of DSD on the 180° radial, maintain 9000. Make three turns in the holding pattern before continuing.
6	The ILS at KRDM is out of service.

CHAPTER

67

Advanced 4: Crossing the Cascades

This flight from Coeur d'Alene, ID (KCOE) to Arlington, WA (KAWO) takes you over the spectacular and widely varied scenery in the Pacific Northwest via a route best flown in a high-performance aircraft. The trip of about 260 nm (see Figure 67-1) requires about 1 hour and 30 minutes of flying time in either the Malibu (X-Plane) or the Baron (FSX).

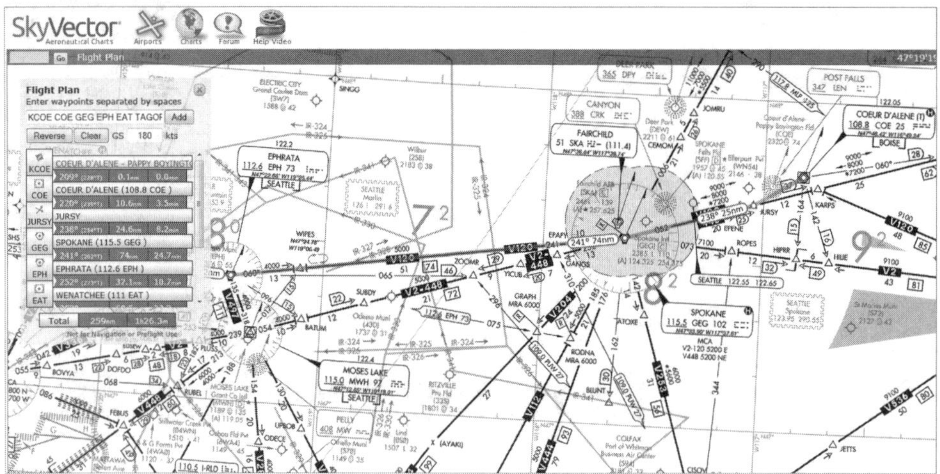

Figure 67-1: First part of the route from KCOE to KAWO on the L-13 en route chart as shown on SkyVector

Charts and Information

To prepare for this flight, review the following charts and other references. You can find the IFR procedure charts for this flight in `IFR_Charts.pdf`, available at this book's website. You can find Airport/Facility Directory (A/FD) information and online charts at `http://SkyVector.com`.

CHARTS	REFERENCES
KCOE COEUR D'ALENE ONE departure	A/FD: KCOE and KAWO
En route L-13 IFR chart	
En route L-1 IFR chart	
Seattle Sectional North	
KAWO LOC RWY 34	

CROSS-REFERENCE **For more information about the references and resources that complement this book, see Chapter 2.**

Preflight Briefing

This lesson begins with your aircraft ready to depart runway 23 at KCOE for the flight to KAWO.

Because the weather throughout the area is IMC, you must include an alternate airport in your IFR flight plan. Follow the sequence below for this flight:

- Fly the COEUR D'ALENE ONE departure. Join V120 to GEG and continue on the flight plan route.
- At PAE, join the charted transition to fly the LOC RWY 34 approach at KAWO (see Figure 67-2).

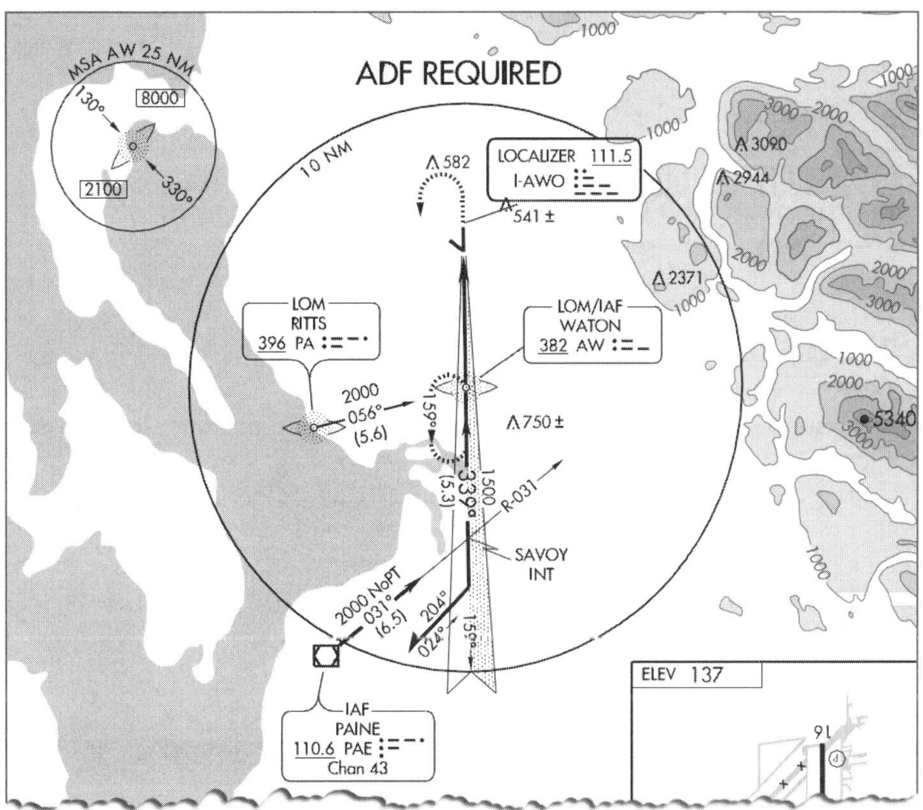

Figure 67-2: Plan view of the approach at KAWO

Clearance

For this lesson, assume that Everett, WA (KPAE) is your alternate airport.

- Cleared to KAWO via the COEUR D'ALENE ONE departure, V120 TAGOR, direct PAE. Maintain 12000. Contact Spokane Departure on 132.1. Squawk 4200.

Weather

The bases of the clouds throughout the area are at about 500 ft., and flight visibility below the ceiling is about 1 mile. The wind is out of the southwest at approximately 10 knots.

Situations and Flights

This lesson uses the following files for X-Plane and FSX:

- X-Plane: `Wiley-Advanced-04.sit`
- FSX: `Wiley-Advanced-04.flt`

CROSS-REFERENCE **For more information about using Situations (X-Plane) and Flights (FSX), see Chapter 10.**

What-Ifs

You can use the "Dice-Based Failure Scheme" described in Chapter 8 to create additional challenges for this flight.

At any point during the flight, roll a die, draw a number from a hat, or use another method to select a random number between 1 and 6. Using Table 67-1, find the corresponding problem to solve, and then take the appropriate action. If the challenge is a failure of an aircraft system or instrument, use the failure options in X-Plane or FSX to replicate the problem.

Table 67-1: Random Challenges for This Flight

NUMBER	RESULT
1	Vacuum system failure
2	Alternator failure
3	Communications failure en route to KAWO
4	Weather at KAWO is below the minimums for the LOC RWY 34 approach.
5	ATC requires you to hold as published at STILY intersection, northwest of KAWO. Maintain 4000. Make three turns in the holding pattern before continuing.
6	The WATON NDB at KAWO is out of service.

CHAPTER

68

Advanced 5: Medford, OR, to Astoria, OR

This flight is from Medford, OR (KMFR) to Astoria, OR (KAST).You must fly a challenging departure procedure at KMFR, but the reward is cruising up the scenic Oregon coast, where better weather may await. The trip of about 250 nm (see Figure 68-1) via Eugene (EUG) and Newport (ONP) requires about 1 hour and 25 minutes of flying time in either the Malibu (X-Plane) or the Baron (FSX).

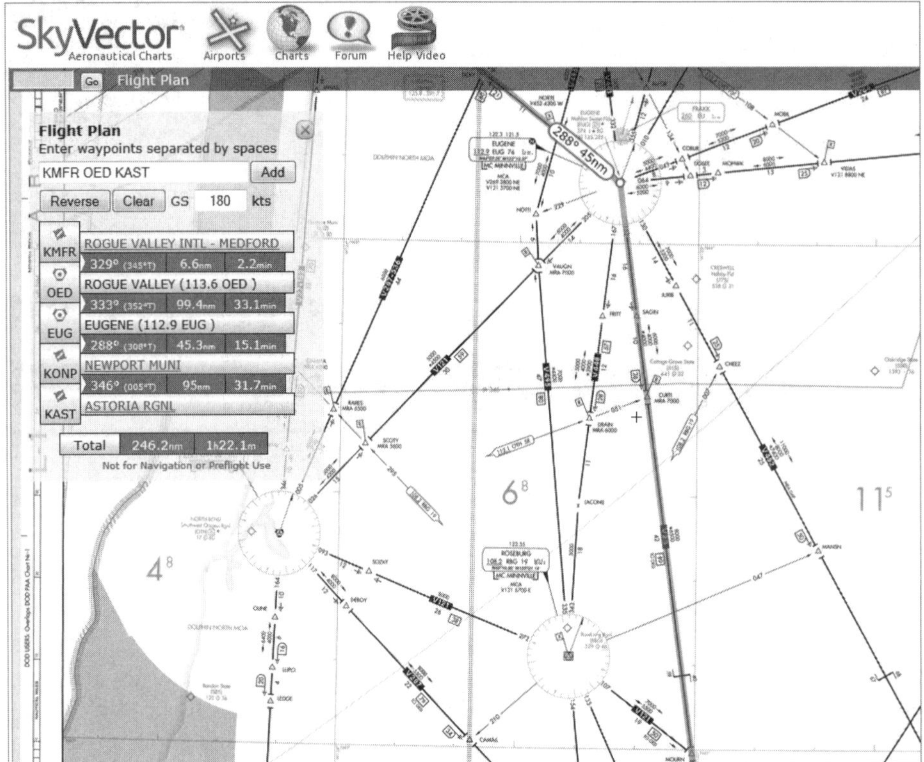

Figure 68-1: Part of the route from KMFR to KAST on the L-1 en route chart as shown on SkyVector

Charts and Information

To prepare for this flight, review the following charts and other references. You can find the IFR procedure charts for this flight in `IFR_Charts.pdf`, available at this book's website. You can find Airport/Facility Directory (A/FD) information and online charts at `http://SkyVector.com`.

CHARTS	REFERENCES
KMFR airport diagram	A/FD: KMFR and KAST
KMFR BRUTE FIVE departure	
En route L-2 IFR chart	
En route L-1 IFR chart	
Seattle Sectional North	
Klamath Falls Sectional North	
KAST ILS RWY 26	

CROSS-REFERENCE For more information about the references and resources that complement this book, see Chapter 2.

Preflight Briefing

This lesson begins with your aircraft ready to depart runway 14 at KMFR for the flight to KAST.

The weather is IMC at KMFR, so you must fly the BRUTE FIVE departure procedure (which you practiced in Lesson 17 in the instrument rating syllabus) — this time in a high-performance, complex aircraft. Use the following sequence for this flight:

- Fly the BRUTE FIVE departure, MOURN transition, and then the flight plan route.
- As you approach AST on V27, join the AST 19 nm arc and fly the ILS RWY 26 approach at KAST (see Figure 68-2).

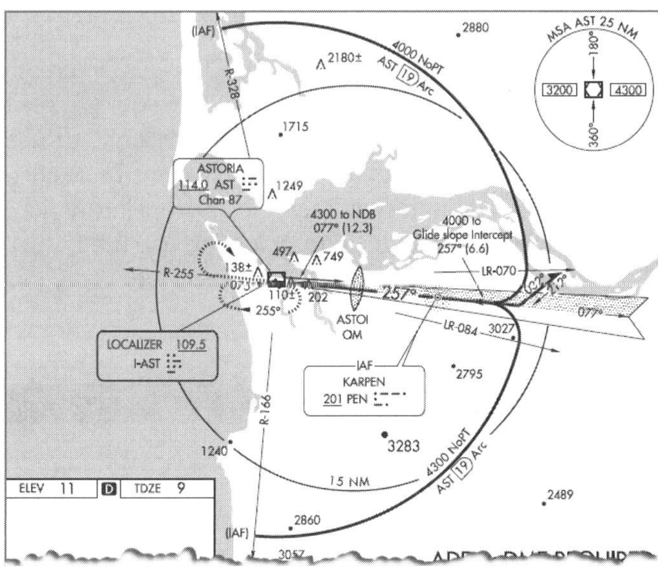

Figure 68-2: DME arcs from AST as shown in the plan view for the ILS RWY 26 approach

Clearance

For this lesson, assume that OLYMPIA, WA (KOLM) is your alternate airport.

- Cleared to KAST via the BRUTE FIVE departure, MOURN transition, V23 EUGE V452 ONP V27 AST. Maintain 12000. Contact Cascade Departure on 124.3. Squawk 4200.

Weather

The bases of the clouds throughout the Medford area are at about 500 ft., and flight visibility below the ceiling is about 1 mile. The wind is out of the southwest at approximately 10 knots.

Situations and Flights

This lesson uses the following files for X-Plane and FSX:

- X-Plane: `Wiley-Advanced-05.sit`
- FSX: `Wiley-Advanced-05.flt`

CROSS-REFERENCE **For more information about using Situations (X-Plane) and Flights (FSX), see Chapter 10.**

What-Ifs

You can use the "Dice-Based Failure Scheme" described in Chapter 8 to create additional challenges for this flight.

At any point during the flight, roll a die, draw a number from a hat, or use another method to select a random number between 1 and 6. Using Table 68-1, find the corresponding problem to solve, and then take the appropriate action. If the challenge is a failure of an aircraft system or instrument, use the failure options in X-Plane or FSX to replicate the problem.

Table 68-1: Random Challenges for This Flight

NUMBER	RESULT
1	Vacuum system failure
2	Alternator failure
3	Communications failure en route to KAST
4	Weather at KAST is below the minimums for the ILS approach.
5	ATC requires you to hold south of AST on V27, maintain 6000. Make three turns in the holding pattern before continuing with the ILS approach.
6	The ILS at KAST is out of service.

Glossary

This glossary includes a sample of key abbreviations and terms from the following sources:

- The Pilot/Controller Glossary (published with the AIM)
- The FAA handbooks described in Chapter 2

To learn more about a wide range of aviation-related abbreviations and terminology, see the glossaries included with each of the FAA handbooks and other technical documents available via the links at this book's website.

A/FD — *See* Airport/Facility Directory.

Aeronautical Decision-Making (ADM) — A systematic approach to the mental process used by pilots to consistently determine the best course of action in response to a given set of circumstances.

Air Route Traffic Control Center (ARTCC) — A facility established to provide air traffic control service to aircraft operating on IFR flight plans within controlled airspace and principally during the en route phase of flight. When equipment capabilities and controller workload permit, certain advisory/assistance services may be provided to VFR aircraft.

Airplane Flight Manual (AFM) — A document developed by the airplane manufacturer and approved by the Federal Aviation Administration (FAA).

It is specific to a particular make and model airplane by serial number and it contains operating procedures and limitations.

Airplane Owner/Information Manual — A document developed by the airplane manufacturer containing general information about the make and model of an airplane. The airplane owner's manual is not FAA approved and is not specific to a particular serial numbered airplane. This manual is not kept current, and therefore cannot be substituted for the AFM/POH.

Airport/Facility Directory (A/FD) — A publication designed primarily as a pilot's operational manual containing all airports, seaplane bases, and heliports open to the public, including communications data, navigational facilities, and certain special notices and procedures. This publication is issued in seven volumes according to geographical area.

Airspeed — Rate of the aircraft's progress through the air.

Airway — An airway is based on a centerline that extends from one navigation aid or intersection to another navigation aid (or through several navigation aids or intersections); used to establish a known route for en route procedures between terminal areas.

Altimeter setting — Station pressure (the barometric pressure at the location the reading is taken) which has been corrected for the height of the station above sea level.

Altitude — The height of a level, point, or object measured in feet above ground level (AGL) or from mean sea level (MSL).

Angle of Attack — The acute angle formed between the chord line of an airfoil and the direction of the air striking the airfoil.

ATC — Air Traffic Control.

Attitude — The position of an aircraft as determined by the relationship of its axes and a reference, usually the earth's horizon.

Attitude Indicator — An instrument which uses an artificial horizon and miniature airplane to depict the position of the airplane in relation to the true horizon. The attitude indicator senses roll as well as pitch, which is the up and down movement of the airplane's nose.

Attitude Instrument Flying — Controlling the aircraft by reference to the instruments rather than by outside visual cues.

Automatic Terminal Information Service (ATIS) — The continuous broadcast of recorded noncontrol information in selected terminal areas. Its purpose is to improve controller effectiveness and to relieve frequency congestion by automating the repetitive transmission of essential but routine information.

Axes of an Aircraft — Three imaginary lines that pass through an aircraft's center of gravity. The axes can be considered as imaginary axles around which the aircraft rotates. The three axes pass through the center of gravity at 90° angles to each other. The axis from nose to tail is the longitudinal axis (pitch), the axis that passes from wingtip to wingtip is the lateral axis (roll), and the axis that passes vertically through the center of gravity is the vertical axis (yaw).

Below Minimums — Weather conditions below the minimums prescribed by regulation for the particular action involved; e.g., landing minimums, takeoff minimums.

Calibrated Airspeed — The speed at which the aircraft is moving through the air, found by correcting IAS for instrument and position errors.

CDI — Course deviation indicator.

Ceiling — The heights above the earth's surface of the lowest layer of clouds or obscuring phenomena that is reported as "broken," "overcast," or "obscuration," and not classified as "thin" or "partial."

Center of Gravity (CG) — The point at which an airplane would balance if it were possible to suspend it at that point. It is the mass center of the airplane, or the theoretical point at which the entire weight of the airplane is assumed to be concentrated. It may be expressed in inches from the reference datum, or in percent of mean aerodynamic chord (MAC). The location depends on the distribution of weight in the airplane.

Changeover point (COP) — A point along the route or airway segment between two adjacent navigation facilities or waypoints where changeover in navigation guidance should occur.

Circle-to-Land Maneuver — A maneuver initiated by the pilot to align the aircraft with a runway for landing when a straight-in landing from an instrument approach is not possible or desirable. At tower-controlled airports, this maneuver is made only after ATC authorization has been obtained and the pilot has established required visual reference to the airport.

Circling Approach — A maneuver initiated by the pilot to align the aircraft with a runway for landing when a straight-in landing from an instrument approach is not possible or desirable.

Clearance Limit — The fix, point, or location to which an aircraft is cleared when issued an air traffic clearance.

Common Traffic Advisory Frequency (CTAF) — A frequency designed for the purpose of carrying out airport advisory practices while operating to or from an airport without an operating control tower. The CTAF may be a UNICOM, Multicom, FSS, or tower frequency and is identified in appropriate aeronautical publications.

Constant Speed Propeller — A controllable pitch propeller whose pitch is automatically varied in flight by a governor to maintain a constant RPM in spite of varying air loads.

Controlled Airspace — An airspace of defined dimensions within which ATC service is provided to IFR and VFR flights in accordance with the airspace classification. It includes Class A, Class B, Class C, Class D, and Class E airspace.

Controlled Flight Into Terrain (CFIT) — A situation in which a mechanically normally functioning airplane is inadvertently flown into the ground, water, or an obstacle.

There are two basic causes of CFIT accidents; both involve flight crew situational awareness. One definition of situational awareness is an accurate perception by pilots of the factors and conditions currently affecting the safe operation of the aircraft and the crew. The causes of CFIT are the flight crews' lack of vertical position awareness or their lack of horizontal position awareness in relation to terrain and obstacles.

Critical Angle of Attack — The angle of attack at which a wing stalls regardless of airspeed, flight attitude, or weight.

Cross-Check — The first fundamental skill of instrument flight, also known as "scan," the continuous and logical observation of instruments for attitude and performance information.

Crosswind Component — The wind component measured in knots at 90 degrees to the longitudinal axis of the runway.

Cruise Clearance — An ATC clearance issued to allow a pilot to conduct flight at any altitude from the minimum IFR altitude up to and including the altitude specified in the clearance. Also authorizes a pilot to proceed to and make an approach at the destination airport.

Dead Reckoning — Dead reckoning (sometimes spelled *ded reckoning* as derived from *deduced reckoning*), as applied to flying, is the navigation of an airplane solely by means of computations based on airspeed, course, heading, wind direction, and speed, groundspeed, and elapsed time.

Decision Altitude (DA) — A specified altitude in the precision approach at which a missed approach must be initiated if the required visual reference to continue the approach has not been established. The term "Decision Altitude (DA)" is referenced to mean sea level and the term "Decision Height (DH)" is referenced to the threshold elevation. Even though DH is charted as an altitude above MSL, the U.S. has adopted the term "DA" as a step toward harmonization of the United States and international terminology.

Decision Height (DH) — A specified altitude in the precision approach, charted in height above threshold elevation, at which a decision must be made either to continue the approach or to execute a missed approach.

Density Altitude (DA) — This altitude is pressure altitude corrected for variations from standard temperature. When conditions are standard, pressure altitude and density altitude are the same. If the temperature is above standard, the density altitude is higher than pressure altitude. If the temperature is below standard, the density altitude is lower than pressure altitude. This is an important altitude because it is directly related to the airplane's performance.

Departure Procedure (DP) — Planned IFR ATC departure, published for pilot use, in textual and graphic format.

En Route Low Altitude Charts — Aeronautical charts for en route IFR navigation below 18,000 feet MSL.

Feeder Route — A route depicted on instrument approach procedure charts to designate routes for aircraft to proceed from the en route structure to the initial approach fix (IAF).

Final Approach Fix (FAF) — The fix from which the IFR final approach to an airport is executed, and which identifies the beginning of the final approach segment. An FAF is designated on government charts by a Maltese cross symbol for nonprecision approaches and a lightning bolt symbol for precision approaches.

Fix — A geographical position determined by visual reference to the surface, by reference to one or more radio NAVAIDs, by celestial plotting, or by another navigational device.

Flight Director — An automatic flight control system in which the commands needed to fly the airplane are electronically computed and displayed on a flight instrument. The commands are followed by the human pilot with manual control inputs or, in the case of an autopilot system, sent to servos that move the flight controls.

Flight Level (FL) — In the U.S., a measure of altitude (in hundreds of feet) used by aircraft flying above 18,000 ft., with the altimeter set at 29.92" Hg.

Flight Visibility — The average forward horizontal distance, from the cockpit of an aircraft in flight, at which prominent unlighted objects may be seen and identified by day and prominent lighted objects may be seen and identified by night.

Forward Slip — A slip in which the airplane's direction of motion continues the same as before the slip was begun. In a forward slip, the airplane's longitudinal axis is at an angle to its flight path.

Glideslope (GS) — Part of the ILS that projects a radio beam upward at an angle of approximately 3 degrees from the approach end of an instrument runway. The glideslope provides vertical guidance to aircraft on the final approach course for the aircraft to follow when making an ILS approach along the localizer path.

Ground Visibility — Prevailing horizontal visibility near the earth's surface as reported by the United States National Weather Service or an accredited observer.

Groundspeed — Speed over the ground, either closing speed to the station or waypoint, or speed over the ground in whatever direction the aircraft is going at the moment, depending upon the navigation system used.

Heading — The direction in which the nose of the aircraft is pointing during flight.

Heading Bug — A marker on the heading indicator that can be rotated to a specific heading for reference purposes, or to command an autopilot to fly that heading.

Heading Indicator — An instrument which senses airplane movement and displays heading based on a 360° azimuth, with the final zero omitted. The heading indicator, also called a *directional gyro (DG)*, is fundamentally a mechanical instrument designed to facilitate the use of the magnetic compass. The heading indicator is not affected by the forces that make the magnetic compass difficult to interpret.

Headwind Component — The component of atmospheric winds that acts opposite to the aircraft's flight path.

Ident — A request for a pilot to activate the aircraft transponder identification feature. This helps the controller to confirm an aircraft's identity or to identify an aircraft.

IFR (Instrument Flight Rules) — Rules that govern the procedure for conducting flight in weather conditions below VFR weather minimums. The term "IFR" also is used to define weather conditions and the type of flight plan under which an aircraft is operating.

Indicated Airspeed (IAS) — The direct instrument reading obtained from the airspeed indicator, uncorrected for variations in atmospheric density, installation error, or instrument error. Manufacturers use this airspeed as the basis for determining airplane performance. Takeoff, landing, and stall speeds listed in the AFM or POH are indicated airspeeds and do not normally vary with altitude or temperature.

Indicated Altitude — The altitude read directly from the altimeter (uncorrected) when it is set to the current altimeter setting.

Initial Approach Fix (IAF) — The fix depicted on charts where the instrument approach procedure (IAP) begins unless otherwise authorized by ATC.

Instrument Approach Procedures (IAP) — A series of predetermined maneuvers for the orderly transfer of an aircraft under IFR from the beginning of the initial approach to a landing or to a point from which a landing may be made visually.

Instrument Flight Rules (IFR) — Rules and regulations established by the Federal Aviation Administration to govern flight under conditions in which flight by outside visual reference is not safe. IFR flight depends upon flying by reference to instruments in the flight deck, and navigation is accomplished by reference to electronic signals.

Instrument Landing System (ILS) — An electronic system that provides both horizontal and vertical guidance to a specific runway, used to execute a precision instrument approach procedure.

Instrument Meteorological Conditions (IMC) — Meteorological conditions expressed in terms of visibility, distance from clouds, and ceiling less than the minimums specified for visual meteorological conditions, requiring operations to be conducted under IFR.

Localizer (LOC) — The portion of an ILS that gives left/right guidance information down the centerline of the instrument runway for final approach.

Manifold Pressure (MP) — The absolute pressure of the fuel/air mixture within the intake manifold, usually indicated in inches of mercury.

Marker Beacon — A low-powered transmitter that directs its signal upward in a small, fan-shaped pattern. Used along the flight path when approaching an airport for landing, marker beacons indicate both aurally and visually when the aircraft is directly over the facility.

Minimum Altitude — An altitude depicted on an instrument approach chart with the altitude value underscored. Aircraft are required to maintain altitude at or above the depicted value.

Minimum Crossing Altitude (MCA) — An MCA is the lowest altitude at certain fixes at which the aircraft must cross when proceeding in the direction of a higher minimum en route IFR altitude. MCAs are established in all cases where obstacles intervene to prevent pilots from maintaining obstacle clearance during a normal climb to a higher MEA after passing a point beyond which the higher MEA applies.

Minimum Descent Altitude (MDA) — The lowest altitude, expressed in feet above mean sea level, to which descent is authorized on final approach or during circle-to-land maneuvering in execution of a standard instrument approach procedure where no electronic glide slope is provided.

Minimum En Route Altitude (MEA) — The lowest published altitude between radio fixes that ensures acceptable navigational signal coverage and meets obstacle clearance requirements between those fixes.

Minimum Obstruction Clearance Altitude (MOCA) — The MOCA is the lowest published altitude in effect between radio fixes on VOR airways, off-airway routes, or route segments that meets obstacle clearance requirements for the entire route segment. This altitude also ensures acceptable navigational signal coverage only within 22 NM of a VOR.

Minimums — Weather condition requirements established for a particular operation or type of operation; e.g., IFR takeoff or landing, alternate airport for IFR flight plans, VFR flight, etc.

Missed Approach — A maneuver conducted by a pilot when an instrument approach cannot be completed to a landing. The route of flight and altitude are shown on instrument approach procedure charts. A pilot executing a missed approach prior to the missed approach point (MAP) must continue along the final approach to the MAP.

Missed Approach Point (MAP) — A point prescribed in each instrument approach at which a missed approach procedure shall be executed if the required visual reference has not been established.

NAV/COM — Navigation and communication radio.

Navaid — Navigational aid.

Navigational Aid — Any visual or electronic device, airborne or on the surface, that provides point-to-point guidance information or position data to aircraft in flight.

Nondirectional Radio Beacon (NDB) — A ground-based radio transmitter that transmits radio energy in all directions.

Nonprecision Approach — A standard instrument approach procedure in which only horizontal guidance is provided.

Notice to Airmen — A notice containing information (not known sufficiently in advance to publicize by other means) concerning the establishment, condition, or change in any component (facility, service, or procedure of, or hazard in, the National Airspace System) the timely knowledge of which is essential to personnel concerned with flight operations.

Obstacle Departure Procedure (ODP) — A procedure that provides obstacle clearance. ODPs do not include ATC related climb requirements. In fact, the primary emphasis of ODP design is to use the least onerous route of flight to the en route structure while attempting to accommodate typical departure routes.

Outer Marker — A marker beacon at or near the glideslope intercept altitude of an ILS approach. It is normally located four to seven miles from the runway threshold on the extended centerline of the runway.

Pilot in Command — The pilot responsible for the operation and safety of an aircraft during flight time.

Pilot's Operating Handbook/Airplane Flight Manual (POH/AFM) — FAA-approved documents published by the airframe manufacturer that list the operating conditions for a particular model of aircraft.

Pilotage — Navigation by visual reference to landmarks.

Precision Approach — A standard instrument approach procedure in which both vertical and horizontal guidance is provided.

Prevailing Visibility — The greatest horizontal visibility equaled or exceeded throughout at least half the horizon circle (which is not necessarily continuous).

Procedure Turn — The maneuver prescribed when it is necessary to reverse direction to establish an aircraft on the intermediate approach segment or final approach course. The outbound course, direction of turn, distance within which the turn must be completed, and minimum altitude are specified in the procedure. However, unless otherwise restricted, the point at which the turn may be commenced and the type and rate of turn are left to the discretion of the pilot.

Procedure Turn Inbound — That point of a procedure turn maneuver where course reversal has been completed and an aircraft is established inbound on the intermediate approach segment or final approach course. A report of "procedure turn inbound" is normally used by ATC as a position report for separation purposes.

"Roger" — Communications term meaning "I have received all of your last transmission." It should not be used to answer a question requiring a yes or no response.

Roundout (Flare) — A pitch-up during landing approach to reduce rate of descent and forward speed prior to touchdown.

Runway Visual Range (RVR) — An estimate of the maximum distance at which the runway, or the specified lights or markers delineating it, can be seen from a position above a specific point on the runway centerline.

RVR is normally determined by visibility sensors or transmissometers located alongside and higher than the centerline of the runway. RVR is reported in hundreds of feet.

Scan — The first fundamental skill of instrument flight (also known as "cross-check") — the continuous and logical observation of instruments for attitude and performance information.

Scenario-Based Training — SBT is a training system that uses a highly structured script of real-world experiences to address flight-training objectives in an operational environment. Such training can include initial training, transition training, upgrade training, recurrent training, and special training.

Sideslip — A slip in which the airplane's longitudinal axis remains parallel to the original flight path, but the airplane no longer flies straight ahead. Instead, the horizontal component of wing lift forces the airplane to move sideways toward the low wing.

Single Pilot Resource Management (SRM) — The art and science of managing all resources (both on-board the aircraft and from outside sources) available to a single pilot (prior and during flight) to ensure that the successful outcome of the flight is never in doubt.

Skid — A condition in which the tail of the airplane follows a path outside the path of the nose during a turn.

Slip — An intentional maneuver to decrease airspeed or increase rate of descent, and to compensate for a crosswind on landing. A slip can also be unintentional when the pilot fails to maintain the aircraft in coordinated flight.

Slipping Turn — An uncoordinated turn in which the aircraft is banked too much for the rate of turn, so the horizontal lift component is greater than the centrifugal force, pulling the aircraft toward the inside of the turn.

Special Use Airspace (SUA) — Airspace in which flight activities are subject to restrictions that can create limitations on the mixed use of airspace. Consists of prohibited, restricted, warning, military operations, and alert areas.

Spin — An aggravated stall that results in what is termed an *autorotation* wherein the airplane follows a downward corkscrew path. As the airplane rotates around the vertical axis, the rising wing is less stalled than the descending wing, creating a rolling, yawing, and pitching motion.

Stabilized Approach — A landing approach in which the pilot establishes and maintains a constant angle glidepath towards a predetermined point on the landing runway. It is based on the pilot's judgment of certain visual cues, and depends on the maintenance of a constant final descent airspeed and configuration.

Stall — A rapid decrease in lift caused by the separation of airflow from the wing's surface, brought on by exceeding the critical angle of attack. A stall can occur at any pitch attitude or airspeed.

Standard Instrument Departure (SID) — A planned instrument flight rule (IFR) air traffic control (ATC) departure procedure printed for pilot/controller use in graphic form to provide obstacle clearance and a transition from the terminal area to the appropriate en route structure. SIDs are primarily designed for system enhancement to expedite traffic flow and to reduce pilot/controller workload. ATC clearance must always be received prior to flying a SID.

Standard Rate Turn — A turn in which an aircraft changes its direction at a rate of 3° per second (360° in 2 minutes) for low- or medium-speed aircraft. For high-speed aircraft, the standard rate turn is 1½° per second (360° in 4 minutes).

Standard Terminal Arrival — A planned instrument flight rules (IFR) air traffic control arrival procedure published for pilot use in graphic and/or textual form. Standard Terminal Arrival Routes (STARs) provide transition from the en route structure to an outer fix or an instrument approach fix/arrival waypoint in the terminal area.

Standard Terminal Arrival Route (STAR) — A planned IFR ATC arrival procedure published for pilot use in graphic and/or textual form.

Trim Tab — A small auxiliary hinged portion of a movable control surface that can be adjusted during flight to a position resulting in a balance of control forces.

True Airspeed (TAS) — Calibrated airspeed corrected for altitude and nonstandard temperature. Because air density decreases with an increase in altitude, an airplane has to be flown faster at higher altitudes to cause the same pressure difference between pitot impact pressure and static pressure. Therefore, for a given calibrated airspeed, true airspeed increases as altitude increases; or for a given true airspeed, calibrated airspeed decreases as altitude increases.

Turn Coordinator — A rate gyro that senses both roll and yaw due to the gimbal being canted. It has largely replaced the turn-and-slip indicator in modern aircraft.

Turn-and-Slip Indicator — A flight instrument consisting of a rate gyro to indicate the rate of yaw and a curved glass inclinometer to indicate the relationship between gravity and centrifugal force. The turn-and-slip indicator indicates the relationship between angle of bank and rate of yaw. Also called a *turn-and-bank indicator*.

Vector — A heading issued to an aircraft to provide navigational guidance by radar.

Very-High Frequency Omnidirectional Range (VOR) — Electronic navigation equipment in which the flight deck instrument identifies the radial or line from the VOR station, measured in degrees clockwise from magnetic north, along which the aircraft is located.

VFR Conditions — Weather conditions equal to or better than the minimum for flight under visual flight rules.

Victor Airways — Airways based on a centerline that extends from one VOR or VORTAC navigation aid or intersection, to another navigation aid (or through several navigation aids or intersections); used to establish a known route for en route procedures between terminal areas.

Visibility — The ability, as determined by atmospheric conditions and expressed in units of distance, to see and identify prominent unlighted objects by day and prominent lighted objects by night. Visibility is reported as statute miles, hundreds of feet, or meters.

Visual Approach — An approach conducted on an instrument flight rules (IFR) flight plan that authorizes the pilot to proceed visually and clear of clouds to the airport. The pilot must, at all times, have either the airport or the preceding aircraft in sight. This approach must be authorized and under the control of the appropriate air traffic control facility. Reported weather at the airport must be ceiling at or above 1,000 feet and visibility of 3 miles or greater.

Visual Approach Slope Indicator (VASI) — A visual aid of lights arranged to provide descent guidance information during the approach to the runway. A pilot on the correct glideslope will see red lights over white lights.

Visual Descent Point (VDP) — A defined point on the final approach course of a nonprecision straight-in approach procedure from which normal descent from the MDA to the runway touchdown point may be commenced, provided the runway environment is clearly visible to the pilot.

Visual Flight Rules (VFR) — Rules that govern the procedures for conducting flight under visual conditions. The term "VFR" is also used in the United States to indicate weather conditions that are equal to or greater than minimum VFR requirements. In addition, it is used by pilots and controllers to indicate type of flight plan.

Visual Meteorological Conditions (VMC) — Meteorological conditions, expressed in terms of visibility, distance from cloud, and ceiling, that meet or exceed the minimums specified for VFR.

VOR — A ground-based electronic navigation aid transmitting very high frequency navigation signals, 360 degrees in azimuth, oriented from magnetic north. Used as the basis for navigation in the National Airspace System. The VOR periodically identifies itself by Morse Code and may have an additional voice identification feature. Voice features may be used by ATC or FSS for transmitting instructions and information to pilots.

Waypoint — A predetermined geographical position used for route/instrument approach definition, progress reports, published VFR routes, visual reporting points or points for transitioning and/or circumnavigating controlled and/or special use airspace, that is defined relative to a VORTAC station or in terms of latitude/longitude coordinates.

Zulu Time — A term used in aviation for coordinated universal time (UTC), which places the entire world on one time standard.

Index

A

B

C

D

G

L

M

T

U

V